Remaking the Presidency

Peri E. Arnold

Remaking the Presidency

*Roosevelt, Taft,
and Wilson, 1901–1916*

University Press of Kansas

© 2009 by the University Press of Kansas
All rights reserved

Published by the University Press of Kansas (Lawrence, Kansas 66045), which was
organized by the Kansas Board of Regents and is operated and funded by
Emporia State University, Fort Hays State University, Kansas State University,
Pittsburg State University, the University of Kansas, and Wichita State University

Library of Congress Cataloging-in-Publication Data
Arnold, Peri E.
   Remaking the presidency : Roosevelt, Taft, and Wilson, 1901–1916 / Peri E. Arnold.
      p.   cm.
   Includes bibliographical references and index.
   ISBN 978-0-7006-1659-6 (cloth : alk. paper)
      1. Progressivism (United States politics)—History. 2. Roosevelt, Theodore,
1858–1919. 3. Taft, William H. (William Howard), 1857–1930. 4. Wilson, Woodrow,
1856–1924. 5. Progressive Party (1912) 6. United States—Politics and government—
1901–1909. 7. United States—Politics and government—1909–1913. 8. United
States—Politics and government—1913–1921. 9. Wilson, Woodrow, 1856–1924.
I. Title.
   JK2316.A76 2009
   973.91092'2—dc22   2009015242

British Library Cataloguing-in-Publication Data is available.

Printed in the United States of America

10 9 8 7 6 5 4 3 2 1

The paper used in this publication is recycled and contains 30 percent postconsumer
waste. It is acid free and meets the minimum requirements of the American National
Standard for Permanence of Paper for Printed Library Materials Z39.48–1992.

This book is dedicated to the memory of Alexis Arnold Quinn

Contents

Preface

THIS BOOK PRESENTS three related perspectives on the Progressive Era's distinctive presidents and their leadership projects. I examine in detail Theodore Roosevelt's, William Howard Taft's, and Woodrow Wilson's approaches to leadership. In a step back in time, I explain these presidents in a temporal, Progressive Era context. Then I take a long view, to see how these extraordinary presidents relate to the presidency's modern development.

An apparently simple question launched the project that became this book. While serving in a time of relatively modest and unmemorable presidencies, how did Theodore Roosevelt and Woodrow Wilson use the office to gain iconic status in presidential history? The period of Republican dominance in which they appeared, stretching from Lincoln through Hoover, exhibited congressional primacy, presidential passivity, and hostility to governmental activism. Why and how did these two presidents construct activist leadership in a context that was apparently inhospitable to such activism?

Unlike Lincoln, Roosevelt had no war to make his fame. Had Wilson managed to avoid World War I, his domestic initiatives themselves would have secured his fame alongside Roosevelt. Why did Roosevelt differ from his immediate predecessor, William McKinley? Why did Wilson differ from his immediate successor, Warren G. Harding? And how are we to understand the role played by the apparently forgettable William Howard Taft, sandwiched between Roosevelt and Wilson?

We are a century past Roosevelt and Wilson, but finding answers to these questions is important if we are to understand why these two presidents remain vitally relevant within today's political discourse. Both presidents have symbolic significance, and Americans of varied political tendencies invoke them as allies. Theodore Roosevelt of the "Big Stick," the Panama Canal, and the strong navy is a hero for conservatives, while liberals also prize the conservationist and trust-busting aspects of Roosevelt. Woodrow Wilson's expansion of federal regulation over banking and business makes him a liberal hero, but his foreign policy idealism has also influenced conservatives such as Richard Nixon, Ronald Reagan, and George W. Bush.

Thus to understand how these presidents governed is itself an important goal, shedding light on how these influential presidents affected change in American government at a time of political uproar. In addition, understanding their leadership could offer us larger insights into the transformation of American government from a system of checks and balances and minimalism in the nineteenth century to expansive government and presidentialism in the twentieth.

To get to these larger questions we must begin with a close-up examination of the early twentieth-century presidents and their contexts. But questions arise at the start: Is the salient difference between McKinley and Roosevelt merely a difference in personality? Was the latter more gifted for leadership than the former, and can we say the same of Wilson in comparison to Harding? Our conventional discourse about leadership assumes that individual-level characteristics can predict presidential success. But every presidential campaign demonstrates the confusions in our public discourse about *what* characteristics are associated with presidential success. Is it intellect or the "common touch," military service or elite education, executive experience or legislative service? Is eloquence required, or plain speech? In fact, are any of these variables applicable to explaining Roosevelt's or Wilson's experience in office?

It is not simply a matter of whether enough scholarly attention has been paid to Roosevelt or Wilson, since biographers and historians have lavished attention on both. But biographies are only a starting point for our purposes because they do not present a sufficient explanation for these presidents' novel leadership. Biographers characteristically attribute presidential leadership to a set of individual-level characteristics. Thus, like ballet, leadership may be seen as an expression of personal skills and talents. For example, one historian characterized Roosevelt and Wilson as "heroic" in their uses of leadership.

As we shall see below, individual characteristics have an important place in my story, but my starting point is the office occupied by these presidents. *Why* did Roosevelt and Wilson seek an activist role at a time when the presidency's norm was relative passivity? *How* did they gain the means for effective, activist leadership in a role that had not heretofore supported such leadership? The Progressive Era separates Roosevelt and Wilson from McKinley on one end and Harding on the other, and its reformist energies and political disruptions might explain the appearance of new sources for presidential energy. But if the period's roiled politics help explain Roosevelt and Wilson, how shall we fit in Taft? He is chronologically as much a Progressive Era president as the others, and if we have a contextual explanation for their leadership, it must also relate to the apparently less active and less successful Taft. This is where my book begins, setting the presidency into the Progressive Era and discovering that Taft is as much a puzzling figure as Roosevelt and Wilson. The chapters that follow will reveal how emerging forms of American politics affected the presidency and how three presidents improvised novel leadership projects to use the presidency's new possibilities.

During my graduate studies at the University of Chicago, Grant McConnell inspired my interest in the Progressive Era's politics and ideas. Decades later I remain indebted to McConnell for his penetrating scholarship and passionate teaching.

A visiting research professorship at the University of Virginia's Miller Center for Public Affairs during 1993–1994 gave me time to begin thinking about the Progressive Era presidency. I am grateful to Kenneth Thompson and the center for its support and to the University of Notre Dame for supplementary funding during that year. I am also grateful to Notre Dame's Institute for Scholarship in the Liberal Arts for its support of indexing for this volume.

Several different institutional venues offered opportunities for presenting my work at various stages of its development: the Miller Center, Notre Dame's Kellogg Institute for International Studies, the political science departments of Western Michigan University and Princeton University, Brandeis University's Program in Constitutional Government, and panels at annual meetings of the Midwest Political Science Association and the American Political Science Association. In these settings I profited from criticism and generous advice. I am grateful to Matthew Dickinson, Fred Greenstein, Morton Keller, David Lewis, Scott Mainwaring, Sidney Milkis, Guillermo O'Donnell, Mark A. Peterson, Daniel E. Ponder, Jos Radschelders, Howard Reiter, Bill Ritchie, Colleen Shogan, Stephen Skowronek, Norman C. Thomas, and James Sterling Young. Evidence of my obligation to many political historians is plain to see in my citations. However I must acknowledge two historians, Lewis Gould and Michael McGerr, to whose work I am particularly indebted.

Fred Woodward encouraged this project, supplied smart advice, and helped me see an end to it. He has made Kansas a major imprint for work on the presidency, and I am proud this book joins his list. Several readers for the Press served my book well, helping correct weaknesses and better focus its strengths. My very dedicated and careful production editor, Jennifer Dropkin, transformed a stack of manuscript pages into this handsome book .Of course, I am responsible for the remaining imperfections.

I gratefully share the adventure of family life with my wife Beverly and our daughters, Emma and Rachel. They lovingly remind me that there is life beyond my intellectual distraction of the moment. This is dedicated to the memory of my sister, who is always with me.

"DELIGHTED!" Roosevelt is caricatured here as transforming for
political purposes from Knickerbocker gentleman to Rough Riding
hero. (*Harper's Weekly*, June 18, 1904, p. 923; provided courtesy of
HarpWeek, LLC)

1

The Progressive Era and the Presidency

The New Nationalism regards the executive power as the steward of the public welfare.
Theodore Roosevelt[1]

D ESPAIRING OF PRESIDENT MCKINLEY, Theodore Roosevelt wrote privately in 1897 that if the United States "could be ruled by a benevolent czar we would doubtless make a good many changes for the better."[2] Four years later McKinley was dead, and Roosevelt had the opportunity to be a different kind of president. John Morton Blum observes, he "reshaped the office of the presidency, used it intentionally to improve the conditions of life in America, and mobilized it in periods of major national involvements in world affairs."[3]

Roosevelt, along with Woodrow Wilson, "reshaped" the presidency amidst the swirling politics of Progressivism. From the 1890s to the beginning of World War I a loose coalition of reform movements put forward new ideals for society, new demands on government, and higher expectations for the performance of politicians. Was it coincidental that two of the most memorable presidents in American political history served during that brief period? If the demands for reform associated with Progressivism influenced Roosevelt's and Wilson's presidencies so profoundly, why was McKinley not similarly affected? Then there is the easily overlooked William Howard Taft, sandwiched between Roosevelt and Wilson. If the forces of the Progressive Era significantly influenced Roosevelt's and Wilson's memorable presidencies, why wasn't Taft also lifted to great achievement?

These questions denote a puzzling quality about presidential leadership. Do we look to context and institutional role to understand a president's performance in office, or do we look to the president's personal characteristics? Did the Progressive Era context influence these presidents, and if so, through what mechanisms? Or, was it just the variation of individual characteristics that determined differences among McKinley, Roosevelt, Taft, and Wilson? To examine only a president's personal characteristics masks the opportunities and constraints within which he or she works.[4] But, to examine only the president's role and its political context is to miss *how* an individual functions within a given role and context.

This book's goals are to explain the differences among the three presidents of the Progressive Era, to show how that period's ferment affected the presidency and its incumbents, and to examine how they, in turn, affected progressive politics. Where should we start in considering the influence of context and individual characteristics in forming presidential performance? This duality is not a chicken-and-egg problem. The starting point is clear. Our inquiry should begin with context and role. If the Progressive Era's reform politics affected the presidency's role, we should be able to identify the mechanisms at work therein. Then we can ask, why did some presidents respond differently than others to Progressivism's contextual and institutional effects upon the executive role?

The Old Presidency and the New

Contemporaries recognized Theodore Roosevelt's presidency as a break from the past. Herbert Croly's 1909 manifesto for progressive nationalism celebrated him as "the founder of a new national democracy . . . [and] his influence and his work have tended to emancipate American democracy from its Jeffersonian [individualist] bondage."[5] Roosevelt's primacy in Croly's account calls to mind Clifford Geertz's insight that to Americans the presidency represents one of the "master fictions" sustaining our mental maps of the social order.[6] In his time Roosevelt symbolized a quest for a new America. But why did that quite accidental president gain such acclaim? What made his leadership novel?

Roosevelt differed from his predecessors in two clear ways. First, he took the presidency to be a platform for his own policy preferences. He entered office amidst a clamor for solutions to new economic problems, and he was the chief executive over an expanding and changing executive branch—an administrative state. Expanded administrative responsibilities brought new capacities into the executive branch. The administrative state, in turn, increased the president's policy responsibilities and justified his expanded efforts at setting the policy agenda.[7]

Second, deep changes in American political life divided Roosevelt and his successors from McKinley and his predecessors. In the late 1890s, organizations, relationships, and interests that had formed American politics since the 1830s were displaced by new relationships, new forms of organization, and new kinds of popular communication. Since the 1830s presidents had been bound to mass parties by mechanisms of nomination, campaigning, elections, and patronage.[8] Consequently, presidents of the party period, or third-party system, were as much satellites and captives of their parties as they were party leaders.

My point is not that party period presidents were passive (and thus unmemorable) while Roosevelt invented activism (and became memorable). Rather, the activism of party period presidents was qualitatively different than what came afterward and was expressed within the norms and domain of the political parties.[9] Parties nominated presidential candidates for their loyalty and electability. That nominee's success depended on the party's capacities for voter mobilization.[10] Samuel Kernell writes those presidents were "the manufactured products of political machines."[11] Party period presidents communicated to the public through the partisan press, and their policy advocacy was pursuant of the party's platform.[12] Additionally, serving in an era of minimal national governmental responsibilities, these presidents were not managers of administrative apparatus as much as they were managers of unruly factions within decentralized mass parties.[13]

Party factions competed over distributive policies that were the government's primary product in post-bellum America.[14] Factions sustained themselves through the currency of "spoils." And their factional leaders, often members of Congress, sought and husbanded that currency.[15] National government regulated rarely, and then regulation was adjudicated through the federal courts and not administrative agencies.[16]

The distributive policies the parties sought to control were, for example, the veterans' pensions, subsidies for the railroads, the letting of contracts to supply government, and the support for public works as well as the partisan distribution of government employment.[17] The political stakes were material, and the political battle was fiercely and closely fought. The five presidential elections from 1876 through 1892 saw the winning candidate average 47.72 percent of the popular vote.[18] Republicans occupied the presidency for all but two terms in the post-bellum party period and usually held the Senate as well. But Democrats controlled the House for nine of the eleven sessions from 1874 through the 1894 election.[19]

The "patronage state" privileged Congress.[20] In whatever form taken, the distribution of patronage is mechanical, virtually automatic, requiring no elaborate administrative apparatus. Distributive policies like high tariffs, land grants, or veterans' pensions were disaggregated to allow Congress to distribute rewards among many constituencies and different party factions. Through legislative formulas Congress made certain it would control distributive policy. When these formulas insufficiently rewarded political allies, Congress provided its own version of administrative discretion through private bills. In the 49th Congress, sitting from 1885 through 1887, 40 percent of the House's legislation and 55 percent in the Senate consisted of private bills to bestow the veterans' pension on individuals.[21] One might think presidents of the period would have at least controlled personnel appointments through the constitutional appointment power. However, Senate leaders stripped even that element of presidential discretion. President Rutherford B. Hayes complained that fellow Republicans in the Senate substituted the "Senators' doctrine" of appointment for the president's appointment power. He wrote that the senators held: "We will appoint the officers and our officers shall rule the party, and party shall rule the country."[22] Yet no sensible politician in the presidency could break with his party. Close electoral competition and frequently divided government reinforced presidents' subordination to party; to split with the party would be to weaken the electoral prospects of party and president.

The presidency's subordination to party was reinforced by the outcome of the "war" between the Republican Congress and President Andrew Johnson. Johnson's impeachment and trial were ultimately about which branch would control Reconstruction. The crises of secession had opened political space for Lincoln's assertive presidency, and Congress closed that space in rejecting Johnson's effort to control reconstruction.[23] Congressman Benjamin Butler (R-MA) recognized the interbranch struggle as central to the episode, charging that Johnson "was trying to overthrow Congress and establish an absolute dictatorship."[24]

The Old Way Exemplified: McKinley

William McKinley's public rhetoric exemplifies how the party defined the president's policy stance.[25] Second only to the embattled Andrew Johnson, McKinley was the nineteenth-century president most given to rhetorical promotion of public policy.[26] Yet his rhetoric exhibited party period norms, promoting Republican principles and policies.

Consider McKinley's first inaugural address. On March 4, 1897, he spoke to a citizenry divided by "the electoral maelstrom of 1896."[27] McKinley explained his intentions and gave reasons why the losers of 1896 should accept Republican leadership. McKinley spoke to the issues that defined 1896's battle lines, echoing the Republican party platform. Promising prosperity, defending a protective tariff policy, and promising to seek a moderate bimetallism as a salve to the silverites, McKinley seconded the 1896 platform. Then he said: "Immunity should be granted to none who violate the laws."[28] McKinley denounced business misbehavior by illegal combinations, or "trusts." Bryanite Democrats had vowed to break the trusts. McKinley's speech signaled he was sensitive to the dangers of illegal combinations, but the 1896 Republican platform had not addressed trusts.

McKinley could not assume authority to promote a policy independently of his party. Because the 1896 platform was silent about business combinations, McKinley turned to an earlier Republican platform to gain authority to speak. He quoted the 1888 platform that promised wary surveillance of "all combinations of capital organized in trusts" and recommended "such legislation as will prevent the execution of all schemes to oppress the people by undue charges."[29] It is notable that calling upon the earlier platform, McKinley quoted exactly its language on trusts, as if paraphrasing the language would not sufficiently demonstrate its legitimacy and his right to proclaim it.

Party period presidents were also limited by the antique organizational arrangements of the old executive branch. Speaking to the condition of the presidency in the party period, Louis L. Gould writes:

> The White House itself was a ramshackle building that was showing its age. On the verge of assuming world responsibilities, the presidency was understaffed, and the facilities at the disposal of the nation's chief executive were minimal.
>
> That was how the American people wanted their president treated. He was "Our Fellow-Citizen of the White House," not a dominant presence set apart. . . . At the same time the chief executive could walk around Washington in relative safety on his own. . . . The president was far from the national celebrity he would soon become.[30]

Of course, the party period presidents had not had great need for effective executive organization. Morton Keller writes, these "presidents had little say over the estimates, appropriations, expenditures, and the policies of government bureaus and departments."[31] In 1885 Woodrow Wilson wrote about the office he would one day occupy: "The high office has fallen from its first estate of dignity because its power has waned; and its power has waned because the power of Congress has become predominant."[32]

Wilson was hardly alone in lamenting the state of the presidency or conceiving the importance of presidential leadership for the public interest. Such notions entered middle-class opinion, and that spread was itself a harbinger of changes to come. In 1898 Henry Jones Ford wrote: "Ideas are the sap from which institutions obtain their growth."[33] Normative ideas about presidential leadership appear during the controversies over the "money question" in Grover Cleveland's second term. By the standards of the party period, Cleveland was failing, increasingly opposing his own party's program and wielding the negative power of the veto as his last resort. Yet Cleveland's independence was praised in the quality press.

Cleveland entered office in 1893 opposing the 1890 silver purchase act, requiring that government issue money backed by silver. Hard money interests in both parties supported Cleveland's position, and the Republican *Chicago Daily Tribune* and the Mugwump *New York Times* editorially backed the Democrat Cleveland. Both papers promoted the president as the presumed initiator of change *and* the official most able to recognize and articulate the public interest. For example, in a remarkable editorial the *Tribune* urged Cleveland to call a special session of Congress for repeal of the silver purchase policy but ruefully noted the power of silver sentiment in the Senate. The editorial observed that Cleveland was not likely to unilaterally suspend silver purchases, unlike Jackson "might have done . . . if he thought it for the best interests of the country."[34] Executive unilateralism would make for good government! In an editorial the *New York Times* also stressed the virtues of an independent presidency, writing: "The present situation . . . brings out very clearly the peculiarity of the Presidential office" because it demonstrated the importance for prosperity of the president's judgment. "It can hardly be asserted with confidence that Congress would be equal to the task."[35]

That same preference for presidential independence is evident in the work of intellectuals at the century's end. For example, Henry Jones Ford argued that American government's evolution weakened the Framers' constitutional plan and that strong executive government was both necessary and, in fact, emergent. He wrote: "To take care of the government, to attend to its needs, to shape its policy, and to provide for its responsibilities is the special business of the

President."[36] The party period had not imposed such demands upon presidents, but that was changing.

The New Way: Roosevelt, Taft, and Wilson

There are few moments in American political history when the character of presidential leadership changed as dramatically as after Theodore Roosevelt's entry to office in September 1901. Unlike McKinley, Roosevelt promoted his own policy initiatives, even more freely after election to his own term in 1904. In his 1905 inaugural address, he told his conservative and pro-business party that the conditions that created enormous material wealth and economic progress "have also brought the care and anxiety inseparable from the accumulation of great wealth in industrial centers."[37] As illustrated by his December 1907 annual message, Roosevelt assumed authority to address the economic problems he diagnosed, much to his party leaders' chagrin. In the message he announced:

> The fortunes amassed through corporate organization are now so large, and vest such power in those that wield them, as to make it a matter of necessity to give to the sovereign—that is, to the Government, which represents the people as a whole—some effective power of supervision over their corporate use. In order to insure a healthy social and industrial life, every big corporation should be held responsible by, and be accountable to, some sovereign strong enough to control its conduct.[38]

Roosevelt's independent initiatives are associated with the Progressive Era's striking outpouring of novel legislation. David Mayhew finds that the period 1905–1916 is one of four "lawmaking surge" eras in American political history. It was "as if the system's volume could somehow be turned up to a pitch of accelerated change."[39] Probing for explanations of that Progressive Era surge, Mayhew finds it not well explained by the "usual suspects," elections, political parties, or economic fluctuations. Rather, a public "mood change" is associated with the surge. That same mood change, the public's rising expectations for reform, created a receptive constituency for presidential leadership. Thus conditions appeared at the century's opening that made possible newly independent and active presidential leadership. But how did that era's demands for change stimulate novel presidential leadership?

Chapter One

Context and Role

In 1908 Woodrow Wilson described the presidency quite differently than he had in 1885. He wrote, "The President is at liberty . . . to be as big a man as he can. . . . His capacity will set the limit."[40] Wilson had in mind two presidents flanking the divide between the party period and the Progressive Era, Grover Cleveland and Theodore Roosevelt. More than Wilson recognized, what made these presidents distinctive and "big" revealed a great deal about the presidency's path of change.

Wilson admired Cleveland for his integrity and his use of presidential powers to block what he found objectionable, claiming him as "an exception to the . . . prevailing rule of presidential mediocrity."[41] Cleveland issued by far the most vetoes (584 in eight years) of any president, a record that would stand until Franklin Roosevelt's 635 over twelve years.[42] Cleveland's use of the veto to block Republican bills appealed to the Democrat Wilson, but Wilson also admired that he withstood the demands for inflationary currency policy from Democrats as well as some Republicans. Cleveland claimed his authority derived not from partisan loyalties but from "the people," an idea akin to Wilson's evolving theory of presidential leadership as an interpretive process.[43] At a time when the norm was presidential loyalty to party, the *New York Times* editorialized that Cleveland conflicted with congressional Democrats because as "the chief representative of the people—the President of the United States—will, in their name, accept nothing but what the people justly and imperatively demand."[44]

Cleveland's case also demonstrated the power of the party period's constraints on presidents. His first term saw strains within his party over patronage and currency. In his second term his sharp break with his party over currency policy undermined his partisan authority for leadership.[45] Cleveland was left without party support but had no claim to an alternative source of authority to sustain his leadership. He was not an agenda setter. Nor did he appeal openly to the public for support, despite his claim to represent "the people." And his operation of the presidency was "backbreaking and primitive," leaving him little energy for independent initiatives.[46]

Nothing demonstrates the differences between Cleveland and Roosevelt better than their uses of the presidency's unilateral tools, the veto and the executive order. The former is the presidency's most potent means to block Congress, and the latter is the most potent tool for unilateral direction of the executive branch. In contrast to Cleveland's 584 vetoes in two terms, Roosevelt issued 82 vetoes in just under two terms. Turning to executive orders, Cleveland issued 253 during his two terms, but Roosevelt issued 1,081. In the term in which he succeeded McKinley he issued 251 orders, and he issued 830 in the term to which he was elected in his own right.[47] Cleveland's action was negative—to block Republican patronage and inflationary legislation; whereas Roosevelt's action was positive—setting an agenda and directing the work of a nascent administrative state.

Wilson's claim that presidents can "now" be as big as they want implied institutional and contextual causes for changing presidential leadership. He thought that the increasing complexity of the national government's tasks, particularly after the war with Spain, heightened presidents' importance.[48] Wilson recognized that Theodore Roosevelt's novel presidency was not just an expression of an outsized personality. But he offered no clues about what specific factors caused the changes he mentions.

The Presidency in a Transforming Context

A potential explanation for the changes Wilson observed is that the presidency was adapting to exogenous forces of modernization, such as expanding industrial capitalism, urbanization, and America's new international role. In effect, government had lagged behind change in the economy and society and was now catching up. The historian Lewis Gould's account of the modern presidency's emergence exemplifies a modernization explanation. Gould sees in William McKinley's presidency (and the role in it of his secretary, George Cortelyou) the beginnings of systematic rationalization of presidential work and the extension of presidential influence on executive agencies along with notably more public presidential travel and rhetoric. Gould notes that as McKinley entered office the forces of change were already at work. Far more than McKinley's personal characteristics, it was the expanding industrial society, the growth of mass communications, and, of course, the Spanish war and consequent new territories that enhanced the presidential role McKinley occupied.[49] Over time these factors continued to expand and shape the institution into a modern presidency.[50]

The modernization thesis productively links change in the presidency with other institutions and societal sectors. It is translatable into terms and causes that explain change in other sectors, such as the managerial revolution in the American economy. However, there is a serious flaw in this perspective. It offers no clear causal link between its independent variables and the specific presidential actions and role changes we seek to explain. James March and Johan Olsen say of functionalist theories such as this one that they are "indifferent to the be-havioral reality of the micro processes that are assumed."[51]

The weakness of that modernization explanation is apparent when we con-sider William Howard Taft, the often-overlooked president sandwiched between Roosevelt and Wilson. Historical judgment makes Taft a mediocrity. [52] But that as-sessment assumes a new criterion for success. Taft failed to meet expectations for his presidency stimulated by Roosevelt's performance in office as well as the period's mood of political reform.[53] However, as we shall see below, he was not simply a throwback to an earlier constrained presidency. A wave of important pro-gressive legislation continued during his term in office. But Taft failed very pub-licly to comprehend the presidency's new responsibilities for popular leadership.

A theory that satisfactorily accounts for presidential leadership in the Pro-gressive Era should link large changes in the political system to variations in be-havior among incumbents. We are challenged to explain what forces affected all three presidents and how all three differed from predecessors. Then at the indi-vidual level we must explain the differences among Roosevelt, Taft, and Wilson *within* the large-scale forces at work in Progressive Era politics. That first chal-lenge invites us to consider the forces that disrupted American political institu-tions at the end of the nineteenth century.[54]

Around 1900 fundamental changes occurred in institutions salient to the presidency. The erosion of the third-party system changed the relationships of the presidency to the parties, Congress, and the electorate. Simultaneously, the kinds of changes in the economy and society identified as most salient by mod-ernization theory posed new challenges for the federal government. After the long era of relatively stable politics and modest governmental function, a new system of pluralist interests and bargaining politics emerged. As the stable insti-tutional arrangements of the party period eroded, the presidents' ties to the par-ties loosened. The emerging context of new political actors and new political challenges presented new norms and expectations for presidents, a "new script," so to speak.[55] In what follows we shall note changing institutions that framed a new institutional order after 1900 and, in turn, created new possibilities for presidential leadership.

First, a changing economic order consolidated firms into national corpo-rations producing greatly concentrated wealth, substantial power over prices in some industries, and the world's first mass-market, consumer economy.[56] To take the example of one industry, in 1890 the American Tobacco Company was formed, merging more than two hundred small firms and dominating the national market for tobacco products. After 1900 national, consolidated corporations represented a seventh of the nation's manufacturing capacity and most of them controlled substantial market share in their industries.[57] That corporate reconstruction created new great firms and business groups that affected government outside the realm of party control.[58] Interest groups increasingly became the main participants in public policy battles, displacing party organization.[59] It was also a development that established new identities, relationships, and obligations among many in the urban middle class. Samuel Hayes notes: "This systematization of human relationships in . . . centralized corporate activity . . . constituted still another process of decision-making which affected political parties adversely."[60] It immersed Americans in rationalized administration, and identification with rational organizations such as firms and interest groups undermined "the compulsive identification with a political party . . . opening the way to various forms of nonpartisan and interest-group politics."[61]

The emergence of an urban middle class further disrupted stable party allegiances. Those citizens made new demands for broad reforms in government, society, and the economy to transform their environment into a middle-class ideal. Experiencing the turmoil of economic and social change, middle-class Americans sought a new way of politics, embracing "a dynamic set of new ideas and a driving desire to reform society . . . by reworking domesticity, fostering association, and developing the power of the state."[62]

The urban middle class at the turn of the century constituted about a fifth of American society.[63] Its political weight, in addition to its propensity to seek reform, was related to the decline of electoral turnout that paralleled its rise. Turnout of eligible voters in the 1896 election was 79.3 percent but fell to 65.2 percent in 1904. Walter Dean Burnham explains low-income voters were dropping out of the electorate, giving greater leverage at the ballot box to the emergent middle class.[64]

Another great institutional change at the end of the party period was the transformation and expansion of newspapers. Papers were now independent of political party organizations and had grown to be major businesses depending on advertising revenues and newspaper sales. The quality press, such as the *New York Times,* the *Chicago Tribune,* and the *Washington Post* pioneered the production of factual journalism for middle-class consumption. They informed citizens, and they also provided a means for broadcasting, so to speak, the president's message in a way that was not immediately dependent on his political party. Finally, these newspapers, as commercial enterprises reflecting the sentiments of their readers, provided to politicians something they had never had before. In an era before scientific polling, the newspapers offered a rough and ready indicator of public opinion.[65]

The growth and professionalization of the administrative state further eroded the old party order. Civilian employment in the federal government expanded almost five-fold between 1871 and 1901, from 51,020 civilian employees in 1871 to 239,476 employees in 1901. These employees were increasingly subject to civil service protection and jobs were removed from party distribution. In 1871 there was not yet a competitive civil service, but in 1901 44 percent of government's employees were under the civil service.[66] As important, the work of the executive branch agencies after the turn of the century was increasingly specialized and depended on specially skilled employees.

The emergence of pluralist politics was the consequence of these changing institutions eroding the organizational solidity of the third-party system. The decline of parties and electoral competition in the early twentieth century "meant that extra party groups . . . increasingly enjoyed greater structural openings to *directly* influence . . . policymaking."[67] That was dramatically becoming clear in agricultural regions, formerly the heartland of majoritarian, reformist electoral politics. After 1900 farm politics increasingly took the form of interest group activity displacing the last gasps of agrarian radicalism. In 1919 the Farm Bureau Federation was formed, representing the virtual dominance of farm politics by a business-oriented interest group. Similarly, the embrace of political neutrality by the new American Federation of Labor reflected that same logic of interest group politics versus partisan politics.[68]

Amidst chaotic urban life and threatening new economic institutions, middle-class Americans worried about the character and health of their society. For them parties, courts, and Congress were yesterday's political institutions, bent on preserving the governance style of the party period and unresponsive to the needs of cities and the middle class. When addressing reform, Congress was more likely to respond to agrarians' demands and less likely to respond to urban-middle-class citizens' needs, given that both houses overweighed rural representation.

When Congress did produce reform legislation, it had little capacity to maintain a coalition of support for reforms beyond those that most concerned agrarians.[69] There was no majority support for labor-friendly legislation except during a brief period, 1914 into 1916, and little interest in urban social problems.[70] Beset by the changing economy, corrupted local governments, a maldistribution of wealth in the face of growing poverty, overwhelming waves of immigrants, and a threatening urban environment, middle-class Americans saw government as necessary for solving social and economic problems.[71] In contrast to the parochial Congress, it was the presidency that presented a possibility for leadership to address what middle-class Americans identified as the public interest. Highlighting the presidency's importance for reform in the early twentieth century, Robert Harrison writes: "Congress was all too liable to give way to the centrifugal tendencies that were implicit in its composition . . . direction could only come from outside, and most obviously from the White House."[72] That institutional preference by progressive reformers is exemplified by an April 1902 editorial in the *New York Times* noting Roosevelt's difficulties with Congress. It observed: "The Administration is much more in accord with public opinion and much more responsive to it than the nominal 'representatives' of that opinion."[73] As the party ties that bound presidents were loosened in the emergent pluralist system, presidents had expanded opportunities to use the symbolic status of their office to reach out to "latent national constituencies," dispersed among numerous legislative districts and seeking representation beyond congressional parochialism and party loyalties.[74]

Contextual Change and the Presidents

What are the links and cues that would connect the macro-level institutional changes of the Progressive Era to the actions and decisions of the presidents? Contextual explanations for presidential leadership attempt to explain "when the political system spurs presidential action and times when it bars action" and "when the president transcends contextual limitations to change his or her context."[75] What do we learn from the changing political context after 1900 that provides clues to presidential behaviors and ideas about when presidents might attempt to transcend those conditions?

The developments that weakened the political parties' grip on national government did not simply give birth to new institutions and relationships. Those changes created new opportunities for presidential leadership, but none of this should be thought of as simply historically determined. Robert Harrison writes that the Progressive Era state "was not a product of autogenesis, emerging spontaneously from a peculiar conjunction of . . . forces."[76] The clash of institutional orders and ideas created political space and possibility for new presidential leadership, but it remained for politicians to recognize and act upon these opportunities.

Consider William McKinley, the last of the party period presidents, and Theodore Roosevelt, the first Progressive Era president. In respect to Executive Mansion operations, relations with reporters, and his exercise of commander-in-chief responsibilities, there was much that McKinley innovated in a manner that was modernizing, that is, bringing the presidential operation up to date.[77] Yet, in his understanding of his role, McKinley was a man of the political past, just as he was the last Civil War veteran elected as president. He was not blind to the emerging challenges in this context. For example, he may have made some effort to deal with the trust issue had he not been assassinated early in his second term.[78] However, his recognition of that problem, seen through his partisan lens, was slow and grudging. He was a traditional Republican politician forced, perhaps, to deal with an issue about which populists and then progressives were clamoring. To argue that like his successors McKinley was moving to a progressive reformist stance belies everything about his own political background and habits. About the idea that McKinley might be seen as a progressive, Eric Rauchway wryly notes that it envisions "a bloodless . . . progressivism . . . unrecognizable to the voters of the early 1900s. These progressives do no standing at Armageddon, they harbor no fierce discontent, they make not the slightest reference to other people's money."[79]

McKinley and Roosevelt occupied the presidency back to back. They had the same sparse staff resources and nonexistent organizational capacities for acquiring information and conducting analysis. They both served at a time of a changing party system and emergent pluralist politics. In short, there is no contextual or institutional difference between these two very different presidents. Then why did they differ? To answer that question we require an explanation based in individual-level variables. We need an account of what opportunities each president saw in his context and how he chose to respond.[80]

Opportunity and Incongruity

What most obviously distinguishes Roosevelt from McKinley has to do with Roosevelt's different generational background, his different career path, and his consequently different relationship to the Republican party. McKinley came to the presidency up a ladder of offices, pushed by a determined Ohio Republican party and managed by a brilliant party operative, Senator Mark Hanna (R-OH). Whatever McKinley "saw" was through the lens of being a Republican of the Civil War generation, his organizational experience as a party man and governor in Ohio, and his role as a Republican leader in Congress. Theodore Roosevelt came to the presidency by accident and saw its possibilities through his very different political perceptions and ambitions. Roosevelt's career was idiosyncratic, juggling party loyalty *and* the impulse to reform in government and economy. Thus he entered the same office McKinley had occupied but saw new ways to use it because he saw more clearly than McKinley the implications and possibilities of the changes around him.

The new institutional economics gives us a framework for analyzing the individual-level differences we see between McKinley and Roosevelt. In a foundational contribution to studying the presidency, Terry Moe describes mid- and late-twentieth-century presidents finding "incongruence" between their individual political goals and the organizational context they find in the presidency. He hypothesizes that these presidents increase "congruence" between their goals and the institutional role through personnel appointments and organizational restructuring.[81] All modern presidents attempt to impose their policy initiatives and oversee their implementation, and all of them are "driven by these formidable expectations to seek control over the structures and processes of government."[82]

The post–World War II presidency Moe analyzed was an organizationally dense executive system whereas the office McKinley and Roosevelt occupied lacked organizational resources. Nevertheless, Moe's concept of congruence-seeking presidents is fully applicable to changing presidential leadership after 1900. In that earlier context, innovation-seeking presidents would have to find or adapt resources to achieve their new policy goals. The party period presidents, like McKinley, were dependent on party platforms for policy goals and congressional party organization to achieve the party's goals. In that relationship, the president was not an autonomous actor with his own policy agenda, and his primary responsibility was to support and enable his party's policy efficacy.

In contrast to McKinley, Roosevelt sought goals beyond his party's agenda. He was an "orthodox–innovator," in Stephen Skowronek's account, who was "dedicated . . . to defending and confirming the commitments of an established political regime, but within that frame, he negotiated the first major departures from the institutional forms and routine operations of American party governance."[83] He was "unmatched in presidential history for his mastery of orthodox innovation."[84] Occupying the same office, cheek to jowl in time, and sharing party affiliation, McKinley and Roosevelt had different goals for their presidencies, attributable to differences in their histories, talents, and perceptions of the world outside the Executive Mansion. Roosevelt's incentives for innovation were the same forces that disrupted the once-stable relationships of institutions and interests within the third-party system. Politically independent newspapers and magazines were widely distributed and could broadcast his language and actions. Middle-class adherents of a reform-oriented politics offered a new constituency for his presidential leadership. And, not least, the emerging problems of a burgeoning urban industrial society gave Roosevelt material for a new policy agenda.

The Search for Strategic Resources

A president pursuing progressive reform after 1900 would find an incongruity between his goals and the political resources available in the presidency to achieve those goals. A president articulating his own policy goals lacked the bare necessities to sustain presidential policy autonomy, resources such as organizational support, expert staff, informational and analytic capacity, and means to publicize the president's message.

Circa 1900 the presidential staff comprised two secretaries and a handful of clerks and messengers. Presidents lacked capacities to sustain leadership and policy initiatives apart from the party. Of course, those were not the needs of the party period presidents, whose leadership roles were integrated with party leadership and organization.[85] Progressive Era presidents, however, would have to identify and acquire scarce political resources to facilitate their goals.[86] That was easier said than done in the rapidly changing political context of the Progressive Era.

Strategic analysis is the process whereby presidents identify and acquire resources to overcome asymmetry between their goals and their capacities. That process would be complicated not only by the presidency's lack of resources in-house, so to speak, but also by the lack of precedent for independent resource acquisition by presidents. Thus the process of acquiring political resources within the Progressive Era would be highly contingent upon a president's own skills. With their dilemma of strong incentives for independent initiatives and inadequate political resources, the progressive presidents would operate with a high level of uncertainty. They lacked sufficient information about available political resources, they could not be sure about the consequences of the policies they promoted, and they were necessarily uncertain about the consequences for their party of their leadership innovations. These are the characteristics of a highly "ill-structured decision situation." Describing that situation and its implications for decision making, the decision theorist K. J. Radford writes: "Two different individuals involved in the same ill-structured decision situation may decide on different approaches . . . may make different recommendations . . . [and] each may legitimately claim to have acted in a subjectively rational manner in the circumstances as he or she perceived them."[87] It is within that ill-structured situation that the Progressive Era presidents employed their leadership styles to overcome uncertainty and build progressive leadership.

Constructing Progressive Era Leadership

Our story began with the effect on the presidency of the transition from the party period to the pluralist period of American politics. The story's denouement brings us to the incumbents within that presidency. Macro-level changes created new incentives for presidential autonomy and policy initiative. But the presidency's institutional structure and resources did not change over that short period of time. Thus there was incongruence between new demands for presidential leadership and the presidency's organizational means to enable independent action. A president's success was contingent upon his ability to overcome that gap.

We now have a general explanation for why Progressive Era political change affected the presidency *and* differentially affected presidents of the period. At first one might see differences in presidential performance from McKinley through Wilson as a random walk, simply one idiosyncratic president following another. As an alternative I offer a theoretical account that incorporates individual performance into the changing institutional and political contexts of the period. Now it remains for us to conceptualize how those incumbents formed their leadership, attacking the problem of incongruence in ways that produced marked differences in their respective performances.

Structure and Agency

After 1900 the party period's presidential norms were collapsing, including what had been criteria for qualifications to vie for a major party nomination.[88] Outlandishly, from the perspective of the party period, a major party might even nominate for the presidency a professor of political science! The old norms gave presidents a relatively clear script for leadership, and their erosion gave presidents latitude but with few clear guides about how to use their office in a time of change.

Chapter One

Leadership Style

How the Progressive Era's presidents used the office's open script and addressed incongruence was determined by what I shall call their "styles of political leadership." By that term I mean to designate a politician's tool kit of skills combined with his or her conception of presidential leadership. Within the tool kit I include specific abilities that affect presidents' success, including skills at negotiation, public rhetoric, organizational management, and, not least, comprehension of both political processes and issue substance. These "tools," in turn, are put to work promoting an incumbent's conception of leadership. That conception includes the incumbent's ideas about the presidency's place in American politics and governance, ideas about the president's proper relationship to the people, and, finally, the incumbent's public policy goals.

Scholars of political psychology have established several different approaches for analyzing presidents' behavior, focusing upon the elements of personality from which an adult character and work style is assembled. [89] In that research tradition, "leadership style" is often defined as how individual personality traits affect the president's work. My approach here differs, starting not with basic elements of personality but rather with a president's observable and mature style of political work.[90] Through biographical examination and cases of policy leadership for each president, we will examine the origins of their individual political styles and then analyze how they accomplish their political work in an ill-structured context.

The following chapters examine Roosevelt's, Taft's, and Wilson's leadership projects. For each president one chapter is devoted to the formation of the future president's leadership style. Then for each, a second chapter analyzes that president's search for congruity between his key policy goals and political resources. For each president I focus upon two issues of high priority that he addressed early in the first term to assess the formative stage of his presidential leadership project.[91]

Claiming Authority for a Progressive Presidency

Roosevelt, Taft, and Wilson were men of different backgrounds, sensibilities, and skills, constructing leadership projects anew within a rapidly changing political environment. Each was challenged to experiment with the presidency's new potential for political independence from party and Congress and to assemble the capacities and justifications to use that independence.

In addition to their strategic problem of matching resources to their new political goals, these Progressive Era presidents had to justify their authority for innovative leadership projects. Presidents have powers, based in the Constitution and statute law, and manifested, as well, informally through their skills. But power alone is insufficient for legitimate leadership in the American constitutional system. Presidents must have authority to legitimately wield power and govern. Therefore to understand how a president will govern, it is necessary to identify his or her claim to authority. That claim not only signals the leadership project to be pursued; it is also a window onto that president's relationship to the Constitution, predecessors in the office, other governmental institutions, and the public.[92] Stephen Skowronek writes: "Before a president can formulate a strategy for action, he needs to construe his place in history and stake claims to certain warrants for the exercise of power within it."[93] In a period of stable politics and structures, presidents' authority claims will predictably invoke immediate past practices and contemporary norms about the limits and uses of presidential power. During the flux of changing institutional order, as old norms fade or become irrelevant, we would expect presidents to make innovative authority claims as they seek to legitimate bolder leadership projects responding to an unsettled context.

In 1897 William McKinley stretched backward to the 1888 Republican platform, in partisan obedience to legitimate his inaugural language criticizing trusts. His Progressive Era successors were temporal neighbors, yet their claims to authority, and their party ties, signaled a widening gap between themselves and McKinley.

We shall see that Theodore Roosevelt claimed authority in pragmatic terms, justifying his actions as principled and necessary in light of the times in addition to espousing Republican fealty. William Howard Taft initially pursued a reform agenda in the face of opposition from his party's leaders. His response was more complicated than Roosevelt's balancing act between orthodoxy and innovation. Taft invoked a partisan warrant for authority while adopting a moderate reform stance. He aspired to move Republican leaders closer to moderate reform, but his embrace of partisan authority also made Taft politically responsible for the Republican Congress's legislation. Unlike Roosevelt's balancing act and Taft's failed effort to make traditional partisan authority new, Wilson turned a traditional claim of partisan authority into the basis for strikingly novel presidential leadership.

Thus, in Roosevelt, Taft, and Wilson we have three distinctive cases of presidents negotiating the choppy crosscurrents of changing institutions and politics at a time when the old way of presidential leadership was inadequate to new chal-lenges. Motivated by new opportunities for leadership in that period, these presi-dents constructed three very different leadership projects, in effect, three different experiments attempting to make a progressive presidency. Those "experiments" produced three very different outcomes, in terms of contemporary judgments as well as in historical retrospective. In the following chapters we shall examine and compare these remarkable efforts to solve the incongruities of the Progressive Era context and construct a presidency for a time of reform.

2

The Political Education of Theodore Roosevelt: Partisan Loyalty, Reform, and the Politics of Self-Display

Here a President who by tactics still significant resolved the persistent problems of his office; here a master among men who make things political work. . . . Apart from anything Roosevelt attained, this virtuosity compels attention.

John Morton Blum[1]

A MOMENT IN LATE SUMMER 1898 illuminates Theodore Roosevelt's extraordinary self-promotion, foreshadowing a time when personal appeal would displace partisanship in presidential elections. American troops returning by ship from the Cuban battlefield disembarked at Montauk, on Long Island. The isolated site, 120 miles east of New York City, was used to quarantine the arriving troops.

Creating a Political Spectacle

Thousands of soldiers poured into Montauk, worn from the Cuban campaign and ill with dysentery, typhoid fever, and malaria. They were processed and confined to hastily prepared camps.[2] In sparsely populated eastern Long Island, the arriving troops found a low-key reception, "admiring but silent," as reported by the *New York Times*.

But one unit received a very different reception. Theodore Roosevelt's volunteer brigade, the Rough Riders, disembarked to "tumultuous cheering, loud shouts of 'welcome home!' and words of encouragement."[3] The excitement about Roosevelt's Rough Riders was so intense that a small group arriving a few days prior to Colonel Roosevelt and the main brigade received "great cheering and enthusiasm, coupled with loud calls for 'Teddy.'"[4] When Roosevelt finally arrived, reporters wrote that although the troops appeared weary, the Colonel gave "no evidence of having passed through the tortures of the Cuban campaign." Roosevelt told reporters that he was "disgracefully healthy."[5]

Roosevelt was famously robust, edgy with aggression, and bristling with intelligence. As he spoke to applauding citizens and reporters in Montauk, Roosevelt was aware of his extraordinary celebrity. Earlier that year, the mention of Roosevelt's plan to form the Rough Riders drew lively press interest. A reporter wrote that Roosevelt would remain assistant secretary of the navy until actual hostilities began because such a position offered "more risk and peril and better opportunities for adventure" than would a dull military training camp. But, "when the fighting begins . . . he will be found in the front with his dashing band of Western cowboys."[6] Roosevelt's superior at the navy department, Secretary John D. Long, later said of Roosevelt that "he took the straight course to fame, to the governorship . . . and to the presidency of the United States."[7]

While in Cuba, Roosevelt followed the public's fascination with his military heroics through friends' letters.[8] Even while he dashed about in Cuba to create his legend, he ruminated about converting the legend into political currency. He wrote Senator Henry Cabot Lodge (R-MA) that New Yorkers "seem to be crazy over me."[9] Yet, he told Lodge, he was not confident that leading Republican politicians would support his bid for high office in New York. About that he was mistaken.

The New York Republican State Committee met to consider the question of a gubernatorial nominee just five days after Roosevelt landed at Montauk. The incumbent governor, Republican Frank Black, was sullied by a financial scandal over canal-building contracts.[10] Were he to be renominated, it was unlikely that Republicans could retain the governorship or legislative majorities. The committeemen confronted the party's leader, Senator Thomas Platt (R-NY), with a solution. They "were filled with enthusiasm for the Colonel, and they called upon the Senator . . . to lay before him . . . the extent to which the boom of the Rough Riders' hero had grown in the districts they represented."[11]

Meanwhile Roosevelt played the coy warrior brilliantly. From the beginning of his public career he understood that gaining public attention and mirroring public concerns in his actions and language was central to political leadership.[12] Declining to address politics in August 1898, he presented himself as the sturdy leader of heroic men. Of course, as the cultural historian Sarah Watts comments, Roosevelt's presentation as a warrior was itself a powerful appeal to a wholly masculine electorate.[13] After Montauk, Roosevelt returned home to Oyster Bay,

New York. He came home to an uproar of greeting from his townsmen that also drew crowds from outside Oyster Bay, including many politicians, expecting "the launching of a gubernatorial boom." However, Roosevelt spoke only about "the deeds of his beloved Rough Riders on Cuban battlefields."[14]

While eschewing public mention of politics, Roosevelt considered the conditions that Senator Platt might attach to a nomination and the problems he would face as governor in dealing with the party leaders. He wrote in a letter: "I haven't bothered myself a particle about the nomination. . . . I would rather have led this regiment than be Governor of New York, three times over." But, he continued:

> I should be one of the big party leaders. . . . This means that I should have to treat with and work with the organization. . . . the mere fact of my doing so would alienate many of my friends. . . . On the other hand, when we come to a matter like the Canal, or Life Insurance . . . and general decency, I would not allow any consideration of party to come in. And this would alienate those who, if not friends, were supporters.[15]

Roosevelt's Cuban adventure did more than attract public approbation. His artful stance of toughened Rough Rider, combining imagery of the Western frontier and Cuban battlefield, touched a deeper longing in turn-of-the-century America than just the conventional hope for a fresh political face. The *Denver Republican*'s description of Roosevelt's Rough Riders illustrates the myth in the making. They "will go into history along with other immortal fighters. . . . And their names will be fragrant of romance. . . . It is worth something to be one of Teddy's Terrors."[16]

Roosevelt's self-construction as a cowboy warrior signaled to the anxious middle class that here was an unconventional politician prepared to deal with its insecurities and aspirations.[17] If progressivism was "the creed of a crusading middle class," mobilized to fight the many evils of late Gilded Age America, then that class, and its movement for reform, found its leader in Roosevelt.[18] His personal appeal extended beyond Republicans. A group of leading businessmen formed a committee to nominate Roosevelt for an independent ticket in the gubernatorial race. Its leaders explained: "While Roosevelt is a party man, he is one in whom the masses of the people of both parties feel a confidence amounting to devotion."[19] Hesitating, to be sure the Republican nomination was forthcoming, Roosevelt turned down the offer of an independent nomination.[20] At its convention in late September, the Republican party pushed Governor Black aside, and the Colonel was nominated on the first ballot.[21]

The combination of Roosevelt's personal appeal and his intense campaigning won the November election. The party was disadvantaged by scandals and splits between the organization and good-government Republicans. With Roosevelt's nomination the party sought to minimize those deficits. Internalizing both sides of the organization-reform split, Roosevelt insisted that reformers be visibly involved in the campaign, along with the regulars.[22] When the ballots were counted, Roosevelt ran ahead of the rest of the Republican ticket and edged out his Democratic opponent, winning by 17,794 votes statewide. In his own assessment, he had lost votes because of Republican scandals and because many reformers opposed the Spanish War and imperialism.[23] The same innovative, personalist style that launched his electoral career also made Roosevelt a personification of the war.[24]

Roosevelt's Rough Rider performance catapulted him into New York's governorship and then past it. Less than two years after election as governor, he was nominated for the vice presidency. Thirty-three months after entering the governor's mansion, he took the oath of office as president of the United States.

As governor, Roosevelt sought a balance between loyalty to the Republican organization and his own commitments to merit appointments, good government, and public interest regulation. However, there was no such optimal "balance" point. There was no formula defining what constituted an appropriate mix of governance in the public interest and governance in the party's interest. From the perspective of the patronage-driven party, all governance ought to serve the party's interests. That was the goal that energized parties' efforts to win elections. And from the perspective of progressive reformers, good government required total insulation.

Governor Roosevelt quickly saw that for state government to deal transparently and legally with business interests was to undermine the Republicans' economic base. Looking back at his gubernatorial experience, Roosevelt wrote:

> In New York State . . . Platt was the absolute boss of the Republican party. "Big business" was back of him; yet at the time this, the most important element in his strength, was only imperfectly understood. It was not until I was elected Governor that I myself came to understand it.[25]

That insight came after Senator Platt's consistent opposition to Roosevelt's initiatives. After a year at Albany, Roosevelt described Platt as opposed to "the course I had set out to follow, as for instance in the Franchise Tax bill, the Civil Service bill, [and] the superintendency of insurance."[26] For Roosevelt to succeed in his "good government" agenda would be to disappoint and weaken the party organization.

The death of Vice President Garrett Hobart in late 1899 created an opportunity for Roosevelt while also giving Platt a way to rid New York of this uncontrollable executive. Platt promoted him for the vice presidential nomination in 1900 while Roosevelt temporized about entering that elevated but powerless role.[27] At the 1900 Republican convention, Roosevelt drew widespread support. Warming to the idea, Roosevelt entered the convention floor sporting "a Rough Rider–type wide-brimmed hat amid a sea of straw boaters," and his nomination to the vice presidency was approved unanimously.[28] John Morton Blum explains that Roosevelt's ambition made him succumb to the proffered nomination.[29] Of course, a wholly unexpected path to the presidency would open with McKinley's assassination just nine months after his inauguration for a second term.

The Making of an Administrative Politician

Roosevelt brought to the presidency a novel, personalized display of leadership that broke with the norm of restrained presidential public personalities. Less visible, but as important for shaping his presidential leadership, Roosevelt brought to the role skills for administrative management and bureaucratic politics that distinguished him from his predecessors. To understand Roosevelt's use of the presidency, we should follow John Morton Blum's advice and examine first his earlier career "against the background of the institutions in which he deliberately chose to excel."[30]

Earlier presidents had seen service in the Congress, party leadership, the military, and occasionally a governorship. After 1828, Buchanan was the only president to have served earlier in the cabinet. Six of the nineteen presidents between 1828 and 1901 had been governors, and every Republican president since Lincoln was an officer in the Union army. Whatever administrative experience these politicians acquired was within the patronage system of the party period. That world overlapped in time but was qualitatively different than the nascent administrative state in which Roosevelt gained his early experiences in public service.[31]

Also in contrast to his predecessors, Roosevelt's electoral experience was modest for a presidential politician of his era. Before the gubernatorial election, he was thrice elected to single-year terms in the New York State Assembly, and he came in third in the 1886 New York mayoral election. For nine years prior to his Cuban adventure he occupied appointive executive positions in three very different administrative agencies. As he entered the presidency, Roosevelt's career profile was more executive administrator than elective politician. In those three administrative jobs Roosevelt learned the utility of teaching "himself . . . to study complex matters of policy before dealing with them."[32]

In 1889 Republican President Benjamin Harrison appointed Roosevelt to one of the three positions on the U.S. Civil Service Commission. He served four years in that post and was reappointed by Democratic President Grover Cleveland, serving two more years. In early 1895 he was named to New York City's police commission, serving there for two years. In spring 1897 President McKinley nominated him as assistant secretary of the navy, where he served for a year before going to war.

These positions presented Roosevelt with challenges different from those experienced by conventional politicians. Instead of going to school, so to speak, over problems of party factionalism, patronage policies, and electoral tactics, Roosevelt's classroom was the administrative agency. Each of his administrative jobs required that he form procedures and build institutional capacity in underdeveloped agencies.[33] Additionally, these roles required that Roosevelt build a network of support for his agencies to assure their authority and protect their appropriations.[34] Finally, through his official positions Roosevelt became an experienced consumer of specialized rules and technical information, learning Weber's principle that "bureaucratic administration means fundamentally the exercise of control on the basis of knowledge."[35]

The Civil Service Commission

During six years at the Civil Service Commission, Roosevelt fought to implant the new merit system into federal personnel practices that had been habitually partisan and disinterested in ability.[36] He later wrote that he had two aims. "There was . . . the effort to secure a more efficient administration . . . and . . . the even more important effort to withdraw the administrative offices . . . from the domain of spoils politics."[37]

Roosevelt confronted guerilla warfare from party politicians. Having lost the legislative battle over civil service, opponents sought to block the commission's work.[38] Roosevelt's tactics in that struggle depended on tools he found within bureaucracy's rationalized information system. The commission's files armed him to respond to attacks.[39] In a notable example, Roosevelt publicly confronted Senator Arthur Gorman (D-MD), leader of the Senate Democratic caucus. Gorman had claimed that written examinations for postal carriers posed questions irrelevant to the job, citing a qualified constituent who had failed the exam. Roosevelt responded, inviting the senator to see the examinations in question and requesting that he inform the commission of his constituent's name so that his exam could be made public. Gorman was irate, and Roosevelt wrote to him that "after you . . . failed to retract your statement. . . . The only course left me was to publish an authoritative and flat contradiction of your statement. . . . That it should have irritated you I do not wonder."[40] This may not be the best model of congressional relations for an administrator, but it nicely illustrates Roosevelt's grasp of the leveraging power of administrative information.

In another innovation at the commission, Roosevelt conducted field inspections of local postal offices, auditing compliance with the civil service laws and encouraging politically appointed postmasters to implement the merit system. Richard D. White found that the field investigations "caused a sensation, for [they] departed from the more passive enforcement policies of previous commissions."[41] Roosevelt also developed connections with a network of prominent civil service reformers to gather actionable information about personnel practices in federal field offices.

Roosevelt's auditing of merit practices in local post offices triggered an intense conflict with Postmaster General John Wanamaker. Against Roosevelt's charges of merit system violations in the post office, Wanamaker claimed to be "the right type of a civil-service man."[42] In fact, Postmaster General Wanamaker clung to the traditional assumption that local congressmen ought to have priority in deciding personnel matters in the post offices within their districts.[43] Roosevelt had no hesitation in confronting a cabinet officer. However, in contrast to his public controversy with the Democrat Gorman, Roosevelt fought behind the scenes to undermine Wanamaker, a senior official of his own party. He sought President Harrison's support and countered Wanamaker's claims with information from investigations of post office merit system violations.[44]

Roosevelt's civil service tenure honed the moralizing rhetorical style that characterized his leadership thereafter.[45] As Leonard White observed about his commission service: "He brought to it moral fervor, personal independence, physical energy and a complete willingness to fight a good battle for the merit system."[46]

The New York City Police Commission

In spring 1895 Roosevelt accepted appointment to New York City's metropolitan police commission. Reform mayor William Strong named Roosevelt to clean up the corrupt and inefficient police department.[47] The commission's three other members chose Roosevelt as the panel's president. He served for two years, applying personnel reforms learned at the civil service commission while gaining new experience managing a large, politically contentious, service delivery agency.

Reform of the great city's police department entailed problems of corrupt practices and inefficiencies related to a rapidly changing demography and intense social maladies. It meant establishing order in the unruly and ethnically heterogeneous city.[48] New York City's rapid change and crime created anxiety in middle-class citizens who demanded increased police protection and social order. Here was also Roosevelt's first experience with the range and intensity of the Progressive Era's demands for social reform. The historian Robert Gregg observes that during this period, the New York police "underwent considerable reform . . . to deal with . . . alcoholism, prohibition, disease, and violence . . . in short, the threat of anarchy and immorality that new urban dwellers . . . were believed to be bringing to . . . 'moral' communities."[49] Thus the challenge for Roosevelt was to not only reform the police department but also to make the department an instrument of social hygiene.

Roosevelt's ability to change the department was compromised by its organizational structure and a state law. The fragmented authority of a multi-headed commission and a state law dividing the department's accountability to both mayor and governor limited the commission's power over personnel. Roosevelt wrote that the department was "based on the desire to establish checks and balances so elaborate that no man shall have power enough to do anything very bad."[50] What the department needed, Roosevelt saw, was single-headed authority or, at least, centralized authority in a very few hands with a line of accountability directed to one elected executive, either the mayor or governor.[51] However, as commission president, Roosevelt acted as if he had authority over the department and often managed to carry a majority of the commission in his wake.[52] The *New York Times* wrote that while he reformed the commission's work, introducing division of responsibilities among the commissioners, "everything of any consequence goes through . . . Roosevelt's hands."[53]

His initial goal was to eliminate political influence in appointments and establish a robust merit system. He developed rudimentary investigative techniques to evaluate the processing of written examinations. Tracking a group of applicants along each step, he reviewed the application, evaluation, and appointment processes to detect variations from proper procedures.[54] He also used field investigation to monitor the behavior of police on the streets, adding a touch of self-dramatization. With the reporter Jacob Riis as a guide to the city's impoverished neighborhoods, Roosevelt took late-night walks to observe police on their rounds.[55] Replicating his use of civil service reformers as informants while at the civil service commission, Roosevelt used Riis's knowledge of New York's slums to assess police activity and to guide policymaking.[56] Of Riis, Roosevelt said he was the person who was "closest to me" in his work as police commissioner.[57] That work was a crucial step in his evolution from an upper-class Gilded Age reformer to a progressive reformer. Speaking of his nighttime investigations, Roosevelt wrote: "I was well awakened to the need of making ours in good faith both an economic and an industrial as well as a political democracy."[58]

Along with fighting corruption, Roosevelt expanded the department's capacities through establishing bureaucratic routine. He initiated close scrutiny of the department's $6 million budget, and he initiated competitive bidding for purchases of material and services.[59] Roosevelt also saw the political utility of his administrative activities. The police commission was his stage. He adopted a public style that fascinated New York City's reporters and the public. In addition to his pronouncements and his nighttime jaunts, he adopted a black silk sash and pink, tasseled shirts as his uniform. Reporters were naturally drawn to his "raucous, explosive, moralistic manner" that "matched his imposing physical presence."[60] And reporters "loved the copy he generated with his combative mien, his self-righteous rhetoric, and his flair for the dramatic."[61] In New York, the politician as bureaucrat became, as well, the politician as performer.

At the Navy Department

President William McKinley's victory in 1896 occasioned Theodore Roosevelt's appointment as assistant secretary at the navy department. His political friends, particularly Senator Lodge (R-MA), pressed the new president for the appointment. As Roosevelt's name was mentioned, the *Washington Post* expressed surprise because "Roosevelt has established a reputation as a trouble maker."[62] Roosevelt feared that Senator Platt would block him.[63] In fact, Platt welcomed the appointment as a way to be rid of him from New York City, observing that he "has been a disturbing element in every situation to which he has been a party. . . . But he . . . can probably do less harm to the [party] organization as Assistant Secretary of the navy than in any other office."[64]

Roosevelt's year at the navy was his most complex administrative job yet, and it advanced his organizational skills. It expanded his repertoire of abilities for managing technical information in decision-making and planning large-scale projects. It was his responsibility to manage the department's quotidian internal operation, but he also took responsibility for initiating several major administrative reforms. Roosevelt was severely constrained by the power of the department's eight bureaus (yards and docks, equipment, ordnance, construction, navigation, steam engineering, supplies and accounts, and medicine), each a virtually autonomous realm headed by a senior officer. Roosevelt's superior, Secretary John D. Long, was an elderly former governor and ex-congressman with no naval experience who was distrustful of Roosevelt's energy and ideas. Additionally, the navy's professional leadership was tradition-bound and wary of reform.[65] To obtain Long's approval for his appointment, Roosevelt had to promise him to not be disruptive.

However, Long's lethargy and age worked in Roosevelt's favor. In mid-June 1897 Long retreated from Washington for the summer. As acting secretary, Roosevelt busily focused on two projects, defining the navy's strategic role in projecting American power and improving the department's organizational effectiveness. By keeping Long informed by letter, Roosevelt discouraged any thought Long might have had of intervening in Roosevelt's activities. For example, in mid-August, Roosevelt wrote: "You must not answer my letters because then I shall feel that I ought not to send them to you, for I don't want you to be bothered at all; but I just want to tell you how things are going."[66]

Roosevelt engaged in conversation Captain Alfred Mahan, a distinguished theorist of sea power, to develop policies for strengthening the United States' strategic position. Roosevelt was thinking about war. The problems of Spanish incursions in Cuba threatened American interests, and Japan flexed its naval muscle in the Pacific. Speaking at the Naval War College just a month into his new job, Roosevelt explained his view of the navy's strategic role. He said: "We ask for a great navy . . . because . . . no National life is worth having if the Nation is not willing . . . to stake everything on the supreme arbitrament [sic] of war, and to pour out its blood, its treasure, and tears like water, rather than submit to the loss of honor and renown."[67] Roosevelt discussed with Mahan specifics such as the assignment of warships to Asian waters and the relative likelihood of different threats to American security.[68] He acted on Mahan's advice in his own decisions, and regularly pressed his views on President McKinley.[69]

Simultaneously, Roosevelt addressed the navy's administrative organization. Replicating his information-gathering experience at the civil service commission and the police department, he sought information to assess the quality of naval officers "to gather from every source information as to who were the best men to occupy fighting positions."[70] Roosevelt then made personnel assignments upon that information, his promotion of Commodore Dewey to lead the Asiatic squadron prior to the war with Spain being a most prominent example of that exercise.[71] He also gathered advice from those officers most fit for "the fighting positions" for decisions about naval equipment and organizational changes.

Roosevelt's style of work is well illustrated in a problem with an appropriation for ship construction during Secretary Long's absence. Resolution of the problem required both technical information and political judgment. Congress had stalled appropriations for naval armor plate on a warship under construction, balking at prices quoted for the product by its few American producers. To continue construction the builder proposed using thinner plating than specified. Roosevelt had to balance concerns over the capabilities of the important new warship, a heavy cruiser, with the pressing need to quickly expand the navy's deep-sea fleet. In consulting officers in the bureaus of construction and ordnance, Roosevelt received conflicting advice. After information gathering and consultation, he decided in favor of the inferior plating to assure immediate progress in construction.[72] Confronting these kind of complex technical decisions required that Roosevelt learn to identify trustworthy information sources within the navy and learn to assess the quality of advice he received.[73]

Roosevelt simplified administrative reporting for ships' officers. He surveyed and reported on the readiness of state naval militias in the seaboard and Great Lakes states, assessing their readiness to supply manpower in time of war.[74] That summer he also established a board of officers to recommend improvements in the use of dry docks. During the fall Roosevelt organized and led a board of inquiry to recommend reforms in the service's personnel system and its bureaus. Subsequently, Roosevelt recommended three major reforms to the secretary: (1) the separate personnel ladders of engineers and line officers should be merged into one; (2) the promotion of officers should be increased to end stagnation in rank among junior officers; and (3) the treatment of enlisted personnel be improved.[75] The McKinley administration embraced all three recommendations, and the report led to the 1898 naval reorganization bill, "the

Roosevelt bill," as it was termed in the press. The *New York Times* reported the bill's "importance is beyond all question." [76] Roosevelt served just a year at the navy, but what he began there would make him the "man who was to dominate American naval development for nearly a generation," to quote Harold and Margaret Sprout.[77]

Roosevelt's Political Vocation

During 1898 Roosevelt leaped to national prominence. He went from the navy in the spring to war in Cuba that summer and was elected governor in November. More than anything else, what made him a distinctive figure during that year were his talents for self-promotion and self-presentation. However, it was more than appearances that distinguished Roosevelt from other politicians.

The political elite of the late 1890s was composed of men socialized within the patronage-hungry party period. For them, government administration had been a temporary and amateur activity undertaken by "booty politicians," to use Max Weber's term.[78] Administration was subservient to the party organization that controlled government, according to them, and public administrators should be minions of the party. Even while he was a loyal party man, Roosevelt's administrative experiences set him apart from the dominant vocation of partisan politics, winning and its spoils. He was at the forefront of a professionalizing impulse in government administration. Roosevelt strengthened civil service and increased the efficacy of the three agencies he led. His political vocation was identified less with the party machine and more with public policies, the administrative agencies that implement them, and what Weber termed the "sense of status honor" that formed the integrity of merit-based officialdom.[79]

Governor Roosevelt

Roosevelt reveled in his first election victory for high office. He wrote to a friend, "this Governorship . . . is the only post I have ever held that had a blue ribbon attached to it." He added that a "blue ribbon" post was desirable not for its prestige but because it offered an opportunity for an incumbent to accomplish important things, to do "dangerous and hard duty."[80] Because of the "blue ribbon" importance of the office, the governorship brought to a head a problem Roosevelt had so far finessed in his political career.

This office juxtaposed his reform impulses against his partisan orthodoxy in ways he had managed to finesse in prior administrative posts. It required Roosevelt's full attention to his party's interests. He had earlier confessed about his gubernatorial nomination that "there was no possibility of securing [it] . . . unless the bosses permitted it."[81] The party had a tight hold on Governor Roosevelt. Once in office, it would be his task to successfully placate the party leaders and work with the partisan legislature to achieve his policy goals and assure his own Republican political future.

In the late 1890s Moise Ostrogorski observed that American government was inextricably united with machine politics, noting "here . . . is the true explanation of the success of the Machine: it is a government."[82] Roosevelt's own political credentials and loyalties bound him to the Republican party, not only out of practical necessity but also as a matter of principle. When many patricians fled the party in 1884 after the nomination of James Blaine, Roosevelt remained loyal, held his nose, and supported the nominee. He attacked those Mugwumps as "parlor reformers" lacking the "sinewy power" to bring their ideals to reality, and afterward he disdained genteel political independents.[83]

Thus, Roosevelt internalized party loyalty *and* reformist commitments. His guiding principle was that one must not only be a reformer, "but he must be efficient. If he goes into politics he must go into practical politics."[84] Both sides of that dialectic shaped his performance in the governorship and the presidency. Stephen Skowronek characterizes President Roosevelt as "unmatched in presidential history for his mastery of orthodox–innovation."[85] Roosevelt's presidency was a brilliant balancing act between his affiliation to the dominant Republican regime and his impulses to address problems of society and economy. That talent for balance was revealed and first honed earlier at Albany.

Indeed his balancing act had its first real test in the governorship. To observe his effort to resolve the tension between partisan interests and good government we shall examine two episodes in which he asserted public interest in the face of party patronage demands. The first of these was appointment of the state insurance supervisor. The second case was his initiative for taxation of firms holding public service franchises.

Appointing the State Supervisor of Insurance

Executive offices were political plums distributed to the leader's lieutenants. More important, control of executive appointments assured that the party could use public expenditures and regulation to further party interests. In short, gubernatorial appointments would have to be approved by Senator Platt.[86] Roosevelt's appointment decisions confronted the divide between partisan interests and good government principles. That his appointments had to find approval in the Republican-led state senate guaranteed the organization's interests would be protected. A reform-minded governor, a "parlor reformer," could have denied partisan considerations and deadlocked with the senate over appointments. But Roosevelt avoided deadlock and balanced the pressures of partisanship on the one hand and individual qualifications on the other.

The superintendent of insurance case illustrates Roosevelt's successful balancing act. That office supervised the state's insurance industry and was a conduit for a symbiotic relationship between the party organization and the industry. The incumbent, Lou Payn, was Governor Black's appointee, with a fixed term ending in February 1900. He was a former lobbyist and a leader in the Columbia County Republican organization. Harold Gosnell described Payn as "possessing a 'genius' for 'handling things' in the state legislature."[87] Payn's reappointment was unacceptable to Roosevelt. He had too openly flouted civil service rules in the management of his department and had a reputation for dishonesty. Roosevelt's friend, Elihu Root, publicly spoke of Payn as a "a stench in the nostrils of all decent men."[88] Yet, leading insurance industry's executives and Republican papers called for Payn's reappointment.[89] On his own behalf, Payn worked his influence in the legislature and party. He confidently announced at the end of 1899 that no other person nominated by Roosevelt as insurance superintendent would win senate approval.[90]

Platt pressed Roosevelt to retain Payn, and the governor reported to Henry Cabot Lodge that he told Platt he "could not compromise" over Payn.[91] This seemed a zero sum situation between partisanship and competency. Yet, at the end of January 1900, Roosevelt successfully nominated Thomas Hendricks as the new superintendent of insurance, replacing Payn. How had he secured victory from apparent deadlock?

Roosevelt's success depended on information with which he disarmed Senator Platt and then publicly embarrassed Republicans. Through a disgruntled ex-employee of the State Trust Company the governor learned that State Trust had loaned a large sum to Payn while he was regulator of the firm's insurance business. Roosevelt then asked his former associate at the police commission, Avery Andrews, for information about Payn's financial circumstances and the loan.[92] While not enough to prove a violation of the law, the information

Andrews turned up gave Roosevelt leverage to embarrass Platt. At the same time, Roosevelt's offer to Platt was to appoint a "straight organization republican [*sic*]" as long as that person was "honest and efficient."[93] Thus while using his own information sources to indict Payn's honesty and defeat Platt, Roosevelt assured Platt that he would have a veto over the choice of Payn's replacement. And Roosevelt proposed to Platt the name of New York State Senator F. J. Hendricks, a Syracuse Republican. Balking at first, Platt ultimately approved, and Hendricks was confirmed.[94]

Genteel reformers attacked Roosevelt for the Hendricks appointment, accusing him of submitting to the machine. Roosevelt dismissed them as failing to understand the game he was playing. He achieved the great success of replacing a corrupt official with an honest one, albeit one who would cooperate closely with the Republican organization's interests. Providing his own characterization of the case, Roosevelt wrote to a friend:

> If I had done what the *Evening Post* and Parkhurst advised, I would not have had . . . more than six [votes] for the confirmation of anybody. . . . Why I should denounce Senator Platt and the machine when after months of opposition they had come my way, I really do not see.[95]

Roosevelt believed that his ability to operate as governor "depended upon the maintenance of harmonious relations with Platt; at the same time, results worth achieving demanded a vigilant and sustained effort to keep the machine" straight.[96]

The Franchise Tax Bill

While he was governor, Roosevelt awoke to the unhealthy relationships among big business, the political party machines, and government.[97] Early in his term he saw three bills that represented the symbiosis of business interests and machine politics. All three made long-term grants of public rights to rapid transit and utility companies in New York City. These were the Astoria gas bill, the rapid transit bill, and the tunnel bill. Roosevelt agreed that the bills would improve public services in the city. However, he wrote to Senator Platt's chief lieutenant, Benjamin Odell, "there does seem to me to be a question whether we ought not to have some return in the shape of a percentage on the gross earnings of the privileges conferred by these franchises."[98]

The franchise bills mark a further turning point in Roosevelt's ideas as a reformer. With them, he confronted Progressive Era concerns over the depredations of big business in the economy, politics, and government.[99] On March 27, 1899, he sent a message to the legislature proposing creation of a joint committee to design a system of taxation for corporations holding public franchises. He said "that a corporation which derives its powers from the State should pay to the state a just percentage of its earnings. . . . This should be especially true for the franchises bestowed upon gas companies, street railroads, and the like."[100]

Once Roosevelt spoke of taxing corporate franchises the issue took on a life of its own, suggesting that the governor's concerns crystallized already widespread sentiments.[101] And with his taxation statement to the legislature, Roosevelt confronted a political paradox. He depended on continued support from the party for his agenda as governor, and he required party support for the next stage of his political career. He could ignore corruptions of government for the benefit of business and the party machine and secure Senator Platt's support. Or, he could risk Platt's fury by pursuing policies in the public interest.

Roosevelt's choice was to accept neither of these options but to pursue a third alternative through which he would attempt to influence the legislature above the appeals of machine loyalties and simultaneously finesse Platt and the Republican organization to prevent an open break with the "easy boss." Roosevelt's insight was that public, rhetorical leadership could create its own momentum of widespread support for an issue, potentially influencing legislators and restraining Platt from open opposition. "He ventured rebellion only when he could be sure that a majority of the people and a substantial fraction of the party stood with him."[102] His game was to force a vote on a tax on franchises in the legislature while he explained the importance of the issue to the public. Through his promotion of the issue, the people would be interested "and the representatives would scarcely dare to vote the wrong way."[103]

Roosevelt found a legislative vehicle in a bill to tax corporate franchises, introduced in the legislature by Senator John Ford in January 1899. The Ford bill would require that county assessors attach a valuation to, and levy a tax on, the municipal rights held by corporations as franchises. The bill passed the senate, but opposition from the Republican machine sidelined it in the lower house.[104] Roosevelt wanted assessment by a state body rather than the counties, but the Ford bill was the perfect medium to dramatize his position. Thus, as Republicans sidelined the bill in the assembly, Roosevelt addressed businessmen at the Union League Club in Chicago, stating that no franchises should be granted to corporations "unless a return is going to the State."[105] Through the Chicago speech, Roosevelt heightened the profile of his quest for a franchise tax and increased pressure on the legislature. Reporting on that speech, the *New York Times* asked: "Is Governor Roosevelt to be the apostle of a new National crusade for tax reform, with the taxation of franchises as its keynote"?[106]

In late April Roosevelt delivered the coup that brought victory to his tax crusade. Constitutionally, the governor could force a vote on a measure, and Roosevelt delivered a message to the assembly on April 28, requesting a vote on the Ford bill. The bill consequently passed by a vote of 104 to 38, inaugurating what a contemporary tax expert called "a distinct advance in the tax system of New York."[107] It was not a victory over Democrats, reported the *New York Times* about Roosevelt's strategy, but rather "over the organized leadership of his own party." And the news report continued that politicians of both parties were impressed by "the fine politics the Governor displayed in forcing" the vote, "predicting that it will make him . . . a more formidable Presidential possibility than ever before."[108]

To the Vice Presidency

The *Times'* prediction that his victory on the franchise tax brought him closer to the presidency was prescient not only because of Roosevelt's expanding popular appeal. That victory solidified Senator Platt's decision to push Roosevelt from the governorship. After the Ford bill was approved by the assembly, Platt wrote to the governor suggesting to him that he demonstrated an excess of "altruism" in dealing with matters of business and government and urging that he show "very rare and difficult . . . moral courage not to sign" the bill.[109] Roosevelt responded with a closely reasoned letter explaining that the franchise tax was a genuinely moderate measure and any flaws in it could be addressed in a special session of the legislature.[110] The more success the governor achieved, the more likely he was to pose problems for Platt.

Vice President Garret Hobart's death in November 1899 gave Platt a place to honorably sideline Roosevelt. The situation was ripe for Roosevelt's nomination as vice president. His public appeal had grown enormously, and many Republicans thought his reform record and zestful campaign style made him the perfect foil to William Jennings Bryan's renewed candidacy in 1900. Platt thus had the advantage of popular support in the party for Roosevelt's candidacy, masking the awkwardness of pushing him out of Albany.[111] At the June 1900 Republican convention in Philadelphia, with his Rough Riders' campaign hat, Roosevelt reprised the political appeal of his heroic spectacle.[112]

Conclusion

The McKinley and Roosevelt ticket was an odd match. Roosevelt's career centered in government while McKinley's centered in politics. Roosevelt's work in administrative government was harmonious with Progressive Era demands for expanded governmental activity and problem solving. McKinley's stake in politics harked back to the structure of mass parties and their maintenance through the work of government.

The 1900 Republican ticket was as much a pairing of opposites as that of any party's ticket since that time. Not that contemporaries failed to take note of the misfit of the ticket. Mark Hanna's famous comment that now "there's only one life between this madman and the White House" exemplifies how strange Roosevelt seemed to many senior Republican leaders. But what they thought they saw in him, his political idiosyncrasy, they misunderstood. Of course, striking differences in personality and background separated Roosevelt from McKinley and his cohort. The younger man was a socially privileged scion of the old Knickerbocker elite. He was a product of elite education, and he was a much-published intellectual and member of a circle that included Henry Adams, Alfred Mahan, Henry Cabot Lodge, and Brooks Adams. Roosevelt, of course, had also aggressively sought to clean up government during his career, showing less concern for party interests than thought desirable by men like Hanna and Platt. And then there was the cowboy Roosevelt and the Rough Riders. What were the old pols to make of this extraordinary talent for spectacle?

But those notable personal differences between the two running mates masked the greater difference between them that was not understood by the party bosses. In looking at Roosevelt, the bosses failed to see they were looking into the future of American politics. Those differences between Roosevelt and McKinley that were most important related to the emerging systemic divide in American politics. McKinley was a man attuned to the identities and structure of the old system. Roosevelt was a man capable of hearing the demands and seeing the opportunities unfolding in what would be called the Progressive Era.

3

Constructing Leadership to Make History: Anti-Trust and the Navy

I was bent upon making the Government the most efficient . . . instrument in helping the people . . . politically, socially, and industrially. . . . As for the particular methods of realizing these various beliefs, I was content to wait and see what method might be necessary in each given case.

Theodore Roosevelt[1]

SIX MONTHS AFTER INAUGURATION as vice president, Roosevelt was president. As vice president he complained he was "an historical observer who did no work." [2] Now he would make history.

Roosevelt adopted the classic stance of a succeeding vice president, pledging to continue McKinley's policies and cabinet.[3] Nevertheless he worried the business and political elite.[4] The *Nation* wrote, "The ship of state is on its way to unknown ports."[5] The *Washington Post* feared that Roosevelt might overturn the dignity and conservatism of national government:

> What changes will he make? What does the future hold in store? . . .
> Roosevelt, known to be an admirer of what he calls a strenuous life,
> has been chiefly noted in the past for his pugnacious, effervescent
> spirit, his forte for spectacular display. This is the ground for the fear
> that in the White House he may lack the conservatism . . . so essential
> to a successful administration of the nation's affairs.[6]

There was cause for conservatives' anxiety, if they were sufficiently perceptive to read the implications of Roosevelt's leadership style. There were new issues in the political air and new demands for government action that could motivate a president who was responsive to them. And Roosevelt *was* a different kind of politician than McKinley. As the *Nation* characterized the difference, if "McKinley's role was opportunism, his successor's is strenuousness."[7] As we have seen, he was of a different generation, with a different career route, and a less easy relationship with his party than conventional politicians of the party period. He was propelled into the vice presidential nomination, in large part, by his troubled relationship with Republican bosses.

Roosevelt's differences from McKinley were evident not just in personality but in the issues he addressed and the manner of his political work. He calculated issues and their implications with a broader sense of social priorities than his fellow Republicans. Consequently, he was more attuned than his predecessor to middle-class voters' growing demands for reform. Additionally, his political style was a highly public spectacle, communicating his agenda and appeals to a middle-class electorate through popular magazines and major newspapers. Was the role Roosevelt assumed as president one that would be imposed on anyone who occupied the presidency at that time?[8] Would McKinley, in his second term, have become "Rooseveltian"? The journalist William Allen White thought not and attributed Roosevelt's presidency to his own personal characteristics and style. He wrote that he "is president . . . solely because of his unsullied integrity. And he was put there by his enemies who loathed the virtues that made him strong."[9]

In some respects McKinley was also innovative, but his most important innovations were related to party organization and campaigns. He and Mark Hanna had innovatively unified and controlled the Republican Party. They reinforced Republicans as a conservative party tied closely to emergent corporate capitalism. Under Hanna's guidance, major corporations became cash cows ensuring the dominance of a conservative Republican Party. Matthew Crenson and Benjamin Ginsberg characterize McKinley as a "discreet insurgent."[10] His innovations were toward strengthening the party's conservatism rather than responding to new demands.[11] "McKinley made the divided authorities of the government function more effectively in the interests of business expansion."[12]

Personal Characteristics and Political Role

Roosevelt responded to the changing character of American politics and its implications for presidential leadership. He was a Republican loyalist, committed to continuity of Republican control of national government. Yet, his recognition of changing forces and demands in national politics positioned him to adapt his partisan commitments to new political challenges.

His own propensity toward innovation joined with newly expanding possibilities in the presidency. As the forces holding together the structure of the party period weakened, political space opened for new kinds of political organization and new constituencies. The innovative presidency Roosevelt crafted synthesized his personal political style with new opportunities for presidential leadership. Macro-level changes in the political system created new incentives for leadership but required politicians with new sensibilities for those incentives to be recognized.

The general outline of Roosevelt's vigorous presidency has been told and retold. My purpose is not to repeat it again but to investigate the intersection of role and individual leadership that help us understand his impact on the office and government. The question is how did Roosevelt construct innovative leadership within the same very limited office occupied by McKinley, Cleveland, and Harrison? It was an office "small in scale and limited in power . . . caught up more in . . . party politics and patronage than in the formulation and conduct of public policy."[13]

What this chapter seeks to explain is Roosevelt's use of office to establish a policy agenda, promote that agenda, define specific applications of policy, and then implement policy. All of that contrasted to his Gilded Age predecessors in "the small scale and limited" office. So we seek to understand how Roosevelt confronted the incongruity between his goals and the office's paucity of resources, turning the old office into a platform for policy leadership.

Two Cases of Presidential Policy Leadership

Historians commonly divide Roosevelt's presidency into a restrained "McKinley" term and an activist "Square Dealing" term following his 1904 election. After the 1904 election, H. W. Brands writes, "he blew what Wall Street could only interpret as a charge."[14] My approach differs in that I focus on specific, revealing cases of Roosevelt's leadership early in his presidency rather than its overall contours. What Roosevelt accomplished early set the public expectations for his leadership and established his pattern of governance. What followed later was a recurrent pattern of leadership applied to increasingly ambitious goals.

Cases exemplifying Roosevelt's efforts to shape and effect policy will have three characteristics. First, they should be discreet cases of his policy engagement, not policy toward business, for example, but a specific initiative regarding business questions. Second, we are interested in cases in which Roosevelt was the dominant or initiating actor, the agenda setter, and in which his position was at odds with his party's predominant preference. Third, we are interested in cases that reveal Roosevelt's identification of, and communication with, a public constituency.

The cases examined are the *Northern Securities* anti-trust case and the innovation of the all-big-gun battleship. In each I will examine Roosevelt's initiative and his acquisition of strategic resources to pursue his policy preference. For each case, I will show how it fits into the larger arenas of Roosevelt's policies of corporate regulation and naval policy, respectively.

The Trust Problem

The 1900 Republican Platform stated an equivocal position on the trust question. "We recognize the necessity and propriety of the honest co-operation of capital to meet new business conditions . . . but we condemn all conspiracies and combinations indented to . . . control prices."[15] The 1896 platform had contained no language about trusts, but William Jennings Bryan's attack on trusts in that election, and his likely renomination in 1900, forced a Republican platform response. Yet, as of fall 1900, there was no evidence that the Republicans would use their undivided control of government to regulate consolidation in American industry.[16]

In the prior year, the Republican-controlled 56th Congress "neither did nor intended to do anything inimical to trusts or combines of any description."[17] In his role as the Republican attack dog in the 1900 campaign, Roosevelt mentioned the dangers of trusts far more than other Republicans. Speaking in Grand Rapids, Michigan, he cited his success in using the franchise tax to control public utility trusts in New York State, and he proposed a concrete idea for national assessment of trusts: "We must be able by law to find out exactly what each corporation does and earns. This . . . publicity itself will effect something toward remedying many evils. Moreover, it will give us a clearer idea as to what the remaining evils are.[18]

The turn of the century saw an acceleration of corporate mergers and consolidations. It was in this flux of business reorganizations that the modern American corporate structure emerged. Between 1898 and 1902 there were 2,653 mergers with a capitalized value above $6.3 billion.[19] That process of business concentration and change heightened Americans' anxieties about trusts, their impact on consumers, and their great concentrations of wealth. During the 1890s several conferences on the trust problem received widespread press coverage. And popular magazines such as *McClure's* and *The Century* published exposés of trusts.[20] Yet McKinley was unresponsive to these concerns. The federal government's only tool for dealing with business concentration was the Sherman Anti-Trust Act of 1890. Its utility was in doubt as Roosevelt entered the presidency. The act brought common law doctrine of unfair limitation of competition to bear on the expanding scale of American firms. The law was not meant to impose a new regulatory force onto the economy but rather to end concentration when it harmed the public welfare.[21]

There were just eighteen Sherman Act cases initiated by the federal government prior to 1901, and four of these aimed at labor unions.[22] Not only had past administrations been hesitant to use the law, but the first case under it to reach the U.S. Supreme Court limited its utility against manufacturing combinations in restraint of trade. In *U.S. v. E. C. Knight,* 156 U.S. 1 (1895), the Court constricted the act even while recognizing Congress's unchallenged powers to regulate interstate and foreign commerce.[23] The American Sugar Refining Company controlled four major sugar refiners, achieving a monopoly on the manufacturing of refined sugar in the United States. The court ruled first that holding companies were under state not federal jurisdiction. Additionally, the court distinguished manufacturing from commerce; only the latter is "interstate" activity.[24]

Two Supreme Court cases after *Knight* created further complexity for Sherman Act litigation. In *U.S. v. Trans-Missouri Freight Association,* 166 U.S. 290, a 5–4 Court found that the Sherman Act did apply to combinations of interstate railroads that restrained trade. And a court divided 5–3 in *U.S. v. Joint Traffic Association,* 171 U.S. 505, affirming the act's application to interstate commerce and sustaining its declaration that any restraint of trade, not just those judged "unreasonable" by common law standards, were prohibited by the act.[25] Thus Roosevelt found an incoherent state of affairs regarding business combinations, public policy, and the law.[26] There was a quickening of concentration in the burgeoning American economy, and the law stated that all such (nonmanufacturing) combinations in interstate commerce violated the law.

Roosevelt immediately addressed the disparity between law and policy. In his annual message of December 3, 1901 he stated an intention to act on the antitrust question. The message itself was remarkable, "one of the most ambitious by any American president."[27] It was distinctive on several counts. Rather than compiling departmental reports, Roosevelt wrote the message himself. It promoted the president's independent policy initiatives, apart from party priorities. On all these counts the message parted company with those of post-bellum presidents like Cleveland, Harrison, and McKinley that were composites of departmental reports and party-supported initiatives.[28]

The trust problem was his first topic. In his characteristically dialectical rhetoric, Roosevelt spoke of the productivity of business and the necessity of leaving capitalist invention unhampered. But, "it is also true that there are real and grave evils." He admitted that many Americans thought "the great corporations known as trusts are in certain of their features . . . hurtful to the general welfare." And, he insisted, these views were well founded. What was to be done, he suggested, was creation of a federal supervisory system for corporations in interstate commerce to assure that there was made public "full and accurate information as to their operations."[29] Toward that end he recommended a new cabinet department of commerce and industries "to deal with commerce in its broadest sense; including . . . whatever concerns labor and all matters affecting the great business corporations."[30] Roosevelt saw two distinct ways of acting on the trust issue: through the Sherman Act, to preserve a vanishing individualism in the economy, which he thought was futile; or by recognizing that combinations are central to modern business and supervising them.[31] Thus Roosevelt, as no president had done before, frontally addressed the gap between economic reality and policy.

With his message Roosevelt had broken his pledge to conform to McKinley's policies and people. In September he had embraced McKinley's presidency as the ground of his own authority. Now he set out an independent claim for his pursuit of anti-trust policy, invoking two justifications. The first was a pragmatic response to the challenge of new business power. The determination of a policy's soundness was "tested in experience in view of . . . observable outcomes, as opposed to being measured against some standard that is atemporal and external to experience."[32] Having no already established authority for domestic policy initiatives, Roosevelt used pragmatic reasoning to give his preferences the justification of social efficacy.[33] Roosevelt's second strategy was rhetorical, using the threat of anarchy and disorder to prove the necessity of his pragmatic authority for addressing trusts. His discussion of business regulation followed a long denunciation of anarchy that had opened the message (McKinley had been assassinated by a self-proclaimed anarchist). The juxtaposition of social disorder with the restraint of business through regulation italicized Roosevelt's pragmatic reasoning by linking regulation and order.

On the franchise tax issue Governor Roosevelt had faced a question of economic monopoly. His preparation of the 1901 annual message's trust initiative paralleled his preparation of his franchise tax initiative. Before sending the message to Congress, he circulated drafts and consulted widely with two goals in mind. First, he aimed to build support for a policy initiative. Second, he sought to co-opt potential critics by offering the opportunity for advising the president on the trust problem. Just as he had done as governor, he consulted and built support, primarily with those to his right: business leaders, conservative journalists, and orthodox Republican legislators, his party's reform-wary leaders. This consultative style broke with McKinley's practice in speech and message preparation. Typically McKinley quickly dictated a speech or message and read it to one of his associates. For example, he dictated his second inaugural during one week and then read it to Secretary of War Elihu Root.[34]

Through October and November 1901 Roosevelt received a parade of visitors to read drafts of his message and advise on its provisions. Among these were personal friends such as Columbia University's president, Nicholas Murray Butler, who Roosevelt invited to come to the White House to discuss an early draft.[35] He invited the historian Brooks Adams because he wanted to discuss with Adams how to include in the message "one or two ideas of your *Atlantic Monthly* article."[36] Among the many others invited were A. J. Cassatt, president of the Pennsylvania Railroad; Roman Catholic Bishop John Ireland; Harry Chapin, president of the Boston and Albany Railroad; and Paul Morton, a Chicago railroad executive.[37] Republican congressional leaders were consulted. For example, in late September he wrote to Senate majority leader Nelson Aldrich: "Before I write my message, I should like to . . . go over certain subjects with you." [38]

Similar letters were sent to eight other senior Senate Republicans, inviting their views. To other Republicans Roosevelt invited consultation about their specific issue interests. He asked of Representative George W. Ray: "Is there anything that I should put in my message about bankruptcy?"[39] To Wayne Mac-Veagh, a former attorney general, he wrote: "I shall want your advice over the constitutional side of the corporation business."[40] Roosevelt also sought out reporters. He invited Lyman Abbott, the editor of *The Outlook* magazine, to "go over certain questions of my general policy." Paul Dana, editor of the *New York Sun,* was urged to "come down . . . as there are so many things I would like to talk over with you." Charles Miller, editor of the *New York Times,* was also invited to discuss Roosevelt's policies, as was Whitelaw Reid of the *New York Tribune* and St. Clair McKelway of the *Brooklyn Eagle.*[41]

Many of those Roosevelt consulted advised against his draft language on supervising corporations. But he had the assurance of Attorney General Philander Knox that the proposed legislation would pass constitutional muster. He responded to Connecticut Senator Orville Platt's complaint about the proposed policy that "Mr. Knox believes that a law that can stand could be devised . . . I will get you together with the Attorney General . . . to see if we can devise such a law."[42] To Paul Dana, who sharply disagreed with Roosevelt's criticism of business generally and the plan for supervision in particular, Roosevelt explained it had Knox's approval and had been also reviewed by Secretary of War Elihu Root, "the most influential senators and . . . at least a dozen prominent businessmen."[43]

Through his give and take with others about the message, it was clear that Roosevelt's strategy of consultation was far more an effort at co-optation than it was a search for accommodation with conservatives. He fended off efforts from powerful business figures and party leaders at softening his stance. When his banker brother-in-law, Douglas Robinson, told Roosevelt that George W. Perkins, J. P. Morgan's chief lieutenant, wished to see him to express his opposition to the trust language of the message, Roosevelt responded, "Perkins may just as well make up his mind that I will not make my message one hair's breadth milder."[44]

As Roosevelt resisted opposition, he was playing to another, larger audience. As in the New York franchise tax case, he understood that action on trusts was a winning issue with the public. Conversely, Roosevelt seemed to understand that to disappoint the public on the trust issue would deflate his leadership. In this regard, his annual message was intended for the public's eyes as much as it was meant for Congress. As Roosevelt remarked to Paul Dana: "You have no conception of the revolt that would be caused if I did nothing in the matter."[45] That this strategy succeeded is demonstrated in a later remark by the president of the Rock Island Line that Roosevelt "had so aroused the people" that it was impossible for the railroad executives to resist Roosevelt's regulatory efforts.[46]

In his *Autobiography* Roosevelt wrote of his alternative to winning over his conservative critics: "I was forced to abandon the effort to persuade them to come my way, and then I achieved results . . . by appealing over the heads of the . . . leaders to the people."[47] That the message reached the people is demonstrated by praise for it from newspapers of various political stripes. The independent Democratic *San Francisco Bulletin* stated, "Not since Lincoln has there been a President who so thoroughly represents the democratic spirit of the American people." The Democratic *Detroit Free Press* wrote: "It is a message which every American . . . can read with pleasure." The Republican *Topeka Capital* reported: "It is one of the strongest messages ever sent to Congress by any President."[48]

Two months after sending his message to Congress, Roosevelt shocked the financial community by announcing an anti-trust suit under the Sherman Act. He saw a ripe target in the recently organized Northern Securities Corporation, formed by J. P. Morgan and James Hill to hold securities of the Northern Pacific and Great Northern railroads. The two roads ran parallel between Midwest shipping centers and the Pacific Northwest. The apparent aim of Northern Securities was to coordinate operations and eliminate competition between the two railroads.[49] Roosevelt saw the suit as a direct challenge to the use of holding companies as instruments for the restraint of trade. The *E. C. Knight* decision had held that the "sugar trust" holding company had not violated the law, and Roosevelt observed that Northern Securities was a holding company controlling "railway transportation throughout that vast territory exactly as the Sugar Trust had acquired control." Thus this suit sought to force the Supreme Court to reconsider the status of holding companies formed to restrain trade.

Roosevelt's decision on the *Northern Securities* case seems inconsistent with his message's acceptance of business combinations and proposal for federal supervision. The suit relied on the categorically anti-combination position of the recent Court decisions. However, to focus on that inconsistency is to miss what was most innovative in Roosevelt's action.[50] He was early in the process of formulating a coherent policy toward business combinations, and the suit was not the mechanism for achieving coherence. Rather the suit, like his idea for federal supervision of trusts, was a move to impose executive discretion on anti-trust policy. The Supreme Court might continue to fail to distinguish between productive and detrimental trusts, but the president could impose consistency on the application of the Sherman Act through discretion over what cases to initiate. Martin Sklar writes that Roosevelt's "selective enforcement of the Sherman Act . . . openly renunciatory of the law as the Supreme Court had construed it [was] an executive usurpation of the judicial function, and in effect . . . of the legislative function as well."[51]

Roosevelt's action against Northern Securities shocked the financial community. Most Sherman Act cases were initiated by the relatively independent federal district attorneys and not by the administration in Washington. On February

19, 1901, it was Attorney General Philander Knox who announced the suit against Northern Securities. Business leaders accused the president of acting capriciously, and the stock market fell.[52] A second cause for surprise was the expectation that a properly conservative administration would communicate its intentions to business leaders, as Roosevelt had consulted over his message's trust language. The *New York Times* reported that some businessmen said that this was the first time in decades that "Wall Street was completely surprised by the action of the Government at Washington."[53] In fact, Roosevelt reached the decision about the suit with little consultation. Attorney General Philander Knox, who would lead the government's case, was the only cabinet member consulted. Not even Roosevelt's friend and distinguished corporate attorney, Secretary of War Elihu Root, heard of Roosevelt's intention before the public announcement.[54]

The lack of consultation about the suit indicates Roosevelt's certainty of purpose in pursuing it. Knox had assured him the case was legally justified. About his larger policy purpose in launching the suit he required no advice. It was a step in asserting presidential control, and there is no advisor who can see the stakes entailed in the decision as clearly as the president.[55] In addition, his own thinking about business combinations had been formed at Albany during 1899 and 1900 through consultations with experts E. R. A. Seligman of Columbia University and Jeremiah Jencks of Cornell.[56]

To a correspondent who complained that there was no public warning of the suit, Roosevelt responded: "What we did was . . . give . . . public . . . warning" in announcing the suit.[57] The suit was even more surprising in its motivation than its suddenness.[58] The public drama of the suit's announcement was an assertion of unbridled presidential authority.[59] A leading historian of the origins of American anti-trust policy describes the business world's reaction to the suit:

> The business world and . . . the Old Guard felt that the vagueness of the [annual] message . . . justified a sigh of relief. . . . [But] those who assumed that Roosevelt's message was to be taken as a . . . discussion on a plane far from everyday industrial realities were . . . mistaken. The era of trust-busting was officially initiated . . . on February 19, 1902.[60]

With the message and the suit Roosevelt wholly appropriated the trust issue for the executive. There was no hint of presidential modesty here. Noting that something new was afoot, the *New York Times* asked if "corporate enterprise in this country is to be dependent hereafter for the untrammeled conduct of its

business not upon the plain reading of the statutes but upon the will of a President."[61] Nor was there any hint here of party period presidential modesty about
taking public positions. Through the suit Roosevelt responded forcefully to
widespread public fears about trusts. While business voices were tremulous, the
public embraced Roosevelt's leadership. For example, the progressive Oregon
state Republican platform announced united support for "the war . . . President
Roosevelt has inaugurated against the giant combinations of incorporated capital."[62] The *Philadelphia Press* observed the appearance that big business was
above the law was most dangerous for business in general. Praising Roosevelt's
intentions and actions, the newspaper wrote that "the only escape from this
peril is in the . . . regulation of great combinations."[63]

As Roosevelt wielded presidential resources—the message and the suit—to
resolve the policy confusion regarding trusts, a Supreme Court vacancy appeared serendipitously. Illness forced Justice Horace Gray to resign in July
1902.[64] Roosevelt saw the vacancy as an opportunity to shape the Court's decision in the *Northern Securities* case. To Senator Henry Cabot Lodge Roosevelt
identified the criteria he had used in nominating Oliver Wendell Holmes Jr., the
chief justice of the Massachusetts Supreme Court. The president lauded
Holmes's several pro-labor decisions because he valued a judge who had "broad
humanity of feeling . . . for the class from which he has not drawn his clients." He
added that "Holmes' whole mental attitude . . . is such that I should naturally expect him to be in favor of those principles in which I so earnestly believe."[65]
Roosevelt's selection of an appointee on the basis of his policy views was of a
piece with his assertion of presidential authority over anti-trust policy. As governor, Roosevelt had said that "the courts [are] not necessarily the best judges of
what should be done to better social and industrial conditions."[66] As president
he had the appointment power to improve the Supreme Court. And Roosevelt
took credit for improving the Court when it approved his policies. When in
April 1903 the Court found constitutional the franchise tax that Roosevelt had
sponsored as governor, the president said: "The courts can be educated just as
the public can be educated."[67]

Roosevelt's use of judicial appointment to affect judicial outcomes broke
with past presidential practice. The judicial appointment criteria of the party
period included party loyalty, some legal distinction, demonstrated commitment to property rights, personal connection with party leaders, and state representation.[68] However, Roosevelt's goal for this appointment was the outcome
of the *Northern Securities* case in the likelihood that it would reach the Court.

And Roosevelt was to be famously disappointed with his appointment of Oliver Wendell Holmes to the Court.

The *Northern Securities* case was decided in the government's favor by the federal circuit court in Minneapolis, sitting as a trial court. The court found the trust was a plan to restrain commerce that had the capacity to manipulate rates and that the Sherman Act "declares illegal every combination" with these effects.[69] The case was appealed to the Supreme Court and argued in December 1903. The Court reported its decision on March 14, 1904, upholding the circuit court.[70] The decision validated Roosevelt's initiative in anti-trust policy, but ironically the justice chosen as policy insurance was among the four dissenters to the majority opinion. Holmes read the anti-trust act more narrowly than did the majority. To his eye it did not declare all combinations illegal but allowed those that did not establish a monopoly. More threatening to the president's assertion of national power over trusts, Holmes argued that Congress's power to regulate commerce did not extend to questions of the ownership of stock in companies simply because those companies engaged in interstate commerce.[71] Roosevelt felt betrayed, telling Senator Lodge that Holmes "has been a bitter disappointment."[72] Nevertheless, Roosevelt had succeeded in imposing executive control over anti-trust policy.

The first annual message and the *Northern Securities* case laid the foundation for Roosevelt's activism toward big business. After initiating the suit, Roosevelt and Knox announced to great acclaim a Sherman Act investigation of the "beef trust." The recent development of refrigerated freight cars enabled meat packers to supply fresh meat throughout the country, undermining local butchers and creating dominance of the industry by several large firms. Rising meat prices seemed to confirm the malign influence of the "trust." In Philadelphia, local butchers allied together to resist its power.[73] Newspapers reported the rebates on freight rates that railroads were giving to the major meat-packing firms, demonstrating their market power against competitors. The *Washington Post* wrote, "Against such scandalous discrimination it has been . . . impossible for independent butchers and packing houses to successfully contend."[74] Simultaneously, the secretary of agriculture announced that there was no "beef trust" but was met by open skepticism in press reports of his remarks.[75]

In mid-April 1902, in the midst of rising public dismay over this new trust and rising prices, President Roosevelt directed Attorney General Knox to initiate an investigation of the major meat-packing firms, focused through the U.S. attorney's office in Chicago. A suit was subsequently initiated in the Northern

District of Illinois. In late April Roosevelt was hailed by a *Washington Post* editorial for initiating the suit. The paper admitted that it often saw the benefits of modern industrial combinations, however the meat packers demonstrated "ruthless and intemperate rapacity." About the president, the editorial said:

> Mr. Roosevelt . . . will establish a new claim upon the esteem and confidence of the American people. . . . He will be regarded . . . as the champion of the oppressed—as the one Chief Magistrate who, in the whole history of the anti-trust agitation, has substituted action for the . . . hairsplitting platitudes of the past.[76]

It was a signal of Roosevelt's success with the business issue that in his paper, *The Commoner,* William Jennings Bryan attacked the "beef trust" suit for using the Sherman Act's provision for a suit in equity rather than its provision for a criminal indictment. Bryan ranted that a prison cell would be a more effective deterrent than fines. But the attack suggested that Roosevelt's activism was marginalizing the thin-skinned Bryan, who was attempting to demonstrate that he was purer than Roosevelt.[77] The meat-packing case was decided in the government's favor in May 1903 and affirmed by the Supreme Court in 1905.

In summer 1902, a strike across the eastern anthracite coalfields opened another opportunity for presidential intervention. The strike threatened the East's winter supply of heating fuel. The United Mine Workers would accept arbitration, but the major coal firms, acting together, refused to recognize the union. Despite advice from the attorney general that he had no authority to intervene, Roosevelt met with management and labor on October 3, 1902, but he could not move the companies to arbitration.[78] While using emissaries to pressure the mine owners, Roosevelt told his cabinet that if the strike were not resolved he would use federal troops to run the mines.[79] That was a far cry from Cleveland's use of troops to suppress workers a few years earlier in the Pullman Strike. Roosevelt's rationale for intervention was that his role was to favor neither labor nor management but to protect the public. The threat brought management to accept a mediation commission, and workers returned to the mines.[80] The *Washington Post* editorialized: "The President deserves all praise and gratitude. More glorious than winning a battle is this triumph of peace and order snatched by a strong, brave hand from the very jaws of defeat."[81]

At the end of 1902 President Roosevelt's annual message proposed supervising business combinations with a new bureau of corporations in a new department of commerce and labor. During the 1903 session Congress fulfilled that request. The 1902 message also requested, for the first time, appropriated funds for the enforcement of the anti-trust law.[82] The anti-trust division of the department was consequently established and funded during 1903, and the fortified justice department continued to bring anti-trust suits, the most celebrated being against Standard Oil in 1906.

To summarize, beginning with his 1901 annual message and the *Northern Securities* suit, Roosevelt dominated anti-trust policy and reformulated it to one of bringing trusts into the service of the nation.[83] He said: "We are not hostile to them; we are merely determined that they shall . . . subserve the public good."[84] Simultaneously, Roosevelt's trust policy was an extended performance through which he responded to public anxieties and demonstrated his unique role as president, capable of protecting the public interest in a way that neither Congress nor the Courts had managed. To maintain public support, he deftly gained favorable news coverage for his evolving anti-trust policy.[85]

That Roosevelt managed this policy arena so deftly depended upon several elements of his leadership style and experience. He had already gained experience with the trust problem as governor and initiated the public franchise tax. He had learned through that experience that the trust problem, while delicate for Republicans, motivated public support. Finally, through his initiatives Roosevelt built an unparalleled presidential position regarding policy toward big business. A year before the 1904 election, an influential Republican editor estimated Roosevelt's reelection as "certain" because "he has possession of the country as no other President in time has had it."[86] At the end of the nineteenth century the problems of relations among corporations, consumers, and producers had gone beyond the capacities of courts and, as Morton Keller observes, "required political rather than judicial solutions."[87] Responding to that challenge, Roosevelt initiated a multifrontal attack through legal, political, and administrative means. And he built a policy edifice within the executive branch where there had been none.

Building a New Navy

In anti-trust Roosevelt innovated within a nebulous policy system. In naval policy he captured existing, highly structured institutions and policy. He shifted control of the navy from Congress to the presidency and upward from the naval bureaus to the Executive Mansion. Control of naval policy lay traditionally in congressional committees and the heads of the eight naval bureaus. In his 1885 annual report Secretary of the Navy William Whitney wrote, "We have nothing which deserves to be called a navy."[88] Until the 1890s the navy was a minor force, invested in sails and the limited goals of guarding American ports and shipping.

The navy changed by fits and starts. The civil service replaced political patronage for civilian employees. Steel ships became standard. At the end of the 1880s Congress authorized construction of the first (three) armored ships, and steam eventually conquered wind. But administratively the service was mired in the past. The eight bureaus were autonomous, and the secretary was correspondingly weak. Above all, the navy had no doctrine of development and strategic purpose to guide it. Weaponry was being modernized, but there was no conception of goals for that development.[89] While the naval victories of the Spanish War made Americans proud, no expert would claim that the U.S. navy matched any major seagoing power. Roosevelt aimed to change all that.

Roosevelt's interest in the navy was motivated by ideas about the relationship of sea power to national strength. Roosevelt's interest began with his senior thesis at Harvard, a study of the naval war of 1812, later published in book form.[90] His mature writing and letters exhibit what William Harbaugh termed "the cult of military valor," a world-view shared by others of his circle, Brooks Adams, John Hay, Henry Cabot Lodge, Oliver Wendell Holmes Jr., and, not least, Alfred Mahan.[91] For Roosevelt the cult of valor was a good in itself. He said in a speech at the Naval War College: "All the great masterful races have been fighting races" and for a "race" to lose its fighting virtues is to lose "its proud right to stand as the equal of the best."[92] Roosevelt's war talk could be abstractly romantic, but its goal was practical, national expansion. Roosevelt and his circle were committed to the right of a powerful people to expand beyond continental limits, over the hemisphere, and across the oceans.[93] The war with Spain, in which he had the dual roles of instigator while at the navy department and warrior on the Cuban battlefield, expressed that destiny.

Thus, Roosevelt's challenge was to build the means to control the hemisphere and project power across the oceans. At a time when naval power was *the* currency of world power, and the great battleship the ultimate strategic weapon, the American navy's weakness reflected America's weakness.[94] But, for all Roosevelt's ambition, the presidency lacked tools for building and managing the navy. The incongruity he faced was that he sought change in the service, but with no specialized staff, no access to technical information, and no control over budgets, the president was at the mercy of the navy's traditional, Congress-centered decision-making system.

Planning and decision making were dispersed among the bureaus, the chief of each being a senior officer selected largely on the basis of connections to influential politicians. Promotion was based on seniority, and the senior officers were attached to old ways. Commonly in the 1880s senior commanders had opposed armored ships. As one officer at the time predicted, soon "ships of war will throw off their armor and fight in the lightest rig."[95] The navy's primary responsibility was coast and harbor defense. As late as the Spanish War there was a widespread hysteria among the public and politicians when American warships were being marshaled at sea to confront the Spanish at Cuba and in the Pacific rather than positioned to protect American cities and harbors.[96]

Naval appropriations and policy decisions were negotiated between the bureaus' chiefs and the congressional committees, with special influence for representatives and senators of seaboard states. Beginning in the late 1880s, the navy secretary occasionally intruded upon the naval bureau–congressional committee nexus. The first battleships were authorized for the navy, and a naval policy board was established, in 1890. The board brought together the bureau chiefs with several other senior officers attempting to achieve increased organizational coherence. Presidents had no formal role in that system.

Roosevelt's leadership would transform those relationships and the navy itself. Harold and Margaret Sprout observe: "The naval policy of imperial America was . . . the naval policy of Theodore Roosevelt."[97] He was "the first president to think consistently and coherently about the link between military technology, national military power, and foreign policy."[98] And he reshaped the navy according to those ideas. In an office that was bereft of staff resources, organization, and expertise, how did he overcome incongruity?

Entering office, Roosevelt found a navy expanded by the enthusiasms of victory. In 1898 Congress authorized three battleships along with four monitors, an antiquated design dating to the Civil War.[99] In 1899 three more battleships were authorized along with three armored cruisers and six light cruisers; and in 1900 two more battleships were authorized in addition to three armored and three light cruisers. In 1901 congressional enthusiasm waned and no ships were authorized.[100] The postwar navy was now bigger but lacked a coherent strategic vision. Congress still referred to the new battleships' missions as coastal defense. Ships cruising on the high seas were still assigned to cruise a "station," such as the China station in the Eastern Pacific, rather than coordinate in fleet movement. The Sprouts observe that "three years after the war . . . one could observe little progress toward a comprehensive restatement of American naval policy, in the light of war experience and . . . our commitments."[101]

Six weeks into his presidency, Roosevelt wrote to a former naval secretary: "No greater calamity could happen to this country . . . than to stop building up the navy."[102] In his first annual message he pressed his case: "No one point of our policy, foreign or domestic, is more important than this to the honor and material welfare, and above all to the peace, of our nation in the future." Toward that end Roosevelt made several recommendations. First, there must be more battleships and heavy cruisers, along with a proportionate number of lighter ships. Next, there must be an expansion of naval manpower, officers as well as enlisted men. Four thousand additional seamen and a thousand additional marines were needed immediately, along with coordinate expansion of the officer corps. Third, the navy's ships and crews must be pressed into extensive experience on the high seas and engage in "incessant gunnery practice." Fourth, the old practice of ships operating individually at foreign stations must end; instead, they "should be maneuvered in squadrons."

Not only did Roosevelt's message give priority to naval policy, it was striking for its detailed overview of the service and its specific recommendations in contrast to his predecessors' treatment of naval affairs.[103] The president called not just for generally "upbuilding" the navy. He also specified necessary reforms in the details of gunnery practice; the assignment of officers to sea duty, with civilians doing land-based administration; and active cruising for the fleet. Roosevelt concluded with the challenge that Americans "must either build . . . an adequate navy or . . . accept a secondary position in international affairs."[104] In the past, presidents had voiced their recommendations for the navy as approval of recommendations coming from the navy secretary. By contrast, in his message Roosevelt spoke as a naval authority.

Six different men occupied the navy seat in Roosevelt's cabinet, with a median tenure of just over a year.[105] It was a place to park those deserving cabinet-level appointments, and none of them had any qualifications for the job. Throughout his tenure it was Roosevelt who decided naval policy matters and secretaries who followed his orders. His response to the presidency's organizational limitation was to reach outside the office. He assembled a proto-staff to provide salient information and to give him a capacity for affecting activities within the navy department. His authority in pursuing his expansive naval policy and his innovative, informal staffing was underlined by his public stance as a warrior. Harold and Margaret Sprout write that Roosevelt "combined an almost fanatical desire for a big navy, expert knowledge of naval affairs, an extraordinary flair for showmanship, and a fighting spirit."[106] Without "showmanship," Roosevelt would have had a more difficult time than he did selling Congress and the people on a course of greatly expanded naval appropriations. The cowboy-warrior had a potent credibility for explaining the strategic necessity of a strong navy. Ironically, all his Republican predecessors were officers in the Civil War and had battlefield experience, but among them only Roosevelt was an avatar of war.

Roosevelt's message of the link between American destiny and naval power was well received across the country. After the 1901 message to Congress, the *Atlanta Journal* pronounced that the president gave sound justifications for naval expansion and that the "outlying possessions and the protection of our commerce are sufficient reasons for this policy."[107] On the opposite coast the *Los Angeles Times* wrote approvingly that Roosevelt "is set upon doing all he can to give this country a powerful navy."[108] In gaining public support for naval expansion Roosevelt had two advantages beyond his own showmanship. The first, of course, was national pride in the naval victory over Spain. The second advantage was a climate of opinion influenced by the ideas of the naval officer and geopolitical theorist, Alfred Thayer Mahan. Beginning with his *The Influence of Sea Power upon History*, Mahan promoted a theory of the relationship among national power, mercantilist imperialism, and naval power.[109] His scholarship influenced military and political elites, and he popularized his views through popular magazine articles.[110] Within that receptive public opinion Roosevelt pushed effectively for naval expansion, improved battleships, and better training.

We can understand the sources of Roosevelt's "showmanship," but what was the source of his knowledge about naval affairs and his ability to use it for an "intimate influence" on the U.S. navy?[111] It was Roosevelt's ability to employ expertise that gave him intimacy with naval policy and decision-making unmatched by any predecessors. The historian Matthew Oyos puzzled over the fact that Roosevelt "never acquired the expertise of a naval engineer, but for a busy chief executive his ability to digest and then repeat data and principles of ship design was astounding."[112] His intellectual background was a foundation for his intervention in naval affairs. But neither his writing on the naval war of 1812 nor his reading of Mahan could supply expertise regarding modern ship design, naval training, or organization of the service. Yet, he marshaled essentially esoteric information to directly affect each of these subjects. During his tenure as assistant naval secretary in 1897–1898, might he have absorbed sufficient information to control naval policy as president? That seems unlikely, given the rapid change of naval technology in the early 1900s and the limits of what Roosevelt could have absorbed in that hectic year. And there was nothing in the presidency to facilitate bringing technical information and expert advice to bear on decision-making.[113]

It was Roosevelt's earlier Weberian lesson that he called upon to shape naval policy. He had learned that technical information is the special province of bureaucracies and control of that information is the realm of the career official. In each of his administrative posts Roosevelt had used information to further the agency's mission and ward off political enemies of that mission. He reached out for policy-salient information through subordinates and nonofficial experts, and he had supported those subordinates. None of his administrative posts had been well supported with staff. Consequently, he had made use of diverse resources—other actors, civil service reformers, journalists, ministers, and back channels to subordinates—to collect information for enhanced policymaking. In short, he established proto-staffs in organizations that lacked staff support. It was this practice that President Roosevelt reprised for shaping naval policy.

He reached out to several lower and mid-rank naval officers for technical information to support his naval policymaking. As assistant naval secretary he had learned the service's organizational culture and met disaffected junior officers. The navy's encrusted bureaus and seniority-based promotions alienated junior officers who might remain midshipmen into middle age, becoming lieutenants at forty-five or fifty.[114] Enthused about naval modernization, they were potential accomplices with Roosevelt's goal for naval reform. Among the handful of younger officers with whom Roosevelt communicated, two were most active as proto-staff, William S. Sims and Albert Lenoir Key. Both were naval academy graduates of the early 1880s and remained lieutenants two decades later. They were motivated by self-interest and professional dedication to a technocratic, modernizing regimen for the navy. In Sims and Key, Roosevelt discovered informants whose interests were fully symbiotic with his own goals. We shall see the importance of these proto-staffers in the president's interventions in gunnery practice and the design of battleships.

Roosevelt's tactics in the civil service and the police commission depended on knowledgeable and interested people who had no official relationship to those agencies. In the navy, President Roosevelt set out on more delicate proto-staff relationships with officers far beneath him in the chain of command. They were also dangerously far beneath the navy secretary and senior officers whose work they could be charged as undermining. As one naval historian reported with distaste, "Roosevelt . . . fell into the habit of accepting correspondence directly from a few junior officers."[115] This practice was impossible to keep confidential and sparked the resentments of senior officers. Rear Admiral Charles Thomas wrote his wife that Roosevelt had an "insane penchant" for "pushing young men to the front."[116] The president's "pushing forward" his naval proto-staff was unavoidable precisely because their relationship with Roosevelt could not be wholly covert. Their careers would be ruined had he not protected them. As a bonus for him, through their promotion, Roosevelt achieved the kind of leadership he sought for the navy.

In 1904 Roosevelt replaced his naval aide, who had been his brother-in-law, Commander William Cowles, with Albert Key. Cowles was a traditional naval aide, primarily providing social graces in the Executive Mansion. Key's appointment changed the role. He provided Roosevelt with a steady flow of ideas for naval reform, particularly regarding the navy's personnel system. Key, for example, espoused a performance-based evaluation system for the promotion of officers. An indicator of his influence was that Roosevelt's 1904 and 1907 annual messages presented Key's ideas for reforming personnel policy.[117] However, Key's main service for the president would come later and entail questions of battleship design and construction rather than personnel.

Lieutenant William Sims's advising relationship to the president began by chance. In the mid-1890s he was in the eastern Pacific as an intelligence officer, reporting on the naval clashes between Japan and China. In late 1896 he was assigned as naval attaché to the American embassy in Paris. His reports from Paris to the navy command stressed the weaknesses of the American navy compared to the major European powers. He later said, "I first went to Paris with the idea . . . that the American Navy was the hottest stuff." After observation of European forces, he admitted that the American navy was "not in it at all, either in design or in marksmanship, and I made report after report."[118] Senior officers in Washington dismissed him as an alarmist.[119] But Assistant Secretary of the Navy Roosevelt took Sims's reports to confirm his own suspicions of American weakness. When Roosevelt left his navy post, Sims lost the most avid reader of his reports. They were, instead, "muffled in the long corridors of the Department."[120]

In 1901 Sims was back at sea, concerned with the accuracy of naval gunnery. Systematically examining gunnery practice, he discovered that U.S. gunnery was far less accurate than British gunnery. He promoted his findings among "insurgent" mid-career officers but found little interest among senior officers. In November 1901 Sims sent to President Roosevelt a letter describing his gunnery report. In it he also told the president that improvements in gun training that had begun while Roosevelt was at navy had been abandoned.[121]

The president checked Sims's bona fides regarding gunnery and found that he had a sterling reputation.[122] Then he wrote to Sims that he would "always be pleased to hear from you, in criticism or suggestion."[123]

The impact of Sims's letter is evident in Roosevelt's first annual message. There he calls for keeping warships on the high seas for longer tours and that "gunnery practice should be unceasing."[124] This would be a fateful partnership. Elting E. Morison writes that the "shock of the combination [of Roosevelt and Sims] shattered the tranquility of the United States navy."[125] Roosevelt used Sims's gunnery report for his first intervention into naval training procedures. He sent it to Admiral Henry Taylor, who he knew was an ally for naval reform.[126] To Taylor he wrote that marksmanship must be improved because "in any great war the trivial differences of type in the battleships will be as nothing compared with the effect produced by . . . differences in . . . gunnery."[127] Simultaneously, the president also intervened in personnel affairs, normally the purview of the bureaus and congressional committees. He made Taylor chief of the bureau of navigation, which he called "the most important position in the navy."[128]

In March 1902 Sims sent Roosevelt more evidence of poor naval gunnery. He also listed the reports on gunnery that he had sent to the bureau of navigation over the last eighteen months without a reply. Roosevelt forwarded this to Admiral Taylor and ordered Taylor to prepare a summary of Sims's reports and distribute them to all seagoing commands. The president wrote Taylor that he had large expectations of him. "If there is any basis . . . for Sims' complaints . . . we must carefully go into the facts and take . . . measures for correction."[129] Sims's past reports were distilled into a single memo and distributed with the warning proviso that it be kept confidential.[130] When Sims completed sea duty in late 1902, Roosevelt intervened again in the personnel system to place him in charge of naval gunnery practice. The intervention in this instance was bold. Admiral Taylor was initiating a new system of gunnery practice and had chosen Lieutenant Commander A. P. Niblack to oversee it.[131] Roosevelt overruled Taylor and directed that Sims get that place instead, a post he held until 1909.[132]

For Roosevelt, the issue of naval gunnery was a component of the larger goal of creating a powerful navy. The number, size, and quality of a navy's battleships were the essential metrics of its power. A battleship is a massive platform of many guns with the capacity to deliver tons of explosive shells in a single barrage. The battleship was also a symbol of a state's naval ferocity. Assuming effective marksmanship, the "platform" with the largest guns, the greatest speed, and the most protection will dominate the seas.[133] Unlike England, Germany, France, Italy, Russia, and Japan, the United States had not chosen to compete for dominance.

The U.S. navy requested its first armored battleship in 1890. Congress authorized three ships that year but qualified their designs to limit them to "seagoing coastline" duty. The chair of the House naval affairs committee explained that "we should avoid the . . . apprehension of jingoism in naval matters."[134] Policy was formed within two constraints. The first was the practice that congressional committees determined the parameters of ship design. The second constraint was an American hesitation at projecting naval power. By the end of that decade, relatively light coastal-protection battleships were the American fleet's mainstay. One or more battleships were authorized each year of the 1890s, with the exceptions of 1891 and 1900. The first of these was the *Iowa*, displacing 11,346 tons. The three battleships Congress authorized at the beginning of the war with Spain each displaced 12,500 tons.[135] After the Spanish War, Congress authorized three battleships that were somewhat heavier and slightly faster than those built during the 1890s.[136] Thus, by 1901 there were a number of U.S. battleships (albeit on the light side), but there was not yet a change in the navy's mission of coastal and merchant marine protection.

In 1901, the U.S. navy's battleships were inferior to those built in other nations. In addition, the navy's construction program lagged behind other countries' programs. In 1901 the United States initiated construction of 23,850 tons of warships while Russia began construction of 54,835 tons, France 41,872 tons, and Britain 116,620 tons.[137] The U.S. navy's ranks of officers and sailors were also notably smaller than the navies of the leading powers. In 1900 the U.S. navy counted 23,453 officers and men compared to Japan's 26,108, Germany's 30,386, France's 49,775, and Britain's approximately 100,000.

President Roosevelt reformulated naval policy to compete with the major seagoing powers. The navy had to be able to project power across both oceans. To accomplish that goal, the navy must do more than shoot straight. The power of the American navy depended on gunnery *and* on the range of those guns and the quality of the ships carrying them. To gain adoption of his goals, the president had to beat the drum for more ships, and he had to make sure that those new ships were competitive with the best of Britain, Germany, Japan, and France. [138] He was also not above using a war scare to move public opinion, as he did about Japan in 1908.

Until 1906 Congress gave Roosevelt the major ships he requested. It authorized four battleships in 1902, five in 1903, and one in 1904. Congressional resistance increased after the 1904 election. Two battleships were authorized in 1905 but only one each in 1906 and 1907 and two in 1908.[139] By 1906 numerous legislators caviled at the cost of Roosevelt's big navy. Opposition peaked when Roosevelt recommended four new battleships in both his 1907 and 1908 annual messages. In 1908, after a bitter legislative battle, Congress authorized two battleships. In the Senate, Roosevelt's supporters had fought for the four battleships but were defeated by a coalition of Old Guard Republicans and Democrats, united by concerns over the economy, fears that a big navy would lead to war, and growing irritation with Roosevelt's independence.[140] During 1909 Congress again authorized only two battleships.

In his annual messages Roosevelt made his best case for naval expansion. Additionally he wielded his showmanship, communicating a vision of a big navy to the public, thereby building public expectations to prime congressional action. Several of his public addresses during 1902 and 1903 vividly illustrate his use of public communications, as he prepared the political ground for Congress's approval of five battleships during 1903. In May 1902 Roosevelt used the Naval Academy's commencement address to spell out his conception of the navy's purposes. He argued that great naval power maintained the peace. But, should war come, a great navy was necessary for victory. He then spelled out the constituent elements of a great navy: a combination of skilled officers and well-trained crews manning the best-designed and technologically advanced warships.[141]

Another theme of Roosevelt's reinforcement of the big navy program was his forceful embrace of the Monroe Doctrine. As he said in a speech during September 1902, "The Monroe doctrine will be respected as long as we have a first-class, efficient navy, and not much longer."[142] The Monroe Doctrine was Roosevelt's foil again in April 1903 when he told a large audience in Chicago that "if the American Nation will speak softly, and yet build and keep at a pitch of the highest training a thoroughly efficient navy, the Monroe Doctrine will go far." Roosevelt asked Americans to consider whether they could come to any other conclusion but his. His position, he continued, was "so obviously sound that only the blind can fail to see its truth and only the weakest and most irresolute can fail to desire to put it into force."[143]

The height of Roosevelt's dramatization of his naval policy was his decision to send an American battleship fleet around the world. In December 1907 he ordered the Atlantic fleet, constituting the bulk of U.S. warships, on a long distance exercise to the Pacific Coast, via the Strait of Magellan. It was a time of heightened tensions with Japan over California's treatment of Japanese immigrants.

Roosevelt's message in moving the fleet was that the Pacific was as much an American ocean as the Atlantic.[144] The president saw the fleet depart from Hampton Roads, Virginia with great celebration on December 16. Sixteen battleships, a squadron of six destroyers, and a number of gun boats made the passage, stopping with fanfare at several Latin American ports and then undertaking fleet exercises and gunnery practice off Washington State. Then Roosevelt ordered the fleet westward to Hawaii and the Philippines, then on to Japan, the next leg of the round-the-world cruise. No large modern battle fleet had ever accomplished that feat, and it announced America's arrival as a major naval power. While Roosevelt had geopolitical purposes for the world cruise, his main purpose was "to impress the American people" with the importance of their navy and the necessity for continuing its expansion.[145]

Roosevelt's single most important priority for the navy was the design of new battleships. His project was to revolutionize design, and he initiated the "all-big-gun ship." To accomplish that change in ship design required technical knowledge that was not "on tap" for the president. Consequently, the case of his influence on the new ship design illuminates Roosevelt's use of protostaff for technical information. American battleship design unfolded incrementally between 1890 and 1905. Ships grew in size and speed, but their armament type remained constant. Battleships carried guns of three different calibers, typically four twelve inchers, several eight inchers, and a larger number of six or seven inchers.[146] Each of these categories of guns had a different range of fire. While American ships of the period were gaining in competency, they "were built with certain constructional defects that were much criticized during ensuing years."[147] The traditional battery of mixed-caliber guns was itself problematic because in battle the three different ranges of fire compromised accuracy.

Roosevelt knew the thinking of some officers, including Sims, about new battleship architecture.[148] Seeking a design that would overcome problems that plagued even the latest U.S. ships, in 1904 Roosevelt asked Sims for his thoughts regarding the all-big-gun design.[149] Earlier Sims had prepared a report for the naval board of construction criticizing current battleship design, particularly regarding the placement and design of gun turrets.[150] His response to Roosevelt reflected that report as well as the thinking of fellow officer-reformers. He reported that officers most knowledgeable about gunnery and design questions "have long . . . been convinced that this is the only logical battery for a fighting vessel."[151] A battleship with main guns of a single caliber could be fully coordinated in its targeting because the guns could be aimed along the same range of fire.

Congress approved two conventionally designed new battleships during 1905, and the next year rebuffed Roosevelt's request for more. Then events intruded giving Roosevelt an opening for a ship of the new design. In 1905 the British began construction of the *H.M.S. Dreadnought,* bigger, faster, with more firepower and more armor than any battleship afloat.[152] During 1906 another wave of anti-Japanese actions in California led to the segregation of Japanese immigrant children in school, economic sanctions against Japanese immigrants, and efforts to end Japanese immigration completely. The resulting diplomatic protest from Japan sparked some war fever and Congress decided to authorize a new battleship with the displacement Roosevelt requested.[153] The *Delaware* was the American answer to the *Dreadnought.* It would displace 20,000 tons, 25 percent more than the next largest U.S. battleship. Its top speed would be twenty-one knots, two knots more than the next fastest U.S. battleship, and its main armament would consist of ten twelve-inch guns. The *Delaware* would equal the *Dreadnought*'s speed and gunnery while displacing 2,100 more tons.

As the *Delaware* was under construction there remained opposition from some influential members of Congress and senior naval officers. By 1906 Congress's post–Spanish War enthusiasm for naval spending was diminished. Some legislators who had backed Roosevelt's naval "upbuilding" grew wary of more spending. Foremost among these was Senator Eugene Hale (R-ME), chairman of the Senate's naval affairs committee. Adjusted for inflation, the cost of one battleship rose about 20 percent in just seven years.[154] As Roosevelt envisioned more and bigger ships, critics suggested that behind his program were the selfish interests of the navy, ship builders, steel makers, and the arms industry.[155] Critics also questioned Roosevelt's argument that stronger weapons assured a stable peace. A *Boston Globe* editorial mused that "nations in the future which have . . . these mammoth war vessels will be very likely to desire an opportunity to use them."[156]

More dangerous to the president's policy than congressional skepticism was opposition from senior officers. Much of the naval establishment, including heads of the bureaus of construction and navigation, had opposed the *Delaware.* Ironically, Roosevelt's ally, Admiral Alfred Mahan, emerged as the most vocal and prestigious critic of the president's big ship program.[157] During 1906 Mahan published an essay in the *Proceedings* of the American Naval Institute analyzing the recent Japanese defeat of the Russian fleet in the Sea of Japan. He interpreted the battle as showing that victory depended on the ability of warships to engage effectively at very close range while producing large volumes of gunfire. The long-range guns and great speed of the big battleships, he pointed out, were unnecessary and detrimental to effective maneuvering in battle. Additionally, he charged, these great ships were frivolously expensive.[158] Thus, the lesson of that battle was that *Dreadnought*-like battleships were disadvantaged in large-scale naval warfare.

Mahan's attack on the all-big-gun design was a potential deathblow to Roosevelt's project, legitimating criticism from skeptics in Congress. Roosevelt asked Sims to respond to Mahan's article. Sims accessed later reports of the Battle of the Sea of Japan that Mahan had not seen, and with that new information he faulted the facts of Mahan's essay and showed that his conclusions were not consistent with the facts. Sims's analysis left Mahan's argument against the all-big-gun design looking like mere prejudice.[159] Seeing Sims's effective rejoinder to Mahan, Roosevelt had him publish the paper in the Naval Institute's *Proceedings*.[160]

Sims's article was sufficiently authoritative to undermine Mahan's credibility on the issue of large battleships. The controversy reached Congress, and the Senate naval committee printed the articles as a report and held a hearing. The controversy also played out in the public press with both the *Washington Post* and *New York Times* editorializing that the "all-big-gun" program best served the national interest.[161] Having public sentiment on the side of his battleship program, Roosevelt moved to control the key details of planning for the character of the big battleships. He had Sims draw up a memo that explained the key advantages of an all-big-gun ship.[162] Roosevelt, in turn, used Sims's memo as the basis for a letter to the House and Senate naval committees urging final approval by Congress of the *Delaware*'s design and authorization of another ship of the same class.[163] Later in 1907 Congress authorized construction of the second all-big-gun battleship, the *South Dakota*.

As a counterfactual exercise, if we remove William Sims from this narrative of Roosevelt's leadership in naval policy we are left with a president with large intentions lacking means to affect policy. Sims was an information provider as well as a source of analysis of naval questions. It is also notable that Sims's intense focus on the accuracy of naval gunnery became a priority for Roosevelt. Not only did Sims offer to Roosevelt information and analysis, he shaped Roosevelt's own policy agenda. Without Sims in the picture, it is difficult to see Roosevelt successfully framing and accomplishing his agenda for naval policy.

However, had there been no Sims, Roosevelt would have found other proto-staffers from among the insurgent officers. I have focused primarily on the Sims-Roosevelt relationship because it was central to Roosevelt's battleship program, but Sims was not the only proto-staffer engaged with Roosevelt. As naval aide, Albert Key worked on naval organization and personnel issues for Roosevelt. In late 1907 Roosevelt had Key assigned to his first seagoing command, the new cruiser *Salem,* naming Sims to replace Key as his naval aide.

The *Salem* was under construction at the Fore River shipyard in Massachusetts, where the *Delaware* and *South Dakota* were under construction. Key's first responsibility was to supervise the *Salem*'s completion and initial testing at the shipyard. Nothing in the archival records proves that Roosevelt assigned Key to Fore River to have a trusted officer follow the construction of the new battleships. However, Key assumed that role. He observed flaws in the new battleships that were not corrected in the construction phase. For example, the gun turrets and ship's magazine were connected by unbroken passages, potentially allowing fire in a turret to reach the magazine. The thick armor belts that girdled the vessels' hulls were misplaced, likely to ride too high in the water and exposing unprotected hull to enemy torpedoes or shells. Key wrote a report on these problems for senior officers and distributed it to Roosevelt and Sims. In it he charged that these ships would "be wholly unable to hold [their] own against a foreign 'Dreadnought.'"[164]

As an epilogue to this case of Roosevelt's battleship program, we must note that the reliance of Roosevelt on younger officers like Sims and Key naturally empowered them to actions beyond their proper station in the navy. Once convinced of the problems with the first two big ships, and finding the navy's bureau of construction unresponsive to their claims, they went to Roosevelt. The insurgent officers turned the design problems of the battleships into a crusade to attack head-on the navy's stale administrative structure and its conservative senior officers.

Rebuffed by the senior command, and facing the end of Roosevelt's presidency, Sims, Key, and other insurgents chose to go public with an attack on naval business as usual.[165] Their instrument was a prominent naval illustrator and journalist, Henry Reuterdahl, with whom they shared their many criticisms. In January 1908, just as the battleship fleet was setting out across the Pacific, Reuterdahl published "The Needs of Our Navy" in *McClure's*.[166] The article "dropped like a well-aimed bomb."[167] The Senate naval committee held hearings on the article's charges, and that hearing was followed in July 1908 by a conference of naval officers at the Navy War College to consider the charge of flaws in the *Delaware* and *North Dakota*.

Roosevelt ordered the Newport conference in response to Sims and Key's charges.[168] However, these two were no longer serving Roosevelt's interests and needs. His aim was to expand the battleship program by gaining authorization for four more all-big-gun ships.[169] They, by contrast, expanded conflict within and around the navy that could only complicate Roosevelt's program. They no longer served the president with "a passion for anonymity," to use a phrase coined thirty years later.[170] The conference was stacked with officers unsympathetic to the insurgents. After days of wrangling and extended sessions, the conference recommended only minor changes in the *North Dakota*.

His naval proto-staff was no longer useful for Roosevelt after mid-1908, but he ensured that both Key and Sims secured prestigious assignments. Key already had his first seagoing command. And, in 1909, Roosevelt ordered that Sims take command of the battleship *Minnesota*. That was a striking intervention in the personnel system, violating the conventional requirement that a battleship command required the rank of captaincy while Sims was then only a commander.[171]

Context, Progressive Goals, and Roosevelt's Leadership Style

Two questions frame a president's leadership project. First, what are his or her opportunities and constraints within a given temporal and political context? Second, having chosen goals, through what process and with which resources can the incumbent achieve these aims? Placing this frame over Theodore Roosevelt, we find him in the first place interrogating a rapidly changing and chaotic political context to locate his goals, then finding the presidential office barren of resources for pursuing the goals he would choose.

The context in which Roosevelt identified his opportunities and set goals was identical to President McKinley's context. Roosevelt was aligned with the same Republican regime, and they had both run on the same ticket. Upon succeeding to the presidency Roosevelt pledged fealty to McKinley's policies and people. Nothing about that shared context predicts why one was a loyal articulator while the other was "an orthodox–innovator rubbing hard against the boundaries of a politics of articulation."[172] What *was* different was how Roosevelt "saw" his context and related to it, making it functionally different than the political context McKinley experienced. Roosevelt saw political incentives where McKinley had not. McKinley was aligned with the old party and its commitments while Roosevelt "saw" an emergent "radical center" as a new constituency for himself and for a reformed Republican Party as well. Consequently he set goals and sought strategic resources to speak to the interests of those clamoring for government activism and reform in economic life.

It is those goals that formed his leadership project. How he pursued those goals is what we term his "leadership style." Now we can sum up our examination of Roosevelt by looking more closely at that style. We shall analyze its components, beginning by asking what led Roosevelt to more responsiveness than other Republicans to emergent progressive reform demands. Then we shall examine the characteristics of his style through which he won support, acquired strategic resources, and accomplished some of his goals.

Roosevelt was far more responsive to reform demands and middle-class anxieties than the Old Guard Republican leaders for two reasons that emerged centrally in Chapter 3. The first reason is generational. He was born three years before McKinley marched off to the Civil War, and his political sensibilities were formed in the urban settings of the Northeast during the great industrial expansion of the late nineteenth century. In his initial experience with political office, as a New York State assemblyman, Roosevelt joined a coalition of anti-machine reformers. In contrast, beginning in his early thirties McKinley entered Congress as an ultra-orthodox Republican. Roosevelt's appointment to the federal civil service commission was a total immersion experience in the values of merit appointment and the pervasive evils of patronage while McKinley was a specialist in those practices.

As president of the New York City police commission Roosevelt promoted politics-free merit appointment in the police department. As police commissioner he also had his first intense experiences with the depths of urban poverty and disorder and, parallel to those experiences, he also learned of middle-class anxieties about new immigrants, disease, poverty, and disorder. Then at the navy department he was responsible for a very large and complex administrative system. Finally, as New York's governor, Roosevelt experienced a range of prominent issues that pitted reform concerns against traditional politics. By contrast, McKinley's service as governor in Ohio from 1893 to 1897 was marked by executive passivity and the occasional use of the state militia against striking workers.

Roosevelt's pre-presidential experiences sensitized him in two ways to new political issues. First, his political stance from the beginning was reformist and at each stop along the career path his reform sensibilities were heightened. But his reformist sensibilities were not those of the late Gilded Age reformers he resembled closely in social background and education. Those reformers heralded honesty in government and small government, laissez-faire ideas. They had little to no interest in economic problems, no concern with poverty, and no empathy with the plight of labor. However, Roosevelt was as perceptive of anxieties about economic change as he was about honesty in government, and as governor he saw political corruption and business dishonesty operate as symbiotic evils.

Roosevelt not only "saw" new political issues and demands. He demonstrated the political skills to achieve goals responsive to those demands. In our examination of the *Northern Securities* case and the all-big-gun battleship, we saw him succeed through several different tools that were quite novel for a president, including public communication, administrative control and information, and proto-staff recruitment.

Roosevelt became a highly visible public communicator, *and* he associated his public image with his policy agenda. In other words, we might think of Roosevelt as innovatively making the presidency a stage (not just "a bully pulpit") upon which he would model the importance of his policy goal. Past presidents understood the office's symbolic importance. But Roosevelt was the first to use the office's symbolic possibilities to promote substantive policy goals. That is most obvious in the navy case. His self-presentation as the heroic warrior gave him a potent veracity in promoting naval strength. His actions in assembling fleet-level exercises, which he attended, made publicly visible the grandeur of naval power. Finally, of course, the remarkable *chutzpa* (to use a most appropriate word) of ordering the Atlantic fleet to sail around the world, by way of the West Coast and then Japan, at a time of unsettled relations with Japan was a gesture of operatic grandeur.

The *Northern Securities* case presents less vivid examples of Roosevelt's dramaturgy, but they are no less important. His secretiveness in preparing action against Northern Securities and then the announcement of the Sherman Act suit hit the business community like a shot. The surprise attendant to the announcement amplified the news to the larger public, demonstrating vividly that there was a new sheriff in town to police business behavior. While the *Northern Securities* case was proceeding through the courts, Roosevelt modeled his stance of law enforcer over business in other ways, particularly in the anthracite coal strike during the summer of 1902. Therein his public language, his intervention, and his blustery remarks about the coal companies' insensitivity to the public interest all heightened his stance as responsive to public anxiety and aspirations for reform.

If public performance won support for Roosevelt's goals, his deft use of executive branch capacities provided strategic resources to achieve them. In the *Northern Securities* case we see Roosevelt initiating the lawsuit from the top of the administration, relying only on the attorney general's advice, instead of the usual process whereby cases under the Sherman Act were initiated by local U.S. attorneys in federal district courts. Notice also his use of the judicial appointment power attempting to place on the Supreme Court a justice who (Roosevelt thought) would support the government's side of the *Northern Securities* case when it reached the Court. But there was even more at play in Roosevelt's use of the case. His aim through unilateral action was to clarify the currently muddled anti-trust law, pulling into the president's arena policy issues that were conventionally in the purview of Congress and the judiciary.

In the naval case Roosevelt's intervention seems at first more conventional than in anti-trust. After all, the navy department is within the executive branch and the president is commander-in-chief. However, the convention of the time was that naval policy was formed outside the president's purview and within a triangle of senior officers at the navy's bureaus, the relevant congressional committees, and the secretary of the navy. Thus, as with anti-trust, Roosevelt's interventions in naval policy not only were focused on the immediate issue of battleship design or gunnery training but also, more profoundly, aimed at shifting the center of gravity on naval policy toward the executive from Congress and up toward the president from the naval bureaus and secretary.

The naval case presents a clear-cut example of the president using information as a strategic resource to leverage power and affect decision outcomes. The information that Roosevelt marshaled was esoteric, ranging from data about gunnery practice training and results to facts and interpretation of sea battles in the Russo-Japanese War. Here is where we find Roosevelt's potent use of what we have called a proto-staff. Lacking staff facilities in the presidency, Roosevelt used his existing knowledge of the navy to identify appropriate young officers to serve informally as his informants. Through what was seen by many senior officers as deeply inappropriate meddling in the service, Roosevelt found information through which to fulfill his goals for naval modernization.

The anti-trust case does not so much exhibit a proto-staff for information gathering as it reveals Roosevelt's vigorous outreach to independent actors within relevant elites for a combined purpose of gaining information and winning support. Roosevelt did not need technical information in the *Northern Securities* case; the justice department provided that. What he did need was information about the receptivity of different business and political leaders to regulatory ideas. Roosevelt's vigorous outreach in preparation for his first annual message was precisely for that purpose, signaling the general outline of his ideas and giving leaders a chance to feel they were heard in the consultative process.

It is important also to notice what was *not* present in Roosevelt's leadership style. In neither of these cases, nor more generally during his presidency, did Roosevelt take the role of party leader to mobilize support for his goals. His own career path made him an outsider to Republican Old Guard leaders. As a president who was receptive to new issues and demands he was often at odds with the interests of Republican congressional leaders. Well into his own elective term after 1904 Roosevelt attempted to manage and limit his tension with the Republican Old Guard but never became one with them. At the same time, he carefully avoided making himself the standard bearer for the minority of insurgent Republicans in Congress. Thus he remained an outsider to Republican congressional leaders rather than a party leader they looked toward.

The consequence of Roosevelt's success responding to new issues and demands is illustrated by a dyspeptic remark by the *Nation*. Eight months after Roosevelt entered office, the magazine wrote there was "an unhappy political tendency . . . the resort to the President in every time of trouble."[173] Roosevelt's success at representing Progressive Era anxieties and promoting responsive policies launched him into a landslide victory for what was essentially a second term. But his success also impacted the presidency, expanding its place in American politics and government. Roosevelt's political goals and his leadership style affected Americans' expectations about what the presidency should be— the leader who responds "in every time of trouble."

Finally, Roosevelt's effect on the presidency went further even than encouraging expectations of greater executive activism. His dramatic personal responses to issues of reform identified government substantively with progressive issues, validating the demand for reform while at the same time adding energy to the movements for reform. Thus Theodore Roosevelt passed on to his chosen successor and friend, William Howard Taft, expectations about government, reform, and presidential activism that were greatly different than those existing when he entered office in 1901.

The Political Education of William Howard Taft: Toward a Brilliant Career

Like every well-trained Ohio man I always had my plate the right side up
when offices were falling.
  William Howard Taft[1]

IN JANUARY 1903 William Howard Taft's mother, three brothers, and aunt convened in New York City. Their purpose was to consider if William should go to the U.S. Supreme Court or remain governor of the Philippines. Meanwhile Taft awaited advice in Manila. As a public man, William Howard Taft was a creation of his family's tightly knit relationships and their loyalty to the Republican party. In Taft's relationship to his family we shall find a key to his political sensibilities and his approach to political work.

Who Was Taft?

We retrospectively picture Taft as a jovial conservative, more Gilded Age than Progressive Era in his sensibilities. But fat, jolly, and conservative is more a caricature of Taft than reality. Before 1909 Americans were more likely to see him as a model of energetic competence. As one newspaper wrote of his qualifications for the presidency:

> He is . . . a jurist of eminent qualifications. . . . As a Cabinet officer he has been brought into close relations with almost every department of the government; as a diplomat he has rubbed elbows with the statesmen of the world. . . . In the far-away islands . . . he has ruled the strange . . . peoples whom fate and . . . war have placed under the care of our spotless flag, and his rule was gentle and just and wise. [2]

Yet, we look back at Taft as hobbled by a conservatism that kept him from achieving the successes of Roosevelt and Wilson.[3] If his ideology so limited his presidency, why did it not hamper his notable pre-presidential accomplishments under the innovative Roosevelt? Or, did his conservatism just appear, full-blown, at his inauguration to the presidency, making him a misfit in a progressive context? To look critically at the factors shaping Taft's presidential leadership we must survey the relationship between his earlier career and his later presidential performance.

Rather than constituting a career of accumulating expertise, each office Taft occupied before the presidency entailed very different challenges and demanded different skills. He was adept at understanding requirements for success in these roles, succeeding in them through great effort and—most important in his view— by pleasing his superiors. In each role we find Taft with a political outlook that was appropriate to the role. Yet, over time, he seemed to form no coherent political vision of his own. He was an eminently adaptable functionary, a superb subordinate.

Taft's family motivated his career and opened doors to his appointments. Additionally, through the Taft family's political loyalties we see the ties binding William to the norms of the party period. Family and party set the parameters of his career. It was a family project.

W. H. Taft and the Family Enterprise

The Tafts were a leading, politically prominent family of Cincinnati, and William was born into patronage opportunities, an heir to his father's Republicanism. The members of his family made opportunities for him, and he was attuned to their guidance. William's three surviving brothers were notably successful and participated in his career. The eldest, a half-brother, Charles Taft, gained wealth through marriage and was owner-publisher of the *Cincinnati Times-Star*. Henry was a year younger than William and was a prominent Wall Street lawyer. Taft's youngest brother, Horace, was founder and headmaster of the Taft School in Watertown, Connecticut.

Alphonso Taft, the family patriarch, was educated at Yale and arrived in Cincinnati in 1838 to practice law. His sons followed him to Yale and subsequent legal training. Alphonso was a judge on the Ohio Superior Court and then secretary of war and attorney general under President Grant. After losing the 1875 Ohio gubernatorial race he was appointed minister to the Austrian-Hungarian Empire and in 1885 as minister to Russia. Alphonso raised his sons with expectations for their great success and with strong emotional bonds. Touchingly, William recalled his father on his deathbed saying to him: "I love you beyond expression."[4] Alphonso had particularly high expectations for William. He announced to his family, "Mediocrity will not do for Will."[5] As William began his studies at Yale, his father's expectations weighed on him. He wrote to Alphonso: "You expect great things of me but you mustn't be disappointed if I don't come up to your expectations."[6]

There is more here than the dynamics of a loving but demanding father and his talented sons. Alphonso Taft's ambition was for the family to achieve distinction through the "brilliant" careers of its men. Near the end of Alphonso's life, Charles Taft wrote to William, "We boys are all trying to push . . . toward success if for no other reason than to convince Father . . . that he has not spent a life in vain."[7] In particular, the father hoped the family might produce "brilliant political careers." At an 1874 extended family gathering he said that such careers "have not been characteristic of the Tafts . . . [but] it is not safe to say what may yet be in store."[8] Three of his sons achieved brilliant careers in the private sector. That left William to carry his father's hopes that one of his sons would have a successful public career, and it was the family's project to help him fulfill that hope. Helen Herron Taft gleefully joined that family enterprise through her marriage to William in 1886.

Yet Taft's career began without much brilliance. After Yale, he studied law at Cincinnati Law School, passing the Ohio bar in 1880. Trying newspaper reporting first, he later moved on to local patronage jobs doled out by the Republican organization. He was an assistant solicitor for Hamilton County, county election supervisor in 1884, and then federal collector of the internal revenue for Cincinnati. In contrast to Roosevelt's pre-presidential stance in tension between reform and partisanship, Taft's career was built on a foundation of partisan loyalty. Roosevelt was opposed to the patronage norms of the party period, and he worked in key jobs within the nascent administrative state. Taft, on the other hand, was rewarded for conformity with the norms of the party period. Henry Pringle writes that Taft was "inexplicably . . . pushed from office to office without . . . doing much about it himself."[9] But the path of his career was not inexplicable. Taft's family and Republican loyalty enabled it.

State Court Judge

In 1887 Governor William Foraker named the twenty-nine-year-old Taft to Ohio's Superior Court, where Alphonso had once been seated. The next year William was elected for a full term on the court. He thrived as a judge and demonstrated a talent for dogged legal research. His opinions were verbose but could clarify difficult issues through their logic and citations of obscure precedents. His views were pro-business, but in his most notably pro-business appellate decision he affirmed the rights of workers to control their labor and to withhold labor in dispute with management. In that case of 1890, *Moores & Co. v. Bricklayers' Union,* Taft ruled against a union's secondary boycott. He reasoned that labor could not be withheld with "malice" against third parties not involved in a dispute. In later years, Taft cited the case as likely to harm his chances for electoral success because he had opposed organized labor. However, his ruling on a secondary boycott was consistent with precedent, and the Ohio supreme court upheld his anti-boycott decision.[10] Nothing about his Superior Court service went beyond respectably conservative, Republican views of the time.

Alphonso Taft's pride in his son's judgeship validated William's own satisfaction. With Alphonso resettled in San Diego, California for his health, Taft sent frequent letters, including drafts of opinions, which, he said, were often "altogether too long . . . but I . . . must make plain my reasons for my conclusion."[11] Taft might have remained on that court had not his family encouraged him to a precocious aspiration for a U.S. Supreme Court seat. In spring 1889 Horace wrote to William that Representative Benjamin Butterworth (R-OH) was promoting William for appointment to a U.S. Supreme Court vacancy.[12] Taft then learned that the Ohioan favored for the seat withdrew his candidacy. Taft enlisted a senior colleague on the state court who was also a friend of Alphonso's, Judge Hiram Peck, to "get letters . . . to the President."[13] He called on his brother Charles to promote his availability to Secretary of State James G. Blaine. Taft wrote to his father that he thought his "chances are excellent."[14] Taft's efforts to gain the appointment were sufficiently visible that the *Los Angeles Times* commented on the well-connected Judge Taft's candidacy, noting also his very tender years.[15]

Taft called on help from Ohio's governor William Foraker, requesting an introduction to President Harrison during a scheduled visit to Cincinnati.[16] Letters on William's behalf had been showered on President Harrison, including one from Foraker.[17] In meeting Harrison Taft hoped to leave the president with a good impression of the aspiring justice. Later, describing to his father the meeting with Harrison, Taft seemed deflated; it did not quite fulfill Taft's expectations. He wrote that despite the work of his supporters his "chance of going to the moon and of donning a silk gown at the hands of President Harrison are about equal." In a candid aside, he said that were he president, "I would not approach a man of my age and position to that Bench and I felt as if he were even less likely than I should be to do such a thing."[18] But, sixteen months later, Taft wrote what could stand for the guiding principle of his career: "Judgeships like that don't lie around loose, and if you don't get them when you can, you will not get them when you would."[19]

The actual getting of the office might depend on timing and luck, but the possibility of the "getting" of an office depended on the positional advantages Taft had through his family. Through its influence and support Taft pushed forward to a "brilliant career." However, the prize won was not necessarily the target at which he aimed. In 1890 President Harrison, impressed apparently by what he had learned about Taft regarding the Supreme Court vacancy, decided what he saw in Taft was the next solicitor general of the United States.[20]

Though a young person of slight legal experience, Taft had achieved success on the state court through diligence. His success as a judge demonstrated his ability to rise to the demands of a job for which he was only modestly prepared. His performance was energized by expectations for high performance by those closest to him. Most of all, Taft had to impress his father, who had sat on the same court.

Solicitor General of the United States

The *Washington Post* announced Taft's designation as solicitor general, noting, "He was not an applicant for the office."[21] Taft was ambivalent about the proffered position, and his wife Helen (or Nellie) decided for him. She was eager to move from Cincinnati into the larger world of the "bigwigs" as she would say. In her diary, she wrote: "I was very glad because it gave Mr. Taft an opportunity for exactly the kind of work I wished him to do . . . I looked forward with interest, moreover, to a few years in Washington." [22] Alphonso also advised that his son take the proffered appointment. He admitted that at first he "hesitated whether you ought to take it" because it would be very hard work "and your present place is so satisfactory." However, he explained, it was an office of great honor and "preparatory . . . for a high national position."[23]

The solicitor general's office was established in 1870 within the new department of justice to assist the attorney general in all his duties.[24] In practice, the solicitor general was responsible for managing cases and representing the government before the Supreme Court. Newly arrived in Washington, Taft was greatly anxious about his ability to perform his duties. To Alphonso he admitted being ill prepared, natural for a young lawyer, but peculiar for someone who had recently sought appointment to the Supreme Court. Taft wrote:

> Considering that I have had no experience in [the Supreme Court], and am entirely unfamiliar with the rules of practice, that I have very little familiarity with the decision of the court, and the Federal statutes, the prospect of work is rather overwhelming. However, I suppose I can worry through it in some way.[25]

A year later Taft wrote that he had grown in depth of knowledge of federal law and practice, and "I have made some very valuable acquaintances, have come into exceedingly pleasant relations with the Supreme Court, and have had an occasional glimpse behind the scenes of . . . the government."[26] His family's connections assured his access to the political elite. February 15, 1890 was Taft's first day at the justice department. As he sorted through his new office, U.S. Senator William Evarts (R-NY), a distinguished attorney and former secretary of state, burst in. Evarts explained that Alphonso was a Yale classmate and an old friend. He then invited Taft to a dinner at his home that night where Taft joined Senator and Mrs. Henry Cabot Lodge, and Mr. and Mrs. John Hay, among others, at the Evartses' table.[27]

Taft's taste for hard work compensated for inexperience. Alphaeus Thomas Mason observes he was undistinguished as solicitor general.[28] Yet judged by the outcomes of his cases he was at least competent. After twelve months in the office he had argued eighteen cases in front of the Supreme Court. Of those already decided, he had won eleven and lost two.[29] His work was an accelerated course in federal public law and also gave him exposure to leading Republicans. Most fatefully, he became friendly with the young chairman of the civil service commission, Theodore Roosevelt. With an eye on future possibilities, Taft also cultivated social relations with the Supreme Court's members.[30]

Yet, after a year as solicitor general Taft was looking for another plum job. In March 1891 Congress created new federal appellate judgeships, one in each circuit. Taft pushed himself forward for the new seat in the sixth circuit, which included Ohio. Ten months after arriving in Washington Taft wrote that "I . . . have my eye on the Circuit Judgeship."[31] His old colleague Judge Hiram Peck organized prominent Cincinnati Republican judges and attorneys to promote "the appointment of Solicitor General Taft to the new judgeship for the Ohio Circuit."[32] Charles Taft communicated to Senator John Sherman (R-OH) that he "thought it was queer that Sherman had never done anything for him" and that what he wanted was "his assistance in the matter of the Circuit Judgeship."[33] The campaign was successful, and Taft took his new job in March 1891.

Taft's new plum depended, in part, on his success as solicitor general. In Washington he was acutely attentive to pleasing his superiors. The attorney general had to be satisfied. But Taft looked beyond him to the Supreme Court justices for approbation. He enthusiastically described social interactions with the justices, taking their regard for him as demonstrating his success. For example, with a possible opening impending, Justice Henry Brown let him know that he and "Justice Jackson . . . are very anxious that I should be the fortunate one."[34]

U.S. Circuit Court

Taft served on the federal appellate court for eight years, finding professional and personal fulfillment on that bench. He had space to research and apply the law from a dispassionate place, and he liked a judge's passive role. He preferred sitting behind the bench to arguing in front of it. "I find it quite embarrassing to change from the easy position of sitting on the bench to the very different one of standing on your legs before it, and I do not find myself at home . . . in presenting one side of a case at Court."[35] Taft saw his judgeship as "a fine position to hold" and had the added advantage of being "in the line of promotion to the Supreme Court."[36] There was disagreement among his closest advisers over his next move. His parents were pleased with his elevation to the federal bench. His wife saw it differently. Nellie claimed judicial life was stultifying and said, "Once more I saw him a colleague of men almost twice his age and, I feared, fixed in a groove for the rest of his life."[37] Lamenting her own situation as much as Taft's, she complained that the circuit judgeship "will put an end to all the opportunities you . . . have of being thrown with the bigwigs."[38]

Through his solicitor general experience Taft won an esteem that made him seem deserving of the federal circuit. The *Chicago Daily Tribune* wrote that Taft "has made a reputation since he came to Washington."[39] He went on to win the esteem of leading lawyers as he moved among the circuit's legal elites and addressed cases arising from the era's intense economic conflicts. He served simultaneously as dean of the Cincinnati Law School. Taft summed up his feelings about his circuit court service: "I love judges, and I love courts. . . . They are my ideals, that typify on earth what we shall meet hereafter in heaven under a just God."[40]

It was in his federal appellate opinions that scholars cite strong evidence of Taft's conservatism. He served at a time of great labor unrest and heard strike-related cases. He privately expressed bitterly anti-labor views. For example, to Nellie he wrote strikes "seem to be in the hands of the most demagogic and insane leaders and they are determined to provoke a civil war." Taft frequently imposed injunctions against strikes and boycotts. However in several areas of the law Taft took more liberal positions on labor questions. He broke new ground on the issue of employers' responsibility for worker safety. Existing precedent held that workers themselves assumed the risks of their workplaces.[41] However, in the case of *Narramore vs. Cleveland , C.C. & St. Louis Railroad Co.,* Taft ruled in 1889 for a worker suing his employer for injuries resulting from unprotected railroad tracks. Ohio statutes required that tracks be protected. Taft's opinion stated that to decide for the employer in this case is "to enable it to nullify a . . . statute and is against public policy."[42]

Taft also expanded application of the Sherman Anti-Trust Act. In 1895 the Supreme Court limited that law's reach over manufacturing firms, deciding they are not in interstate commerce.[43] But in 1898 Taft decided *U.S. vs. Addyston Pipe,* ruling against a group of manufacturers of iron pipe for fixing prices among the Ohio Valley states. Taft distinguished this case from *United States vs. E. C. Knight,* deciding that price fixing directly affected interstate commerce.[44] The headline that appeared in the *New York Times* read, "Iron Pipe Trust Illegal: The First Case in Which Manufacturing Combination Had Been Found Guilty."[45] In a railroad rate case of 1899 Taft ruled to expand the Interstate Commerce Commission's (ICC) power to halt discriminatory freight rates. The East Tennessee, Virginia, and Georgia Railway charged more for goods from Eastern cities to Chattanooga than from Chattanooga to Nashville, a significantly longer distance. The ICC had sued to end the discriminatory rates. The question before the court was whether the commission had the legal power to act against rate discrimination, and Taft decided for the commission. The *Washington Post* called it "the most important case ever decided in favor of the Interstate Commerce Commission."[46]

In these cases Taft displayed a more nuanced view of the relationship of government and business than is usually attributed to him.[47] All the while he nursed ambition for elevation to the Supreme Court. He maintained ties to the justices and hoped their esteem would recommend his appointment. Justice John Harlan wrote to Taft he hoped "that the time is not far distant when we may welcome you into our judicial family."[48] After visiting the Court during a trip to Washington, D.C., Taft reported to Nellie: "I held quite a levee in the courtroom. . . . Then the court came in and I got a bow from them. . . . Then all the notes began to come down, first from Harlan and then from Jackson."[49] While Taft aimed for a seat on the Court, his family promoted him for whatever plum appointment came open. In early 1896, assuming a Republican victory later that year, Charles Taft pushed his brother for attorney general. He also assured William that should he be appointed to the next cabinet, he would "stand by you financially so that you can fill the position creditably and without embarrassment."[50]

However, McKinley did not choose William Taft for his cabinet, and in 1899 Henry Taft attempted to push his brother through another open door. Yale's presidency was vacant, and Henry wrote to William, "All the sentiment of the liberal element in the corporation is centering upon you as the fit man for the place, and some of the men . . . are very anxious to know . . . what your attitude will be."[51] Denying his fitness for the post, William explained that he was unqualified both by his professional training and his Unitarian affiliation.[52]

A call from McKinley came on January 22, 1900, with a telegram asking Taft to meet with the president in Washington. The telegram did not mention the purpose for the meeting.[53] There was no current vacancy on the court, and Taft went to Washington unsure of what plum could be in the offing. McKinley's offer was appointment to the new Philippines commission to create a civil government for the Philippines and to become civil governor once the ongoing insurrection was suppressed. Taft was taken aback by the president's offer. Nellie Taft later wrote, "Mr. Taft was strongly opposed to taking the Philippines" as a prize of war, and perhaps even more disqualifying, he "knew just about as much about the Filipino people as the average American knew in those days."[54] When Taft returned to Cincinnati for family consultations President McKinley exerted pressure on him to accept the post. A letter from Secretary of War Elihu Root awaited his arrival in Cincinnati, explaining it was his duty to accept the job and to not yield to his own ease in a judicial career.[55] McKinley also sent Supreme Court Justice William Day to convince Taft of the assignment's importance.[56]

Nellie Taft needed little convincing and looked forward to the great adventure.[57] Taft's brothers urged him to take the job. Horace wrote, "You can do more good in that position in a year than you could on the bench in a dozen."[58] Henry counseled William with a long view toward the acclaim he could gain: "The opportunity of great distinction from . . . establishing of a wise government is so unusual that I hardly think, at your age, you would be justified in refusing to embrace it."[59] Taft accepted, motivated in part by the president's promise that should he be reelected in 1900 he would appoint Taft to the Supreme Court when a vacancy occurred. Looking out for his brother, Henry advised that while the promise was "direct assurance of appointment," Taft should nevertheless get it in writing.[60]

Colonial Governor

As the Tafts departed for Manila, Nellie observed that what lay ahead of them "came to mean more to us personally than any other event in our times. The whole course of my husband's career was destined to be changed"[61] Taft now had a challenging job with large risks. The United States had occupied the Philippines after defeating Spain, acquiring an archipelago of many language groups and a tense division between a Catholic majority and Muslim minority. An armed insurgency smoldered, and Taft's assignment was to replace military occupation with a civil government that would incorporate Filipinos and draw support from the population.

Taft and his four-member commission embarked from the United States in mid-April 1900, carrying detailed directions from Secretary Root. That document was "the germ of all future government and advancement" for the islands, and his mission was to implement its instructions.[62] Taft, who had high anxieties entering his first judgeship and the solicitor general post, was surprisingly matter-of-fact about the new mission. His confidence seemed rooted in a wholly unfounded assumption that his training as a lawyer was precisely the prerequisite for the challenges he would face. He said to Root that he saw the task ahead as work for a lawyer because it required framing government and drafting new laws.[63]

The commission began its work in September and assumed executive responsibilities from the military governor in summer 1901. Taft's role as colonial administrator was a world apart from his own background and social setting. Nothing in his past prepared him for it, and his notion that legal training was the right background amounted to whistling in the graveyard. But against great odds he succeeded famously. What he began in 1900 as a little-known jurist turned him into a heralded national figure with proven credentials for high office.

Bound for Manila, Taft and the commission stopped over at Honolulu. His observations about Hawaii hint at his lack of preparedness for engaging a native culture in a colonial context. Commenting on the selection of a new governor for the territory, he preferred that Sanford Dole be chosen because he represented the "missionary influence, which is . . . criticized, and yet the missionaries have made all there is out of the islands." Taft noted that the alternative to Dole "would probably make a good governor" but was too ingratiated with the "native element, which being in the majority, would better be restrained than encouraged."[64] He failed to see the local resentments aimed at the oligarch Dole, and he overlooked that the 1900 Hawaiian Organic Act would enable large-scale native participation in politics.

When Taft arrived in the Philippines the military governor was General Arthur MacArthur. He exercised authority over the Filipino population and commanded 65,000 U.S. troops engaged in jungle warfare.[65] The general and the judge's relationship quickly soured.[66] MacArthur resented the commission's meddling, as he saw it, and he resisted its recommendations.[67] An example of that disagreement occurred over Taft's plan for a native constabulary. It would maintain order, freeing American troops for combat service. But more important for Taft, the constabulary would establish a native role in civil government. Taft sent the proposal to Secretary of War Root, but MacArthur resisted the idea. Taft said, "The military man is never pressed with a desire to hurry matters, at least this military man is not."[68] In a demonstration of Taft's influence that further angered MacArthur, Secretary Root accepted the proposal for the native troops and gained appropriation for a force of 12,000. [69]

Taft saw Filipinos and their prospects in a way that contrasted with the general's view. Taft said that MacArthur saw his mission to be "conquering eight millions of recalcitrant, treacherous and sullen people."[70] The army treated Filipinos with contempt, as an inferior race. In one of his reports to Root, Taft described a visit to a provincial town with his wife and sister-in-law, noting that the military was "shocked at the idea" that the natives of the town would be allowed to shake hands with the white ladies.[71] These racist attitudes, he realized, fueled the insurrection. In place of the inferiority Taft had recently seen in native Hawaiians, he learned to see in Filipinos the promise of eventual self-government and an eagerness for self-improvement. To Secretary Root in August 1900, he described Filipinos as having "an aptitude for education" but also being weighed down by superstition and following "unscrupulous leaders," but "a large majority longed for peace."[72] Taft assumed the role of a gentle and understanding tutor; these people were "our little brown brothers."[73]

Consequently, he included Filipino elites within government and encouraged the formation of political organizations among "responsible" Filipinos. He practiced democratic openness contrasted to the caste-like behavior of the U.S. military and the aristocratic pretensions of the former Spanish governors.

Nellie Taft recalled that she and her husband "insisted upon complete racial equality for the Filipinos, and from the beginning there were a great many of them among our callers and guests."[74] Yet, tensions between his inclusiveness and the military's disparagement of Filipinos did not diminish. At the end of 1901 Taft wrote that as he appointed Filipinos to government positions, "it has . . . disappointed the army and there has been constant grumbling."[75]

Despite struggles with MacArthur over jurisdiction and authority, Taft progressed toward building a colonial government that included Filipinos. He added two Filipino members to the commission, and in building a new judicial system for the islands, he made a Filipino chief of the supreme court, though most of the judiciary was American.[76] He also exhibited openness in government by having the commission hold public hearings on proposed legislation.[77] At the end of 1901 there were 765 town governments established under new laws, with municipal officers elected by all Filipinos owning property valued at $250, or paying an annual tax of $15, or literate in Spanish or English.[78]

As colonial governor Taft confronted issues on which he moved with far greater governmental activism than did American presidents or state governors of the time. For example, he confronted a financial scandal in the Philippines' major bank, an institution owned by Catholic institutions and controlled by the Vatican's representative to the islands. As he reported to Secretary Root, if the bank is unstable "we shall pass additional legislation . . . to take charge of the bank."[79] Thus, Taft's mission in the islands entailed a wide range of internal governance issues faced by a national government, and his responses to issues as they arose belie his image in our historical imagination as a rigid conservative.

On another Church-related matter, Taft conducted highly sensitive diplomacy with the Vatican.[80] Under the Spanish, Catholic religious orders controlled education, agriculture, and large sectors of the economy. For Taft, "The friars ceased to be religious ministers . . . and became political bosses."[81] The orders, or "Friars," owned 400,000 acres of prime fertile land farmed by 60,000 tenant farmers, and they were widely resented by Filipinos.[82] The Friars' properties were politically sensitive. Reformers sought to redistribute the land to tenants, but the Vatican's representative, Archbishop Chapelle, was unmovable about these properties. He accused Taft of anti-Catholic motives and charged that Americans were introducing liberalism, threatening the Church and good order. Archbishop Chapelle told Taft "all the conservative, wise and serious minded men, both here and in America" agreed with his view of Taft and his policies.[83] Undeterred, Taft proposed a decisive resolution of the problem. The United States should purchase all the Church lands and evict the orders, replacing them with American priests. He recommended to Secretary Root and the president (now Roosevelt) that they send an emissary "to Rome to negotiate a purchase of these lands." And he wondered, "Have we a man competent to do the business"?[84] President Roosevelt decided Taft was the man.

After stopping in the United States to consult Roosevelt and Root during May 1902, Taft traveled to Rome. The mission was delicate; he had to avoid offending American Catholics *and* not imply official United States diplomatic recognition of the Vatican. During nearly three months of negotiations, he succeeded in establishing the outlines for an agreement, finally concluded in November 1903. He then returned to the islands and colonial governance.

In his performance as governor Taft exhibited a tenacious grasp of policy details, a close supervision of subordinates, and a concern for communicating clearly the ideals of American occupation. Consider two examples that reflect his engagement with the quality of colonial government. Hearing of harsh actions by the American warden at the national prison, he wrote to him a gentle but clear directive. Noting the prison's "clean and satisfactory condition," Taft continued: "I understand the necessity for discipline . . . but I also understand that strict discipline is quite consistent with courtesy and kindly treatment."[85] Another example concerns the public schools established under American supervision. He saw American teachers as exemplars of citizenship. In instructions for the staff, Taft wrote: "The opportunity . . . for the American school teacher[s] . . . to ingratiate themselves with the Filipino people exceeds that of any other class of servants of Government." The teacher who fails to "wield influence among the people for their good is missing half the purpose of his being here."[86]

Taft's success demonstrated to Republicans that he was a highly credible presidential candidate. Theodore Roosevelt described him as eminently qualified to be "a first-class President of the United States" and "a first-class Chief Justice of the United States." Praising Taft's accomplishment in the Philippines, Roosevelt observed:

> Few more difficult tasks have devolved upon any man of our nationality . . . and it may be doubted whether among men now living another could be found as well fitted as Judge Taft to do this incredibly difficult work. . . . Every American . . . who is proud of his country and jealous of her honor, should uphold the hands of Governor Taft. [87]

Taft's service and great success as a colonial pro-consul was his first experience in an office that approximated the issue breadth, issue complexity, conflict, and high visibility of great executive office.[88] In what respects was the Philippine experience preparation for the presidency? As much as it shone on Taft the spotlight of political stardom, there are several aspects of his experience in the islands that distinguished it from what he would face in the presidency.

First, in the islands he was the imperial pro-consul with no official barriers to his authority. There were no checks and balances, no competing political parties, and no legislature to impede him because he and the commission held the legislative power, not the Philippine assembly. In initiating reforms, Taft benefited from a second aspect of the role that made it different from the American political scene. His role was unaffected by the agendas and interests of political parties. He was able to rule in Manila without obedience to his party's policy agenda and platform, except in the most general sense that the Republicans supported American possession of the islands. His fundamental partisan views remained in place. He had a near-hysterical fear of Bryan defeating McKinley in 1900 and inspiring the Filipino insurrectionists to think that they would win independence,[89] It was because the Manila context removed him from issues that would trigger his powerful partisan impulses that he was freed to deal pragmatically with matters of governance. For example, when the Spanish Filipino Bank fell into disarray, Taft's response was regulatory intervention, violating hallowed Republican principles.

A third element distinguishing his performance in Manila, and perhaps the most important, was that he worked within a detailed framework of goals and direct supervision. For all his appearance of imperial autonomy, he was in fact working under the guidelines and immediate supervision of the secretary of war. Taft departed the states with a detailed plan of colonial governance. Secretary Root's biographer, Phillip Jessup, describes the documents as "more than instructions . . . they were the outline and the framework within which the civil government of the Philippines was to be formed and to develop."[90] Taft later described Secretary Root as the person "who more than any other one man initiated our Philippine policy."[91] Root wrote that his purpose in drafting the document was:

> to determine and prescribe the framework of insular government, to
> lay down the rules of policy to be followed upon the great questions of
> government as they are foreseen or arise, to obtain the . . . ablest men

. . . to distribute and define their powers, and then to hold them responsible for the conduct of government in the islands with the least possible interference from Washington.[92]

Taft sent Root reports describing his activity, problems, and decisions. Root responded either by letter or cable, providing the governor with a continuing sense of satisfaction in pleasing his superior. Root wrote that his reports were "most instructive, interesting and comforting."[93]

Taft's assignment in the Philippines was far larger than anything he had done up to that time, but like his judgeships and brief service as solicitor general, this role also entailed specified goals and clear supervision. Of course, none of that diminishes the brilliance of Taft's performance. He was a superlative subaltern.

In late 1902 President Roosevelt offered Taft the prize of appointment to the Supreme Court. What ensued reveals his reliance on his family as well as his ambivalence about leaving Manila for the Court's comfortable prestige. His initial reaction to Roosevelt's offer revealed the intensity of his need for the president's approval. He feared that Roosevelt sought to "kick him upstairs," having become dissatisfied with his work in Manila. Consequently, Taft asked his brother to gain clarification about Roosevelt's motive. Eventually relieved of that fear by messages from his brothers and Roosevelt himself, he was ambivalent about the offer of a place on the Court to which he had aspired.[94]

There were several sources for Taft's indecision. He was committed to his work in the islands. He thought that conditions there were, as he wrote his brother Charles, "just as critical as they have been for the last two years."[95] But there was also a matter of ascertaining his optimal career path. Would Taft continue on the path of executive politics, or would he take the best plum available for a judicial career? His wife urged him to pursue the executive path toward the White House.[96] His ambivalence about the judicial post suggests more interest in an executive career and elective politics than has been typically attributed to him. The press reaction to the rumor of his possible appointment to the Court demonstrated his eminent public reputation. The *Washington Post* wrote the appointment would be "a reward for his long and arduous service" in the islands.[97] When it had become public knowledge that Taft was resisting the president's pressure to take the Court appointment, the *Chicago Tribune* wrote: "It is doubtful if the history of American politics furnishes many such examples of a man deliberately sacrificing his own career for the sake of his desire to do his full duty by his country and by millions of brown men."[98]

Taft's uncertainty about Roosevelt's offer returns us to the Taft family conference of January 1903. In his indecision—stay in the Philippines or take the Court appointment—Taft turned to his family. He asked brother Harry "to go to Washington to find out whether [it] was the case" that Roosevelt wanted to remove him from Manila.[99] Roosevelt's response to Taft's resistance was to force the issue, not because he wanted him out of Manila but because he wanted him on the Court. Consequently, Taft wrote to brother Charles that he seemed to have no choice but to accept the Court.[100] Amidst the flurry of messages among the president, Taft, and his brothers, the family met in New York City. The question of whether William should take the Court position was subordinated to the question of his prospects for a presidential nomination. In meetings with President Roosevelt, Secretary Root, and others in Washington, Henry Taft garnered the information that was grist for the family's decision mill. The most important intelligence for the family was that both Roosevelt and Root had mentioned their estimation that William would be an ideal Republican nominee for the presidency after Roosevelt's last term.[101]

Thus the family saw a path to greater distinction for William were he to not take the Court appointment. In the discussion, Taft's mother and aunt both favored his remaining in politics. Charles, enunciating the core principle of party-period career planning, advised that Will should "take what happens to be within your reach." Henry, conveying Root's advice that William would be "the surest candidate as Roosevelt's successor," advised against the Court. He pointed out that his brother had demonstrated great abilities for executive and legislative leadership that went far beyond what would be used on the Court. And, Henry added, "I really cannot quite reconcile myself with your finally choosing a judicial career at your age."[102]

As Henry was writing to William with the family's recommendation on his decision, events in Manila reinforced his own preference to remain. Six thousand Filipinos of various classes demonstrated in front of the Malacanan Palace to celebrate Taft and demand that he continue as governor. As he said about the event, "The Filipino people have taken the matter in hand and we have had great doings out here. All the elements . . . have united to protest against my retirement."[103] Roosevelt consequently allowed him to remain in Manila. That experience of public acclaim also underlined for Taft the psychic rewards available to him along the path of elective executive politics.[104]

He was now on track to the presidency, with his brothers back in the States managing his progress. William's new political prominence created problems as well as opportunities for his managers. For example, Henry reported that Republicans hostile to progressive reform were floating Taft's name as an alternative to Roosevelt for the 1904 nomination. Henry wrote, "You might wish to put an end to this talk," and that, in any case, Roosevelt's nomination was safe.[105] Charles sent news of a promising political opportunity: Ohio Republicans hoped to draft William for the next gubernatorial race.[106] Brother Horace wrote to William in late January urging that William put aside his ambition for the bench until he returned home "and we can all have a whack at you." Horace was not "possessed with the idea of your being president" but hoped that William could return to a position in which he could "do a lot of good."[107]

In March 1903 Henry passed on to William news that Secretary Root was to leave the war department and Roosevelt would ask him to fill the place.[108] In another signal that Taft achieved the stature of "presidential timber," pro-Roosevelt Republicans promoted him for the vice presidential nomination in 1904.[109]

War Department and Washington

In calling Taft to return to Washington and join his cabinet, Roosevelt flattered him, saying that he and Root were the two men in public service about whom he felt most strongly. Roosevelt assured Taft that as war secretary he would remain in charge of Philippine policy. He also gave him time to wrap up his work: "I want to ask you . . . if I can persuade Root to stay until a year hence . . . come back and take his place."[110] Implying how well he understood Taft's personality, Roosevelt asked him to "not mention this to a soul," presumably to prevent another round of demonstrations in Manila. He also wrote, "I desire your decision on your own thought and on the proposition's merit by itself," obviously hoping that he might decide this by himself rather than in conference with his family.[111] Incapable of complying with the latter request, Taft circulated Roosevelt's letter to his brothers and mother. Their response was, as he later wrote to a friend, "unanimous in the demand that I should accept the place and come home."[112]

Taft had personal reasons for returning to the States and a cabinet position. His health deteriorated in the islands, and he was satisfied that he could guide the Philippine policy from a distance. Nellie also urged him to accept, seeing the cabinet as an appropriate next step for her husband. She later wrote: "This was much more pleasing to me than the offer of . . . Court appointment."[113] Finally, he was attracted to the cabinet post because he would work closely with Roosevelt.

Chapter Four

Returning to Washington, Taft needed his family enterprise for more than advice and emotional support. The war secretary's official salary was $8,000, in contrast to the colonial governor's compensation of $20,000. In Manila the Tafts had needed sufficient funds for an imperial style of life, maintaining the Malacanan Palace, many servants, a large stable of horses and carriages, and expansive entertainments.[114] The return to Washington would see a fall in their standard of living from imperial to bourgeois. Roosevelt blithely advised his new war secretary to accept the lifestyle change and live frugally in Washington, as he had while solicitor general.[115] The Tafts dismissed that advice as outlandish, and Charles stepped forward. Earlier in Taft's career, Charles had given him frequent monetary gifts. Now he gave his brother a continuing income, assuring that William would annually receive $6,000.[116]

Once the Tafts were resettled in Washington, the war department would be an insignificant part of William's work as secretary of war. Roosevelt wanted him because he trusted his competence and judgment, and his primary role would be as Roosevelt's chief problem-solver, to take responsibility for overseas problems as they arose. Taft's political celebrity also made him a useful presidential surrogate in the 1904 electoral campaign.

The war department of 1904 was ready to sustain an absentee secretary. Root achieved sweeping reforms in the U.S. army and the department's organization during his tenure. He changed the officer corps, army organization, and the relationship of the army to civilian control. He eliminated seniority as the basis of promotion. He introduced the general staff, with a supporting set of younger officers, serving the president and replacing the old single post of the general of the army. He built mid-career education for the army, reforming the existing staff colleges and creating the Army War College. Root also established administration for the possessions won from Spain. Finally, he had insisted on strict adherence to civil service for civilian employment at the department, and for upper-level administrative appointments he insisted on quality and experience before politics.[117]

Thus, Taft took on a department that was sufficiently stable and well staffed to operate without his frequent intervention. He served Roosevelt as a special emissary and, in effect, as deputy secretary of state, filling a vacuum created by Secretary of State John Hay's declining health. His experience in Asia had proven his fitness as a substitute secretary of state. Adding to his appropriateness for a role in foreign affairs, the war department was responsible for American overseas possessions. His first major assignment was the Panama Canal project for which the president gave him oversight for planning and construction. Having no background on either Panama or civil engineering Taft had to catch up, as he said, to discuss "the matter on the stump."[118] He would soon have to do more than explain and defend the policy. In November 1904 Roosevelt sent Taft to Panama to assess design alternatives and also to reassure Panamanian leaders about American intentions toward the small country.

Taft was a quick study. His report to Roosevelt demonstrated a command of the political and legal aspects of the canal project and some general understanding of the engineering issues. The historian Ralph Minger writes:

> With an amazing capacity for detail, he surveyed the physical
> aspects of canal construction. He offered opinions about the
> various individuals involved . . . evaluating their technical abilities.
> Although conceding a lack of expertise in engineering problems, he
> offered . . . conclusions on the scope of the project. . . . What
> emerges from the pages of this report is the figure of a man
> possessed of enormous vitality.[119]

Before departing for Panama, Taft's main job was to promote Roosevelt on the campaign trail. His role in the campaign was symbolically important. He was a major Republican figure in his own right and was frequently cited as an example of the "safe" and wise advisers guiding Roosevelt. As Senator Orville Platt (R-CT) said, the charge that Roosevelt was "unsafe" was preposterous: "Who stand as his supporters and admirers? Let me name three of them who all men honor, all men trust—Elihu Root, John Hay, and William H. Taft."[120] On October 1, Taft opened the Ohio Republican campaign and campaigned without stop for the next month. He traveled the campaign circuit across Ohio and into Indiana, Illinois, West Virginia, New York, New Jersey, Connecticut, and Maryland. Taft's charge was to defend the administration policies, but his favorite subject to which he turned in every speech was the Philippines and how it represented the administration's high aspirations.[121]

After his inauguration in March 1905 Roosevelt went west to hunt, announcing that all would be well in his absence because he "left Taft sitting on the lid." The most sensitive matter for Taft in Roosevelt's absence was applying Roosevelt's broad understanding of the Monroe Doctrine to the Dominican Republic (then called Santo Domingo). Because Santo Domingo could not service its debts to several European countries, there was a threat of intervention into that Caribbean nation by its creditor states. With dubious legal authority Roosevelt placed an

American officer as the country's collector of customs to organize repayment of creditors. Taft implemented that arrangement, avoiding the question of legality by telling the American officer to consider himself an agent of Santo Domingo, but for good measure, to report regularly to the war department.[122]

After Roosevelt's return, Taft took a congressional delegation to the Philippines, building support for eliminating tariffs on Filipino products. Roosevelt ordered him to also stop in Japan.[123] Russia and Japan had agreed on American mediation of their ongoing war, and his assignment was to sound out the Japanese about their conditions for peace. After meeting the Japanese foreign minister, Count Katsura, in late July 1905, he described the meeting in a cable to Roosevelt. Katsura assured Taft that Japan supported American occupation of the Philippines. In turn, Taft assured him that the United States supported continued Japanese occupation of Korea. The two men also discussed the desirability of American, British, and Japanese cooperation in the Eastern Pacific. Taft said that without a treaty it was impossible for the president to join in a formal agreement to that end. However, Taft said, "he felt sure that without any agreement at all . . . the United States . . . could be counted on . . . as if the United States were under treaty obligations."[124] These are the terms of loose construction proposed by the man later described as a narrow legalist. The entourage then continued on to Manila. The whole trip drew great public interest because the party included Roosevelt's lively daughter, Alice, and during the trip she began her romance with Ohio Representative Nicholas Longworth, leading to their marriage.[125]

Taft returned in early fall to his Panama Canal work. He pushed Congress for appropriations to begin canal construction. After the bill passed, Taft claimed credit for it, telling his brother Charles, "If I had not gone to Panama, and had not made the long speech I did explaining the situation . . . the difficulty of getting the matter through . . . would have been greater."[126] The congressional junket of summer 1905 and Taft's success with the Panama bill offer evidence for his ability to deal with Congress.

In late 1905 Taft resolved to "take a little more part in the administration of the War Department than heretofore." Now, he thought, it would be a good idea "to change the regulations so that more of the details shall come before me" and relieve his assistants of the job of running the department. He wrote that he "had so much outside work . . . but now I think I am about ready to take up matters in that Department."[127] But that did not happen. During early 1906 Taft could only intermittently attend to the department. His main concerns were now with a bill lowering tariffs on products from the Philippines and appearances before congressional hearings on matters relating to the Philippines and Panama. He managed to gain passage for the tariff bill in the House but lost in the more protectionist Senate, even after intensive lobbying by Taft and his brothers.[128]

In March 1906 Taft was given another opportunity to join the Court. Justice Henry Brown was to retire, and the press speculated the president would name Taft to his place.[129] But that was not yet a settled decision for Taft and his family. Charles wrote to him after publication of the impending appointment, "You seem to have many knotty points to settle . . . I am . . . in favor of your taking it . . . but I should want it understood that this is no bar to your being promoted to the Chief Justiceship." Charles added that he thought Court appointment would not preclude "the possibility of being a presidential candidate."[130] Horace Taft responded to the news reports, telling William that they "discouraged" him because he feared the Court would destroy his presidential prospects.[131]

Nellie opposed her husband entering the Court, and she spoke with Roosevelt to insist she wanted William to remain on track to the presidency. Taft called together a family conference, which drew sufficient public attention to be reported in the *New York Times*.[132] After consulting the family, he again chose to forgo the Court. He expressed his decision indecisively. He hoped that the president could put off the decision over appointment till the end of 1906, explaining that his important executive work kept him from his true love, appointment to the Court.[133] There is a view of Taft as always disappointed in his yearning for the Court. However, the fact is that each time he had an offer to join the Court he chose to continue on an executive path. In fact, with family encouragement, he was increasingly thinking of the presidency as his foremost goal. And Roosevelt encouraged that ambition. He told him that in the difficult political circumstances he foresaw, wherein selfish wealth clashed with angry radicalism, Taft "would be the best possible leader. . . . In such a contest you could do very much if you were on the bench; you could do very much if you were in active political life . . . I think you could do most as President."[134]

In fall 1906 the president sent Taft to Havana to arbitrate conflict threatening civil war between the country's two major parties. Cuba gained independence after the Spanish-American War, but the Platt amendment gave the United States authority to intervene in its domestic affairs. Taft arrived in Havana in mid-September, and over the course of several difficult weeks managed to bring the two parties to end hostilities.[135] The rebels pledged to put down their weapons and pursue peaceful politics. In turn the party in power agreed to new elections. Privately Taft was not optimistic about the agreement and thought that instability would return. He wrote to Nellie that Cuba was "no more fitted for self-government than the Philippines."[136]

Despite Taft's own skepticism about the island's future stability, his success in Cuba was acclaimed upon his return to the states. *Collier's Weekly* called him the "secretary of peace."[137] Putting his fame to work for the Republican party, Taft began a speaking tour for the 1906 congressional campaign, simultaneously weighing the prospects for his own 1908 presidential campaign. He rallied Republicans across the Midwest and West and found that if Roosevelt was not to be a candidate for a third term, there were many people for whom Taft would be the clear choice.[138] Thus, his presidential race began during the 1906 campaign. He designed speaking trips with an eye to building delegate support for the 1908 convention, and he initiated his campaign organization, looking to Charles Taft for money and leadership.[139]

Taft remained disengaged from the war department even as the Brownsville incident roiled the army and divided public opinion. In August 1906 African American soldiers in Brownsville, Texas were said to have fired shots in the town killing one white citizen and injuring several others. Although he had no reliable information about who had actually fired the shots and why, President Roosevelt dishonorably discharged 160 African American soldiers, six of whom held the Medal of Honor. Roosevelt acted without consulting Secretary Taft, and the latter only learned fully the case's details when he returned from the campaign trail. He feared Roosevelt's action might harm his own wooing of Southern African American convention delegates. He also thought that the case deserved more careful consideration than Roosevelt had given it.[140] Taft suggested to Roosevelt a rehearing of the case, but his advice was ignored. Taft reasoned that the president ignored him "because I had not been cognizant of the facts on which the order was issued I do not think he paid as much attention to my suggestion as he otherwise would."[141]

During 1907 Taft campaigned for the nomination with a pause for a round-the-world mission. As a presidential candidate he gave even less attention to the department of war than he had earlier. As Nellie described him, he was working with "the men who were conducting his 'boom.'"[142] Early in the year he fought Senator Foraker for control of Ohio's delegates. After winning them he began an extensive speaking tour, beginning in St. Louis and continuing on to Wisconsin, Kansas, Iowa, Minnesota, the Dakotas, and back to Washington by the end of

June.[143] After a month's respite at his Murray Bay, Quebec vacation home, Taft set out for Japan and the Philippines, returning across Russia to meet with the German emperor.[144] Embarking from Seattle, he whistle-stopped his way west. Nellie joined him at Yellowstone National Park and said of the remainder of the whistle stop tour: "I got completely worn out as a mere onlooker, and as I saw Mr. Taft encountering the throngs at every stopping place, speaking until his voice was a hoarse whisper . . . my political enthusiasm waned slightly, though temporarily."[145]

We think of protracted campaigns as a modern development. Martin Van Buren argued that one of the merits of nominating conventions was that they would limit the "intrusion of electoral politics into the normal processes of governing."[146] However, Taft was campaigning for the nomination sixteen months prior to the convention. Why was he so early into the campaign? That was not the behavior one would expect from a hesitant candidate, as Pringle and others have described Taft. He was in fact energized by the campaign. It became his next job, and he invested it with the same dedication he had invested in every other role. As Taft began the speaking tour toward Seattle, Roosevelt advised him to pay his domestic travel himself. Roosevelt suggested, "In this particular situation you and Charley had far better pay any expenses within the United States for any trip which [critics] can even assert to be political, rather than have them paid out of Government appropriations."[147] He was now more of a presidential candidate than he was secretary of war.

Taft was the leading candidate, but he ran as if he were a dark horse. In June 1907 the *Washington Post* wrote that of the possibilities for nomination—Taft, Philander Knox, and Charles E. Hughes—Taft was the favorite. "Were the politicians . . . to express their views . . . they would unquestionably declare that Secretary Taft was a 2 to 1 shot."[148] Roosevelt assured Taft that he was most likely to obtain the nomination.

However, Roosevelt's assurance was sufficiently qualified to unsettle the insecure Taft. Roosevelt told him that "men of prominence" were promoting Roosevelt for a third term. He also mentioned that leading reactionaries were likely to oppose Taft as an extension of Roosevelt. Taft was also under attack from "standpatters" convinced that he was not reliable on "protection."[149] Roosevelt had also informed Taft that commerce secretary George Cortelyou would seek the nomination. Roosevelt sketched an unpredictable political landscape, and most frightening, and the threat Nellie most feared, Roosevelt might steal the nomination for himself.[150] In the face of these anxieties, all Taft could do was campaign more energetically.

Chapter Four

What Did Taft Learn? A Subordinate's Skills

Three themes run through Taft's pre-presidential roles. First, opportunities fell on him. Second, he demonstrated perseverance, energy, and ability in every role. Third, he exhibited no clear ideological stance across these roles. Through inquiry into each of these characteristics we will understand the political skills and inclinations that he brought to the presidency, for good and ill.

1. "There Is a Reward for the Righteous"[151]

Taft's public positions were rewards for his connections and his loyalty. As time passed, these plums also revealed his abilities. Thus, good things came to him just as rewards come to the righteous, though the reward was for his Republicanism rather than his righteousness. In Taft's world one was the equivalent of the other.

Beyond his extraordinarily good fortune in his rewards, there was nothing unusual about Taft's career path. He was a product of orthodox Republican loyalties and a recipient of family influence and party favors. He explained to William Allen White that good things had come his way because "I always had my plate the right side up when offices were falling." He elaborated further that "right side up" meant he had a prominent family and was himself "hail-fellow-well-met with all of the political" men.[152] Observing American political parties at the end of the nineteenth century, Moise Ostrogorski wrote that office seekers know "there is no salvation save" in the party leader who is the master of patronage.[153] As we follow him into the presidency, what makes Taft's characteristic patronage career notable is that he brought into the Progressive Era context norms and habits formed in the party period.

2. Perseverance, Mission and Authority

There would be no second best for William. In each public office prior to the presidency, he was driven to succeed and driven also to please his superiors. During Alphonso Taft's life, William struggled to please him. After his father's death, Taft's superiors and brothers became the looming figures he sought to please. Notice how Roosevelt's offer of the Supreme Court seat in 1902 unsettled him, throwing him into a paroxysm of self-doubt about the president's intentions.

Allied with Taft's need for approval was his ability to clearly identify what each position demanded of him. Clarity of mission was a prerequisite for pleasing his superiors. Until the Philippines, his roles engaged and applied his legal training, and he worked within his comfort zone. But that changed with the Philippines assignment. We might imagine Taft ensconced at the Malacanan Palace wielding imperial discretion. In reality he was to implement the instructions Secretary Root had drafted. Taft brought great energy to the job and unusual sympathy for Filipinos, but the job he performed had specified goals.

Taft's hypersensitivity about approval by superiors made him an ideal factotum for Roosevelt. Whether it was diplomatic concerns with Japan, instability in Cuba, oversight of canal construction in Panama, or just "sitting on the lid" of government, Taft accomplished what Roosevelt set out for him. Each task was a specific goal, and for each he expected the president's clear approval. Any sign of Roosevelt's disapproval pained him. For example, during the 1904 campaign Taft mentioned in his speeches the need for ending tariffs on Philippine products. Roosevelt then asked him to not wave a tariff reform flag during the campaign because it unsettled the "stand patters." Taft responded bizarrely, offering to resign: "If my presence in the Cabinet embarrassed him I would retire at once."[154]

3. Pragmatic Conservative

Taft's views were conventionally Republican, and he adapted them to his official roles. He was less liberal on the federal circuit court and more liberal in Manila. Pringle sees President Taft constrained by legalistic conservatism, believing: "We have a government of limited power under the Constitution and we have got to work out our problems on the basis."[155] Alpheus Thomas Mason describes Taft as "a thoroughgoing Social Darwinist, an outspoken critic of governmental regulation."[156] The historian Donald F. Anderson offers a more nuanced view of Taft's conservatism but also defines him as "preeminently a man of the law and the Constitution."[157] This conventional view of Taft is framed by his debate with Roosevelt over presidential powers, represented by Roosevelt's *Autobiography* and Taft's *Our Chief Magistrate and His Powers*. Both were written after 1912, and both justify their authors' conduct of office. Roosevelt famously forwarded his "stewardship" view of the office, claiming that anything not barred by the Constitution was within the president's power. He contrasted his view with what he called a Buchanan/Taft view. Taft responded that Roosevelt was an ignoramus about the law; presidents could exercise no power that was not located in "some specific grant of power or justly be implied." [158] These books continue in print the political struggle of 1912. The reality is that Taft's view of the presidency was not so simple or static; it evolved "through three basic stages—pre-presidential, presidential . . . and post-presidential."[159]

It was not just his views of the presidency that had evolved. His ideas about government's role changed as he moved through his pre-presidential roles. Upon the bedrock idea of safeguarding private property, Taft's notion of what would constitute policies appropriate to that end were contingent upon the office he occupied and the problems he faced.

The place to begin in understanding Taft's conservatism is to see how conventional it was. For example, his lurid language about strikers while a circuit judge—"it will be necessary for the military to kill some"—was merely a sentiment that was widespread among those of his class, including Theodore Roosevelt, at the time of the Pullman Strike and the Haymarket Riot. What in fact characterized both Taft and Roosevelt was a propensity for pragmatic balancing of conservative political instincts with efforts to solve real problems to satisfy conflicting interests. For example, in his *Autobiography*, Roosevelt balanced individual and property rights. He wrote: "The right to use one's property as one will can be maintained only so long is it is consistent with the maintenance of certain fundamental human rights."[160] How different is this view from Taft's willingness, as we have seen above in the *Narramore* case, on the federal circuit, to balance the property rights of the railroad with the right to safety of the worker?

In the Philippines Taft exhibited political nuance that also belies the portrait of a legalistic conservative. He was, so to speak, a good political anthropologist, comprehending the characteristics of the diverse Filipino cultures, the importance of a relatively expansive governmental role there, and the necessity for representation of Filipinos in new mechanisms of government.

A plethora of evidence from Taft's four years as war secretary suggests both the evolution and plasticity of his views. Sitting in Roosevelt's cabinet he agreed with Roosevelt's moderate reformist agenda and supported his use of executive power. His harmony with Roosevelt undermines the portrait of him as a rigid conservative. Consequently, Henry Pringle offered an almost comical explanation, saying that his agreement with Roosevelt was a personality aberration that undermined Taft's consistency of thought. "One searches in vain for a major issue on which Taft took a stand, even in private, against Roosevelt." And the explanation for that was that he "no longer viewed the President objectively."[161] Sometimes ideas and actions are just what they appear to be. Taft's public agreement with Roosevelt was affirmed in his private correspondence, and his letters from his brothers display agreement with Roosevelt's policies.[162] In needing to psycho-analyze Taft's agreement with Roosevelt, his biographers miss two important elements of his views. First, they miss his pragmatism, his willingness to adapt ideas to the requirements necessary for solving problems. Second, we must take into account the perspective through which he identified policy problems.

Roosevelt, and Taft as well, divided society not into two camps, conservatives and radicals, but into three camps. That third camp represented those at the irrational extreme, reactionaries who opposed any changes that would ameliorate social and economic conditions and radicals who would turn to socialism and anarchism. We see this model in Roosevelt's expression to Taft of his anxiety about growing social conflict:

> The dull, purblind folly of the very rich . . . their greed and arrogance
> . . . and the way in which they have unduly prospered . . . often
> through the weakness or shortsightedness of the judges . . . these facts,
> and the corruption in business and politics have tended to produce . . .
> excitement and irritation in the popular mind, which shows itself . . .
> in the enormous increase in the socialistic propaganda.[163]

Taft's agreement with those thoughts is evident in the following from his 1906 address at Yale University, warning students that the laissez faire principles they learned in class would need to be qualified as they confronted public problems after college:

> I think these principles . . . are still orthodox and still sound, if only
> the application of them is not carried to such an extreme as really to
> interfere with the public welfare. Experience will show that there are
> fields of business action which the Government can better cover than
> private enterprise; and there are also fields over which, because of
> probability of abuse by private enterprise, the Government should
> assume control, not by way of initiation and administration but by
> way of effective regulation.[164]

Conclusion: Experience and the Limits of Taft's Political Education

As Taft returned in late 1907 from his round-the-world trip, the *New York World* editorialized that "in addition to his own eminent qualifications, [Taft] rightfully inherits whatever political strengths Mr. Roosevelt's politics . . . command in the public mind."[165] Strikingly, his boom seemed to strengthen while he was abroad. This latest assignment from the president kept Taft's qualifications in the public mind more than what he might have achieved by campaigning at home.

The trip highlighted his qualifications for the presidency. He had extensive executive experience in the Philippines and the war department. His diplomatic travels prepared him for the presidency in a time when the United States emerged as a world power. As a judge he engaged issues of an expanding industrial capitalism. Thus, if experience predicts performance, William H. Taft was prepared for presidential success. But is it possible Taft's political education did not prepare him for the presidency? As Richard Neustadt observed about the presidents of the later twentieth century, experience was necessary but not sufficient for success in the presidency: "By no means is it a place for every politician."[166]

The first great limitation of Taft's experience was the absence of politics. If politics is defined as the struggle among individuals occupying separated roles but sharing powers, then Taft rarely experienced political life and its rules. It is notable that until the 1908 presidential election he had only been an electoral candidate once, in 1888, to retain his state court seat. But that was not his most serious political deficit. Rather, it was that Taft never experienced the institutional politics of the legislative or executive roles he would have reached as an elected official.

Taft's judicial experiences attuned him to reinforcing separation of powers but did not expose him to the political implications of separated institutions sharing powers. But what of his Philippine experience, in which his commission served as lawmaking body, and he subsequently became civil governor? What he learned in Manila were lessons that did not carry over to the presidency. He was a lawgiver without resistance. On the executive side, he was the instrument of Secretary Root. The policies of Taft's colonial government were givens from above. They required of Taft no priority-setting or discernment among opposing possibilities. Taft's inexperience in dealing with the turmoil of American politics was made acute by the fact that from 1900 until his own election campaign he was insulated from the intensely domestic issues of Progressive Era politics. While he was governing the Philippines, overseeing the Panama Canal, and conducting diplomacy with the Japanese and the Vatican, Americans were angered over trusts, horrified by the adulteration of meat, and demanding relief from high prices. Unfortunately for Taft, his first intense exposure to having to deal with those issues came after his inauguration as president.

Did he not get an education in executive-legislative politics through four years in the cabinet? That might have been the case had he actually administered the war department. Had he Root's experience at the department, reforming organization and gaining new legislation, Taft would have acquired skills relevant to the presidency. But his four years as war secretary were spent as President Roosevelt's emissary and troubleshooter. His correspondence of the period contains few references to his department. He worked on the president's priorities and at the president's direction. The tasks to which he was set required negotiating skill and diplomatic subtlety. However, the cabinet years left him without any independent experience in choosing priorities from competing possibilities and setting his own course of action.

Finally, the essential character of Taft's pre-presidential career was at odds with the challenge he would face as president. In a sense his career had been passive. Patronage lifted him from place to place. Contrast his pre-presidential passivity with Roosevelt's entrepreneurialism. Roosevelt held nontraditional offices in civil service and at the New York City police commission. Then he fought for appointment to the navy department and used his Cuba adventure to win the governorship. By contrast, Taft's career floated on party regularity. With some hyperbole Pringle writes, "Fates were, as always, pushing Taft higher and higher. Perhaps he was the only man in American political history who can . . . be described as a creature of destiny."[167]

Taft was one of many political men pulled along a path of patronage appointments. What distinguished him from those others was that his talents conspired with partisanship to push him into increasingly prestigious jobs through which he proved his fitness for the presidency. Thus William achieved the "brilliant political career" that Alphonso Taft envisioned for him.

"UNCLE SAM—BILL, YOU'D LOOK SO MUCH BETTER IN YOUR OWN CLOTHES." Taft is caricatured as fitting badly into Roosevelt's progressive political agenda. (*Harper's Weekly*, June 13, 1908, p. 3; provided courtesy of HarpWeek, LLC)

Improvising for Continuity:
The Tariff and the Blow-Up at Interior

The qualities shown by a thoroughly able and trustworthy lieutenant are totally different . . . from those needed by the leader.
  Theodore Roosevelt[1]

WILLIAM H. TAFT'S 1908 VICTORY was a triumph for Roosevelt's policies as well as the Republican party. As in 1896 and 1900, the Democrat William Jennings Bryan ran against a personable Ohio Republican, but much was different about the 1908 election. The earlier Bryan was a populist fire-breather who offered the panacea of silver-backed currency, attacked trusts, and denounced the protective tariff.[2] In contrast to Bryan, McKinley stood foursquare upon Republican orthodoxy, promising prosperity through protection.

In 1908 Taft's promise of continuity with Roosevelt's reforms constrained Bryan, who quipped, "I find it difficult . . . for if I make a straight-out democratic speech, . . . the president [Roosevelt] makes one of the same kind."[3] On most issues, Bryan and Taft seemed to be on the same page. The *Chicago Daily Tribune* reported, "It is a remarkable thing that on no single [issue] . . . are the parties diametrically opposed to each other."[4]

The Campaign

Taft's campaign was a family affair. Brother Charles Taft headed his campaign organization, brother Henry Taft raised money from his circle of corporate executives, and his wife Nellie coached Taft's rhetorical efforts. Roosevelt also eagerly advised his heir. After the election Taft complained he had "been the subject of a coterie of bosses the demands of which left me no duty but to respond from 6 o'clock in the morning till midnight to the calls of the populace."[5]

Chapter Five

At first intending a McKinley-like front porch campaign, Taft switched to match Bryan's barnstorming.[6] While campaigning across America, he promised lower tariff rates to consumers who linked tariffs and price inflation.[7] Thanks to Charles Taft's organizational skill, the campaign organization exceeded the staff Taft would find in the White House. He traveled with a personal assistant, a public relations specialist, a physician, and a stenographer, plus agents of the Republican national committee.[8] In contrast, Bryan traveled with a few supporters. Taft's advantage reflected his access to unlimited money from the coffers of both his brother and the party. The Republican war chest nearly tripled what Bryan had raised, $1.65 million compared to the Democrat's $620,000.[9]

Taft disparaged campaigning but was a dedicated campaigner. He approached campaigning as he had his earlier offices, with a large capacity for work and great energy. In this case he was eager to please his brother Charles, Roosevelt, and Nellie. He could not match Bryan's rhetorical power, but he projected a comforting amiability and thoroughly enjoyed the friendly crowds. Roosevelt praised the campaign in unqualified terms: "Taft has made a great canvass and his work on the stump has told tremendously in our favor."[10] Taft's victory did not match Roosevelt's 1904 landslide over Judge Alton Parker, but his majority was greater than McKinley's in 1896.[11] Republicans also won 56 percent of the House, equal to the 1900 majority but lower than 1904. In the Senate the Republicans won 66 percent of the seats, a larger share than in the preceding three presidential elections.

An "Ill-Structured" Role

Taft saw immediately that the presidency was different than any role he had occupied previously and expressed uncertainty about its demands. He said:

> I know the difficulties that will arise in my new career, and I know that
> questions will arise that I do not know of now, and that times will
> come when my friends here will shake their heads and say, "poor Bill,"
> but all I ask is suspension of judgment until the situation has been
> understood.[12]

The president's responsibilities are ill defined in that no set script awaits a new president. Presidents wield "the executive power" and see "the laws are faithfully executed." But to what end? Every incumbent faces the question, how will I use my presidency? And over time the answer is contingent upon context and the incumbent's leadership skills. In the party period, platforms and parties' organizational needs guided and constrained presidents. But Taft's context contained confusing signals. Roosevelt had veered from the post-bellum party era's model of Republican leadership and fashioned a personal presidency. How would Taft respond to the confused signals and rising progressive expectations for the post-Roosevelt presidency?

Taft brought three strong commitments to the presidency. The first was a commitment to the law, the second was a commitment to party, and the third was loyalty to Roosevelt. He wanted to believe these commitments were harmonious with each other, but in office he would be forced to make choices among them as he confronted the presidency's challenges. In the campaign he spoke as if the law was an adequate decision-making guide for presidents. Once in office he saw that he would have to do more than follow the law. He admitted, "If I were now presiding in the Supreme Court . . . as chief justice, I should feel entirely at home, but with the troubles of selecting a Cabinet and the difficulties in respect to the revision of the tariff, I feel just a bit like a fish out of water."[13] Taft had discovered: "The White House is a bigger proposition than one imagines."[14]

That remark displays Taft's difficulty in conceptualizing the unstructured character of the Progressive Era presidency. If implementation of law could define the president's responsibility, then the office could be understood through his commitment to law. But Taft had to impose his priorities on the role in a context of clashing values, conflicting interests, and insufficient information. In that decision context there is no objectively rational calculus to produce an optimal outcome. The best the decision maker can do is use experience, available information, and judgment, a "subjectively rational" course of action.[15]

Taft's second commitment was to his party. His partisanship had formed in a time when partisan identity merged with constants of ethno-cultural identity. Despite the emergence in the 1880s of liberal critics of party machines (among them, brother Horace Taft), Taft's partisan commitments had not changed, abiding by the principle that "unswerving allegiance to a party was the first commandment of politics."[16] He aspired to use his party commitment to give order to his presidency. It would guide his selection of appointees, although the uncertainties therein plagued him. He also took the party platform as setting his agenda as president. Taft explained that partisanship is essential to democratic governance. "The existence of parties, their maintenance, and their discipline are essential to the carrying on of any popular government."[17] And partisan unity was an imperative for him: "A useful party cannot be formed unless those who are members . . .

yield their views on the less important . . . principles, and unite with respect to the main policies for which the party is to become responsible."[18] However, despite his apparent embrace of the party period presidency, Taft's third commitment would clash with his assumptions about political partisanship.

Just as he was committed to the law and his party, Taft was equally committed to Roosevelt's agenda. He promised continuity with his predecessor and mentor. He proclaimed that he shared Roosevelt's ideas of government.[19] Proclaiming his perfect loyalty, Taft said of Roosevelt that he acted exactly as Lincoln would, were the latter president in the same circumstances.[20] Roosevelt, in turn, saw Taft as a political clone. He wrote: "Taft was nominated solely on my assurance . . . that he would carry out my work unbroken."[21]

Taft was consistently supportive as Roosevelt's subordinate. He agreed with Roosevelt's initiatives, even those crossing boundaries of clear legality, as in the Santo Domingo customs intervention. In the Cuban crisis Taft willingly wielded American influence with only loose treaty language for legal cover. Taft agreed when Roosevelt explained presidents can decide how an appropriation will be spent unless Congress directs that a specific course be followed."[22] But, Taft was not simply a deluded pushover. Along with Root, he was the cabinet member with the most influence over the president.[23] As a presidential candidate Taft separated from Roosevelt on only one substantive issue, the tariff. And that difference was a matter of tactics not substance.[24] Roosevelt feared that tariff reform would divide the party, whereas Taft thought lower rates had sufficiently clear benefits to win over most Republican legislators.

Transitioning to Govern

No longer subordinate, Taft had to name his own subordinates and set his own priorities. Between the election and inauguration he had four months to accomplish all this. But fatigued from the long campaign, his first goal was to rest and golf at leisure. He announced he would transact as little business as possible while at Warm Springs. That Taft felt little need to worry about preparing for his presidency is implied by Nellie's remark to a reporter: "We can make no especial arrangements for taking up our new duties, For if we are not prepared for them now it would be hopeless to try to prepare ourselves."[25] Later the Tafts moved to Augusta, Georgia, for more rest and golf. The president-elect announced that golf, which he played daily, would be a presidential priority. "I am going to do my part to make golf one of the most popular outdoor exercises."[26]

The *Los Angeles Times* headlined a story about Taft's activities: "In Training for His Work in White House, Spends His Days Riding and On Links."[27] His new dedication to leisure was a topic at a Taft family gathering, with Nellie present but the president-elect absent. Horace later wrote to his brother, "The discussion began innocently enough, but before we got through we had Nellie defending you against the charge of laziness."[28] Taft's lethargy was in fact atypical of him. He had launched himself energetically into prior jobs with a combination of eagerness and anxiety. But now he appeared to go to ground, as if the path ahead was not yet clear.

In December the demands of the upcoming congressional session intruded on Taft's leisure, and he was forced to consider cabinet appointments and plan his first legislative initiative, tariff reform. He discussed names for the cabinet and sought support among legislators for tariff reform. He drew out the process of deciding upon names for the cabinet, and rumors about likely appointees were rife.[29] In a burst of enthusiasm after his nomination Taft had promised Roosevelt to keep his cabinet intact.[30] Roosevelt also had requested that Taft retain a number of Roosevelt's men below cabinet rank. Later, when Taft ignored the promise to retain his cabinet, Roosevelt had to implore him to inform those who would not be kept.[31] Taft's delay seriously bruised feelings within Roosevelt's circle; Interior Secretary James Garfield, for example, learned only in late January that he would not be kept on by Taft. And Taft gave him that news not in a face-to-face communication but in a brief note.[32]

Names for the cabinet that were made public just before March 4 disappointed progressive Republicans and Roosevelt's friends in particular. The former expected inclusion of more of their own kind, and the latter were disgruntled at how few of Roosevelt's cabinet were retained. The nine people Taft chose included three holdovers, George von L. Meyer at navy (moved from the post office), James Wilson at agriculture, and Philander Knox, appointed at state (originally Roosevelt's attorney general and then a senator). Ironically, the only appointee with strong progressive credentials was Secretary of Interior Richard Ballinger. Seven of the nine were lawyers.[33]

Many scholars see evidence of Taft's conservatism in his cabinet choices. Donald Anderson writes, "While the electorate was becoming more progressive . . . Taft was shifting the balance of power within his cabinet to the right of center and setting the stage for his own political demise."[34] But Taft was not thinking of his cabinet choices in ideological terms. He was, rather, thinking of the cabinet functionally, picking those with whom he was comfortable, and he was most comfortable working with lawyers. He also chose those who could support his major initiatives. Philander Knox and George Wickersham, both corporate lawyers by background, favored anti-trust and railroad rate regulation.[35] Experienced lawyers would reinforce Taft's commitment of vigorously enforcing the laws regarding business behavior. A letter from Taft to Philander Knox gives us a glimpse of his thinking:

> What we shall have to do is reorganize the Dept. of Justice, the Dept. of Commerce and the Interstate Commerce Commission with a view to . . . cooperation in the enforcement of . . . antitrust law and I need a cabinet of as many experienced lawyers as I can get to draft the statutes for congressional consideration in December 1909 . . . and . . . see if we can [win] the support of the leaders of the two houses. But lawyers of experience we need in the cabinet.[36]

Taft's Inaugural: Goals and Warrants

Taft's inaugural address was second in length to Benjamin Harrison's.[37] Yet it impresses more by its specificity of progressive policy commitments than by its length.[38] Taft explained that his address would "give a summary outline of the main policies of the new administration." And, "I should be untrue to myself, to my promises, and to the declarations of the party platform upon which I was elected . . . if I did not make the maintenance and enforcement of those reforms a most important feature of my administration." During the campaign Taft promised to present an agenda "to Congress the means by which the Roosevelt policies shall be clinched."[39] Of course, his Congress would be little different than the Congress with which Roosevelt conflicted in 1907 and 1908. Thus Taft's agenda was also likely to conflict with the Republican leadership's preferences. Yet his inaugural address insisted on major legislative reforms; anti-trust policy required new laws and the tariff had to be reduced immediately because uncertainty about tariffs harmed the economy.

Taft's call for tariff reform broke with long-standing Republican orthodoxy. He argued fair rates should adjust the difference between cost of production of imports and the production cost of the equivalent American-made goods. The tariff should not shelter inflated prices. Complicating matters, the tariff was the major source of government's revenues. Should rate reduction cause a revenue decline, Taft recommended establishing new taxation. He promised government economies in that event but said "the scope of modern government . . . has been widened . . . and this widening has met popular approval." These activities must be paid for, including business regulation, conservation of resources and reclamation of arid lands, building great public works like the Panama Canal, and expansion of the navy. In short, he promised that the Roosevelt agenda would be continued and paid for.

Taft called also for monetary policy reform to create more flexible currency. He argued for a postal saving system to secure small savers, important in light of the banking panic of 1907.[40] He closed with issues important to labor, increasing government's responsibility for injuries of its workers and regulating the use of injunctions. Taft's agenda was straightforwardly progressive. He promised continuation of Roosevelt's politics, but on the tariff he ventured onto policy terrain that had been too dangerous for Roosevelt.

Taft had political and substantive motives for seeking tariff reform. The first was defensive, to defuse a charge that the protective tariff fostered monopoly conditions, the "mother of trusts." The second was a commitment that over time rates should decline as American industries gained economic strength. In the campaign he explained that the protective tariff reduced production costs and increased capital investments and labor productivity. Because of those salutary benefits, he said, "the necessity for maintaining the tariff at the former rate has ceased."[41]

Taft claimed robust authority for his leadership by invoking Roosevelt, the Republican platform, and his electoral mandate.[42] He was an affiliate of a resilient regime, to borrow Stephen Skowronek's terminology, and he was successor to an innovatively popular president. Taft had decisively beaten Bryan and carried in a Republican Congress. And, not least, he was an eminently respected figure. No mere politician, he was a man to be trusted, learned, judicious, and proven competent in challenging assignments.

Taft's Leadership Project: Fifteen Months Later

Fifteen months after the inauguration, Taft wrote to Roosevelt as the latter returned from a year abroad:

> It is now near a year and three months since I assumed office and I have had a hard time. I do not know that I have had harder luck than other presidents but I do know that thus far I have succeeded far less than have others. I have been conscientiously trying to carry out your policies but my method of doing so has not worked smoothly.[43]

He itemized his troubles. The tariff act was not as "radical a change" as he favored but had been unfairly attacked. The corporation tax he had achieved was criticized by business. Congress blocked his expansion of Interstate Commerce Commission (ICC) powers. On the touchiest subject, his firing of Roosevelt's friend, Gifford Pinchot, as head of the forest service, Taft said only that Roosevelt would have to judge the circumstances of the removal. Taft saw several causes for his troubles. Republican insurgents had worked to "defeat us." Democrats in Congress opposed Taft's reform. Newspapers attacked him because the tariff act had not abolished rates on newsprint. And, sadly, his wife's illness was a heavy burden for him.[44]

There were three more fundamental reasons for Taft's sinking presidency. The first will be briefly mentioned while the second and third will occupy the remainder of this chapter. First, Taft's warrant claims were less robust than they first appeared. Second, he had failed on two iconic issues for Progressives, even though he was also accumulating a record of accomplishments. Finally, we have to assess Taft's political skills and his consequent ability to find and use strategic resources to move the most important measures on his agenda.

Taft's authority was fragile. He was the chosen successor of an enormously popular president, but he lacked his predecessor's flair for political spectacle and self-aggrandizement. He was elected with a hefty electoral majority but against an opponent weakened by two unsuccessful runs for the office and with less organization and money; also, no major issue had separated Bryan from Taft. A significant part of his electoral majority would be quickly disappointed because Taft was not Roosevelt. A substantial minority would be disappointed because he tried to be Roosevelt. Indeed, instead of holding a potent claim of authority, Taft entered a presidency that would challenge him to patch together support from warring factions.[45]

Removed from the passions of Progressive Era political struggles, and not sandwiched between Roosevelt and Wilson, Taft's presidency would be seen as successful. Compared to the norms of the party period presidency, Taft's initiatives were notably aggressive. He passed more reform legislation in his four years than Roosevelt had in his seven years.[46] He gained a tariff board of experts to guide rate-setting as part of his new tariff legislation. Against conservative opposition, he successfully promoted postal savings. With the Mann-Elkins act he finally expanded ICC supervision of railroads. He oversaw creation of the children's bureau and railroad and mine safety legislation. At one point, Senator Henry Cabot Lodge urged Taft to hold off on introducing more legislation so as to calm business sentiment.[47] But Taft was subject to Progressive Era expectations, and he was wedged between two remarkable presidents. The tariff failure and the conservation controversy during his first year in office poisoned his relationship to Progressives.

Among other successes Taft was also the first president to engage in administrative reorganization and executive budget reform. Throughout his four years in office he conducted a vigorous anti-trust program, bringing more suits than had Roosevelt.[48] Not least, he initiated the income tax amendment to the Constitution.[49] The government under Taft also thrived fiscally. Revenue jumped in 1910 as a consequence of more tariff receipts and the beginning of a flow of returns from a corporate tax, and he saw a 3 percent decline in the federal debt.[50]

To understand Taft's presidency, both why he failed politically in the short run and why his historical reputation has suffered in the long run, we shall focus on how he addressed his most sensitive issues at the outset of his presidency. For that purpose, we turn to tariff reform and the Pinchot-Ballinger controversy.

Leading on Tariff Reform

The protective tariff was a wall Republicans built to shelter nascent American industry from foreign competition.[51] It was the true cross of Republican faith and an anathema to Democrats. It was also "one of the most consistent and enduring partisan, issue–divisions in American history."[52] Dissatisfaction with the rate schedules of the very high Dingley Act of 1897, passed in McKinley's first year in office, was widespread. It was blamed for rising consumer prices and limited foreign markets.

Beyond radicals and agrarians, a wide range of business interests sought reform. For example, a conference on tariff reform meeting in February 1908 was described as drawing "men who are developing the natural resources of the country . . . [and] are also . . . exporters . . . [and] seek the removal of unnecessary obstacles to such commerce."[53] Industries dependent on raw materials favored tariff reduction. Roosevelt had realized there was a constituency for tariff reform. After his reelection in 1904 he had raised the issue with Republican leaders only to be rebuffed. He afterward wrote: "I feel sure that Congress ought to revise the tariff, not so much from any economical need as to meet the mental attitude of the people; but it is not an issue upon which I should have any business to break with my party or with Congress."[54]

Pressure for reform grew as the cost of living rose. During the 1890s lower tariff rates (passed by Democrats) accompanied low inflation. After the Dingley tariff of 1897, prices increased markedly. The cost of living increased 28 percent from 1900 to 1912. In the same period food prices shot up 42 percent.[55] Taft read the issue as one he could not avoid. It is also worth noting that Horace, Taft's Mugwump brother, was critical of protection and argued his views to the president-elect. Horace advised that if Taft would enact real tariff reform "you will have to represent the consumers yourself, using . . . agents of your own" because the committees of Congress would hear only from manufacturers.[56] Horace's advice, in effect, summed up expectations that were stimulated by progressive leaders but also by Roosevelt in making the presidency itself a stage for reform leadership.

However, the Republican Party had not undergone a conversion on the tariff. The tariff reform plank was included in the Republican platform because Taft's agents controlled the platform. It was rumored around the convention that the platform had been "brought from Washington."[57] The standpat Tariff League protested against the tariff plank.[58] Speaker Joe Cannon swore to undo the planks promising tariff reform, a postal savings bank, and limitations on labor injunctions, all of which Taft favored.[59] But Taft won the battle over symbols within the convention, and the reform language remained.

In his inaugural address Taft called for an immediate special session of Congress for tariff revision. He said: "A matter of most pressing importance is the revision of the tariff. In accordance with the promises of the platform upon which I was elected, I shall call Congress into extra session . . . in order that consideration may be at once given to a bill revising the Dingley Act." Taft said the revision should secure the revenue needed by government, and it should adjust rates to do no more than "equal . . . the difference between the cost of production abroad and the cost of production here." He stipulated that he expected lowered rates on many products and higher rates on few, if any.[60]

Taft was the first Republican president to propose reduced tariff rates. Even more threatening to Republican orthodoxy, Taft said that the prime consideration in revising the tariff should be "taxation and . . . revenue," echoing the traditional Democratic language of "tariff for revenue only." Then he ventured further into the apostasy, proposing a corporate income tax to compensate for reduced tariff revenue. Taft claimed authority for his unorthodox stance, stating he acted on "the platform upon which I was elected." Therein he invoked what should have been robust authority—advancing Roosevelt's reform spirit while acting consistently with the party platform and on the basis of a substantial electoral victory. The *Chicago Daily Tribune* headlined: "Taft Seeks Real Tariff Revision: New President Will Force Congress to Carry Out Faithfully Pledges of His Platform."[61] But Taft's real leverage on the tariff was in fact weaker than it at first seemed.

The tariff was an issue for which there was no stable equilibrium within the Republican's coalition of interests. Protective rates were the party's gifts to a long list of economic interests, and protectionism tied diverse interests to the party. E. E. Schattschneider quipped that the tariff was "a dubious economic policy turned into a great political success."[62] Reduced rates would threaten those interests benefiting from the rates while the benefits of reductions were widespread among consumers and promised little political benefit for the party. Thus tariff reduction had little attraction for most Republican politicians.

Created by his allies without full party support, the platform plank did not give Taft strong authority for tariff reform. Henry Pringle described the leadership's acceptance of the platform's promise as merely cynical.[63] Senator Henry Cabot Lodge (R-MA) admitted privately that a new tariff bill would by and large replicate the old Dingley tariff "with some improvement in details and classifications." But he hoped that improving economic conditions would mitigate political disappointment with the new tariff.[64] True to form, in the congressional debate party leaders asserted that "revision" did not mean reduction. Speaker Cannon asked, "Where did we ever make the statement that we would revise the tariff downward?"[65]

Against such resistance, Taft's challenge was to find means to affect the legislative process and secure reform. In the House, Speaker Cannon thought reform smacked of "the Democratic tariff for revenue and anti-trust rhetoric."[66] To further his tariff initiative Taft briefly considered making common cause with insurgents who sought to deny Cannon the speakership.[67] To disarm Taft, Cannon promised he would cooperate on tariff reform.[68] With an understanding that Cannon and Senate Majority Leader Nelson Aldrich (R-RI) would support his tariff reform, Taft promised noninterference in the congressional fight.[69] Having cut the deal, he then conveniently used "the law" to explain to insurgents that it was constitutionally inappropriate for the president to interfere in congressional leadership choices.[70] Taft was also following Roosevelt's advice to him that Cannon and Aldrich could be cooperative if handled wisely.[71]

Chapter Five

Taft opened the special session with a brief message lacking the force of his inaugural address. He said tariffs were no longer adequate for government's necessary revenue. Either the Republicans could raise tariff rates to even higher levels or break with the past and lower tariff rates while enacting another form of taxation. The message posed a stark demand, hinting that the Republican Party's deepest commitment was no longer adequate to government's needs or the economy's health.

Failing at Reform

Tariff legislation occupied five months between April and August of 1909, and Taft signed the Payne-Aldrich bill on August 6. The law lowered rates slightly from the high levels of the Dingley tariff. While keeping rate-setting in congressional hands, the law gave to the president discretion to raise rates if the country of origin discriminated against American goods. It also established an expert tariff commission with only advisory functions. Finally, the law initiated a modest corporate tax. Taft was pleased to win on several issues, reductions in rates for lumber and gloves and the provision for corporate taxation. Yet, the public saw the act's reductions as too small and covering too few products. Consequently Taft appeared to defend the preferences of Republican standpatters rather than those of Progressives.

One week into Taft's presidency, his military aide, Archie Butt, wrote: "If the president continues to transact business as he is . . . now, he will be about three years behind when the fourth of March, 1913 rolls around."[72] But Taft found his purpose when the special session opened, and tariff reform became his main focus. Yet much of his energy on the issue was misspent. He was unable to affect congressional decision making and unwilling to affect public opinion about those decisions. His success on tariff reform would depend on his comprehension of the politics of the tariff, his skill at affecting Congress, and his ability to publicly communicate his own stance. He would fail to fulfill any of these requirements.

Tariff bills contain rates for thousands of imported items, and each rate was defended by an economic interest. Despite widespread public sentiment for change, those narrow interests had far more effect than the public on the legislative decisions that constituted "the tariff." For a middle class seeking reform, Congress was the institution of those narrow interests, and the presidency was attuned to popular opinion. In embracing tariff reform, Taft responded to popular expectations; his task was to overcome Congress's parochialism.

Were he to influence tariff legislation decisions, Taft would need to understand tariff policy. His striking lack of information is demonstrated in a letter to Charles Taft. Mentioning a person who performed poorly as a postal official, Taft wondered whether he might be "a good man to become an expert on the tariff question."[73] His inadequate grasp of policy was recognized widely. Senator Lodge wrote: "Taft wants a tariff that will strike the country favorably . . . but knows little of the question."[74] In short, the president responded to public demands for reform but lacked even the most basic information he would need to affect the legislative process.

Taft's first error was to stay on the sidelines as each house produced a bill. Cannon and Aldrich advised him to weigh in with his preferences to the conference committee.[75] Superficially that deal made sense. The conference would be controlled by the leaders and would reconcile the House and Senate bills. But could he trust them to fulfill their promise to support his reform? He related his anxiety to Horace Taft: "They are going to confer with me, they say, and give my views great influence in the . . . Conference Committee. How much this means and how far they will be willing to go, I do not know."[76] In fact, the leaders misled Taft. With tariff legislation, conference committees were limited to reconciling rates between the House and Senate bills. By dealing only with the conference committee, Taft would be constrained within the high and low rates within the two bills without being able to demand a rate lower than what was already contained in the bills. Thus, he was trapped by his lack of knowledge about the tariff and congressional process.[77]

Taft remained in Washington through the summer, meeting with legislators and industry representatives as if through long workdays he could shape legislation. His military aide described Taft using "the White House as a great political adjunct in the battle."[78] Taft's hopes bounced between high confidence and despair. His letters to Nellie, summering in Massachusetts, display his work and mood. To her he admitted that success—getting "a bill passed that I can defend"—depended on "very acute and expert politicians . . . I am trusting . . . them and I may be deceived; but on the whole I have the whip hand."[79] Taft mentioned that Senator Aldrich said he would follow Taft's lead on lumber rates. But Taft confessed, "I don't know how much he means by that. I told him I would like to have that in writing."[80] In another letter Taft wrote, "If I had more technical knowledge I should feel more confident."[81]

In contrast to tariff rates, Taft intervened effectively in the tariff bill's tax provision. That is explained by the large difference between his knowledge about tariffs and tax policy. Insurgents and many Democrats favored an income tax, but earlier the Supreme Court had found an income tax unconstitutional. Republican conservatives strongly opposed any attempt to again pass an income tax and any attempt to tax corporations. Taft deftly managed these differences playing on the fact that a high corporate tax rate would draw political support to himself from insurgents and Democrats. He then used his popularity on the issue to influence Aldrich and Cannon to accept a moderate corporate tax in the tariff bill.[82]

With no equivalent leverage over the tariff process, Taft signaled the possibility of a veto should rates be insufficiently reduced.[83] Archie Butt said he "does not hesitate to tell each person he meets that he does not fear to veto a bill. . . . I think he is giving it out . . . so as to frighten the high tariff people."[84] Yet he did not seek expert advice for guidance. His regular communication was confined to legislators and his family. A rare example of expert advice that Taft received was from his friend, J. D. Brannan, a professor at Harvard Law School, and he did not pursue further that source. Brannan and his colleagues at Harvard had discussed the tariff situation, and Brannan sent Taft a letter describing the substance of their discussion. He concluded, "The people look to you to veto the bill rather than to disappoint them in their belief that you will do right." He said a veto would be "approved by the people . . . to let such a bill go through . . . will be regarded as a reactionary step and a surrender to the selfish interests against whom you have been fighting with Roosevelt." Finally Brannan urged Taft to see that "a party united for wrong is weaker than a party whose head at least stands for the right."[85] Brannan's advice, we might say, was Rooseveltian, and it went unheeded.

The House bill passed on April 9 and did not fulfill the goal of major reform. It dealt with about four thousand imported products and raised the rates on about 75 items while reducing rates somewhat on another 400. Taft pronounced that bill as acceptable. As the Senate took up the tariff bill, he advised progressive Republicans to stand up for reform, again wielding the veto threat. He told Senator La Follette (R- WI) that he and his colleagues should "amend the bill, cut down the duties. . . . I will keep track of your amendments . . . and when they lay that bill down before me, unless it complies with the platform, I will veto it."[86]

The Tariff End Game

The conference committee's reconciled bill passed both houses in early August. Taft signed it on August 6, claiming it was a triumph. The public did not share his assessment. On balance, the new law slightly reduced a number of rates, but it also raised rates on a number of specific common items. The act's complexity made it impossible to quickly analyze all its rates and their impact. Congress had undertaken no overall fiscal assessment of the bill, and the treasury department concluded it would take at least two months to analyze the law's details.[87] In that period of time the president lost control of the public definition of the tariff issue. What might he have done differently?

As the conference committee neared completion, Taft wrote Nellie: "I don't know whether I will come out all right in this tariff matter or not, but I am in it and I have got to struggle with it." A week later he wrote: "The tariff business is not in a satisfactory condition to me exactly."[88] Yet, as the legislation was completed, Taft rejected his possibilities of affecting it or shaping the public's conception of the legislation and his role in it. He eschewed the veto threat as a way of forcing his views on the conference. He also refused to go public with criticism of the tariff bill. He said to Horace Taft: "I could make a lot of cheap popularity for the time being by vetoing the bill, but it would leave the party in a bad shape . . . and the only person who would gain popularity would be your humble servant, and that at the expense of the party."[89]

Giving up both the veto and the "bully pulpit," Taft revealed why he failed at tariff reform politics. It was not that he was a standpat conservative. Rather, he was operating in a context he did not understand and attempting to achieve legislation with too few tools to affect its outcome. He was torn between commitment to Roosevelt (progressive reform) and party. Out of loyalty to his party he felt constrained from either forcing the issue with the veto or denouncing the legislation. Taft said going public would "only" serve his own interest in "popularity." Therein he revealed he did not understand Roosevelt's innovation in public leadership and did not comprehend that after Roosevelt the interests of a Republican president and the Republican Party were no longer identical.

Taft's insensitivity to the importance of public communication is evident in his correspondence with William Allen White, the prominent Kansas editor. White had advised Taft to keep himself and his agenda squarely in front of the public. Taft responded that he could not do that. Roosevelt, Taft told White, had his "heart . . . on his sleeve, and he must communicate his feeling." Describing his own limitations, Taft said, "After I have made a definite statement I have to let it go at that until the time for action arises."[90]

"The Best Tariff Bill"

Despite the inhibition about going public that he described to White, in mid-September Taft began a speaking tour promoting the new tariff law. His reticence was really a hesitation to promote himself. He was able to publicly promote his party. At Winona, Minnesota, on September 17 Taft declared the Payne-Aldrich Act to be "the best tariff bill that the Republican party ever passed" while giving a painfully long, obtuse, and largely inaccurate account of the law's reduction in tariff rates.[91]

The Winona speech reveals that his reform initiative was smothered by his inability to stand apart from his party. At the end of his incoherent defense of the law, he asked, what was a Republican who believed in reduced rates to do about an imperfect bill? It was, he said, the duty of that Republican to vote for the bill: "In a party those who join it . . . must surrender their personal predilections . . . to accomplish the good which united action . . . secures."[92] The *Boston Globe* reported that at Winona Taft read the "insurgents" out of the Republican Party.[93] Newspapers of all political stripes described the tariff act as a victory for standpatters and a betrayal of reform. Even the strongly Republican *Chicago Daily Tribune* severely criticized the law and Taft's defense of it. It commented that he was defending a law that was indefensible in terms of his own promise. The editorial continued, "*The Tribune* finds itself more loyalist than the king, more Republican than the president in its belief in the inherent ability and purpose of the party to do what is right by the country."[94] Taft's performance demonstrated his promise of reform was hollow, and the public turned negative.[95]

Taft's problem was not a lack of vision for his presidency. His vision was neither small nor "traditional." His pursuit of tariff reform was Rooseveltian in its assumption of executive policy initiative, but he lost control of the issue and the subsequent public discourse. Like his predecessor, Taft articulated an independent policy agenda, and he imposed it as a Republican commitment through control of the 1908 platform committee. His failure to fulfill his commitment to reform was not a failure of ambition. It was a failure of politics.

Pinchot, Ballinger, and Taft: The Crisis in Conservation

As Taft praised the unpopular tariff bill, an obscure public lands issue exploded to further endanger his presidency. The tariff controversy undermined Taft's support, but it alone would not have caused Roosevelt's break with him. Roosevelt knew tariff reform was quicksand for Republicans.[96] However, the Pinchot-Ballinger controversy went to the heart of Roosevelt's own commitments and allies.

The controversy between Chief Forester Gifford Pinchot and Interior Secretary Richard Ballinger broke publicly in August 1909.[97] These men had been at loggerheads since 1907, when Roosevelt appointed Ballinger as chief of interior's general land office. President McKinley had made Pinchot head of the forestry bureau in the agriculture department, and Pinchot turned the bureau into the dynamic and imperial forest service. His role expanded under Roosevelt, who had befriended him while serving as governor of New York. President Roosevelt expanded Pinchot's role, making him informal coordinator of federal land use programs, water resource planning, and forestry conservation in agencies outside of the forest service. With James Garfield as interior secretary and Frederick Newell at the reclamation bureau, natural resource policy was managed through a network of Roosevelt's loyalists. In reclamation Pinchot was responsible for the withdrawal of lands for water conservation. In the public land office he closed commercial access to forest lands and was able to manage forest lands controlled by the bureau of Indian affairs.

Pinchot's influence over interior's land office ended when Richard Ballinger became its chief.[98] Ballinger had been Seattle's successful reform mayor, a respected attorney specializing in land law and a state judge.[99] For Ballinger, reorganizing the land office meant exercising its own legal authority rather than handing it to Pinchot. Ballinger also differed with Pinchot on several specific issues of land policy, in particular, whether it was preferable to allow access to federal coal lands through lease arrangements, as Pinchot preferred, or whether these lands should be sold outright, as Ballinger preferred. As Pinchot sourly described Ballinger in his memoir: "For the T.R. public-land policy, now firmly established, he had little or no use."[100]

Yet Ballinger also considered himself a Roosevelt conservationist and supported vigorous federal policy to direct the efficient use of resources. Roosevelt had seen him in a similar light; in the summer of 1907 he sent Ballinger, along with Pinchot, Garfield, and Newell, to represent the administration's conservation policies at the public lands convention in Denver.[101] Perhaps the largest difference of perspective between Ballinger and Pinchot was that the former was a Westerner, concerned with balancing regional economic development with land and resource conservation.[102] Having reorganized the land office, Ballinger returned to his Seattle law practice in March 1908. Then President-elect Taft named Ballinger to head the interior department, summarily replacing Roosevelt's friend James Garfield. Pinchot looked sourly at the appointment, and he claimed that Ballinger had resigned from the land office because "of his personal hostility to the T.R. land policies."[103] The men's mutual hostility would explode publicly in August 1909.

The issues propelling the conflict into the public arena concerned an arcane mining permit application for Alaskan public land. A minor land office official named Louis Glavis charged improprieties in the mining claims filed initially in 1902 by Clarence Cunningham and others. Those permit applications for mining were set aside when eight million acres of Alaskan lands were withdrawn from entry, requiring reapplications under somewhat closer scrutiny. The Cunningham applications were resubmitted in 1906 and subsequently approved by the general land office. Glavis later charged that Cunningham and other applicants intended to associate their operations, in violation of the law. Additionally, he charged that the Cunningham group was a business front for the dominant mining companies of J. P. Morgan and Harry Guggenheim.[104]

Glavis was twenty-five years old and newly head of the Portland, Oregon bureau of the general land office when he examined the Cunningham claims. After several months spent examining the claims, Glavis was convinced they were corrupt, but his superiors, including Ballinger, rejected his charges. In mid-summer 1909 Glavis took his story to the forest service, claiming that Cunningham's mining operation, if approved, would impinge on national forest land. Glavis received a friendly hearing by forest service officials who helped to sharpen his charges to clearly indict Ballinger instead of just lower-level interior officials. Chief Forester Gifford Pinchot then arranged for Glavis to bring his charges directly to President Taft.

Pinchot saw that Glavis could be made into a weapon against his enemy Ballinger. As Alpheus Thomas Mason put it: "The Chief Forester needed provable instances of wrong-doing in the Interior Department, incontestable facts on which to build his case against Ballinger. Glavis could supply these."[105] Taft heard Glavis's charges in August 1909 and quickly decided that Ballinger was innocent of any wrongdoing. More charges flew, and the controversy exploded into the press. Then for months a congressional investigation of the affair commanded public attention. There was no proof of corruption. There was no smoking gun, to use modern news parlance, but the controversy shattered Ballinger's public reputation, and Taft fared little better. By the time the hearing ended, he was fully alienated from Roosevelt and the progressive public. Senator Robert LaFollette said of Taft that "his attitude upon the tariff question . . . his interference in behalf of Cannon . . . his whole course in the Ballinger affair . . . absolutely alienated the Progressive group."[106]

Conservation and Progressivism

The ideal of conservation connected to Progressivism's diverse reform aims.[107] Thus conservation issues resonated beyond those interested specifically in land and resources policy. The conservation of natural resources harmonized with the promotion of child welfare, the protection of public health, the regulation of corporate power, and the mitigation of great economic inequality. Progressivism sought to "conserve" what we value and to solve both natural and social problems through scientific rationality.[108]

Pinchot's characterization of conservation conveys the centrality of that idea for progressive reform. It is, he wrote, the "movement . . . to make our country a permanent and prosperous home for ourselves and for our children, and for our children's children, and it is a task that is worth the best thought and effort of any and all of us."[109] Pinchot himself was conservation's prophet. He had introduced scientific forestry to the United States and transformed the forest division from a moribund office that fitfully experimented with rainmaking into the highly effective U.S. Forest Service.[110] He was an energetic publicist and organizer, building widespread support for his conservation agenda.[111] To take one example of his influence on public opinion, noting that politicians had called for opening federal forests to farming and grazing, the *Los Angeles Times* responded: "To preserve the forests, to store the floods and irrigate the arid lands has been the war-cry of . . . the forestry bureau for years. It has found lodgment in the consciences and intelligence of the people and that policy is going to be carried out."[112]

For all his prominence as a Progressive Era leader, Pinchot was Theodore Roosevelt's satellite and minion. He wrote: "Conservation policy originated in the Administration of Theodore Roosevelt . . . and . . . was accepted . . . because of him."[113] The two men were bound together as friends and fellow outdoorsmen.

Roosevelt said of Pinchot's loyalty to him, it "is almost fetish worship," and he added his highest accolades: "I do not know the man I would sooner choose to send to some danger."[114]

Taft understood the importance of Pinchot and conservation to Roosevelt. As president-elect, Taft gave to Roosevelt his promise of continuity:

> You can count on my continuing the movement as far as I can, and especially under the influence of Gifford Pinchot, whom I shall continue to regard as a kind of conscience in certain directions, to be followed when possible and to be ignored only with a sense of wrong done to the best interests of the country.[115]

Crisis Management

Having promised Roosevelt that he would support Pinchot, Taft returned Pinchot's nemesis, Ballinger, to federal service. Ballinger was sure to insulate the interior department from Pinchot's influence just as he had done at the land office. Unlike Pinchot, Taft saw Ballinger as a friend of conservation. He had reorganized the land office and fought corruption in its operations, and now as interior secretary he promised continued protection of public lands.[116] Taft had replaced Garfield, an Ohioan, to put a Westerner at interior. But like Ballinger, Taft was critical of Garfield's informal administrative style. Large parts of Roosevelt's conservation policy had rested on informality. As Gifford Pinchot explained, Roosevelt would:

> withdraw sites from entry to keep them safe until Congress could act to protect them . . . T.R. did not have, and could not get from Congress, specific authority for these withdrawals. But neither was there specific authority of law for the Louisiana Purchase . . . or for freeing the slaves by Lincoln, or for the acquisition of the Panama Canal by T.R. himself.[117]

Taft sought instead sought to put conservation policy on a clear legal foundation. However, he did not propose new legislation until January 1910, well into the chaos of the Pinchot-Ballinger controversy.[118]

Taft was divided from Pinchot, Garfield and Roosevelt in his lesser tolerance of administrative discretion. The Roosevelt men used broad discretion in pursuit of good policies. They saw ethical principles and scientific information as fully adequate substitutes for laws. The Roosevelt conservationists shared in

Progressivism's anti-formalism and pragmatism, exemplified in thinkers like John Dewey, Thorstein Veblen, and Charles Beard.[119] The right ends justified efficacious administrative means, even if it required playing loose with the law. That view upset Taft's conception of orderly government, although we can recall that in his role as Roosevelt's subaltern, Taft demonstrated a tolerance for the president's executive discretion.

The Glavis controversy burst on Taft in August 1909, while he vacationed at Beverly, Massachusetts. Taft knew that Pinchot and Ballinger were at loggerheads but he had not yet heard of the Cunningham claims or Glavis's charge. [120] On August 5 Pinchot met Louis Glavis in Seattle to hear the latter's story. Up to that time Glavis had not centrally targeted Ballinger but claimed that Fred Dennett, his superior and chief of the land office field service, was the bad actor. After meeting with Pinchot, Glavis's story changed. Pinchot assigned forest service officials to further develop Glavis's charges, making Ballinger their focus. Pinchot also devised Glavis's immediate strategy dissuading him from publicizing his charges. As James Penick Jr. explains:

> What Glavis had to say was extremely damaging to Ballinger; a confrontation of Taft with the evidence would be more dramatic and . . . more effective. If Glavis won, Ballinger was finished. If Taft repudiated Glavis there would be time enough to think of publication, which then would be even more damaging.[121]

Pinchot sent Glavis to present his charges to Taft. Glavis carried a letter from Pinchot that described his information as so explosive that only the president could properly deal with the issues he raised.[122] Taft received Glavis on August 18, and took for examination his documents. The young land office employee left that meeting with an expanded sense of importance. He waited in Beverly with the hope that Taft would want another meeting with him. Not hearing again from the president, he went to New York City, attempting unsuccessfully to gain Attorney General Wickersham's support. Glavis seemed increasingly obsessive. As James Penick observes, he was "a driven man," and his charges were a "single-minded pursuit of conviction."[123]

Glavis posed two different problems for Taft. First, were the charges true? Second, how would the public airing of the charges affect Taft's political position? After hearing Glavis and examining his documents, Taft consulted several cabinet officers, the attorney general, Naval Secretary Meyer, and Treasury Secretary MacVeagh. Then Taft asked Ballinger to provide a written response to the charges. While Taft was methodically following his judicial impulses, a political storm broke over him. Newspapers published Glavis's charges, and the strongly anti-Ballinger slant of the articles pointed to forest service involvement. In fact, forestry officials continued to act as Glavis's publicists. The *New York Times* warned: "It is more than ever apparent now that [Taft] will have one of the bitterest departmental wars . . . that has worried any Administration in years."[124] The storm warnings were in plain sight for Taft to see.

Ballinger arrived in Beverly on September 6 with a memorandum prepared by interior's solicitor and Ballinger's friend, Oscar Lawler, responding to the charges. Taft examined the case with the attorney general on September 11 and 12 and reached a verdict. As he described his decision to Horace Taft: "I am just now engaged in preparing a letter . . . passing on the issues . . . and ruling with Ballinger on every one of them." [125] Taft then wrote a public letter, addressed to Ballinger, finding him faultless and also removing Glavis from government service. Praising the letter, an editorial remarked that it "exhibits . . . the judicial tone and temper of a magistrate disposing of a case."[126] Taft requested that Attorney General Wickersham prepare a memorandum explaining the grounds upon which Taft exonerated Ballinger. Wickersham subsequently prepared a lengthy document, backdating it to September 11, the date of his meeting with Taft. That decision would prove later to be politically toxic.

Taft ignored the politics of the case as he decided against Glavis. He gave no public recognition of Pinchot's involvement with Glavis's crusade against Ballinger. Yet, his equanimity masked his anger at a "cruel injustice" done to Ballinger.[127] Taft wrote to his wife: "Pinchot has spread a virus against Ballinger widely, and has used the publicity department of his bureau for the purpose."[128] But Taft was slow to see the dangers for himself in the political situation. Newspapers reported his letter as a defeat for the forest service because Glavis's actions were "due to the advice of certain forestry bureau officials."[129] What happened next demonstrated the inadequacy of Taft's judicial mien for protecting his presidency. While he assumed the facts would determine the outcome of the controversy, Pinchot correctly saw that public opinion would determine the winner.

As the controversy escalated, the president disregarded public opinion. Nor did he attempt to influence key actors beyond a flaccid effort to disarm Pinchot. In mid-September he wrote to Pinchot begging him to "not make Glavis's cause yours," and promising that conservation policy would be protected. Fearing the consequences of Pinchot's resignation, Taft said to him: "I should consider it one of the greatest losses that my administration could sustain if you were to leave it, and I . . . hope that you will not think my action . . . is reason" to resign.[130] He feared Roosevelt's ire more than he feared public opinion.

Taft spoke with Pinchot in Salt Lake City during his fall 1909 speaking tour. He again implored Pinchot to cooperate with him and assured that Ballinger would not interfere in forestry matters. Pinchot replied that he had to fight any encroachment on conservation but promised to remain in office. Yet Taft expected the worst, and said he was "convinced that Pinchot with his fanaticism . . . plans a coup by which I shall be compelled to dismiss him and he will . . . make out martyrdom."[131] Following the meeting, Pinchot sent to Taft his bill of particulars against Ballinger, demonstrating that his appeals had not mitigated Pinchot's hostility. Taft finally realized the danger that Pinchot posed yet did nothing to protect himself. He was helpless in this politically chaotic context and without the skills to navigate through the conflict. Without a script, that is, clear goals and means to guide his actions, he relied on his default skill set, judging facts.

To further complicate the president's situation, firing Glavis had not disarmed him. Now Glavis styled himself a martyr for conservation. Using him Pinchot built a movement to destroy Ballinger and undermine Taft. At a time of large-circulation national magazines vividly promoting progressive causes, such as *McClure's* and *Collier's Weekly,* Pinchot and Glavis found a platform.[132] In mid-November Glavis published "The Whitewash of Ballinger" in *Collier's Weekly,* luridly sketching Ballinger's support for "the interests" and implying he was corrupt without actually specifying the charge. Not revealed by the article's title page was the coauthor role with Glavis of forest service publicists Overton Price and Albert Shaw.[133] Prior to that article, most coverage of Taft's decision about Ballinger was positive, but now the balance scale shifted against Ballinger and the president. Respectable publications, from *McClure's* to the *Engineering News,* criticized Ballinger. The *New York Times* reported the *Collier's* article with headlines such as "Glavis Attacks Ballinger Again," detailing Glavis's claim that Taft had not responded to his evidence against Ballinger. Most damagingly, the *Times* quoted long sections of the article with nothing of Ballinger's response beyond his denial.[134]

Taft silently endured the negative publicity. He did not seem the same man who had effectively "gone public" as civil governor in the Philippines and who had been a favorite source for newspaper reporters while war secretary. As a campaigner in 1904 and 1906 and during his own presidential campaign, he demonstrated crowd-pleasing affability. But in the White House, he seemed blind to Roosevelt's precedent of effective public leadership, as if going public would now be undignified. That self-restraint was evident in small ways as well as large. Traveling north from Washington by train a couple of weeks after his inauguration, the president ignored the crowds gathered to see him pass. Archie Butt wrote he "took no notice of the crowd . . . [and] never even went to the platform to wave his hand."[135]

Taft also had little feel for the issues over which Pinchot and Ballinger battled, and he failed to see how conflict over those issues impinged on his interests. Illustrating his inattention to Western interests and conservation, after a dinner in summer 1909 with Western senators and some bureau of reclamation men, he wrote to Nellie: "It was not a very lively party . . . there were quite a number of insurgents there, and some of them were disposed to be rather cheeky . . . the meeting was not altogether a successful one."[136] Taft professed his commitment to the Roosevelt policies, but he lacked an understanding of those policies' meaning in progressive and Western circles.

At the end of 1909 Taft attempted to manage the conflict with the classic move of embattled presidents, stifling information. He ordered that no executive employee provide information to Congress. Simultaneously, Ballinger ordered interior employees to desist from speaking with reporters. Under pressure about his bureau's support of Glavis, Pinchot ended that work, lamenting it was unfortunate some people saw "zealous efforts by the Forest Service to protect the public interest" as attacks."[137] What for Pinchot and his allies was a great fight to save Roosevelt's conservation policy was for Taft a conspiracy against his administration. Indeed, Pinchot was conspiring with Roosevelt's allies and fellow conservationists, circulating Glavis's documents and promoting his cause.

There was press speculation that Taft would end the crisis by firing one or both of the participants.[138] In fact, he did nothing meaningful. While seeing Ballinger often, he had no contact with Pinchot. Rather than intervening between the principals in the fight, Taft sought to use Republican loyalties to protect Ballinger and himself, in effect circling the partisan wagons. He called for a congressional inquiry that would be controlled by the Republican leaders, assuming it would surely clear Ballinger and embarrass Pinchot.[139]

Taft's call for a congressional investigation offers another example of his faith in facts and objective inquiry. He was confident that through a committee investigation "it will . . . be shown just how lenient he has been toward Pinchot."[140]

Taft also assumed the Republican leaders would protect him. The *Washington Post* reported that the party leadership sought the hearings, fearing "the effect on . . . the party and . . . the administration if attacks on the integrity of a member of the President's official family may be made with impunity and . . . unchallenged."[141] While Taft trusted the facts to vindicate him, Pinchot publicized his side of the story. Before the hearing opened, he sent a letter to the insurgent Senator Jonathan P. Dolliver (R-IA) defending the forest service's work with Glavis. He explained that his service's aid to Glavis was justified "unless there are secrets which the people of the United States are not entitled to know . . . concerning . . . the public lands." Senator Dolliver read Pinchot's letter on the floor of the Senate. The following day the president fired Pinchot for insubordination.[142] Simultaneously Attorney General Wickersham sent to Congress his report dated September 11 and other relevant documents on the Glavis charges.

Six members from each house comprised the joint investigative committee, chaired by a party stalwart, Senator Knute Nelson (R-MN). The hearing opened on January 26 and ended May 20. Paradoxically Taft was vindicated by the majority report and politically destroyed nevertheless by the hearings and subsequent press coverage. The committee's seven safe Republicans decided in favor of Taft's decision on Ballinger and Glavis. But, Glavis's attorney, Louis D. Brandeis, undermined Taft's credibility. What the president had failed to realize in trusting an investigation of "the facts" was that each side had its own reading of "facts."

Louis Brandeis entered the case in the employ of *Collier's Weekly*. Fearing a libel suit by Ballinger if the committee found in his favor, the magazine employed the famous liberal attorney to represent Glavis.[143] The joint committee's procedure relied primarily on the attorneys for the principal witnesses, Glavis, Pinchot, and Ballinger, to lead the questioning. Through March, Glavis and Pinchot testified. Both were splendid in the eyes of their supporters. Glavis seemed to have an encyclopedic command of relevant facts and documents, and Pinchot's statements were powerful appeals for conservation values.

Brandeis played to the public beyond the hearing room. Writing to his brother after Pinchot testified, Brandeis said that Pinchot "impressed the Committee." But his larger insight was that Taft "is getting into an ever more uncomfortable position & seems ever more foolish in his actions."[144] Brandeis speculated in another letter that Taft had a means of escape from political embarrassment by claiming he was misled by Ballinger. However, he observed, Taft "insists that he knew and knows it all."[145] The president, he saw, was frozen into a defensive mode but expected the hearings to save him. In early May, the hearing wound to an end. Each camp had gotten out its side of the story, achieving something of a draw. A May 1 *New York Times* editorial mused that what separated Pinchot and Ballinger was not honesty or lack of same but differing principles about how to conduct public policy.[146] Then Brandeis turned the hearings into an inquisition of Taft's actions.

At the beginning of the hearings the administration had submitted to the committee voluminous documents which became a 700-page printed volume. In addition there was the 87-page report, dated September 11, 1909, that had been prepared by the attorney general to support Taft's letter of exoneration to Ballinger, which was dated September 13. Brandeis's great coup began with pointed questions about the attorney general's report. He wondered, how did Wickersham examine all relevant documents and produce an 87-page report in the five or six days between receiving all the documents and the date of his report? Brandeis asked if the Wickersham report had been written later and backdated, and not available to Taft as he wrote his letter exonerating Ballinger, what information did he use to make his decision?

Brandeis reconstructed Taft's, Wickersham's, and Ballinger's activities during September 1909 to determine if their movements could support the claim that the attorney general's memo was prepared in the several days leading up to September 11.[147] In fact, he showed that the memo was written well after September 11. That charge was confirmed when an interior department stenographer named Frederick Kerby testified that he had taken dictation of a relevant memorandum for Taft from the interior department's solicitor, Oscar Lawler. The Lawler memorandum was not among the papers the administration gave to the committee. Brandeis demanded that the Lawler memo be produced, and Wickersham sent it to the committee. Taft's letter exonerating Ballinger incorporated elements of Lawler's memo. Therefore Brandeis charged that Ballinger had prepared his own exoneration through his department solicitor and ally, and Taft had foolishly approved.

The disaster that the hearings visited on Taft is illustrated by a *Chicago Daily Tribune* report. The story began: "Taft's letter of . . . dismissal of L.A. Glavis . . . and exonerating Secretary Ballinger . . . was based upon and in part directly quoted from a draft of a letter written by Oscar Lawler . . . of the interior department, and a subordinate of Mr. Ballinger." Recall that Lawler had also written Ballinger's document to Taft that denied Glavis's charge. The *Tribune* reported that Taft responded to this new revelation, when he was found on the golf course, by claiming he prepared his letter himself, based on his reading of the documents and "upon the report to him of the attorney general."[148] The next day the president changed his story under pressure of the evidence that he had relied on Lawler's memo. He admitted that because of the pressure at the time to prepare for his upcoming speaking trip he requested that Lawler prepare a memo showing the basis for Ballinger's innocence. Ingeniously, he explained he only used part of the Lawler report in his own letter.[149]

Archie Butt observed, "For a President to be forced to offer proofs to substantiate his own statement is reaching the limit."[150] Now Taft, more than Ballinger, Glavis, or Pinchot, was the controversy's central actor and biggest loser. That the hearings produced evidence of his apparent misdeed was flabbergasting to Taft. All he could do was protest the injustice of it all. He knew his actions were proper. He said he asked from Lawler nothing more than a compilation of the facts and had drafted most of his letter to Ballinger by the time he received Lawler's memo. Additionally, he explained Wickersham's memo was dated September 11 because that was the day the attorney general gave Taft his opinion of the Glavis evidence. Finally, Taft knew, correctly as it turned out, that Ballinger was not corrupt and Pinchot and Glavis were manipulative as well as obsessive.

However, for those Americans who feared the "trusts" and sided with Roosevelt, conservation, and reform, the appearance was that Taft had failed in his commitments to continue progressive leadership. Not once during the months the hearing dragged on had he spoken publicly about conservation. He did not counter Pinchot's attacks, nor did he defend his own policies. All the more puzzling, in mid-January he sent to Congress a message on conservation, but he failed to use that opportunity to promote his legislative initiative to the public.

There is more to be puzzled by in the drama's denouement. Taft's replacements for Pinchot and for Ballinger, once the latter resigned in March 1911, were conservationists of the Roosevelt-Pinchot stripe. In early 1910 he appointed Henry Graves as chief of the forestry service. As Ballinger's replacement he appointed Walter L. Fisher. Both men were Roosevelt supporters, close to Pinchot, and devoted friends of conservation. Thus Taft's political ineptness in defending his position throughout this case had nothing to do with the substance of policy. Rather, his failings reflected his inability to improvise effective leadership within an unstructured decision context.

Chapter Five

Role Structure, Authority, and Taft's Leadership Style

Taft's public praise of the Payne-Aldrich Act and defense of Richard Ballinger both undermined his stance as a progressive president. Just a year after Roosevelt left office he skewered his successor for not continuing his progressive agenda, writing to Henry Cabot Lodge that "Taft, Cannon, Aldrich . . . have totally misestimated the . . . movement which we now . . . face in American life."[151] Two years later Roosevelt would attempt to lead that movement back to the White House, destroying Taft's chance for reelection. The former president's outsized ambition might have caused his split with Taft under any circumstance. But Taft betrayed his campaign promise of continuity with Roosevelt and did it without recognizing fully what he was doing and its implications for his presidency. In 1908 he appeared among the most qualified politicians to enter the presidency. Why had he failed so miserably?

Scholars have attributed Taft's failure to his conservative ideology and the straightjacket of his legalist views. However, as we have seen, those ideational explanations caricature the real Taft. Gifford Pinchot was closer to the mark in May 1910: "Everybody . . . recognizes that he moves with absolute accuracy from one blunder by the shortest route to the next."[152] He failed not because of his ideas but because of his leadership style. Contemporaries saw him as error-prone rather than ideological. Henry Cabot Lodge remarked: "The one thing that surprises me about Taft is that he does not know more about politics. With all his great . . . success in administration he does not seem to have got hold of the elements of politics . . . as one of the conditions with which a man has to deal, especially a President."[153] As we have already seen, Taft confessed his own ineptness to Roosevelt: "I have had a hard time" while "conscientiously trying to carry out your policies . . . my method . . . has not worked smoothly."[154]

Taft had promised reform in the 1908 campaign, and he took a huge risk as the first Republican president to seek tariff reduction. He was committed to the continuation of conservation policy, and he successfully initiated policies that conservatives opposed, such as railroad regulation, anti-trust, and postal savings banks. Nor had he been bound in the past by a legalistic straightjacket. In the Philippines and as war secretary Taft gave priority to executive directives from Root and Roosevelt with little thought to legal niceties.

Taft's real failing was the mismatch of his leadership skills and the presidency's demands. He had succeeded in political appointments to roles with defined goals and clear accountability. The presidency was different. Presidents define their own goals and work with less structure than Taft had found as a judge, a colonial administrator, and war secretary. Erwin Hargrove observes presidents "use skills and embrace goals that are congruent with the historical context."[155] Yet Taft had not sought the presidency to fight for his own goals. For him and his family the office would be a capstone of a brilliant public career, a reward not a challenge. Lacking his own strong political and policy motivations, and needing a job description as president, he committed to continuing Roosevelt's agenda. Simultaneously he pledged fealty to his party and its platform; he would continue Roosevelt's policies *and* be faithful to Republican commitments. He failed to see those goals were incompatible. Roosevelt's leadership drove a wedge into the Republican party, leaving it unstable. Even Taft's military aide saw the contradiction that Taft "endorsed the Roosevelt policies, yet in each state he entered he affiliated with the men whom Roosevelt . . . was wont to call the 'Enemy.'"[156]

Political Education, Leadership Style, and Structured Roles

Taft's failure as president can be understood as a failure of his political education. His great successes prior to the presidency occurred in roles possessing several characteristics. First, they were appointive positions for which he qualified through family connection, partisan loyalty, and hard work. Second, they were roles with a clear job description, by the directives of a superior if not by law. Third, in each role Taft was hypersensitive to performance evaluations by superiors. Not only was he seeking approval to assure his next plum, he needed continual approval to confirm he was succeeding in his current assignment. Finally, each role he occupied contained sufficient resources on tap to accomplish the assigned task.

Consequently these jobs gave to Taft a clear structure of work, with specific goals to achieve and means to achieve them along with clear lines of accountability. In these he demonstrated an extraordinary capacity for hard work and challenging tasks. As solicitor general he had to conquer a large backlog of cases while simultaneously teaching himself federal appellate law. At the extreme, in the Philippines, he even incurred severe illnesses without retreating from the challenges he found as a colonial governor.

Leadership in an Ill-Structured Role

In 1909 Taft was inaugurated into a radically different role than any of those earlier assignments in which he had excelled. In a constitutional sense the presidency is relatively "ill-structured," lacking clear cues and accountability. As Harvey C. Mansfield Jr. observes, each president defines the office for him- or herself, in a specific political context. "Thus the Constitution does not determine the behavior of those who govern under it, and is not intended to do so."[157]

Instead, it is political context that goes far in determining the behavior of presidents. For example, the institutions of the party period had provided expectations for presidents' behavior. But Taft's presidency was far removed from party period stability. His context contained expectations for his performance that were stimulated by Roosevelt's use of the office. In the White House Taft would find no job description, no personification of accountability to offer approval, and certainly no supply of political resources sufficient to the goals he set out to achieve. Without external structure, Taft's leadership style failed him. The man who had taken on earlier work challenges with great energy was now lethargic in the absence of clear directions. The man who had struggled mightily to please superiors now had no superior to please but saw critics everywhere. Finally, Taft lacked the sensibilities to identify and acquire political resources to achieve the goals he set for himself.

What Taft did have at the beginning of his presidency were the goals to which he had committed in the campaign, continuing Roosevelt's program and fulfilling his party's platform. Aside from the fact that these goals were incongruent, he early on demonstrated he could not acquire the resources and information to achieve them. He did not understand the congressional process regarding tariff legislation, nor did he understand the risks for him of a long congressional investigation of Glavis's charges. He failed to understand the symbolic importance of conservation for Progressives. And he did not understand that progressive expectations regarding tariff reform would be dashed by his claims of success for the Payne-Aldrich Act. He did not understand the need for expertise on tap. He gave no evidence of using his office with tactical efficacy. In the conservation battle he did not effectively restrain Pinchot, nor did he gently ease out Ballinger. And he was oblivious to expert information when it arrived on his doorstep. Instead of seeking expert guidance when he needed it, he turned to his family for advice that was more comforting than helpful.

In all of the above failures we see the mismatch of Taft's leadership style with the presidency. However, there is yet a more serious flaw in his approach to leadership that doomed his presidency. He did not understand his first obligation was to protect his presidency. For example, as the tariff legislation wound through Congress Taft refused to go public with criticism of Congress because that would benefit him at his party's expense. And in the months of congressional hearings on the Pinchot-Ballinger controversy, he never went public with strong positions on conservation to ward off Progressives' criticism.

Thus Taft did not understand that presidential energy in the Progressive Era depended on connecting the office with the people and their concerns. He did not understand that to make his presidency effective he would first have to protect it from his critics. And, Taft failed to realize his fate as president was apart from the interests of his party and even his family. He entered a presidency reshaped by Roosevelt's performance, and he was on his own within it. He needed leadership skills to shape his own use of the presidency but had not developed appropriate skills within his political education. As Archie Butt said of Taft in this sad situation, with Roosevelt gone, he "will find . . . that his steam has been cut off. He will have to find his own fuel now."[158]

6

The Political Education of Woodrow Wilson: Interpretive Leadership and Expediency

I have often preached in my political utterances the doctrine of expediency, and I am an unabashed disciple of that doctrine.
  Woodrow Wilson[1]

THE NEW JERSEY DEMOCRATIC PARTY gambled on a political novice for the 1910 gubernatorial race. James Smith Jr., the state's Democratic chief, recruited Woodrow Wilson, Princeton University's president, to be the respectable face the party needed to win after fifteen years of Republican control. Smith also needed a candidate who could marginalize several reformers seeking the Democratic nomination. Wilson was a nationally prominent educator, and he was also reliably conservative, promoted by the anti-reform, anti-Bryan Democrats of Wall Street.

Smith's offer to make Wilson a candidate appealed to his aspiration for high political leadership. But to accept that opportunity he so prized, Wilson had to promise to not fight "the existing Democratic organization." He qualified his promise somewhat, guaranteeing to leave the machine unscathed as long as the organization allowed him freedom "in the matter of measures and men."[2] But after securing the nomination and winning his election, Wilson violated his promise. In a major speech delivered before his inauguration, Wilson said the Democratic Party was the mass of Democratic voters, and Smith and his lieutenants were "a system" of corrupt alliances between business and politics. They were a deformity that must be removed from politics and government, and he promised to "cut off the wart . . . it can be done while you wait, and it is being done."[3]

Thus, Wilson's career of public leadership began with a double-cross of his key supporter. During the campaign, as victory seemed close, he embraced progressive reforms. After winning he asserted independence from the machine. So as to make good on his promise to excise the "wart," Wilson blocked James Smith's election to the U.S. Senate by the new Democratic legislative majority. It is not news that a politician would betray supporters to gain advantage; however, Wilson was not a conventional politician. A distinguished academic and university leader, he had prominently advocated the mission of elite university education to form honorable leadership in a democratic society. He was also a prominent Presbyterian and spoke frequently from the pulpit. Wilson's most influential scholarship promoted a normative theory of responsible leadership. How did the double-cross fit into this conception of leadership, and what does it tell us about his leadership style?

To betray Smith was the prerequisite for Wilson's rise from Princeton to the White House. Without loyalty to Smith he could not have been nominated or elected. But without breaking the promise he could not be the celebrated governor backed by Progressives for the presidency. The double-cross was not only required for Wilson's political success, it was justified by his conception of political leadership.

Responsible Leadership: From Congressional to Constitutional Government

All presidents have ideas about leadership, but Wilson was the only president after the founding generation to write systematically about political leadership and American constitutionalism. His writings provide a lens through which to focus on his leadership. Particularly relevant are his ideas of responsible, interpretive leadership that appear in his earliest publications and remain fairly consistent through his last academic publication in 1908. Over a quarter-century Wilson's idea of responsible leadership changed little, but his ideas of how it applied to American government changed markedly.

A responsible leader would both reflect and interpret public sentiment, devising policies addressing the problems of the day. He could not leap far ahead of public sentiment, and it was his task to explain policy to the public. The leader must generate political debate through which to stimulate public sentiments. Finally, the leader is accountable to the public for the success of his policies while opposition parties actively seek to capitalize on his failures.[4] In Wilson's initial view, circa 1880, there was no such leadership role possible in the American constitutional system.

Wilson's leadership ideal was British cabinet government. He had explored English government through Walter Bagehot's work, and he adopted those views wholesale.[5] With Bagehot in mind, Wilson was inspired to ask, to whom were American presidents and high officials responsible? Was Congress an instrument of responsible leadership?

Congressional Government

As a senior at Princeton Wilson wrote "Cabinet Government in the United States," published after his graduation. Five years later he developed those ideas in *Congressional Government.* There Wilson argued that Congress fails the key requirement of a representative government by not conducting the public business in full and open debate. "Nothing can be more obvious than the fact that the very life of free, popular institutions is dependent upon . . . open discussions." Congress "legislates with no real discussion of its business." Wilson charged that real legislative work was done within "irresponsible committees." Government authority had concentrated in Congress and that meant "government by the Standing Committees of Congress."[6] Controlling the allocation of committee memberships and congressional business was the speaker, "a constitutional phenomenon of the first importance."[7] He controlled the invisible work of the committees: "He who appoints those Committees is an autocrat of the first magnitude."[8] What of the president and department heads? They are irresponsible to the people for either policies or their effects.

Contrary to American practice, he said, responsible leadership should be entrusted to interpret the public's sentiments and needs. Wilson observed that "the ear of the leader must ring with the voices of the people," reflecting and fulfilling their will.[9] The post-bellum presidency was a diminished role; its incumbents neither heard the people nor formulated policy. In *Congressional Government* he wrote: "That high office has fallen from the first estate of dignity because its power has waned; and its power has waned because the power of Congress has become predominant."[10]

To create responsibility in American government Wilson would graft cabinet government onto the U.S. system. He said the choice facing us is between congressional and parliamentary government. The former is government by committees, and the latter "is government by a responsible Cabinet Ministry."[11] To achieve the latter, Wilson would require presidents to choose their cabinets from among the members of Congress. He envisioned making cabinets "responsible ministries" that would "form the policies of their parties" that would be debated in Congress.[12]

Wilson was conflicted about his goals as he began college teaching. His scholarship critically appraised the American constitutional system, arguing the necessity for change to achieve responsible government. The Constitution on paper was not in fact the current system of governance. He wrote that while we Americans were "worshipping" our Constitution, "it has slipped away from us" to be replaced by congressional supremacy.[13] He aspired to bring responsible leadership into American practice; his *primary* ambition would be "to take an active, if possible a leading, part in public life."[14] Wilson began teaching and writing "to contribute . . . studies in the philosophy of our institutions, not the abstract and occult, but the practical and suggestive, philosophy which is at the core of our governmental methods." The goal was to write "with such skill and such plenitude of proof that it shall be seen that I have succeeded and that I have added something to the resources . . . upon which statecraft must depend."[15]

Could he fulfill that goal as a professor, writing about politics and nurturing future leaders? Teaching at Bryn Mawr, a women's college, only heightened his frustration. Wilson was not forward-looking about women's education or women's suffrage. He wrote in his diary that teaching "young women . . . on the history and principles of politics is about as appropriate and profitable as would be lecturing to stone-masons on . . . fashion in dress."[16] Perhaps his writing alone could influence the political world, but there was another stumbling block to his search for influence. His critique of congressional government implied the need for constitutional amendment to achieve cabinet government. That was the idea of a dreamer and not a practical statesman.

Constitutional Government

In 1888 Wilson moved to Wesleyan University to teach male students who would vote and could be statesmen. At the same time he began to work out a practical formulation of responsible leadership, inspired by that most practical of presidents, Grover Cleveland. The Democrat Cleveland came to office in 1885 opposed to dominant Republican policies, particularly the protective tariff and the massive use of public revenues for patronage policies. Cleveland's 1887 annual message to Congress was unconventional; it focused on one issue, the protective tariff, as a "vicious, inequitable, and illogical source of unnecessary taxation." The message was so unusual that Cleveland had to justify it:

It has been the custom of the Executive . . . to annually exhibit to the
Congress . . . the general condition of the country, and to detail with
some particularity the operations of the different Executive
Departments. It would be . . . agreeable to follow this course . . . but I
am so much impressed with the paramount importance of the [tariff
question] . . . that I shall forego the addition of any other topic, and
only urge upon your immediate consideration the "state of the Union"
as shown in the present condition of our Treasury and our general
fiscal donation, upon which every element of our safety and
prosperity depends.[17]

Wilson saw this message as "the only voice of courage and decision that had
been heard upon that matter in a generation."[18] He observed, "Mr. Cleveland
had given his party a distinct, unmistakable policy with which to go to the country in the presidential campaign of 1888."[19] Cleveland's return to office in 1893
gave Wilson further evidence of an emerging responsible leadership because of
Cleveland's consistency about the tariff. The Democrats, Wilson argued, returned to power because of Cleveland's clear stance on a controversial issue.
Thus in Wilson's view, Cleveland's performance approximated responsible leadership. However, in his second term Cleveland was also embroiled in currency
issues that split his party, isolating him, and making him increasingly negative
and defensive. Wilson also concluded that after 1893 Cleveland was increasingly
"a President without a party."[20]

Cleveland's unusual policy initiatives, his campaigning on the tariff for reelection, and even his failures that left him "without a party" suggested to Wilson that the American constitutional system was changing toward more prominent and responsible executive leadership. Cleveland did not create a functional
equivalent of cabinet government because he did not bridge executive and legislative activities.[21] But Wilson thought that Cleveland revived the presidency by
pushing it to the center of American politics.[22]

With his new estimation of the presidency, Wilson's scholarship could be
more relevant to statesmen because he could address problems of government
without prescribing constitutional change.[23] In *Constitutional Government*,
based on lectures delivered the year before at Columbia University, he described
the presidency becoming a role exhibiting responsible leadership as a result of
the evolution of government's institutions: "Governments are living things
[and] . . . have their natural evolution and are one thing in one age, another in
another."[24] Cleveland's forceful use of the presidency was idiosyncratic in that it

was shaped by his character. Wilson understood that Cleveland's leadership was a consequence of personality rather than a theory of leadership, but he thought that the emergence of responsible leadership in the presidency was systematic, caused as much by contextual developments as the incumbent's personal characteristics. Responsible leadership would be a synthesis between "the man who occupied the office and . . . the circumstances that surrounded him."[25] In that light, developments at the end of the nineteenth century, in particular the war with Spain, led Wilson to expect an institutionalization of the presidency's importance, placing it "at the front of our government, where our own thoughts and the attention of men everywhere is centered upon him."[26]

Wilson also argued the presidency's enlarged importance would lead to a new relationship between presidents and political parties, making the incumbent a "unifying force in our complex system, the leader both of his party and of the nation."[27] He wrote that presidents are now inescapably party leaders, essentially turning upside down the party period's relationship between party and the president. The president has the nation's attention and leads public opinion. He is the only individual who stands for the whole party, but it is not merely as an organization man that he leads the party. Rather, he is the party's "vital link of connection with the thinking nation," and the people expect the president to interpret the public's sentiments.[28] In turn, the president as interpreter of public sentiment must also be a legislative leader, responsible for his party's legislative work.

This evolved president, Wilson saw, was "at liberty, both in law and conscience, to be as big a man as he can." And he had little fear of an energized president overwhelming constitutional government. Should his leadership lead "Congress to be overborne by him . . . it will be from no lack of constitutional powers on its part, but only because the President has the nation behind him, and Congress has not."[29]

The Limits of Presidential Leadership

Yet Wilson cautioned, there were "illegitimate means by which the President may influence" Congress. These included using patronage to affect legislation and unilateralism circumventing Congress. Among "illegitimate means" Wilson also included political demagoguery, using rhetorical appeals to rouse the public against Congress. Among contemporary politicians prone to such excesses, Wilson counted William Jennings Bryan and Theodore Roosevelt. Bryan he thought was a leader who grasped the problems of the time but had "no mental rudder" to properly guide his leadership.[30] Theodore Roosevelt's propensity for self-promotion and unilateralism, he thought, crossed the line to "illegitimate means." He objected to the numerous commissions Roosevelt created without congressional warrant and his appeals to the public on controversial issues. In this view, what Roosevelt lacked was an ability to interpret the public's anxieties into policy through legislative leadership.[31] Wilson quipped that Roosevelt attempted to wield "all the power that anybody had ever had anywhere."[32]

Across the quarter-century of Wilson's changing view of the presidency, his conception of what constituted responsible leadership remained stable, and cabinet government remained for him the expression of such leadership. His reevaluation of the presidency depended on his seeing it as stimulating a functional equivalent to cabinet government, creating links of responsibility among parties, Congress, and the electorate.

Rejecting Roosevelt's forceful public leadership, Wilson prescribed restraints on overweening presidential action while still encouraging responsible leadership.[33] His solution to the problem was weak institutionally but extraordinarily convenient for his own ambitions. It was the president's personal qualities—character—that would restrain demagoguery. The practical leader, Wilson wrote, "must perceive the direction of the nation's permanent forces. . . . But he cannot . . . do more."[34] He cannot interpret what is not there to begin with. The leader must be principled but also realize that he cannot move any faster than he would be followed.[35] He must be respectful of traditional institutions and modest in his principled claims. As Terry Bimes and Stephen Skowronek observe: "With the promise of institutional solution dispelled and enthusiasm for popular power building anew, Wilson could do little more than repackage the old patrician values of character, balance and refinement and present them as a methodology for guiding leaders thought the inevitable process of 'interpretation.'"[36] In 1908 Wilson wrote, "The country will demand . . . not . . . astute politicians, skilled and practiced in affairs, but . . . a man such as it can trust, in character, in intention, in knowledge of its needs in perception of the best means by which those needs may be met, in capacity to prevail by reason of his own weight and integrity."[37]

This formula for responsible, *constrained* leadership was weak tea in the face of large characters like William Jennings Bryan and Theodore Roosevelt. However, Wilson's formula bolstered his confidence in his fitness for great leadership. He was not a skilled and practiced politician but was a man of knowledge who understood the nation's needs, the best ways to achieve them, and who had a "capacity to prevail by reason of his own weight and integrity." Thinking back to the double-cross described above, by "integrity" Wilson did not mean unbending allegiance to one's words and positions, an old-fashioned integrity that could be seen in a leader like Grover Cleveland. Wilson's idea of integrity was conditioned by the tactical shifts in positions and allegiances necessitated by the leader's work of moving the public in the direction dictated by the nation's needs, as perceived by the leader. To be successful, the leader "must not be impracticable. . . . This is a matter of expediency, not of direction."[38]

"Princeton's Prime Minister"[39]

Wilson's first opportunity for important leadership occurred in 1902 when he was named Princeton's president. Transforming the university made Wilson a national eminence. He had joined Princeton's faculty in 1890, finding it not much changed from his own undergraduate days at the sleepy Presbyterian college. A board of trustees dominated by clerics still made faculty appointments, and the president, Reverend Francis Patton, was an inept administrator. Low admission standards assured sufficient enrollment, and the faculty's quality was decidedly mixed, with few scholars of note and a preponderance of aging clerics. Faculty appointments were influenced by alumni pressure, favoritism, and nepotism. Wilson's own appointment to the chair of jurisprudence and political economy was a result of lobbying from his fellow 1879 alumni.[40] But deciding to work against the grain at Princeton, Wilson quickly became a leader of those faculty members seeking to reform the university.

In 1902 Princeton's trustees gently pushed Patton aside and named Wilson to be the university's first nonclerical president. It was a momentous change for the university and would also be transformative for Wilson. Up to then he had theorized about leadership. Now he would exercise it.

Reforming Princeton

Wilson described his new job as "hard work . . . for Princeton is to be handled at a crisis in her development."[41] Before his inauguration he presented to the trustees his agenda for reforming Princeton. First was the necessity for strengthening the faculty through recruitment, the reduction of classroom hours, and increased salaries. The end product of an improved faculty, he noted, would be expanded research: "A true university is a place for research as well as instruction." His second goal was curricular reform to achieve a coordinated organization of courses. Third, a new method of instruction was required, a modified form of the English tutorial system. Fourth, departments and schools must be strengthened. Added faculty members were necessary in history, economics, and biology. The school of science required an increased budget, and new schools of electrical engineering and jurisprudence should be established as well as a museum of natural history. Additionally, Princeton's graduate school would be established at the heart of the university so as to "stimulate and set the pace for the whole University." To achieve all this, Wilson aimed to raise the unprecedented sum of $12,500,000 as an addition to Princeton's existing $4,000.000 endowment.[42]

Arthur Link observes that, had one "studied carefully Wilson's career as president of Princeton University," he or she "might have forecast accurately the shape of things to come during the period when Wilson was president of the United States."[43] He writes:

> In both cases he drove so hard, so flatly refused to delegate authority, and broke with so many friends that when the inevitable reaction set in he was unable to cope. . . . His refusal to compromise in the graduate school controversy was almost Princeton's undoing; his refusal to compromise in the fight in the Senate over the League of Nations was the nation's undoing.[44]

Link's observation prompts us to examine Wilson's Princeton presidency for insights into his successes as well as his failures. His experience at Princeton also sheds light on the evolution of Wilson's political ideas. He entered the presidency as a stout conservative whose ideas were reinforced by wealthy alumni, donors, and trustees.[45] But eight years later, during his gubernatorial campaign, his views were increasingly progressive.

Accounts of Wilson's Princeton presidency focus primarily on the related controversies over the quadrangle plan and the location of the new graduate school complex. However, as we see in the extent of his 1902 agenda for reform, Wilson's presidential "platform" entailed more than those causes of intense conflict. In his early successes, as much as in his later failures, Wilson exhibited qualities of leadership that reappeared later in his governorship and presidency.

Wilson was one of a small group of university presidents transforming the nineteenth-century college into the modern university, among them Charles W. Eliot at Harvard, Daniel Coit Gilman at Johns Hopkins, Nicholas Murray Butler at Columbia, and William Rainey Harper at Chicago. Yet, Wilson's educational philosophy was distinct from his peers' views. In contrast to those other universities' rapid development of technical specialization and graduate training and increasingly diverse student populations and faculties, Wilson at Princeton sought reforms to immerse undergraduates in a humanistic culture. Princeton's heart, he thought, was in undergraduate education pursued through close faculty-student interaction in a communal, Protestant Christian residential setting. That education would be highly attentive to literature, meaning imaginative and creative work broadly understood. The end goal of Princeton's education for Wilson was the formation of men who would lead, men of learning, intuition, and ease of communication. In his inaugural address, he envisioned Princeton's education "for the minority who plan, who conceive, who superintend, who mediate between group and group and must see the wide stage as a whole."[46]

Curriculum reform was first on Wilson's agenda, to be followed by a strengthened faculty and then reform of Princeton's social organization.[47] Bliss Perry, a friend and colleague, said Wilson was a man of "superb confidence" but crossed into "tragic overconfidence" later in his Princeton presidency. Perry also observed that "on the larger issues of his policy in that office, I believe him to have been right."[48]

Reforming Princeton's Curriculum

During 1901 a faculty committee that included Wilson proposed curriculum reform to attack "the low state of Princeton education," but President Patton blocked the changes.[49] Patton's obstreperousness triggered a rebellion against him that put Wilson into the presidency.[50] President Wilson renewed the effort for curricular reform, forming a new planning committee, which he chaired. It reported its recommendations in April 1904, and in faculty meetings considering the reforms, Wilson served as prime minister, advocating his reform agenda.[51]

The committee proposed a structured first two years of study followed by concentration on a major. The normal semester course load would be reduced to five courses, each meeting for three hours per week. An honors designation was created, giving meritorious seniors a seminar and research experience. During faculty debates about the plan Wilson's temper occasionally flared, but he was quick to apologize and smooth ruffled feathers. In one meeting Wilson responded angrily to criticism from Professor George M. Harper but later caught up with Harper and apologized for his intemperance.[52] Henry Bragdon describes Wilson as open to counsel throughout the process and "eminently democratic."[53] After the faculty approved the reform, Wilson told his wife: "It is not . . . exactly the scheme I at the outset proposed, but it is much better."[54] His leadership in curriculum reform was flexible. The rigidity that famously characterized him later in the quadrangle plan and graduate school was absent. He accommodated diverse views and respected colleagues' disciplinary expertise. The recollection of Bliss Perry is informative. He recalled Wilson as warm, desirous of conversation, but perhaps a bit reclusive.[55]

Wilson's next goal was to change the pedagogy common at Princeton and other American universities. A Princeton degree was not necessarily a reward for scholarship. Courses were lecture-based, thin of content, and too often little was expected of students. The historian James Axtell observes: "Unfortunately too many faculty members were complicitous and cultivated a 'take-it-or-leave-it' attitude."[56] To correct the situation, Wilson sought a variant of the British tutorial system. Guided by "preceptors," a student would be set on a course to educate himself through reading, recitations of ideas, and writing. As distinct from the curriculum reform, Wilson presented his preceptorial plan in final form to the trustees and faculty. Yet the proposal was no surprise to either body. Wilson had long advocated tutorials, and once he presented the plan he met with departments and faculty groups to win support for it. In this process Wilson reshaped his ideas in response to faculty comment. Hardin Craig writes, "It was easy to see that his original ideas had undergone some modification through the advice of the faculty."[57]

There would be fifty preceptors, a faculty rank below professorial positions appointed on a five-year contract. Wilson initially sought to endow the program, but failing that he used smaller donations and a commitment from an alumnus to underwrite any shortfall. He was sufficiently confident that the trustees would adopt his plan that the recruitment of preceptors began prior to its approval in June 1905.[58] Wilson delegated recruitment to senior colleagues and their departments. The academic departments recruited and approved candidates before recommending them to Wilson.[59] Through these new positions and decentralized recruiting, Wilson built faculty support for the preceptorship scheme.

Wilson also moved unilaterally to rid the faculty of some of its worst performers. The trustees gave him authority for "reorganizing the teaching force to create such vacancies . . . as he may deem for the best interest of the University."[60] After removal of several professors, he also presumed that the power of removal inferred a power of appointment. He aggressively sought out senior scholars at other universities, often committing to appointments before the trustees voted approval.[61] He aimed to build "departments . . . at the very front, not only in scholarship, but in influence and leadership."[62] Faculty support for Wilson's early reforms can be seen in an address to alumni by Professor George M. Harper, the same colleague who Wilson had dressed down at one of the faculty meetings on the reform plan. Harper said that Wilson gave Princeton a new life, ending "easygoing methods. . . . Now it is the strenuous life, the rigorous ideal." He praised the new preceptors as instilling in students "obligation to live up to the highest ideal," and he added that Wilson "had the enthusiastic support of all the faculty and the undergraduates, and he trusted he would receive that of the alumni."[63]

We can see Wilson's idea of interpretive leadership in his Princeton presidency. He had important constituencies whose views he sought to represent and interpret, the alumni foremost. He worked assiduously to draw their support, traveling the circle of Princeton alumni groups to explain his conception of the university and show how his agenda for reform would make Princeton more illustrious. Wilson also used the visits with alumni groups for more broadly publicizing Princeton's (and his own) stature. Consider his travel to alumni meetings in upper New York State in 1904. At Albany he spoke to alumni and then addressed a meeting of the Presbyterian Union on the subject of "The University and the Church." A day later he spoke to Syracuse alumni followed by a public address at Syracuse University on "True Patriotism."[64]

Wilson's work drew national attention. The *New York Times* editorialized that the tutorial reform was "perhaps the most radical change that any American university has ever made in its methods and organization."[65] With the close of the 1905–1906 academic year, Wilson was triumphant. The new curriculum and the preceptorial system were both successful. He had won over trustees, faculty, students, and alumni to his vision for Princeton, and he had become the best-known university leader in America. He was "Princeton's most valuable asset."[66]

Wilson became a name to be considered for national political leadership. In February 1906, in a speech at New York's Lotos Club, Colonel George Harvey, the conservative editor of *Harper's Weekly,* proposed Wilson for the 1908 Democratic presidential nomination.[67] He then put Wilson's picture on the cover of his magazine.[68] Harvey saw Wilson as an antidote to Bryanism, and Wilson's public stance against radical reform and Bryan made him a natural candidate for the Bourbon Democrats. Harvey assembled wealthy enthusiasts for Wilson, such as the utilities magnate Thomas Fortune Ryan and the Louisville publisher "Marse" Henry Waterson. The *Wall Street Journal* wrote, "People are proposing Woodrow Wilson . . . for the Democratic nomination for President" and lauded his program for business, applying "old fashioned morals to new-fashioned business."[69] Yet Wilson was not yet ready for political life. In 1906 he declined an offer from New Jersey's machine Democrats to stand for a U.S. Senate seat.[70]

Remaking Princeton's Culture

At the height of his success Wilson took a turn that would alienate his Princeton constituencies and undermine his position. Having strengthened Princeton, he now sought to transform it. He envisioned a Princeton composed of residential learning communities, called "quadrangles" (or the "Quad Plan"), including students of all four years, a resident master, and preceptors. Each quadrangle would create " a sort of family life [for students] . . . as comrades at meals and in many daily activities—the upper classes ruling and forming the lower, and all in constant association with members of the Faculty."[71] Like the tutorial initiative, this plan was inspired by the ancient British universities. The plan was also Wilson's response to an acute problem in Princeton's undergraduate life.

Princeton's thirteen private eating clubs dominated undergraduate life. These intensely selective clubs enrolled about three-quarters of the upper classmen. They, in turn, spurred formation of underclass clubs, preselecting students for the eating clubs. In 1907 the Princeton student paper wrote about the club system that the university was "face to face with a social crisis."[72] In December 1906 Wilson gave the trustees a plan for reorganizing student life. It envisioned the university taking over the senior club buildings and incorporating them within new quadrangles. The trustees formed a study committee with Wilson as chair, and in June 1907 gave their approval to the plan. The trustees also gave to Wilson discretion to implement it. On June 24 Wilson gave an address in which he made the plan public. Nothing, he said, could bring more distinction to Princeton, "throughout the university world" than the reform of the clubs into the Quad Plan.[73]

Despite the trustee's approval, Wilson's initiative had two potentially fatal defects. First, it threatened the social privileges and loyalties of powerful alumni and donors. As word of the plan to abolish the clubs spread, opposition mounted. Second, key Princeton faculty members objected to the plan because they saw the costly proposal preempting the standing commitment to build a graduate school complex. Dean Andrew West of the graduate school and his trustee ally, ex-President Grover Cleveland, were most prominently opposed. Consequently, other trustees had second thoughts about the Quad Plan. The plan was tangled with the graduate school not only because it competed for resources but also because Wilson sought to integrate the graduate school complex with undergraduate quadrangles. He envisioned graduate students and undergraduates mingling to enrich the undergraduate educational experience. However, Dean West sought to build a graduate quadrangle at some remove from the undergraduate campus, seeking a preserve of higher studies, protected from undergraduate hurly-burly. Underlying it all, Wilson saw West threatening to undermine him if Wilson did not master him first.[74]

In late 1907 the trustees reversed their approval of the Quad Plan.[75] Wilson felt betrayed, but the cause of his failure lay substantially in his own leadership. As much as he had accurately interpreted his constituents' views in the curricular and preceptorial reforms, he failed as an interpretive leader with his Quad Plan and the subsequent graduate school imbroglio. The Quad Plan threatened Princeton's social order. It was too radical a solution for what was widely agreed to be a problem of undergraduate life. He had not prepared his constituents through consultation, and he delivered the plan to the trustees as if out of the blue. After the plan's approval, Wilson's stance was unbending about its implementation.[76] Even after the trustees reversed themselves, Wilson continued the fight against what he now described as the undemocratic privileges of Princeton's club system. Failing to hold the trustees' support, he went public to win alumni support.

Wilson was confident his plan was the only solution to Princeton's intractable problems. He wrote to an acquaintance, "I cannot help thinking that it will be found necessary in the end to do substantially what I proposed."[77] In addresses to alumni groups and educators during fall 1907 and early 1908 he advocated his ideas articulately and passionately. Wilson called opposition to the Quad plan undemocratic. He explained to an alumni group that a major goal of university education was for students to develop "democratic thinking," which he defined as thinking everyone was on the same plane with "no favor for anybody." Additionally, to achieve that goal "you must organize the life of your Universities also in that spirit." But the clubs forced young men into stereotyped conformity to fit in. They created status differences, and they separated students' living conditions and their educational life. The "object is to unite these," which "cannot be done by the present system."[78]

The graduate school was the next of Wilson's great defeats. A graduate school with its own dean, Andrew West, was established in 1900. Wilson endorsed the graduate school as a priority for making Princeton a serious university, and in 1903 he reiterated his support for Dean West's graduate school plans, writing a fulsome preface to a fundraising brochure West prepared. [79] However, West's plans languished while Wilson pursued the curriculum reform, the preceptorial system, and then proposed the Quad Plan.

West's opposition to the plan fueled Wilson's suspicion that West threatened his authority.[80] The main issue between West and Wilson was over differing visions of the graduate school. Dean West's control of the existing graduate school was near total.[81] He had raised funds to lease an estate, Merwick, next to the campus and established there a residence for students and a faculty master along with seminar rooms. The lifestyle was formal, with the high point reached every Wednesday evening when Dean West appeared for dinner and formal dress was required.

Wilson thought the graduate school should be in the middle of campus, and its style should be plain rather than aristocratic. The conflict boiled up on campus, among the trustees and alumni, and finally in public from 1907 into 1910. The issue's outcome was decided through three substantial donations. In 1908 a quarter-million dollar bequest from the Swann estate seemed to settle the issue. It specified that the complex should be built on campus, and Wilson sought and gained trustee approval for its location. Over the next two years, West solicited two larger gifts through which he regained control of the graduate school's location. The first of these was half a million dollars from William Procter that specified that he must approve the site, and he was allied with West. Wilson requested that the trustees reject the gift but was denied. He realized his influence at Princeton was plummeting.

Wilson then offered to use the Swann gift for a graduate dormitory on campus while the Proctor gift built a graduate complex at a distance, but Proctor rejected that compromise. On December 22 Wilson wrote to Moses Pyne, the most powerful of the trustees, complaining that by accepting Proctor's gift the trustees had taken Princeton's guidance out of his hands, and he "had come to the end."[82] Several days later Wilson reiterated that position in a letter to all the trustees. He chose to take his stand on the principle of democracy in education, the same principle he embraced in losing the quad battle. He argued the forces of privilege defeated the Quad Plan and now distorted the grad school.

Wilson explained to a *New York Times* reporter that West, Proctor, and his opponents among the trustees represented "social exclusiveness" and wealth against "a life ordered upon a simpler plan under the domination of real university influence and upon the basis of real democracy."[83] But in the end, Wilson's campaign against the power of money was defeated by money. In May 1910 Isaac Wyman, an alumnus of 1848, left his estate of several million dollars to be used by West for the graduate school. Wilson told his wife, "We can't fight the dead. The game's up."[84]

Toward Progressivism

Until his gubernatorial campaign, Wilson's pronouncements on public issues were conservative. He opposed government regulation of business, woman suffrage, and labor unions. Bourbon Democrats and party bosses considered Wilson politically safe, and he also had the stature to attract respectable voters.[85] Yet Wilson's views quickly shifted during 1910, and he gave full voice to progressive reform in what John Gerring describes as his "embarrassingly swift transformation from Cleveland Democrat to Bryan Democrat."[86] No doubt that change was a pragmatic adaptation from what it took to get nominated to what it would take to get elected. However, his battles at Princeton foreshadowed those later liberal views. As class privilege and donor money weighed against his preferences, Wilson increasingly voiced democratic values. [87]

Several days after writing to Moses Pyne that he was unalterably opposed to the Proctor gift, Wilson spoke to the New Jersey Teacher's Association. His topic was the relationship of the citizen to government and the role of education. Wilson said, "Modern economic society means . . . the pooling of men's judgments and . . . consciences. And yet if modern economic society is going to be saved . . . it is . . . by the rising up of men who will say, 'I am indeed a part of this organization; but I will not allow my moral consciousness to be crushed by it.'"[88] Wilson seemed to be speaking for himself as a principled man against concentrated organizational pressures at Princeton.[89] Several days later he spoke at Franklin and Marshall College, warning that social distinctions and wealth were invading college life. Thus, he argued, "the college is going to lose its democratic feeling; and if the college loses its democratic feeling and . . . character, it shall have ceased to serve the nation."[90] The formerly conservative university president was becoming a champion of democracy.

Chapter Six

Prime Minister at Trenton

By spring 1910 Wilson's position at Princeton was no longer tenable.[91] Simultaneously the opportunity appeared for public leadership. Colonel Harvey, playing Wilson's political manager, plotted to gain for him New Jersey's Democratic gubernatorial nomination. Early in 1910 Harvey promoted Wilson to his friend James Smith Jr. Very much for reasons of his own needs, Smith agreed that Wilson would be an attractive candidate.[92] Harvey then secured from Wilson a promise that should the nomination be offered he "would give the matter very serious consideration."[93] With that, Smith built support for Wilson within the Democratic organization.

Of course, in the bargain Wilson had to pledge loyalty to Smith's party machine. Regarding policy the conservative Smith could be comfortable with Wilson's views. But, would Wilson be "safe" for the party organization? Wilson indirectly assured Smith of his reliability. Through a friend, John M. Harlan, Wilson sent the message that he "would be perfectly willing to assure Mr. Smith that I would not . . . set about 'fighting' . . . the existing Democratic organization."[94] Smith's backing for Wilson's nomination now branded him as the machine's man. Reform-minded Democrats used Wilson's record of public statements to depict him as opposed to economic reform and clean politics. Most telling perhaps, the reformers used Wilson's anti-labor views to alienate workers from his candidacy. Countering that threat, Wilson unabashedly denied his earlier statements. Asked by the editor of the *American Labor Standard* to explain his view of unions, he declared that the claim he was anti-union was a lie and that "I have always been the warm friend of organized labor."[95]

At the mid-September convention, reformers fought against Wilson and the bosses. However, the machine controlled sufficient delegates to secure the nomination for him. Then, in his acceptance speech to the convention, Wilson pivoted and signaled that to be the machine's man for the nomination did not mean he would run or govern as the machine's man. He said if elected he would enter office "with absolutely no pledge of any kind to prevent me from serving the people." He promised to strengthen New Jersey's corporation laws "by scrutinizing very carefully the enterprises she consents to incorporate." He promised that he would go to the voters pledging that Democrats would be "servants of no special group of men or of interests."[96] Then he added: "The time when you can play politics and fool the people has gone by; now it is a case of put up or shut up."[97]

In the words of New Jersey editor James Kerney, Wilson would now "preach a new political philosophy and . . . cast into the discard both Harvey and Smith."[98] In a series of speeches he called for the strictest scrutiny of businessmen and their corporations. He endorsed a strong public utility commission and primaries for the direct nomination of candidates.[99] The notable consistency that Wilson retained from his past statements concerned the means for policing business. He thought punishment for the misbehavior of business must focus on guilty executives and not firms. Yet consistency with his earlier views was not a mark of Wilson's campaign. He repeatedly claimed it was a lie that he had opposed unions.[100] He told the voters he was beholden to only the people and not the machine.[101]

To charges of inconsistency (or worse) with his past positions and his obligation to the Democratic bosses Wilson claimed a virtue in flexibility. He promised not to change his mind only if someone could assure that he would wake up in the morning seeing the world exactly as he had seen it the day before.[102] An excellent example of the candidate's political flexibility, as well as his astuteness about building a winning coalition, can be seen in his confrontation with, and then cooptation of, George L. Record. Record was leader of the Republican party's "New Idea" Progressives and a candidate for Congress. He distrusted Wilson's newly liberal positions, and when Wilson challenged any "politician in the state to a debate upon the public platform," Record accepted the challenge. That threw Wilson's camp into confusion. Knowledgeable Democrats saw him as too dangerous for Wilson to face in debate, and Wilson initially ignored Record's acceptance of the debate challenge.[103]

As a prosecutor and Jersey City corporation counsel, Record fought against corporate privileges and promoted public ownership of utilities. He had drafted reform legislation for the legislature and wrote for liberal newspapers.[104] While Republicans pummeled him for refusing to debate against Record, Wilson devised a semihonorable retreat from his initial offer.[105] He told Record that the Democratic State Committee had completely booked his available time for appearances. Instead, he suggested a public exchange of letters through which Record could pose questions to which Wilson would reply.[106]

Record gave Wilson nineteen questions in a letter published on October 17. The topics ranged from the powers of a public utility commission to Wilson's views on primaries and the direct election of U.S. senators. Toward the end of his letter, Record asked Wilson about the Democratic machine: "Do you admit that the boss system exists as I have described it? If so, how do you propose to abolish it?"[107] Wilson's response turned an embarrassment into victory. His letter was relatively short, and his answers to most of Record's questions were brief and affirmative. About physical evaluation of property for purposes of tax assessment of corporations, "Yes." About the popular election of U.S. senators, "Yes." Does the Democratic platform support primary election for candidates for all elective offices? "Yes, I so understand. If it does not, I do." Wilson promised to fully support progressive causes, be independent of control by any interests but the public, and remake his party as progressive. He said, "I regard myself as pledged to the regeneration of the Democratic party."[108]

The Wilson-Record epistolary debate was a turning point in the gubernatorial campaign. It brought Record to Wilson's side, along with the "New Idea" Republicans that Record led. Link writes that Wilson's answers to Record's letter finally placed him, "baggage and all, in the progressive camp; he had cut loose from every vestige of boss connection that once encumbered him from scaling the most formidable heights of progressivism."[109] Reformers took Wilson's letter as a statement of faith. James Kearney wrote that the letter "ended the campaign and branded Wilson as a genuinely upstanding radical."[110] The Reverend Joseph Howell wrote to Wilson: "I am a Republican; but have been fighting this very 'Boss System' . . . over our elections . . . for the last ten years . . . I am heartily glad that a Moses has arisen to lead New Jersey out of the mire of prostitution to 'Special Interests' . . . into the open field of civic righteousness."[111]

Curiously, machine Democrats and their Bourbon allies also applauded Wilson's letter as a bold political stroke strengthening his candidacy. Harvey wrote to Wilson effusively praising it as "the most effective political document I have ever read." He added that he had also read the letter aloud to Henry Watterson who was delighted with it.[112] What were Harvey and Smith to make of Wilson's newfound progressivism, and what of his pledge to Smith? In the short run to the election it was perhaps comforting for Harvey and Smith to think that Wilson's letter was merely tactical. On election day Wilson's margin of victory was the second largest in the state's history, and Democrats controlled the assembly by a large margin and were only a few seats short of a majority in the state senate.[113] The victory was so deep that it swept away Republicans in local offices across the state.

Wilson versus Smith

Wilson's promises and skills were tested immediately by James Smith's candidacy for an open U.S. Senate seat. He had served one term in the Senate from

1893 to 1899, and with Democrats again in control he reclaimed his seat.[114] Smith had a rival for the seat in the person of James E. Martine, the winner of the low-key, nonbinding primary election.[115] Martine was an easily dismissed, voluble Bryanite who had run in eleven prior elections without a victory.[116] However, he had won the primary for the U.S. Senate nomination, and popular selection of nominees was a central principle for Progressives. Would Wilson act on that principle on which he had campaigned, or would he repay Smith? Wilson additionally might have been attracted to supporting Smith's claim to get him to Washington and out of Trenton.

Wilson's conservative backers supported Smith while his progressive supporters pressured him to back Martine.[117] His initial impulse was to seek a respectable alternative, mentioning to advisers that he preferred John Hardin, a conservative corporation lawyer.[118] However, there was no room for finesse on this problem. Reformers of both parties demanded that he endorse Martine. Wilson's new assistant, Joseph Tumulty, had been Martine's manager in the primary, and he urged Wilson to support the primary victor.[119] In early December Wilson announced he could not support Smith because: "I know that the people of New Jersey do not desire Mr. James Smith, Jr., to be sent again to the Senate."[120]

Wilson's success in the subsequent campaign to defeat Smith and elect Martine exhibited the same means through which he would win his legislative agenda in 1911. Influencing legislators first required patronage. Wilson stood above that shabby work, giving Tumulty the patronage portfolio. Tumulty was a young Irish American attorney, active in reform politics in Jersey City and steeped in New Jersey's political customs. He also knew the rules of transactional bargaining while Wilson was a naïf about the trade-offs required by political deal making. Wilson did possess a strong political weapon in his rhetorical skill, and in the Senate fight Tumulty had Wilson deliver speeches in the districts of obstreperous legislators. "Certain legislators," he said, "cannot be made to fully realize the vital importance of this question in any other way than . . . a forcible presentment."[121] Consequently Wilson wrote a friend that his concerns were "Smith, Smith, Smith all the days through," and that his work in that regard would be "terribly plain spoken speechmaking."[122]

Although a neophyte, Wilson delivered a knockout blow to Smith and his minions. Beyond his speeches against Smith, Wilson met with Democratic legislators to convince them of the party's obligation to the primary's result. Tumulty also led Wilson through the cultural complexities of New Jersey politics. For example, he directed Wilson to visit Robert Davis, the Democratic boss of

Hudson County and a Smith supporter. Davis was elderly and ill, and Wilson's visit signaled a respect for the old boss that influenced his loyalists. Wilson then invited the Hudson County legislators loyal to Davis to Princeton to meet with him and won them over to Martine.[123]

On January 25, 1911, the New Jersey legislature elected Martine as the U.S. senator. The *New York Times* editorialized, "Wilson has won a victory for the decent people of New Jersey. He has strengthened the hands of the Governor and stiffened the back of the Legislature." The overall lesson to be drawn from the experience, wrote the *Times,* is: "Woodrow Wilson has demonstrated to the Nation that, bravely led, the Democratic Party may be trusted."[124] Having led the legislature to defeat Smith, Wilson also had the means to legislate his progressive agenda for New Jersey. In a few months he had gone from university president to successful reform governor. Observing Wilson from his reporter's perch, James Kerney thought that with Smith's defeat Wilson had become the greatest amateur politician of his time.[125]

The 1911 Legislative Agenda

Wilson became governor at a time of activist reform executives in American states. His reform stance, upsetting New Jersey's gubernatorial norm, was validated by the experiences of Theodore Roosevelt in New York, William S. U'Ren of Oregon, and Robert LaFollette of Wisconsin, among others.[126] During the 1911 legislative term Wilson initiated and passed into law a reform agenda that would impress the nation and lead him to the Democratic nomination for president. Early in the gubernatorial campaign Wilson had defined his stance as one of program and not party, stating in a campaign address: "We are not interested . . . in the success or failure of parties, but in the success or failure of policies."[127] In that same speech Wilson contrasted his view of executive leadership to that of his Republican opponent, Vivian Lewis. Lewis had promised he would be a "constitutional governor" of limited power and eschew legislative meddling. Wilson responded, if that is the definition of a constitutional executive, he promised to be an "unconstitutional Governor," doing "everything that is legitimate . . . that consists in the pressure of reason and persuasion to carry out all the things that we believe in."[128]

Wilson's inaugural address promised great change. He called for redress of the imbalance between employer and worker. He called for greater controls over the behavior of corporations chartered by the state and a public service commission to scrutinize utilities. Turning to political life, Wilson commended the initiative and recall reforms recently passed by Oregon and aimed at putting control of government in the people's hands. He called also for extending the primary election law to cover every office and demanded ballot reform to purify elections, taking the management of ballots away from the parties.[129] Wilson distilled his 1911 legislative agenda to four initiatives. They would be bills on workmen's compensation, public utilities regulation, primaries and election reform, and corrupt practices legislation. He developed an ad hoc legislative steering committee including Tumulty, several Democratic leaders of the legislature, and several other advisers. George Record drafted the election reform bill, and it was the first item on the governor's agenda introduced to the legislature.

The Democratic organization despised the electoral reform bill, and Smith's lieutenant James Nugent came to Trenton to lead the opposition. Yet, for all the heat of that battle, Wilson's "unconstitutional" legislative leadership undercut Nugent and the organization legislators. The governor's stance was prime ministerial, meeting with the Democratic caucus on two occasions to win over members to electoral reform and to hold the party to a central promise of its platform. This was the first time in New Jersey's history that a governor had met with a party caucus of the legislature. To protests from machine assemblymen that his presence violated separation of powers, Wilson claimed a privilege based in the governor's duty to recommend "such measures as he may deem expedient."[130] At his second meeting with the caucus, over the course of four hours, he persuaded the legislators to support his overall reform agenda as well as the electoral reform bill currently up for vote.[131] In mid-March the electoral reform bill passed the lower house and then the senate in April.[132]

Next, Wilson sent the corrupt practices bill to the assembly, also drafted by Record. It drew protest from the same sources opposing electoral reform. The bill aimed to regulate the behavior of party organizations, eliminating voting fraud and vote buying. Accompanied by ballot reform and primaries, the corrupt practices act threatened to nullify advantages held by the political machines. Again in the role of prime minister, Wilson led the fight. When several progressive Republicans who sought strengthening amendments blocked it in the Senate, Wilson directed Record to draft a revision that would satisfy them while fulfilling Wilson's goals. The revised bill passed the Senate unanimously. The next two bills were public utilities regulation and workers' compensation. These passed the legislature quickly, and by the middle of April Wilson had achieved all four reforms. Aside from these a number of other reform bills had been pushed through by a bipartisan group of progressive legislators, dealing with subjects as diverse as food inspection, school reforms, and factory inspection. At the end of the legislative session of 1911, on April 22, Wilson appeared in the legislature to "witness the concluding hours of the greatest reform legislature in the history of the state."[133]

Wilson's victories broadcast his reputation beyond New Jersey and fueled expectations of his candidacy for the 1912 presidential nominee. The popular magazine *World's Work* printed a profile of Wilson, saying: "No one can listen to [him] . . . without feeling that he is witnessing the beginning of a political revolution, and that its prophet and captain stands before him."[134] Wilson's subsequent month-long speaking trip to the South and West opened his national campaign, causing other potential candidates to begin organizing.[135] Before Wilson's departure, a Boston paper characterized the trip as aiming "to give the people a chance to 'size him up' as presidential timber."[136] Back at home, Wilson directed William F. McComb to open a New York City office to deal with contacts, financial issues, and publicity connected with his exploratory bid for the nomination.[137]

A brief article about Wilson's tour in *The Outlook,* a regular venue for Theodore Roosevelt's writing, exhibits Wilson's bipartisan appeal among contemporaries. It said:

> The programme of legislation secured under his leadership . . . has few parallels in American political history. The people . . . value a man of deeds as well as words, and, without regard to section or party, have done honor to Governor Wilson because he is Progressive not only in principle but also in achievement.[138]

Wilson's prime ministerial–like leadership in New Jersey during the 1911 session presumed, in effect, a Progressive Party. By defeating Smith Wilson divided Democrats and simultaneously reinforced the bond he had formed with the "New Idea" Republicans. His appeal crossed partisan lines, uniting Progressives in both parties. He said there was no one kind of Democrat or Republican; "they are progressives or standpatters, and there are standpatter Democrats as well as standpatter Republicans."[139]

Governor without the Majority

Wilson returned from the West in June 1911 to an executive office that was no longer prime ministerial. The legislature would not return to session until early 1912. Until then Wilson faced the dreariness of appointments and executive management. Yet, his political identity was now bound up with the crusade for political reform and not mundane administration. Shunning normalcy, in summer 1911 Wilson launched into another reform campaign. Leaving daily state business for Tumulty, Wilson promoted adoption of the commission form of government by New Jersey's cities. He went from city to city, passionately urging that progressive-minded citizens reform their local governments. As he said in Trenton: "We are here to discuss a matter of principle that concerns the city of Trenton, but we are really here discussing a transaction that concerns mankind. If America fails in the making of city government . . . to whom shall the men of the nations look?"[140] In Hoboken, Wilson said that the vote for commission reform would "illustrate . . . the impulses and the purposes, the vision and the hope of a great people."[141] Of Wilson's public rhetoric about city reform during that summer, Arthur Link writes, "He used his favorite device of elevating the local issue and expanding its importance into universal proportions."[142]

The thrust of Wilson's new crusade was against the same evil he had opposed in the Senate battle and afterward, the political machines. But this time the machines won. As the commission plan of city reform came to the vote in city after city it was defeated, opposed by the effective party organizations that it aimed to destroy. Wilson attributed the failure to the machines of both parties and called instead for rule by the people, saying: "There is only one instrument of effective self-government, and that is the instrument of public opinion."[143]

Defeated on city reforms, Wilson turned to yet another crusade. Looking toward the September primary and November legislative election, Wilson campaigned for progressive Democrats. He successfully supported the nomination of reform Democrats, but in the November general election the Democrats lost their assembly majority, and Republicans returned to power in both houses. This was James Smith's revenge. Even though Democrats drew more votes than normal in Republican areas, Smith led all the Democratic legislative candidates to defeat in populous, Democratic Essex County. Thus, Smith assured Wilson would be a prime minister without a parliamentary majority in 1912.[144]

During the 1911 legislative session Wilson asserted party leadership, controlled the Democratic caucus, *and* appealed to Republican Progressives.[145] But in the face of the new Republican majority, Wilson seemed disarmed. Given the bipartisan appeals of his 1911 agenda, he might have influenced the 1912 legislature with appeals for reform above partisanship, but he made no such effort. He proposed no new legislative goals. Nor did he attempt to lead the Democratic minority, making no appearances in the party caucus.

In sharp contrast with his 1911 message opening the session, Wilson's 1912 message focused on economy and efficiency. He called for creation of a commission to reorganize state government, and he proposed that state charitable and correctional institutions be placed under one board. Absent from the message were any hints of major legislation.[146] It was as if the person delivering the message was a different man than the governor who delivered the 1911 inaugural address. The 1912 session was an exercise in vetoes rather than legislative leadership. It was closer to Grover Cleveland's negative activism than Wilson's 1911 gubernatorial prime ministership. Wilson's attention turned to the presidential race and the national scene. He spent much of the first eight months of the year traveling to build support, leaving his staff strained to work on his campaign and tend to state government.

Flexible Ideas, Inflexible Process

Wilson, the academic leader and governor, was never particularly wedded to a specific idea or proposal. In both those roles his aims were transformational, and the exact content of the transformation could be negotiated, as with Princeton's new curriculum or the details of New Jersey's incorporation law. But his leadership required a process and a constituency within which Wilson's authority was unquestioned. He was a transformational leader who required a constituency that demanded transformation.

Wilson himself recognized that his leadership style required a supportive and approving constituency. In a gubernatorial campaign speech, he said: "I always think I am right, and although I try to be courteous to the men I differ from, I am always sure they are wrong; and if you make me governor, you may expect me to proceed upon [my] programme."[147] Yet by that self-description Wilson made himself sound more rigid then he would be in practice. The Wilson we have observed in early Princeton reforms and in the 1911 legislative session demonstrated accommodation and compromise *within* a context of broad support for his leadership and his agenda. That support enabled what Wilson understood as responsible, interpretive leadership. Losing support, as he had in the Quad Plan and in the 1912 legislative session, Wilson lost what he understood as a parliamentary vote of confidence.

Finally, we turn to the issue with which this chapter began. What does Wilson's "double-cross" of Smith tell us about his leadership style? It is a commonplace of popular political culture that the truth is the first casualty of political competition. Was Wilson, in the flexibility of his policies and commitments, merely a conventional politician? We gain insight on this matter by considering Lincoln's famous utterance, "My policy is to have no policy." Therein Lincoln meant flexibility is necessary for a politician with far-sighted goals. Similarly, Wilson's policy was one of great flexibility through the process of "interpretive leadership." His political expediency, as he called it, was a mechanism for adjusting his views to public moods and what he saw as the nation's great needs. Simultaneously, expediency protected Wilson from excesses of rigidity to which he was all too prone, particularly in the face of declining support.

Coincidently, Wilson's principle of expediency conveniently allowed him to shift ideas and policies when such shifts benefited him. John Morton Blum perfectly captured Wilson's principled flexibility, writing that he "believed in the principles of his campaign as soon as he began to preach them. Of his sincerity, although he moved with the wind, there can be no doubt."[148] Now the great question was, how would Wilson's leadership style and very limited political experience translate onto the national campaign stage and into the Progressive Era presidency?

"IT TAKES GRIT TO REMOVE GRIME." Promoting Wilson for the presidency, *Harper's* portrayed the governor as reformer of corrupted state government. (*Harper's Weekly*, November 11, 1911; provided courtesy of HarpWeek, LLC)

A Parliamentary Presidency: The Tariff, Bank Reform, and Anti-Trust

We know our task to be no mere task of politics but . . . whether we be able
to understand our time and the need of our people, whether we be indeed
their spokesman and Interpreter.
   Woodrow Wilson[1]

W oodrow Wilson had always yearned for a great public position. Since
   childhood he had imagined himself as a statesman. As an academic his
abiding concern was the possibility for responsible leadership in the American
system. Suddenly, machine politics and a quick conversion to progressivism
made the dream real.

Wilson did not think of himself as power seeking. Idealism fueled his ambition, allowing him to think of his presidential candidacy as above mere politics.
His idealism and austerity drew supporters because he seemed to make visible his
own "God-lashed energies . . . [and] contagious self-righteousness."[2] For Wilson,
the 1912 campaign was to be a struggle between his purity of purpose and his
opponents' dishonorable purposes. About the political opposition he wrote:

> The war upon me . . . is to be heartless. . . . For I am greatly feared.
> Every illegitimate force instinctively dreads the possibility of my
> becoming President. They know that I am "on to them" and that I can
> neither be fooled nor bought.[3]

Few presidential elections have been more complicated than the one in
1912.[4] Republicans feared their loss of the House in 1910 foreshadowed defeat in
1912. Seeing Taft's vulnerability, Theodore Roosevelt attempted to grab the nomination.[5] Failing that, he launched the Progressive Party as a vehicle for his candidacy. The split in the party gave the Democrats a prospect for their first presidential win in twenty years, and major figures sought the nomination. Senator

Chapter Seven

Oscar Underwood of Alabama and Ohio's Governor Judson Harmon represented the party's Southern and conservative voices. Speaker of the House Champ Clark appealed to agrarian interests, invoking the party's Jeffersonian ideals while appealing also to northern machine Democrats. The Alabaman Underwood undermined Wilson's own claim to Southern support, [6] while Clark threatened to edge out Wilson in the West[7] and Harmon controlled Ohio's delegates.

The campaign was tangled further by the Socialist Party's nomination of Eugene V. Debs for president.[8] Debs was a hero of the labor movement, former president of the American Railway Union, a stalwart of the Industrial Workers of the World, and leader of the 1894 Pullman strike. In November's vote Debs achieved the historical high-water mark for a party of the left in an American presidential election, drawing 6.4 percent of the popular vote total. Thus Wilson's route to the nomination and presidency wound through a crowded landscape of personalities and complex political conflicts. The election's full story is outside this chapter's focus, but to understand Wilson's leadership project, his possibilities, and the constraints he faced, we must briefly trace his route to victory.

A Candidate-Centric Campaign

The 1912 election was the first in which primaries played an important role for the nomination. Wilson began 1912 thinking he was ahead of other aspirants for the nomination but lost early primaries to Clark and Underwood. In several nonprimary states Clark's workers also outmaneuvered Wilson's for delegate selection. Wilson saw those setbacks not as a weakness of his candidacy but as proof of a conspiracy against him. He said to his closest advisor, Edward House: "Signs multiply that there is a combination of Clark, Underwood, and Harmon (with a division of territory quite after the manner of the industrial combinations) and the evidence that the combination is being financed from Wall St. falls short only of legal proof."[9]

Psychological interpretations of Wilson can offer important insights into his life and career.[10] However, the suspicions that he described to House and others are better understood as evidence of his sense of purpose rather than as data about his mental state. In his mind's eye, those opposing him were associated with special interests and dedicated to preserving a status quo that he threatened. Such grandiosity, in fact, would seem natural, and useful, to someone seeking the presidency at a time when Roosevelt had already made the office a stage for public performance. There was little difference between the grandiosity of Wilson's self-understanding and Theodore Roosevelt's. And it may be a key to understanding Taft's failure that he lacked certitude of his own special purpose in politics and history.

Indeed, the 1912 election was different than past presidential elections in that candidates were at center stage and not the parties. More than Republican versus Progressive versus Democrat, the race was a battle between Roosevelt's "New Nationalism" and Wilson's "New Freedom." Earlier presidential elections saw great army-like parties mobilizing their forces.[11] There had been earlier glimmerings of candidate prominence: Cleveland in 1892, Bryan in 1896, and Roosevelt in 1904. But in 1912 four distinctive nominees promoted different visions of American political and economic development.[12] Even Taft's personal resignation about the contest, along with his call for saving American institutions, was a self-dramatizing stance. Thus Wilson's crusade of virtue in 1912 was part of a larger drama of novel candidates strutting upon the political stage. That Wilson identified his opponents with malign forces was consistent with an election where candidates personified sharply different approaches to reform and governance.[13]

Seeking the nomination during his second year as governor, Wilson was not initially a compelling candidate. His reforms in New Jersey brought him a national reputation, but he had little to say about the pressing economic issues of the day. His accomplishments at Trenton were largely reforms of government process. But on the national stage his support for the progressive verities of the referendum, initiative, and recall (reversing his earlier, pregubernatorial stand) did not differentiate him from Clark. Wilson could also appear weak because he would quickly retreat from policy positions that drew criticism. He modified his endorsement of the referendum and recall when supporters in Virginia criticized his stance.[14] He also attacked the "money trust," reaching out to Bryanites, but when criticized by some Democrats in New York's financial circles for his "radical" language, he softened his tone.

Wilson's Advisers

A limited grasp of the era's central economic issues disadvantaged Wilson in the fight for the nomination. "The trusts," the organization of business and banking, questions of economic scale and regulation, and the tariff were subjects about which he was poorly informed. Arthur Link writes that "Wilson's appeal had been

Chapter Seven

moralistic and idealistically earnest, but it rarely touched upon the fundamental economic problems . . . demanding solution."[15] Without a clear message about those issues he could not differentiate himself from his opponents or win William Jennings Bryan's approval.[16] It was revealing of Wilson's weakness that Bryan's brother, Charles, wrote Wilson that while he "made a pleasant impression" during his summer 1911 speaking tour, he had better "take occasion to make another speech or two and take the people's side on two or three other questions."[17]

Wilson was limited both by his political inexperience and his disinterest in economics. He had run in only one election and was governor for less than two years. His earlier academic interests had inclined toward cultural understandings of politics. If he was to win the nomination and compete for the presidency, Wilson needed guides to supply the political savvy and policy substance required for his 1912 candidacy.

Political Expertise

Wilson's campaign organization began in spring 1911 with a small group of Southern lawyers and journalists transplanted to New York City. William McCombs, an Arkansas-born graduate of Princeton and Harvard law school, ran the campaign office, raised campaign funds, and began a publicity operation.[18] Later, William McAdoo, another Southern lawyer and businessman, brought into the organization important contacts in the financial community. Those two vied for control, and McCombs's personal instability marginalized him while McAdoo emerged on top. McAdoo became secretary of the treasury in 1913 while McCombs was disappointed in his hope for a cabinet position and served as chairman of the Democratic National Committee.

The person with greatest personal influence with Wilson was the elusive "Colonel" Edward M. House.[19] He was a wealthy Texan with extensive contacts among Democratic leaders, including a close relationship with William Jennings Bryan. House sought to be a king's counselor and chose Wilson as a potential "king." He introduced himself to Wilson in October 1911, conveying the message that important Texas Democrats doubted Wilson's loyalty to past Democratic presidential candidates. House asked Wilson to send him "a line in regard to the matter so that I may inform Senator Culbertson and our friends in Texas generally."[20] Later House wrote to Wilson with a key guaranteeing his access to the candidate, telling Wilson that he was having some success moving Bryan from support for Champ Clark to backing Wilson.[21]

House remained outside the campaign organization even as he became Wilson's closest male friend and trusted adviser. He guided the candidate on strategy and networked for him with party leaders, but at the opening of the 1912 Democratic convention House left the country and was absent during Wilson's end-game struggle for the nomination. After returning from Europe, House helped to resolve friction between McCombs and McAdoo over their respective roles in the campaign and continued his role as personal adviser to Wilson.[22] After the election he became what we would today call the head of the president-elect's transition team.

Policy Expertise

President Wilson would accomplish major policy initiatives on the tariff, banking, and trusts between 1913 and 1915. Yet at the point of winning the nomination he had little knowledge of those issues. His early campaign speeches were vague, attacking the "interests" but lacking policy specifics. He was "searching about for some great issue to carry to the people."[23] The candidate needed advice, and he received advice from many sources, but Louis Brandeis emerged as the influence shaping Wilson's economic ideas.

In 1912 Brandeis was a widely known and sharp critic of business concentration, particularly railroad consolidation. The Boston lawyer was admired and feared as an intellectual powerhouse of progressive economic reform. Eric Goldman observes his "thinking roamed . . . to the connections between law and economics and between economics and democracy."[24] Jonathan Daniels, a North Carolina progressive, and Wilson's secretary of the navy, saw him as a "reformer who knew the bottom facts of every industry. . . . He became *the* authority . . . all progressive movements looked to him for light."[25] Before 1912 Brandeis identified with Republican insurgents. He was close to Senator Robert LaFollette (R-WI), advised Gifford Pinchot during the Pinchot-Ballinger controversy, and was called on by Roosevelt to advise on regulatory legislation.[26] But Brandeis saw in Wilson "certain qualities indispensable to the solution of our problems."[27] He told LaFollette, "Those Progressives who do not consider themselves bound by party . . . ought to give Wilson thorough support."[28] Additionally, Brandeis saw Roosevelt's "New Nationalism," and its embrace of business concentration, as the wrong path to reform. He also feared that Roosevelt's Bull Moose movement would divide progressives and reelect Taft.[29]

Brandeis wrote to Wilson in early August praising his acceptance speech and particularly his remarks about the tariff. Incidentally, David Houston, an economist introduced to him through Edward House, had tutored Wilson about the tariff.[30] Wilson met Brandeis for the first time in an afternoon of conversation at Wilson's summer home. Brandeis later wrote to his brother that Wilson was "strong, simple, serious, open-minded, eager to learn and deliberate."[31] And Wilson found in Brandeis an eager tutor. Thereafter Wilson's views on economic issues gained substance and a Brandeisian flavor. However on a crucial point Wilson would differ with his adviser. Brandeis was scathing on the topic of bigness in business while Wilson remained more sanguine about large-scale enterprises.[32]

The Issues

As a Princeton academic, Wilson's comments on business issues focused on the misdeeds of businessmen rather than problems related to the concentration and behavior of firms. It was the businessman who should be punished for misbehavior and not the firm. Many Democrats shared this view that business policy was ultimately a question of morality more than a matter of economic efficiency.[33] On the other hand, Roosevelt defended business concentration as a natural development and called for its regulation. Roosevelt's commitment to federal certification and regulation of trusts strengthened after 1909.[34] Speaking at the Progressive Party's convention, Roosevelt offered something like a federal licensing scheme for trusts: "A national industrial commission should be created . . . to regulate and control all the great industrial concerns engaged in inter-State business."[35] A day after Roosevelt's speech, Wilson gave his acceptance speech and had little to offer about trusts and business concentration but a repetition of the Democratic platform's call for strengthening anti-trust laws.[36]

> While competition cannot be created by statutory enactment, it can
> . . . be revived in changing the laws and forbidding the practices that
> killed it, and by exacting laws that will give it heart and occasion again.
> We can arrest and prevent monopoly.[37]

Brandeis's influence on Wilson was soon apparent. Wilson gave a Labor Day address that critiqued Roosevelt's ideas about trusts and fleshed out his own ideas. The problem, he said, with Roosevelt's idea for a commission to oversee trusts was that it would join government and big business: "When once the government regulates the monopoly, then monopoly will have to see to it that it regulates the government." Wilson proposed instead to protect competition with regulations to prevent monopolizing behaviors by business. Competition cannot be enforced by law, he admitted, but laws can prevent the kinds of business behaviors that destroy it: "Remedial legislation will so restrict the wrong use of competition that the right use of competition will destroy monopoly."[38]

In late September Brandeis sent Wilson a memorandum on the trust question to develop further his differences with Roosevelt's position. Brandeis wrote: "You have asked me to state what the essential difference is between the Democratic Party's solution of the Trust Problem and that of the New Party; and how we propose to 'regulate competition.'" Brandeis explained the Sherman Act could be revised to make it more effective, leading to clear direction for the federal courts. Finally, he said that a commission should be created to investigate business behavior and supply information to the justice department. But Brandeis meant the commission to have no regulatory power.[39]

Banking and currency reforms were also high on the progressive agenda. Like "the trusts," this issue fit into the progressive moral framework of the big business interests versus the people. Among the fundamental problems needing to be remedied was the financial system's instability. The financial panic of 1907 caused banking failures and severe restrictions of credit, and the solution depended on J. P. Morgan's ability to leverage sufficient credit into the banking system to end the panic.[40] Across the political spectrum it was agreed the banking system had to be restructured and the currency made more elastic to meet changing business conditions.

However, while there was agreement about the need for reform, there was little agreement over *what* reform was needed. In 1908 Senator Nelson Aldrich (R-RI) chaired a National Monetary Commission that proposed a privately controlled central banking system, the so-called national reserve association. The association would establish privately owned regional branches to hold the reserves of commercial banks. The branches would set discount rates on interbank borrowing and issue bank notes based on gold reserves and commercial paper. Directors of the regional banks, in turn, would constitute the board of the national association. For Wall Street and standpat Republicans, the Aldrich plan was the optimal solution to the nation's financial dilemma.[41] The 1912 Democratic platform rejected the Aldrich plan, opposing both private control and centralization of the banking system. The platform favored a decentralized banking system with federal government funds to be deposited not in a few "favored" banks but distributed widely through competitive bidding by national and state banks. In fact, what the platform revealed was that, while Democrats were united in opposing the Aldrich plan, they were not united in supporting any single alternative to it.[42]

Wilson said little about banking in his acceptance speech. He noted that no "mere bankers' plan would meet" the nation's requirements, meaning the Aldrich plan was unacceptable. Then, he promised to consult widely to gain a range of ideas about what ought to be included in banking reform, admitting he did "not know enough about this subject to be dogmatic about it."[43] In his Labor Day speech he stressed that reforms should not put public power in the hands of private experts: "What I fear . . . is a government of experts."[44] In subsequent speeches he returned to the relationship between democratic values and banking issues. On September 20 he called for an expandable, flexible currency to enable business prosperity, and he reiterated reform should not place power in narrow, expert hands. Wilson said a flexible currency is also a democratic currency, and good reforms would enhance public life as well as encourage prosperity. Speaking of the economy constrained by an antiquated currency and banking system, he said: "America is now straining at the leash, and I could name some of the gentlemen who hold the leather thong that is attached to the leash . . . and America is straining to be free. And, God willing, she shall be free."[45]

Like the trust question, Wilson's views of banking began with moral propositions rooted in the Democrats' Jeffersonian principles. But he needed direction on policy alternatives, and as the election approached he consulted Samuel Untermyer, counsel to the congressional ("Pujo") investigation of the "money trust," and he heard from Charles Sumner Hamlin, who favored features of the Aldrich plan (Wilson later appointed Hamlin chairman of the Federal Reserve System).[46] But he had no tutor on banking and currency equivalent to Brandeis's role on business competition. What he heard on banking was a cacophony of quite different perspectives, but running through it was the strong Democratic fear of private, centralized control of banking. Without a firm grasp of policy alternatives, Wilson would lack the knowledge tools he would need for interpretive, interactive leadership of Democratic legislators.

Victory

For all the drama, ideological confrontation, and innovation in what Sidney M. Milkis and Daniel J. Tichenor call the first "modern campaign," its outcome was predetermined by the Republican Party's split.[47] Roosevelt's decision for a third-party candidacy was not meant to be political suicide. He imagined 1912 as a time of challenges and social transformation, much like the period prior to 1860 that opened political space for the new Republican Party, transcending the old party competition.[48] Yet Wilson was the decisive winner with 41.8 percent of the popular vote. Roosevelt gained 29.1 percent of the vote, and Taft placed third with 24.6 percent. Wilson won 435 electoral votes to Roosevelt's 88 and Taft's 8. These results could be read as an election in which Wilson, the minority party candidate, squeezed to victory between the warring factions of the majority Republicans. However, the election result could also be read as a victory that was pregnant with possibilities. Roosevelt's reading of the political terrain was not entirely wrong, but the emergent potential party was not his own new party but a potential coalition of progressives and reform-oriented Democrats. Wilson was the first Democratic president since Cleveland left office in 1897. Democrats controlled both houses of Congress for the first time since 1885. Wilson had won nineteen states that Taft carried in 1908, and while he was only a plurality victor his margin of victory was 15.4 percent over Roosevelt.

In short, the Democrats' 1912 victory could look less like a fluke and more like an opportunity to reorganize the American electoral landscape. Turning to Wilson's claim of authority and his project of progressive presidential leadership, we shall see that he entered office seeking to remake American politics. The key, of course, to making the 1912 election the basis for that transformation was that the Democrats' record should lead to majority victories in 1914 and 1916.

Wilson's Progressive Leadership

In his 1913 inaugural address Wilson promised to reinvigorate democracy and government. He characterized the Democratic victory as a decision by the nation to use the party to change government and address problems anew. Wilson observed America had achieved great progress, but "evil has come with the good. . . . With riches has come inexcusable waste." We have wasted our natural resources. Industrial success has come with large human costs. Governments are corrupted and serve private rather than public purposes. It was the Democratic Party's duty "to cleanse, to reconsider, to restore, to correct evil without impairing the good." Progress led the nation to think selfishly, he said, but "the scales of heedlessness have fallen from our eyes," and now the nation must align government with its highest ideals. "Our work is a work of restoration."

Chapter Seven

Wilson promised tariff and banking reform to make consumer goods more affordable and to ease the availability of credit to every region. He also committed to protecting competition in business. He promised policies to improve agricultural productivity and stabilize the rural economy. He promised conservation of natural resources and called on government to uplift Americans: "This is the high enterprise of the new day: to lift everything that concerns our life as a nation to the light that shines from the hearth-fire of every man's conscience and vision of the right." Wilson said the people now expected progressive government, committed to enhancing national life, and governance committed to justice. He added, these "shall always be our motto." His victory happened because "the nation has been deeply stirred . . . by the knowledge of wrong, of ideals lost, of government too often debauched and made an instrument of evil."[49] Thus his leadership would strike at Republican dominance and could establish a new Democratic progressive coalition. In his address Wilson walked a fine line between, in Stephen Skowronek's words, "a disastrous preemption and a masterful reconstruction."[50] The Republican split that gave Wilson his victory also gave him the possibility of forming a new majority. The question, then, was would he either adapt to the dominant party's policy commitments as a preemptive or minority president or attempt leadership toward building a new progressive majority?[51]

Constructing Wilson's Government

Wilson's transition into the presidency paralleled his entry to the governor's office. He welcomed progressive Republicans into his inner circle and was inclined initially to put a Republican in his cabinet, considering Representative George W. Norris (R-NE), a Roosevelt backer.[52] In late January Wilson met with Progressive Party congressmen, reaching out to expand his ideological majority.[53] Yet Wilson's impulse toward party government overruled his flirtation with bipartisanship. In the end, only Brandeis remained among possible appointees who were not prominent Democrats, and then he was dropped from consideration as Wilson encountered opposition to him among prominent businessmen and lawyers in the Northeast as well as from Massachusetts' Democratic leaders.[54] For the time being, Brandeis would take a role similar to that played by George Record in New Jersey, advising Wilson without having an official position. By 1916 Wilson had gained sufficient confidence in his own authority to overlook opposition and successfully nominated Brandeis as associate justice of the U.S. Supreme Court.

A second similarity with his gubernatorial transition was Wilson's continuing discomfort with patronage. At Trenton, Wilson made Tumulty responsible for patronage. After the 1912 election he gave Colonel House chief responsibility for suggesting and vetting candidates for cabinet appointments. Several names were obvious: Bryan had to have a prominent position and was named secretary of state; and McAdoo, who was central to Wilson's campaign, became treasury secretary. One of Wilson's several early supporters among Texas Democrats would be appointed, and House successfully pushed forward Representative Albert Burleson as postmaster general. House also successfully promoted his friend David Houston for agriculture secretary and James C. McReynolds as attorney general.[55] Wilson had Postmaster General Burleson, House, and Tumulty share the patronage portfolio. And he announced he was not available to meet with job seekers.[56]

Wilson's cabinet appointees were more or less identified with progressive causes and reflected the diversity of the reform camp. The cabinet contained characters as different as Bryan, the rural populist, William B. Wilson, a labor union official and congressman, and Californian and former Interstate Commerce Committee member Franklin Lane for Interior. James McReynolds was a Southern conservative but appealed to anti-trusters because as a U.S. attorney he had vigorously prosecuted anti-trust cases. The cabinet members had wide discretion over their departments while the president's attentions in the domestic sphere were fixed on legislation and managing public opinion.[57] In the words of John Morton Blum, "He left himself free, as in theory his prime minister had to be, to cooperate personally with . . . legislation, free also to go directly to the Congress or the people."[58]

A third and most significant parallel with Trenton was Wilson's prime ministerial conception of the presidential role. Returning from a postelection Bermuda vacation to prepare for the presidency, Wilson consulted congressional Democrats to plan a special session of Congress and encourage them to draft legislation on tariff and banking reform.[59] As Wilson planned his work with Congress and the Democratic caucus, Representative Oscar Underwood (D-AL), chair of the ways and means committee, suggested to him, "I feel there must be in the Cabinet one or two persons who have the implicit confidence . . . of [the Democratic caucus of each house]." The name Underwood proposed was Albert Burleson, who chaired the House Democratic caucus.[60] Wilson at first resisted Underwood's advice, responding that he planned to take no prominent member of Congress into his cabinet. Instead he intended an informal legislative cabinet that he would work with while being present at the Capitol several days a week.[61] However, House convinced Wilson to bring Burleson into the cabinet to reward a Texan who had promoted Wilson's candidacy while also adding to the cabinet his skills at patronage management.

Democrats in Congress supported Wilson's intention to guide legislation. Senator Atlee Pomerene (D-OH) said: "The closer the President and Congress can get in the transaction of public business the better it will be." Senator Ben Tillman of Georgia was more cautious, advising that the president was welcome if he came to advise legislators and not dictate to them.[62] The Democratic caucus was receptive to Wilson's leadership in large part because they had been a minority and looked to the president to succeed and give them greater electoral security. Over a third of the House Democrats were newly elected in 1912, and another significant number had been elected for the first time in 1910. Many of those new members shared Wilson's reform ambitions.[63] The Capitol's President's Room became Wilson's venue for consultations with lawmakers, and with them he made an exception to his rule to not deal with patronage, as he used appointments as currency for bargaining with legislators.[64]

A last feature to mention of Wilson's transition planning was his selection of Joseph Tumulty as White House secretary. Tumulty had served him effectively in Trenton, but Wilson thought him insufficiently cosmopolitan for Washington. He was too immersed in New Jersey politics, too Irish, and too Catholic. Wilson attempted to recruit Newton D. Baker, Cleveland's progressive mayor, for the job but failed in that effort. Then Edward House and Wilson's wife pressed for Tumulty's appointment. In early February Wilson gave the job to him.[65]

After a low-key inauguration (eschewing lavish inaugural balls), Wilson pressed ahead on his legislative agenda. We shall examine three cases of his legislative leadership, occurring during his first two years in office: the Underwood Tariff Act of 1913, the Federal Reserve Act of 1913, and the Clayton and Federal Trade Commission Acts of 1914. These three cases are conventionally identified as the most important legislative accomplishments of Wilson's first term.[66] Tariff reform was Wilson's first legislative initiative, and it established the pattern of his "prime ministership." Its importance to Wilson's presidency justifies adding it as a third case for examination compared to the two leadership cases used for Roosevelt and Taft. Adding the tariff case is useful because it allows comparison to President Taft's efforts on that same issue at the same point in his presidency.

The Underwood Tariff Act

Unified Democratic control of government assured reversal of the Payne-Aldrich rates because the party opposed protectionist tariffs. In 1894 the Democratic 53rd Congress reduced rates with the Wilson-Gorman Act. The Democratic House majority, elected in 1910, passed several tariff reduction bills that died in the Republican Senate.[67]

Wilson's inaugural address called for tariff reduction, but there was a gap between the party's principles and the ability of Democratic legislators to agree upon on a reformed rate schedule. Many Democrats were wedded to protection of a specific good, such as sugar, a commodity grown and processed in areas predominantly Democratic. The focus of Republican tariff protection was on the bundle of interests and products of the Midwestern and Northeastern economic "core." In contrast to that, the Democrats' geographic base lay in the South and parts of the West, the "periphery" to the economic core.[68] While Democrats could agree on forcing down the tariffs of the industrial core's manufactured goods, they would fragment into competing interests over protection for farm and lumber products and the few manufactured goods of the periphery, such as cotton textiles. Wilson's great accomplishment in leading tariff reform was his ability to move Democrats to near-consensus on sharply lowered rates.

In late December the president met with Representative Oscar Underwood (D-AL) to plan the special session for tariff reduction. The tariff bills passed by the Democratic House during 1911 were the templates for new legislation, and Underwood promised to produce a new bill in time for Wilson's inauguration in March.[69] The resulting bill contained sharply lower rates from the Payne-Aldrich tariff and included an income tax to regain revenues lost through reduced tariffs. Wilson called Congress to convene in special session on April 7, a month after his inauguration.

Wilson then pushed House Democrats to pass the first bill produced by Underwood's committee, which retained protection for farm products, sugar, shoes, and wool. He requested data about imports from the ways and means committee files and used these, along with executive branch information, to question the initial bill's rates. In contrast to Taft's inability in a similar situation to marshal information about the tariff, Wilson skillfully identified and obtained from the committee information to affect congressional decision-making.[70] Recall that at the same point in the legislative process President Taft had followed advice from Speaker Cannon and Senator Aldrich to not intervene until the conference stage of the tariff bill. With the information Wilson acquired he successfully made his case to the Democrats on ways and means that protective rates on "Democratic" products betrayed the party's campaign commitment.

The sugar rate was an especially nettlesome problem. In the last session the House had eliminated the sugar rate but it had failed in the Senate. Consumers saw sugar protection as directly fueling a rapid rise in the cost of living. At the same time, protection of sugar was crucial for legislators from states that grew cane and beet sugar. Sugar cane was concentrated in the Democratic south while sugar beet growing and refining occurred in the politically diverse agricultural regions of the West and Upper Midwest. Sugar cane was grown in nine states, with Louisiana the largest producer, and Democrats occupied every House and Senate seat in those nine states.[71] To finesse the sugar problem for Democrats, Edward House proposed that sugar get a transition period, temporarily retaining a rate of one cent per pound, and Wilson accepted the idea setting a three-year lead time to ending a sugar tariff.[72] In late March the president read a draft of his tariff message to the cabinet, which then discussed how Democratic constituencies would react to the message and the proposed rate reductions.[73] He also mentioned casually that "he might deliver his tariff message in person . . . but left it as an open question." By appearing in person before Congress Wilson would reverse the tradition beginning with Jefferson that presidents addressed Congress only in written form. Momentous as it was for Wilson to break that tradition, he decided against making it appear as a formal state occasion, telling his cabinet he wished to appear with little formality, "without being attended by the Cabinet Ministers."[74]

Wilson gave his remarkable address to Congress on April 8, explaining he chose to speak in person to show the president as a person and not merely an institution, "that he is a human being trying to cooperate with other human beings in a common service." He said the special session was "a duty [that] was laid upon the party now in power at the recent elections which it ought to perform promptly." He was scathing about existing tariff rates as protection for powerful interests; "we have built up a set of privileges and exemptions from competition behind which . . . it was easy to organize monopoly." Consequently American consumers and small businesses were systematically cheated. It was the Democratic Party's legislative responsibility to abolish "everything that bears upon even the semblance of privilege . . . and put our business men and producers under the same stimulation of a constant necessity to be efficient, economical, and enterprising." Wilson moderated the scale of the reform he demanded only to the extent of admitting that change should be paced and "not revolution or upset or confusion." Finally, he said he would put no other item before Congress until the tariff bill was passed, but soon after that he would ask Congress to take up banking and currency reform.[75]

The Underwood tariff bill moved efficiently to passage in the House. Its success was ensured by the discipline of the Democratic caucus, formed in 1911 to give order to the party's new majority. The caucus bound Democrats to support party measures that received a two-thirds vote in the caucus, allowing defection in the floor vote only for overwhelming constituency interests.[76] Thus Wilson's prime ministership was enabled by the caucus rules that were already in place as he entered office. However, the Democrats' electoral success in 1912 created some difficulties for party unity among House members. More members meant more diverse interests might be promoted for protection. But Wilson's attentive negotiations on the specifics of rates, Underwood's skills, and the power of the caucus passed the bill with few defections.[77] Of the Democrats, 274 supported the bill and 5 opposed. But only 4 Republican insurgents voted for the bill, which passed 281 to 139.[78]

The Senate posed somewhat different challenges for Wilson's tariff reform initiative. Democrats had only a seven-vote majority, large by most standards, but the Senate was traditionally more protectionist than the House. Of course, Senate rules also allowed for more leisurely progress of legislation. Senate Democrats had initiated a formal caucus, albeit with looser rules than those of the House Democrats. After the bill passed the House, a reporter wrote that in the Senate the strength of its Democratic caucus would see the bill through to passage without significant amendment.[79] However, Wilson was less sanguine about the bill's fate in the Senate. Josephus Daniels noted in his diary: "The lobbyists descended upon Washington like the locusts in Egypt."[80] Intense industry lobbying against rate reductions threatened reduced wages for workers or shutdowns if the Underwood bill became law.[81]

Wilson responded to the anti-reform lobbying with an extraordinary public attack on lobbyists and, by implication, the Senate itself.[82] This was one of the episodes of the Wilson presidency that demonstrates the Progressive Era public's receptivity to presidents "going public." As different as their political styles were, Roosevelt and Wilson both had a fine sense for the uses of the White House as a megaphone. At a press conference on May 26 Wilson turned a reporter's question about diplomatic recognition of Mexico to another subject entirely. He said because Washington reporters were insufficiently attentive, they "were missing a lot of stories about the extraordinary lobbying in this town at this time." He said lobbyists were swarming to put private interests ahead of the proper purpose of legislation. Asked if he was accusing lobbyists and legislators of corruption, Wilson responded that it was rather "systemic misrepresentation of the facts" by special interests that most concerned him and threatened to derail good legislation.[83] To make sure that his charges were reported accurately, Wilson followed up with a written statement to reporters extending his diatribe against protectionist lobbying. He stated:

> Money without limit is being spent to sustain this lobby. . . . [Yet] . . .
> the people at large . . . have no lobby and be voiceless in these matters,
> while great bodies of astute men seek to create an artificial opinion
> and to overcome the interests of the public for their private profit. . . .
> The Government . . . ought to be relieved from this intolerable burden
> and this constant interruption of the calm progress of debate. [84]

On a quiet summer day that statement was a cannon shot down Pennsylvania Avenue. To embarrass Wilson, the Republican Senator Albert Cummins immediately offered a resolution calling for an investigation and asking the president to reveal information to support them.[85] Surprisingly, Cummins's resolution passed the Senate, with Democrats choosing to not defend Wilson. The *New York Times* wrote, the Democrats "think it better for the President to be left to bear the onus of his own statement than for the Senators of the party to assume to protect him from the responsibility."[86] But Wilson welcomed the investigation as if it was his idea, announcing he would supply names and information to a hearing.[87]

The balance of opinion shifted after a week of hearings in which lobbyists and members of Congress testified. The revelations supported Wilson's charge; the *Chicago Daily Tribune* wrote the Democrats "believe they have made a political ten strike" with the hearing's revelations. The *New York Times* observed the hearing revealed a lobby that was "insidious to the extent that [its] publicity campaigns are . . . often based on misrepresentation."[88] The lobbying investigation threw tariff reform's opponents into disarray but also delayed the Senate's consideration of the Underwood bill. Debate began on July 19, and it was clear now that the bill would pass without significant amendment. The bill's income tax provision was criticized by many insurgent Republicans and some Democrats for insufficiently taxing the rich. These issues of taxation oc-cupied the Senate floor for more than a month. Then the Senate voted, and the bill carried by a vote of 44 to 37. The two Democratic senators from Louisiana (and cane sugar) defected. Only two Republicans voted for the bill.

The tariff victory was a great achievement. The Underwood-Simmons Act contained the lowest tariff rates since the Morrill Act of 1861.[89] Wilson's achieve-ment was the mirror image of Taft's failure to fulfill his promise for tariff reform. After passage, Secretary of Agriculture David Houston (an expert on tariff pol-icy) wrote to a friend, "A tariff revision downwards—not dictated by the mfgrs.; lower in the Senate than the House. . . . A progressive income tax!! I did not . . . think we should live to see these things."[90] Wilson and the congressional Demo-crats had fulfilled a key campaign pledge. For Wilson, the success was a dramatic achievement of presidential leadership that in turn depended on the discipline of the Democrat caucus.[91] However, as we shall see in all three of the policy in-itiatives of this chapter, the Democratic caucus was also characterized by dispar-ate views on reform that required presidential nuance to counter the Demo-crats' centrifugal tendencies.[92]

The story of the Underwood tariff is not fully told without noting the value-added component of Wilson's leadership. If the Democrats of 1913 were disci-plined in pursuing a legislative agenda, it was because Wilson understood the uses and limits of the caucus for his interpretive leadership. First, Wilson's novel address to Congress heightened the importance of the legislative goal and drew great public attention to it. Second, his frequent interventions with Democrats in the ways and means committee and in the caucus countered and tamed the centrifugal force of regional economic interests. Throughout the process, Wilson's role was to interpret the array of Democrats' positions so as to direct the bill toward consensus in the caucus. Third, and not least, Wilson's attack on "the lobby" labeled opposition to tariff reform as corrupt and eased Senate pas-sage. Charles Forcey writes: "Wilson's genius . . . lay in his capacity to work with Congress, in contrast to Roosevelt whose very ability at marshaling public sup-port often alienated the legislators."[93] And, in contrast to Wilson, Taft had lacked any ability to lead Congress and stood submissively aside from it.

The Federal Reserve Act

Banking reform was next. Wilson's preinaugural consultations convinced him that banking and currency reform were necessarily linked to tariff reduction because increased business activity (as expected by anti-protectionists) required credit and currency flexibility. Concluding his tariff address to Congress, he said: "At a later time I may take the liberty of calling your attention to reforms which should press close upon the heels of the tariff changes, if not accompany them, of which the chief is the reform of our banking and currency laws."[94]

Banking and currency policies posed a far greater challenge for Wilson's leadership than had the tariff. Representative Underwood said of banking reform, "While the Democratic Party had made up its mind what ought to be done on the tariff, currency reform was practically a new question, and it would be impossible to predict how long the House would take for . . . the bill."[95] There were several sharply competing preferences about banking reform. To grasp those several different approaches and negotiate over alternatives, Wilson needed expert advice. After the 1912 election, Edward House had David Houston tutor Wilson about tariff and banking issues.[96] Houston subsequently sent to Wilson a paper with some ideas about banking reform, including an explanation of why banking reform should accompany tariff reduction.

The 1912 Democratic platform on bank reform was simply negative, opposing the Aldrich plan. It called for eliminating banking panics and giving relief to areas requiring expanded credit and demanded more credit to farmers.[97] The platform reflected the ongoing Pujo committee investigation of "the money trust." During 1912 Representative Arsene P. Pujo (D-LA) led a House banking subcommittee investigation revealing control of American banking, credit, and currency policy by a small group of New York City banks and a handful of major financiers who comprised an interlocking directorate of finance and industry.[98] The platform demanded that banking reform remove control from that "trust," but it offered no means for reaching that goal.

If the Democratic platform represented, by implication at least, one pole of banking reform, the recommendations of the National Monetary Commission would constitute the opposite pole. The 1907 financial panic convinced almost everyone, including the bankers, that financial reform was imperative, and the Aldrich plan had emerged from that sense of urgency for change. But the idea of a banker-controlled, centralized system was an anathema to Democrats. [99] In their perspective it was simply a blueprint for institutionalizing the money trust's domination. Yet the agrarians and their more conservative fellow Democrats could not agree on what would constitute an appropriate banking reform.

The challenge for Wilson was to find common ground among these Democrats. What is remarkable here is that he succeeded in leading his congressional party to a legislative outcome that was not foreseeable at the outset. As Elizabeth Sanders notes, Wilson had the largest claim of responsibility for passage of the Federal Reserve Act "since the new legislation enacted a preference held by so few people . . . the creation of a government agency with great discretion to control the supply of money and credit."[100] Wilson succeeded through a skilled mixture of negotiation with legislators, well-timed public appeals, and an insistence on the public control of banking and currency policy.[101]

Representative Carter Glass (D-VA) led a subcommittee to draft the bill for bank and currency reform. The Glass bill would create currency flexibility by making commercial paper a basis for bank notes, and it aimed also to extend American banking facilities internationally to support exports.[102] The bill eschewed any central control for banking, instead establishing regional reserve banks to be owned, in turn, by commercial banks of the region. These regional reserve banks would be federal treasury depositories and hold the reserves of member banks, issuing bank notes on the basis of their deposits and rediscounted commercial paper. Each reserve bank would be independent, but the comptroller of the currency would supervise the system's operation.[103] The Glass plan was a midpoint between the Aldrich plan and the agrarians' demand. The agrarians desired a large number of publicly owned and controlled regional reserve banks with authority to issue credit and currency backed by land and agricultural crops. The Glass plan reflected both the agrarians' fear of Wall Street domination through centralization while also bowing to conservatives with wholly private ownership of the reserve bank system.

Wilson's negotiation of the banking bill depended not on his command of policy details but on his embrace of basic principles that Democrats shared, less to do with his own preferences and more with his ability to interpret and negotiate with the preferences represented in the Democratic caucus. The Bryanites distrusted private bankers at money center banks, particularly New York City. Yet, to work, reform legislation had to engage the support of the banking community, even if given grudgingly. Wilson sought tutoring from Houston, House, and Brandeis to grasp the elements of banking, but he did not need that knowledge to understand the power stakes at play. His operating principle was that a reform bill, whatever its details, had to contain centralized public control of the banking system and currency. That principle attempted to balance two opposed views. It spoke to the agrarians' demand that banking be public. It responded also to conservative bankers' demand that the system be centrally coordinated.[104]

Chapter Seven

In late December 1912 Representative Glass and his economic adviser, H. Parker Willis, conferred with the president-elect. After seeing their draft bill, Wilson responded with one demand. There had to be clear, central federal control of the system of regional banks. Wilson had House consult with Glass to refine the bill, and a federal reserve board of six public members and three members chosen by the regional banks was substituted for loose oversight by the comptroller of the currency.[105] The evolving Glass bill was not alone among Democratic ideas for reform nor was it easily embraced. In May Wilson consulted the cabinet and found Bryan strongly opposed to including private bankers on the national board and opposed to privately owned regional banks issuing currency. Bryan threatened opposition to any bill that did not place banking and currency under federal control. As Bryan went so would most agrarians. In effect, he forced Wilson's hand in favor of even more federal control in the reform plan.[106]

Issues of federal government control and agricultural credits roiled the bank reform discussions. At the end of May three bills contended for attention, including a proposal by Secretary McAdoo. Wilson had to achieve some kind of agreement amidst the flurry of ideas among Democrats. He publicly took up that challenge at his May 29 press conference where he noted the proliferation of reform plans. He claimed he was now responsible for distilling the party's bill out of those contenders, saying, "I am generously invited to make a bill out of the three."[107] In mid-June, the powerful rules committee chair, Representative Robert Henry (D-TX), further confused the issue by charging that the push for currency reform was Wall Street propaganda, and he proposed instead further investigation of the "money trust."[108] Wilson countered he would not tolerate any effort to merge the Pujo committee's inquiry and the banking bill, and with Bryan's aid sidetracked Henry's venture.[109]

During June the president negotiated to find support for the essentials of a bill. Working with Secretary McAdoo, Representative Glass, and Senator Robert L. Owen (D-OK), Wilson had a bill to send to Congress just after mid-June. Then he added an outside political game to his inside game, calling on the public to support his bank reform. Meeting with members of Congress on June 16 at the White House, Wilson stressed that if the public supported the bill there was no question that it would pass. The members dutifully repeated the president's public message as they left the White House, and newspapers broadcast it, for example: "The President believes strongly that the country will back him in his view that the currency system ought to be reformed."[110] On

June 23 Wilson addressed a joint session of Congress about bank reform. He said the new tariff and economic growth required banking and currency reform, and "control of the system of banking and of issue which our new laws are to set up must be public, not private, must be vested in the government . . . not the masters of business."[111]

Throughout the summer, with Bryan on his side, Wilson struggled to repress agrarian and Republican insurgents' efforts to further amend the Glass bill, making it unacceptable to moderate and conservative Democrats.[112] Wilson actively engaged congressional Democrats to maintain their support or to win over the occasional stray. In a way that foreshadowed the staff functions of later presidents, Joseph Tumulty communicated with Glass and other leaders to keep Wilson informed of which members needed attention.[113] A united Democratic caucus beat back amendments, and on September 18 the Federal Reserve bill passed the House 287 to 85. The victory was a signal accomplishment of Wilson's interpretive leadership. The bill that passed was distilled from the preferences and fears that the president found within the Democratic caucus. Additionally, he saw that public sentiment was heavily tilted against private control of the banking system. Through negotiation and public appeals Wilson found the place on the spectrum of banking reform alternatives where Democrats' preferences overlapped, and there he shaped successful legislation. The act's combination of federal control accompanied by political insulation of the Federal Reserve Board (fixed, long tenure for members) recognized the Bryanites' demand for public control as well as the conservatives' distrust of government control.[114]

The challenge of Senate passage remained, and Wilson would face several recalcitrant Democrats on the Senate banking committee who, along with Republican stalling, delayed the Glass-Owen bill's passage. It passed finally in mid-December by a vote of 54 in favor and 34 opposed. The successful bill had been slightly amended to draw agrarian support, and it sped to conference committee and final approval. The bill was delayed because of the seven Democrats on the banking committee just four supported it outright. Three dissenting agrarian Democrats allied, ironically, with standpat Republicans to drag out hearings. That delay in the bill's progress gave the banking lobby time to continue its attacks on the bill, threatening to undermine public support. Wilson said to Senator John Sharp Williams (D-MS) he feared that the delay gave the banking lobby a chance "to make the two houses uneasy in the presence of the bankers' power."[115]

Frustrated by the lack of progress and risk to the bill, Wilson tried various wiles, from threatening public attack on the insurgent Democrats to finally winning them over with some accommodations and soft power. Throughout the process, Bryan, now satisfied at the federal role in the bill, also worked to bring around the several recalcitrant Democrats.[116] The final deal struck was that the banking committee would report on two bills, the Glass-Owen bill and another that drew support of progressive Republicans and the several Democratic dissenters. The Democratic caucus then quickly chose the Glass-Owen bill over the alternative, and it went on to pass the Senate.[117]

What should not be lost sight of in this complicated story of lawmaking is Wilson's extraordinary skill in guiding the process. In late June, the New York *World* said of the Glass-Owen bill that it contained unheard of and extraordinary power for the president: "It cannot be denied that the . . . bill centralizes a tremendous financial power in the President." The newspaper report continued, "The bill makes the Presidency a financial prize such as American institutions have never yet known. . . . Thus the currency question becomes a political question as well, and a political question in the broadest sense."[118] What the *World* writer presciently saw was that the Federal Reserve Act constituted a great expansion of the federal government's role in the economy, and the presidency was at the center of the expansion.

There was another way the bill's passage signaled an expansion of presidential power that was *not* at the time institutionalized. Through brilliant improvisation President Wilson had wielded a prime minister's skills to herd Democratic factions to enable banking reform. Combining negotiating skills, a talent for reasoned public communication, and powerful faith in party unity, Wilson improvised a mode of presidential leadership that, in turn, made possible the "tremendous" extension of institutionalized presidential power that the Federal Reserve Act represented.

Signing the Federal Reserve Act, Wilson said:

> It was the first of a series of constructive measures by which the
> Democratic party will show that it knows how to serve the
> country. . . . The tariff bill was meant to remove those impediments to
> American industry and prosperity which had so long stood in their
> way. . . . Then there came upon the heel of it this bill, which furnishes
> the machinery for free and elastic and uncontrolled credits.[119]

Anti-trust was the next "constructive measure."

The Clayton and Federal Trade Commission Acts

The 1912 Democratic platform stated, "private monopoly is indefensible" and demanded "enactment of . . . legislation . . . to make it impossible for a private monopoly to exist."[120] That plank was adopted by a convention in which delegates divided over candidates but agreed on principles, including the need for further legislation against business concentration.[121] As the banking act passed, Wilson demanded that Congress push forward to fulfill that pledge before the 1914 congressional election.

But what policy should be instituted against trusts? The Sherman Anti-Trust Act of 1890 was thought by most knowledgeable observers to be inadequate to current challenges. It made illegal any action causing "restraint of trade or commerce" among the states or with foreign nations. In the few cases regarding the Sherman Act that came to the Supreme Court before 1901, the Court interpreted restraint of trade broadly, covering most agreements among competitors, even while interpreting "commerce" narrowly as in the E. C. Knight case to apply only to interstate trade literally and not manufacturing more generally. The Roosevelt and Taft administrations vigorously litigated anti-trust cases, leading to a fundamental change in the Court's Sherman Act jurisprudence. In the Standard Oil case the Court introduced the rule of reason, reading into the Sherman Act the common law distinction between reasonable and unreasonable restraints of trade.[122]

No interest was satisfied with the rule of reason. The agrarians distrusted its loophole and were scandalized that unelected, probusiness judges would define what was a reasonable restraint of trade. Businessmen, on the other hand, were left without a guide to what would be a legal restraint of competition. Louis Brandeis, for example, feared that the courts would consequently impede efforts by small businesses to moderate competition so as to be able to compete against bigger business.[123] Many progressive big business leaders feared the rule of reason threatened the efficiency that could be achieved by large-scale integrated firms. Their concerns were represented by Herbert Croly who argued that dominant industrial corporations represented economic progress and called for substituting "cooperative for competitive methods, wherever cooperation can prove its efficiency."[124]

Roosevelt proposed a strong federal commission to regulate business and certify business practices. A far weaker notion of an investigative commission attracted politicians and businessmen located in areas of diverse economies in the Midwest and Pacific Coast. In this view, the commission would gather information to clarify what practices were anticompetitive and illegal. Opposing that approach, Democratic agrarians sought legislation that would fully specify those practices that illegally restrained trade, with criminal as well as civil penalties attached to infractions. Thus the agrarians aimed to limit judicial discretion over anti-trust policy.[125]

Before 1910 Wilson lacked a coherent position on business concentration. During the 1912 campaign his statements reflected the party platform and agrarian preferences. In his first genuinely substantive speech on economic issues, delivered at Buffalo on Labor Day, Wilson attacked Roosevelt's idea of legalizing monopolies rather than prohibiting them. Later the same month Wilson denounced the idea of a regulatory commission as "a smug lot of experts . . . behind closed doors."[126] However, while excoriating monopoly and T.R., Wilson's campaign speeches contained little information about his own policy preferences. In the past he had attributed business misbehavior to the actions of individual businessmen rather than to the organization of firms and industries. Late in the campaign he described an approach that would join agrarian goals with his own preference for policing and punishing individuals. He promised laws "against every specific process of monopoly . . . and then direct the punishment against every individual who disobeys the law."[127]

While Wilson's concept of anti-trust policy seemed vague, his leadership in this policy arena did not depend on expertise. When a reporter asked Wilson if he had a "trust program" to send to Congress, he responded that he had conversations with congressmen about trust issues. But, he continued, he had no "tariff program . . . [or] a currency program. I have conferred with these men who handle these things. . . . That is what I am trying to do in this case."[128]

In the tariff and Federal Reserve acts Wilson had worked with Democratic leaders to form legislation that could gain support of each house's Democratic caucus. Wilson interceded substantively in both cases, for example, in the Underwood tariff, offering a phased reduction of the rate for sugar to decrease producers' pain. In the banking bill Wilson helped Democrats, including Bryan, agree on federal reserve structure with more power at the center (albeit public power) than the party had originally preferred.

But anti-trust posed a larger challenge for Wilson's leadership. The tariff and Federal Reserve acts were based on ideas widely shared within the party over what constituted a desirable policy outcome. There was far less agreement among Democrats about anti-trust policy. The agrarians of the economic periphery sought a statutory checklist of prohibited behaviors accompanied by strong penalties and an aim to dissolve existing trusts. Another group of Democrats representing economically diverse areas rejected any bill prohibiting cooperation among businesses. The Progressive Party presented an added complication because its platform plank favored regulation of business concentration.

Which way would Progressive Party voters move in 1914? Would they retreat back to the Republican Party? Would they stick with the reduced number of Progressive Party candidates who were on the ballot? Or, might they be attracted to the Democrat's progressive program?[129] Taking the progressives into account, and the Progressive Party's commitment to a strong regulatory commission for business, the optimal point for policy compromise on anti-trust could not be within the preferences only of agrarians and other Democrats. Rather, the optimal policy for potentially co-opting Progressive Party voters would be located within a spectrum of options that included the Progressive Party's regulation of bigness in business. Consequently, Wilson was challenged to distill into one bill the quite distinct preferences.

How he confronted that challenge through his interpretive leadership helps us explain the central puzzle in the formation of the anti-trust program of 1914. The legislative process began with initiatives weighted toward the Democratic agrarians' views. Yet, the eventual outcome of this process was a regulatory commission stronger than anything envisioned by most Democrats and a statute, the Clayton act, that was less specific in its prohibitions than agrarians had favored. Wilson returned from a December 1914 vacation announcing that anti-trust legislation was next on his agenda.[130] He met in mid-January with Democratic members to survey their preferences, and this meeting formed agreement on a long list of business practices that would be prohibited by law, such as interlocking directorates, extension of the Sherman Act's statute of limitations from three years to five, and introduction of private liability suits for anti-trust violations.[131] At these meetings Wilson suggested a "trades commission" to gather information and recommend legal action by the justice department. The commission idea would have surprised those who recalled Wilson's attacks in 1912 on a regulatory commission as "government by experts." However, now he had to take into account Progressive Party voters. That these voters were in play is confirmed by Progressive Party attacks on the idea as "theft" by Wilson from the Progressive platform plank, which promised "a strong . . . commission . . . which shall maintain . . . supervision over . . . corporations. . . . doing . . . what is now done for the railroads" by the Interstate Commerce Commission.[132]

Wilson spoke to Congress about anti-trust, but he breathed no Bryanite fire. He described the current atmosphere for legislation as one of "accommodation and mutual understanding." He said that the "vast majority of businessmen" condemn efforts to monopolize and the Democrats will "be their spokesmen." Wilson proposed legislation to prohibit specific activities, including interlocking directorates. He said that there was much that was now known about illegal business behavior and that these actions could be prohibited by law. But, there was more that needed to be done because "businessmen . . . desire something more than that the menace of legal process . . . be made explicit and intelligible. They desire the advice . . . which can be supplied by . . . an interstate trade commission."

Wilson characterized the commission he recommended as an "instrument of information and publicity." It would also support implementation of judicial decisions. This was not yet the Progressive's expert regulatory agency he had criticized in 1912.[133] Wilson heard appeals for such a commission from his own officials. Perhaps most influentially, Joseph Davies, the commissioner of the bureau of corporations, sent recommendations creating "an interstate trade commission" with an informational and investigative role in support of the courts and legislature.[134] A similar recommendation came from Samuel Graham, the assistant attorney general, who proposed it could "answer authoritatively the . . . inquiries now addressed by anxious and law-abiding men to the Department of Justice."[135] These voices joined with Secretary of Commerce Redfield and others, who expressed the need to abate the current uncertainty of anti-trust law.[136]

While Wilson's commission proposal was not Roosevelt's robust commission idea, it went some distance in appealing to Progressives.[137] At the time Edward House urged on Wilson the need to win over Progressive voters.[138] His commission initiative was praised in a leading Progressive magazine, *The Outlook*. The magazine, which was Roosevelt's usual platform, endorsed Wilson's program. The editorial admitted his commission was limited; nevertheless "even in this limited form the Commission should be welcomed."[139]

The electoral incentive of attracting Progressive voters was not the only factor shaping Wilson's initiative and its evolution into the summer of 1914. He also had to wrestle with unstable policy preferences among Democrats. The agrarians were committed to detailed legislation but they could not agree on what that list should contain, and they were also prone to oppose a commission.[140] On the other hand, Democrats in diverse economic regions and the East feared legislative overspecification would stifle business. They sought another approach, such as the commission, and Louis Brandeis's position on anti-trust spoke to the views of those Democrats.[141]

Another factor influencing Wilson's position was his dependence on advisors to guide his own anti-trust views. During the first half of 1914 the president was pressured from several different policy perspectives within his own party as well as from the incentive of attracting Progressives. Lacking sufficient knowledge of the issue to distill a compromise policy initiative, as he had done with banking reform, Wilson was buffeted by competing demands.

The Democrats' fragmented positions on anti-trust produced five House bills that were introduced after Wilson's speech to Congress. One bill established a trade commission; a second outlawed interlocking directorates of corporations; a third bill offered a detailed definition of the Sherman Act's language of "unfair competition"; and a fourth bill defined a number of practices as illegal, including price discrimination meant to injure competitors, refusal by mine operators to sell to qualified buyers, and price fixing. That latter bill also enlarged the grounds for private suits for anti-trust violations. And a fifth bill, yet to come, would empower the Interstate Commerce Commission to regulate railroad securities.[142]

As these bills proceeded to hearings they were large targets for business criticism, and Wilson responded by declaring they were not all "administration bills." The annual meeting of the U.S. Chamber of Commerce in mid-February occasioned sharp criticism from business leaders. The bills were attacked for unrealistically maximizing individual competition over efficiency, prosperity, and fairness.[143] But businessmen generally favored the trade commission. Speaking at the convention Louis Brandeis said of the five bills that they were "not Administration bills." They were the bills of those members who introduced them, and he said. "I find much in them that I would see amended."[144] Brandeis went on to say that President Wilson did not seek regulatory policy to enforce unrestrained competition but rather sought a system of regulated competition.

Through the spring of 1914 competing anti-trust agendas tangled the legislative process. However, Wilson refused to postpone legislation until after the November election. Business groups claimed that apprehension about regulation was depressing business activity. House members yearned to return home to campaign, but Wilson insisted that Democrats must stand for election having fulfilled all three major platform promises. In late January he had announced his intention to keep Congress in session, and he brushed aside House Majority Leader Oscar Underwood's pleas for adjournment.[145] Wilson referred to the administration's task of legislative leadership as attempting "to work order out of chaos."[146] Additionally, Wilson was distracted by revolution and instability in Mexico. In August the European Great War broke out. Finally, he was bowled over by the death of his wife, Ellen, on August 6, after several months of illness. He wrote in May that he felt "amidst the present perplexities and the . . . pressure" he should put up a sign outside his office, "Don't shoot, he is doing his damnedest."[147] Despite all this, Wilson managed to keep his eye on the goal of fulfilling the party's anti-trust commitment.

As the bills worked through committees, the president engaged repeatedly with House and Senate committee chairs and Democratic members seeking agreement to consolidate the bills and present a package to unite Democrats and draw progressive Republicans.[148] He continued to seek advice from officials of his administration and several outsiders to fill in his own blank spots. Some congressmen were offended by Wilson's reliance on expert advisers. Responding to Wilson's suggestions that he knew came from outsiders, the Commerce committee chair, Representative Charles Adamson (D-GA), wrote angrily to the president that his committee "has had full hearings . . . and is satisfied with the bill as reported to the House."[149] Therein is a sign of the limits of Wilson's legislative leadership. It was apparent at the outset of his presidency that he could approach Congress as an institutional equal and insert himself to an unusual extent in the legislative process. However, open reliance on outside experts implied that the president controlled information to guide legislation, leaving the legislators in a subordinate position to process what Wilson dictated.

Despite the political risks, Wilson was inescapably dependent on outside advice. Committed to completing anti-trust legislation, he could not find a stable consensus point within the Democratic caucus, nor did he sufficiently command the issues to build a stable legislative coalition between Democrats and progressive Republicans. Business executives attacked the bills as harsh and insufficient. Railroad executives told the Senate commerce committee that the bills unfairly constrained directors and forced public revelation of internal business planning. Businessmen also protested the Clayton bill's prohibition of agreements over pricing.[150] At the other end of the spectrum, agrarians dismissed business's complaints as disingenuous and fought for more prohibitions and stiffer sanctions. Complicating matters further was the demand by organized labor to exempt unions from the reach of anti-trust legislation. Wilson was unsympathetic, but urban Democrats and agrarians added that exemption to the Clayton bill.[151] From the perspective of Democrats aligned with progressive views, such as Senator Henry Hollis of New Hampshire, the five bills were the work of "radical democrats [who] do not feel sure of their ground."[152]

In mid-June pressure to adjourn Congress increased from businessmen seeking relief from anxiety and Democrats seeking to campaign. The House had passed three anti-trust bills in early June. That set the stage for a change in Wilson's legislative role. Norman Hapgood and Louis Brandeis introduced George Rublee to Wilson, and Rublee sold Wilson on the idea of a robust regulatory commission. Rublee was a corporate lawyer and reformer who had supported Roosevelt in 1912. He worked with Brandeis on railroad regulation and rate issues before the Interstate Commerce Commission, and he aided a first term Democrat, Representative Raymond Stevens (D-NH), to draft a bill to create a strong regulatory trade commission. With that bill Stevens had sought, unsuccessfully, to graft onto the Democratic agenda the progressive vision for a trade commission.[153] The New Hampshireman Stevens was a geographic outlier in the Democratic caucus, holding a normally Republican seat. Facing an uphill election battle to retain his seat, he backed a progressive version of a trade commission.

Rublee, along with Stevens, Hollis, and Brandeis, met with Wilson on June 10. They convinced him to seek change in the commission bill to make the trade commission responsible for determining what practices constituted "unfair competition" rather than relying on legislative definitions. Brandeis, Stevens, and Hollis then fanned out to lobby members of Congress in support of the change.[154] Arthur Link writes of that moment that the president's "conversion . . . was the decisive event in the history of the antitrust program."[155] His advisers' advice gave Wilson a clear position from which to negotiate a legislative resolution on anti-trust. With the Senate bills still in the commerce committee, Wilson proposed that the Covington bill containing the trade commission provision (that just passed the House) be amended, giving the commission power to define what constituted restraint of trade and issue orders to firms to cease such activity. The committee's members were receptive to Wilson's initiative, but two potentially daunting hurdles remained.[156] First, Wilson had to convince other Senate Democrats to support the new measure. Second, he had to manage the bill through conference and House adoption of the Senate package.

Wilson's new initiative drew headlines reporting "Radical Change in Trust Program" and "President Favors Change in Trust Program."[157] Wilson was also described as skeptical about the Clayton bill, which contained the House's efforts at defining anti-competitive behaviors plus a weak exemption for organized labor. In effect, strengthening the trade commission to make it the arbiter of what constitutes "restraint of trade" was to make the Clayton bill definitions irrelevant. However, the Clayton bill's labor exemption by itself made that bill important to a coalition of Democratic legislators and an anathema to businessmen.

The commerce committee passed the newly amended Federal Trade Commission bill with one Democratic dissenter. Senate Democrats were divided on the amendments to the commission bill just as they were about the Clayton bill. However, the congressional Democrats suddenly pulled behind Wilson. To avoid appearing unable to act on their anti-trust promise, the leaders held a meeting of the Democratic caucuses of both houses to plot a strategy for passage of the bills. The *Chicago Daily Tribune* wrote, Democrats "decided to lend immediate assistance to the president, who so far has been combating single handed the countless appeals to postpone action . . . and to 'give business a rest.'"[158]

It was another month before the two bills passed the Senate and went to conference, finally passing in the form Wilson sought. For several weeks they were stalled by those resisting weakening of the Clayton bill, Republicans attacking the retention of that bill's labor provision, and those who were skeptical of the trade commission's powers and discretion. In early August the trade commission bill passed by a wide margin, fifty-three to sixteen, with progressive Republicans joining Democrats. Two intransigent agrarians opposed it, Senator Thomas of Colorado and Senator West of Georgia, aligning with fourteen conservative Republicans.[159]

The Clayton bill passed in early September with forty-six voting for the bill and sixteen opposed. Seven Republicans and a Progressive joined all the Democrats to support the bill. The successful bill omitted the provisions against price discrimination and a definition of restraint of trade that had been in the House version. It retained penalties for directors of errant trusts, prohibitions against tying contracts to reduce competition, and a prohibition against interlocking directorates. The pro-labor language was retained.[160] Wilson urged the conference and House to approve the bills as passed by the Senate. The key measure for him now was the Federal Trade Commission bill. Several agrarians from both parties continued to fight for the original Clayton bill. Senator James Reed (D-MO) denounced the reduced bill in conference as signaling "Peace on earth: good will to the trusts."[161] Nevertheless, the calendar was working against that last sputter of opposition. Congress had been in session for the last eighteen months, and House members needed to campaign before the election. Time, or the lack of it, was with Wilson. The Senate approved the report for a weak Clayton bill on October 5 and the House passed it while rushing to adjournment.

The anti-trust policy and commission President Wilson shepherded into life were distant from the populist fury driving the 1912 Democratic platform. Arthur Link writes, Wilson's "failure to solve the antitrust problem by doctrinaire remedies" reflected the weakness of the New Freedom in addressing the complex problems facing Americans. We can add that it also reflected the limits of Bryanite solutions. What Wilson and the Democrats did accomplish "revealed greater ideological flexibility than they had heretofore shown."[162] Yet Wilson's reversal, from support for strong legislation and a weak informational commission to proposing a strong commission and weak legislative prohibitions, presents a major puzzle of his legislative leadership. That sudden switch in policy positions belied his campaign statements. It was also a reversal of his claim that his role was merely to interpret the Democrats' intentions and not dictate to the party or the country.

This reversal is a key piece of evidence for the corporate liberal interpretation of Wilson's place in the Progressive Era. In that perspective, big business executives sought institutional relations tying corporations to big finance and to the federal government, establishing a system of protection for corporate interests. In this interpretation, Wilson's reversal turned the Democratic Congress away from punitive, anti-trust legislation, substituting a trade commission that with the right appointees would promote a corporate liberal agenda. Thus, Wilson was either himself an advocate of that view or a captive of corporate liberals such as George Rublee.[163] But we should be skeptical of the corporate liberal interpretation as we seek to explain Wilson's actions in anti-trust. Even granting that interpretation of its overall claims, it has a logical flaw in respect to Wilson's intentions and actions. Wilson's actions were consistent with the dominance of corporate liberalism, but this does not explain his behavior. In short, the question is not whether the federal trade commission as established worked harmoniously with big business. Rather, the key question is, why did Wilson reverse course? In corporate liberal accounts of the creation of the Federal Trade Commission we find little attention in fact to Wilson's actions and purposes.

Alternatively, Scott James presents an account of Wilson's reversal that addresses directly his actions and purposes. James builds a strong case for electoral motivation to explain the reversal and Wilson's later liberal social legislation leading up to the 1916 election.[164] He offers substantial evidence for Wilson and other Democrats taking into account the problem of their minority electoral status and aiming to draw Progressive Party voters. As suggested above, however, the electoral incentive was not the only purpose that motivated Wilson's actions in anti-trust, nor necessarily the dominant motive. First, he aimed to fulfill the platform's loose language about trusts. He also sought to reduce what he saw as the grave problem of private influence over public affairs.[165] Not least, Wilson also attempted to maintain party unity and fulfill his ideal of interpretive leadership. Of course, calculation about the electoral appeal of the trade commission to Progressives and insurgent Republicans was intertwined with these other purposes. We cannot understand Wilson's leadership from mid-1914 through the 1916 election without taking account of his electoral incentives. Yet our investigation of the anti-trust case suggests that the electoral incentive was only one of several motives for Wilson's actions, and not the most pressing.

For our purpose, the most striking lesson about Wilson's shift on anti-trust was that it demonstrated the limits of his interpretive leadership. Unlike the tariff and banking reform, Wilson could not find a policy position that represented a stable agreement among the congressional Democrats. To retrieve the party's commitment to produce legislation, and to do it before the 1914 election, Wilson resorted to an idea, vouched for by Brandeis, which appealed to those Democrats from mixed economic regions or the East, as well as most Progressives and progressive Republicans. That coalition constituted a large plurality in both houses. The uncertainty about the new initiative was how agrarians would perceive it. The contents of the Clayton bill became the currency for bargaining with the agrarians. To leave some prohibitions in the Clayton bill was to give them half a loaf. And as the election approached, the appeal to support their president and caucus led most of the agrarians to vote for the bill that represented Wilson's policy reversal.

The President as Prime Minister

Despite very limited experience in public office, Woodrow Wilson brought to the presidency a fully developed leadership style. It had emerged in his Princeton presidency, succeeded at Trenton, and then adapted well to Washington as Wilson found himself leading a Democratic congressional majority. The foundation for Wilson's leadership style was intellectual rather than experiential and was established long before he entered a political office. What is remarkable about his accomplishments as a leader is how adeptly he asserted himself and his priorities in each successive role. There seemed to be no learning curve in these roles, and his successes came quickly and impressively. Yet, as we have seen at Princeton and Trenton, conflicts and failures followed Wilson's initial dominance and successes, and that same pattern would appear in his post–World War I presidency.

We are touching here upon repeated and famously analyzed behaviors that appear across Wilson's successive roles.[166] Such recurrent patterns in individual behavior invite psychological and character-based explanations. However, we have in Wilson's leadership style a sufficient explanation for these patterns at Princeton, at Trenton, and during his first term in Washington. And that style was based not in Wilson's psyche but in his leadership theories and skills. In each of the cases we have examined in Wilson's career, his ability to lead forcefully and convincingly depended on his feeling assured of strong support for his role and goals. At Princeton he was a forcefully effective leader when supported by his university constituencies; and at Trenton he was similarly energized and decisive with legislative and public support for his goals. However, in neither role was Wilson merely a passive recipient of constituency and party support. As Princeton's president he worked the alumni like a campaigning politician and tended faculty relations while developing close ties to trustees. As governor he went public with his goals while also leading the assembly's Democratic caucus.

Making Wilson's initial challenges greater as university head and governor, his agenda in each role was transformational. He sought to upset the established order, and his initiatives required strong backing to be passed. In neither role did Wilson show any interest in "little" or transactional politics, the mode of politics he would be forced into by a loss of majority support. At the same time, he was most confident and relatively flexible leading those who supported his transformational appeals. Wilson's leadership of the progressive coalition in the first few months as governor recalls his early years at Princeton. In each context he assumed a prime ministerial role over a "party" of supporters that shared his goals but would have differing ideas about the best means to reach them. Thus he was able to say after his curriculum reform was adopted that it was improved by amendments within faculty councils. Yet, when his judgment and initiatives were rejected, as in the Quad Plan and during 1912 in Trenton, Wilson became inflexible and defensive in the face of unsupportive constituents and opposition politicians. Aside from whatever psychological trauma Wilson may have experienced through political rejection, that loss of support was the equivalent for him of a no-confidence vote.

Quite remarkably, the pre-presidential pattern we observed of very quick assertion of a leadership stance and immediate success was repeated in the presidency. The three cases examined in this chapter show Wilson in a dominant leadership stance with a strong agenda for progressive reform but with great flexibility for adopting policy approaches that would succeed legislatively. With Democrats controlling both houses of Congress in 1913, he used the presidency, already expanded by Roosevelt, as a leadership stage for innovating legislative leadership, using the presidential role much as he used the governorship during 1911.

But Washington was not Trenton; there was no established routine of legislative leadership by presidents circa 1912. Federal institutional norms implied that a replay in Washington by Wilson of his gubernatorial role would produce criticism that he was acting inappropriately, even violating constitutional norms. Indeed, opponents did criticize him harshly. Because Wilson bridged the separate branches, Senator Albert Cummins (R-IA) declared him a menace, writing that "the President reigns supreme . . . he seems to be of the opinion that he alone is competent to promote the public interest."[167]

In moving his prime ministerial style from Trenton to Washington, Wilson quickly adapted it to his new context. Rather than dominating his party's caucus as he had at Trenton, Wilson presented as an engaged interpreter and respectful partner to the congressional Democrats. He insisted that it was not *his* program that was being legislated. It was, rather, the program of the Democratic Party, and it was his privilege as the Democratic president to engage Congress to give legislative life to the party's commitments.

The tariff, the banking reform, and anti-trust all reveal the relatively low priority Wilson gave to the specific content of legislation. He was neither a legislative craftsman nor a "policy wonk," to use modern parlance. Indeed, he was remarkably flexible about legislative substance, to the point of easily adopting measures contradicting his earlier positions, such as the retention of a sugar tariff or initiating a strong trade commission. Wilson sought to lead his party to fulfill its principled commitments. For example, in tariff legislation the long-standing party commitment for reduced tariffs in every sector guided his actions. In banking reform, the principle of public control of currency and central banking activity was his touchstone. Stymied by his inability to find sufficient agreement among Democrats on anti-trust policy, his purpose seemed more than anything to find what could attract a legislative majority quickly and allow for adjournment. He seemed to believe what worked in 1914, just as he believed wholeheartedly in what he said to be elected in 1910 or 1912. Just as he had conveniently become a progressive Democrat in the 1910 New Jersey election, so Wilson adapted his commitments to the purpose at hand, embracing ideas that could draw Democratic support and achieve legislative success.

At Trenton Wilson had been dependent on others for the content of legislation, and in Washington he continued to need others for policy content while he propelled the process forward. But all was not identical in Wilson's leadership in comparing the cases of Trenton and Washington. Over time his style and skills matured. Consider the anti-trust case in comparison to his abandonment of his legislative leadership in Trenton after Democrats lost the majority. With his party in the minority, Wilson abandoned meetings with the Democratic caucus, made no effort to bring together the progressive factions of both parties, and wielded the veto freely. The deadlock over anti-trust bills in summer 1914 had features paralleling Governor Wilson's loss of the legislative majority. There were strong factional divisions among the Democrats over anti-trust, and the preferences of Republican insurgents were far apart from those of most Democrats. Thus Congress was fragmented and less responsive to Wilson's direction than it had been. Wilson had the executive prerogative of repeating his behavior in 1912, stepping back from his prime ministerial role. Instead, he sought any means to achieve the Democrats' commitment to anti-trust legislation. The solution he found was far closer to the Progressive Party's platform than many Democrats would have wished, but it solved the problem. The Wilson of 1914 was more tenacious, more hardened as a politician, more capable of dealing with the give and take of legislative politics than the Wilson of 1912.

Wilson's leadership on the tariff, banking reform, and anti-trust was a bravura and innovative presidential performance. John Milton Cooper calls it "possibly unmatched" and only rivaled in the twentieth century by Franklin Roosevelt's New Deal and Lyndon Johnson's Great Society.[168] More broadly, beginning with the landmark legislation examined above and extending through 1916, Wilson shaped and fulfilled a large part of the Progressive Era's legislative agenda. About policy he was flexible, accommodating differences within his party and the diverse strands of reform constituting progressivism, but he was determined about the overall agenda and the main direction of government.

In the end, there is a paradoxical quality to Wilson's stunningly successful leadership style. He was both passive and aggressive. His conception of interpretive leadership was passive in two respects. First, his stance presumed he was leader of a majority party in the legislature given the responsibility to govern. Second, he took his interpretive task to be the formation of initiatives distilled from the preferences existing within that party that had been chosen to lead by the people. Thus, Wilson's leadership assumed an existing support system, a legislative majority. When his majority support vanished, Wilson's leadership stance crumbled and with it his authority. He was left then without a constructive alternative stance for leadership and turned hostile toward opponents, at Princeton as well as at Trenton in 1912.

Yet, at the head of a majority, Wilson's leadership stance was also aggressive in that he presumed he had broad authority to frame the legislative agenda, determine its pace, interject legislative content when needed, and lead his party in Congress in every respect short of entering into floor debate. Finally, he presumed the authority to speak to the people, over the heads of his party and Congress, explaining his intentions and interpreting the people's needs. With that "bravura performance," Wilson achieved a culmination of the Progressive Era's expectations of a progressive president, fulfilling what Roosevelt had begun in 1901.

The Progressive Presidents and the Modern Presidency

What the country needs is . . . constructive leadership by a real Executive
. . . leadership which is not afraid to assume responsibility for going before
the people; leadership which will utilize the superior powers of the
Presidency to formulate issues.
  Frederick Cleveland[1]

IT IS USUALLY INDIVIDUAL PRESIDENTS rather than the presidency itself that attract attention, and studies tend to focus on presidents biographically with institutions and context as background. Scholarship on the Progressive Era presidents exhibits this tendency in the extreme. Few books treat more than one of these presidents, and none attempt a systematic approach to all three within their shared political context.[2] The drama of individual presidential leadership easily overwhelms the impulse to analyze the context in which it occurs. Consider Roosevelt; at Osawatamie, Kansas he declared, "The New Nationalism regards the executive power as the steward of the public welfare."[3] But nine years earlier he had pledged to continue the dead McKinley's appointees and priorities, and two years after Osawatamie he stood before the Progressive Party's convention with the tradition-breaking oath, "We are standing at Armageddon and fighting for the Lord."

Roosevelt's journey from promising continuity with McKinley to call for radical presidential activism and then to apocalyptic politics appears at first as a story of personal transformation. He exhibits what Clifford Geertz describes as "what . . . causes some men to see transcendency in others."[4] Seeing that same quality, the historian Michael Beschloss characterized Roosevelt (Wilson also) as "heroic," suggesting that presidential leadership indeed should be understood as a manifestation of some special quality of an individual's character.[5]

Chapter Eight

But Roosevelt's presidency was not a phenomenon insulated from time and context. As a thought experiment, I ask the reader to make a shift in time and imagine Roosevelt as a replacement for President Rutherford Hayes (1877–1881). Would that Roosevelt create new anti-trust policy and build a robust naval power? Would he celebrate presidential power and the New Nationalism at Osawatamie (the place of John Brown's initiation to guerilla war)? The thought experiment turns quickly ludicrous. Roosevelt's attack on Northern Securities, his use of executive power and courts, as well as his "upbuilding" the navy were all possibilities opened to him by a political context of changing power relations and new public expectations. Thus his journey from pledged support for McKinley to "Armageddon" is part of a larger story of three presidents confronting new opportunities in an office suddenly less constraining than it had been for predecessors.

Roosevelt privately thought McKinley to be too weak and passive. In replacing McKinley, he grasped new possibilities for presidential activism. As he pushed at the presidency's limits he discovered the party period's constraints were as much norms internalized by presidents as they were institutional limitations imposed on those presidents; Roosevelt had not internalized those norms as had party period politicians. Thus he created new political leadership within the old office, changing the presidency in the process by stimulating new public expectations for what presidents might do and illustrating the uses of new levers of power.

The party period presidents had not remolded the office through their leadership. In the one instance where a successor attempted to retain something of the unusual authority of his predecessor, Congress swatted away Andrew Johnson's effort to control reconstruction policy. But as Roosevelt crafted progressive leadership in the presidency, he also changed the role to be occupied by his immediate successors. William Howard Taft not only followed Roosevelt but also constructed a leadership that aimed to continue his presidency and meet public expectations for energetic reform leadership. The election battle among Roosevelt, Taft, and Wilson in 1912 was over who would best continue the expanding project of the Progressive Era presidency. Once in office, Wilson governed in a context shaped by Roosevelt's presidency and 1912 candidacy. His leadership and agenda were constructed in Roosevelt's image and extended ideas Roosevelt had introduced.

From the Party Period to the Progressive Era

Rather than seeing Roosevelt, Taft, and Wilson as fascinating, idiosyncratic individuals in the early twentieth-century presidency, we have examined them as

incumbents acting within changing institutions and pushing at the limits of political authority. Parties were weakening as the dominant organizing institutions
of American political life. Competing with the parties for political space were
emerging interest-based organizations representing business, agriculture, labor,
and the professions. At the same time government's expanding responsibilities
were implemented by agencies removed from partisan spoils. Middle-class
Americans surveyed politics and government through information and critical
opinions gained from widely read national magazines and prominent, quality
newspapers. With new political forms overshadowing the party period's norms
and institutions, presidents would look beyond party organization for their
cues, opportunities, and allies.

I have suggested we think of the party period's presidency as a well-
structured role with a highly specific script. That script was defined by the
party's needs and program and reinforced by the incumbent's own socialization
as a party period politician. In contrast to that model, we can see the Progressive
Era's presidency as an ill-structured role with a loosened script. The prerequi-
sites for nomination were loosened, channeling new kinds of politicians into the
office. Thus incumbents performed in the office differently than had their predecessors. Even in the brief period between McKinley's first inaugural address
and Roosevelt's first annual message, the president presumed novel authority
for independent policy initiatives. Recall the example of President McKinley,
aiming in his 1897 inaugural address to reassure the country he was aware of the
dangers of trusts. For authority to address trusts, he invoked party scripture, so
to speak, calling upon the 1888 platform's language. Within the party period's
script McKinley could not address a major issue independently of party.

Progressive Era presidents asserted independence from party and Congress.
However, they had no precedents for how to use that new potential. They confronted new demands for their policy leadership while their formal role provided few resources to plan, push forward, and implement new policies. Thus
each president had to reinvent the office, seeking to acquire strategic resources
that were external to the office. In this study, we have called those efforts to acquire strategic resources a manifestation of the incumbent's leadership style,
and so we have examined how each Progressive Era president improvised his
own means to cope with the presidency's new possibilities. Thus, our theoretical
story that begins at the macro level, tracing changes in power relations and institutions after 1900, becomes a micro-level examination of how three presidents each improvised leadership to use the office's loosened script.

Chapter Eight

Improvising Leadership

There was no user manual and no precedent to guide Roosevelt, Taft, and Wilson through the tumultuous politics of Progressivism. The incumbent's own skills and political experience guided him in remaking presidential leadership. Consequently, Roosevelt, Taft, and Wilson each offered very different approaches to the challenges of Progressive Era presidential leadership. Yet all three had to construct leadership engaging the same three major dimensions of the universe of Progressive Era politics: the party in Congress, the president's relationship to public expectations, and the agenda of policy reforms.

Each of these dimensions constitutes a variable through which we can identify the distance between progressive presidential performance and the party period's norms. First, party in Congress was the magnetic pole of the party period president's universe. Second, the party period president's direct communication to the public was constrained by formality and typically silent about the policy process. Third, the party period's president was loyally bound to his party's policy agenda and platform.

Party in Congress

The changing place of parties in the polity around 1900 was a tectonic shift creating a new playing field for presidents. After the mid-1890s the United States, in the words of the historian Joel Silbey, tipped "over from a partisan political era into a new one of mixed qualities, confusion and ambiguity."[6] Each progressive president addressed those changes in a strikingly different way. Yet underlying their different approaches to leadership was the obvious fact that none of these three men would have been likely to enter the presidency through the conventional selection process of the post-bellum party period. Roosevelt, Taft, and Wilson each came to the office from backgrounds that were strikingly different from the experiences of party period presidents. By the standards of orthodox partisans of the late nineteenth century, Roosevelt was too little the party man and too much the reformer. Taft was too much the jurist and administrator and insufficiently an electoral politician. And most remarkably, Wilson was a university professor who only studied government and leadership! Only in a time of disrupted parties and roiled politics could these men have reached the presidency.

For Theodore Roosevelt loyalty to the Republican Party was highly malleable. Prior to his own election to the presidency in 1904, he was careful to not break with the Republican congressional leadership. But even during his first McKinley term, Roosevelt gave party loyalty secondary consideration. Foremost in his leadership style was a self-constructed spectacle of himself as hero that he displayed to the public. Roosevelt would not openly appeal to Democrats to support his measures; he thought bipartisanship was unprincipled and empty of content. Rather, his stance leaned towards post-partisanship, using the presidency as a platform for a personal leadership above party. Consider his decision to initiate the *Northern Securities* lawsuit. He aimed to clarify and strengthen anti-trust policy through the suit and also to demonstrate his responsiveness to public anxieties about big business. At the same time, because he was acting unilaterally, Roosevelt could stand apart from congressional Republicans and their business clientele, presenting to them a fait accompli.

In the anti-trust and naval cases, occurring early in his presidency, Roosevelt put his own policy goals above party loyalty. And later, during his second term, his relationship with the congressional Republicans was increasingly strained as he vigorously and publicly promoted a progressive reform agenda. Thus Roosevelt's relationship to his party can best be labeled as a presidentialist stance apart from party. He established a strong, personalist reform image that heightened the president's stature without breaking openly with the congressional Republicans. Of the three progressive presidents, it is Roosevelt's example that most resembles modern presidents' plebiscitary performance and ambivalent relationships with their parties.[7]

William Howard Taft's self-identity was thoroughly Republican. His loyalties bound him to the Republican congressional leaders, making him a paradoxical political figure among the progressive presidents. On the one hand his leadership style was closest to party period norms, but on the other hand he willingly embraced Roosevelt's charge to continue a presidency of progressive policy commitments. As we saw in examining his role in the Philippines and as Roosevelt's problem solver, Taft was able and resourceful in challenging assignments. However, the "assignment" of continuing a progressive presidency obliged him to promote reform while remaining loyal to fellow Republicans who were hostile to those reforms. Roosevelt had stood apart from the congressional Republicans without breaking with them. But as we saw in Taft's handling of the tariff legislation, he refused to distance himself from Republican leaders. And when the tariff legislation passed, though he had admitted privately that it was not what he originally envisioned, he dutifully proclaimed the Payne-Aldrich tariff to be the best ever passed by Congress.

Thus Taft did not use the presidency's new possibilities for visibility and performance to signal, as Roosevelt had, his personal commitment to reform. Taft asked, what is the purpose of such actions but to serve his own self-interest? Thus he fatally misunderstood the presidency's new possibilities for autonomy and public visibility. It is ironic that while failing to individuate himself, and failing to understand how Roosevelt had used public performance, Taft had some success pushing forward the agenda he had inherited from Roosevelt. He continued and expanded Roosevelt's Sherman Act litigation. Taft also initiated postal banking, an income tax amendment, and added powers for the Interstate Commerce Commission. As well, he independently initiated innovative planning for administrative and budget reform. Steven Diner captures the irony of Taft's success: "A few years earlier, Taft's accomplishments might have been recognized as substantial progressive achievements, but the national political discourse had changed dramatically under Roosevelt" as had the presidency, and Taft could not enter the terms of that discourse nor could he publicly perform the presidency as Roosevelt had left it to him.[8]

Wilson's leadership displayed yet another kind of relationship of the president to his party and Congress. He was invested in the possibility of a prime ministerial stance within the American constitutional framework. As he demonstrated as governor, his executive leadership gained great authority when accompanied by a legislative majority but deflated when facing an opposition legislature. When the New Jersey legislature turned Republican after the 1911 election, Wilson surrendered legislative leadership and focused on the presidential nomination race.

Had Wilson not entered the presidency accompanied by a Democratic Congress, it is difficult to imagine how he would have constructed his leadership. But he did have the majority, and even before deciding on the cabinet he began planning with the ways and means committee a strategy for tariff legislation. Until American entry to war, Wilson shaped reformist public policy through his legislative majority, and he found the Democratic caucus open to his leadership. Supporting Wilson's initiatives brought success for the congressional Democrats and helped with their reelection. Not least, the Democrats of both houses had also recently adopted caucus rules that enhanced their capacity to be a unified legislative majority.

Wilson's style was ideally adapted for Progressive Era leadership, given a disciplined partisan majority. During his first term Wilson was a dynamo of legislative and public leadership. However, his example is also an outlier in presidential history. His disciplined party majority was rarely replicated in twentieth-century American politics. Thus, while Wilson's presidency was the most productive of important legislation among the three progressive presidents, it was Roosevelt's personal presidency, the executive standing apart from his party, that was closer to the modern norm.

The President and the Public

Theodore Roosevelt's political education gave him a genius for public performance along with a grasp of bureaucratic organization and its capacities. Roosevelt had parlayed spectacle and expertise into successive political appointments and then, after the Cuban military adventure, into the governorship and presidency. His public conduct suggested he was always aware of the platform he occupied and the audience to which he played. For Roosevelt, actions, language, and initiatives were as important for their public example as for their possibility of leading to policy and law. His performance aimed less at Congress than at the maintenance of public support. Leadership on legislation was only one dimension of his role and not necessarily superior to the importance of encouraging the proper attitudes of citizens toward issues and toward Roosevelt himself.

In contrast to Roosevelt's relationship with the public, Taft entered the presidency and shunned its possibilities for public outreach. He had relished public contact in the Philippines and as war secretary, and he campaigned vigorously during 1908. But as president his taste for public performance greatly diminished. While Congress worked on the tariff, Taft eschewed public statements that might have exerted pressure for lower rates and distinguished him from high-tariff Republicans. Then in the Pinchot-Ballinger controversy he maintained a puzzling silence, as if public statements in his defense would sully the dignity of the office. Taft's conduct seemed to replicate the constraints and norms of the party period presidency. While he was committed personally to continue Roosevelt's agenda, his leadership style could not allow for behaviors in office that might have replicated Roosevelt's performance.

If Roosevelt performed for the public, Wilson could be said to seek conversation with it. His conception of leadership entailed an interpretation of the public's needs and values. In practice, his ideas about a symbiotic relationship with the public were played out through his relationship to his party in Congress. Through the party he thought he had a lens on his public's values and needs. In leading the congressional party to fulfill commitments for reform legislation he understood himself to be engaged in interpretive discourse with public expectations. Thus, for Wilson party leadership *and public leadership were two sides of the same project.*

Of course, the prerequisite for Wilson's public leadership was his Democratic congressional majority. As we saw repeated in his Princeton presidency and the New Jersey governorship, his formula of interpretive leadership only worked with a legislative or its equivalent. Wilson could only "interpret" what was loud, clear, and supportive of his authority. Therein was the downside of his prime ministerial conception of leadership. He had no alternative model to accommodate situations of qualified support, outright opposition, or the challenge to "interpret" the views of those who disagreed with him.

Public Policy Initiatives

Party period presidents advocated policy initiatives in harmony with party platforms and priorities. In that respect, the principal norm of the party period president's role was to be an instrument of the party's interests. That relationship changed and even reversed in the Progressive Era as parties and political conditions changed, leaving presidents with the possibility of free agency policy promotion. All three progressive presidents exhibited that free agency to one degree or another.

Roosevelt's policy initiatives were quite apart from the dominant preferences of his congressional party. Anti-trust and naval policy were of little concern for standpat Republicans. He began with his own agenda and then calculated whether and how he could gain support of his party's leaders for his preferences. The issue he chose to not initiate, tariff reform, illustrates that strategy. After his 1904 electoral victory he raised the possibility of tariff reform and met uniform opposition from the Republican congressional leaders. Consequently he dropped the idea and later warned Taft that tariff reform was an issue that would tear apart the party.

Roosevelt acted unilaterally when possible to pursue initiatives that would be bogged down if sent to Congress, such as clarification of the Sherman Anti-Trust Act. Thus he skillfully located strategic resources and identified means to pursue his goals. Transforming naval policy, he reached down into the navy's ranks to acquire expert information, and he went public with arguments for a great navy to strengthen his hand vis-à-vis Congress. Seeking, successfully, to clarify judicial interpretation of the Sherman Act, he acted unilaterally through the justice department when he might have instead requested legislation. He filled a Supreme Court vacancy with an eye on affecting the Court's eventual decision on the *Northern Securities* case. Furthermore, he pursued the *Northern Securities* case with an eye as much on public anxieties about trusts as on the judicial process.

Succeeding Roosevelt, Taft attempted to push forward the progressive agenda, in his own way. Indeed, the tariff reform initiative was daring. With his demand for rate reduction, Taft was clearly acting against the grain of Republican preferences. Moreover, the evidence is strong that Taft initiated reform because he thought it was good policy, both politically and economically. Thus his initiative fit the pattern of an emergent policy independence among the progressive presidents. His failure with the Payne-Aldrich Act was not due to his lack of policy initiative but rather to his inability to comprehend and negotiate Congress's tariff-making process and his failure to understand his stake as president in the legislative outcome. Those same limitations are also apparent in his dealing with the Pinchot-Ballinger controversy.

It is a misperception to see Taft's difficulties as the problem of a party period politician simply misplaced in the Progressive Era. Taft was more complicated. He observed and supported Roosevelt's novel and progressive leadership, and he obviously understood that the presidency he entered in 1909 was a role of expanded possibilities. However, his leadership style did not contain the insights and tool kit he would need to successfully use the presidency of that era. He was bereft of skills to identify strategic resources for achieving his political and policy goals. Given opportunities to achieve a desirable outcome, he seemed to miss the importance of the moment. He eschewed chances to go public and gave up possibilities for pressuring members of Congress. And he was incapable of intervening in political controversy to protect his own interest.

Woodrow Wilson's policy initiatives were tied to his role as party leader. Unlike Roosevelt, his initiatives did not aim at specific policy details but sought to fulfill the public's expectations for reform. He was not motivated by a particular kind of banking reform, for example, but searched for a bill that fulfilled his party's promise and united congressional Democrats in agreement over policy substance. In that respect, Wilson's leadership style was more procedural than substantive, bent on leading a party of reform to fulfill its great goals rather than seeking to achieve specific programs. His great skill at acquiring strategic resources to achieve his goals was inextricably linked to his prime ministerial stance. His legislative leadership skills were his means for achieving his policy ends, and his rhetorical strengths were applied to linking together his public and his legislative leadership.

Toward a Modern Presidency?

As opportunities for executive leadership appeared in the new century, Roosevelt, Taft, and Wilson each represent an experiment in how to use those opportunities. Two of them, Roosevelt and Wilson, were notable successes, and Taft was held to be a failure by the metric of progressive expectations. Indeed, Roosevelt and Wilson were successful on a rather grand scale, becoming exemplars for later generations of citizens and politicians.

Of course, these presidents also fascinated the Progressive Era public and shaped its perceptions of the presidency. Through their language, initiatives, and shaping of press coverage, these presidents created a personalized presidency. Consequently, each created expectations about the office that affected their immediate successors. For example, as Roosevelt's successor, William Howard Taft inherited not only his predecessor's policy agenda but also the expectation that he could match Roosevelt's bold performance. As we have seen, Taft did not fully understand the presidency's new possibilities of public performance. That failure, in turn, invited Roosevelt's intervention in the 1912 nomination process and led to the political collision that opened the presidency to Wilson. Then Wilson, who had decried Roosevelt's propensity for public performance, found his equivalent in highly visible legislative leadership and public rhetoric. Also Wilson fulfilled public expectations for presidential policy initiatives that were originally whetted by Roosevelt's activism. Thus, these presidents brought quite different leadership styles to the challenges of a roiled political context and loosely scripted presidency. In the end, the two presidents who devised successful leadership projects brought to office skills that were foreign to party period politics. In that sense Roosevelt and Wilson were "new men." Taft's failed leadership project, by contrast, reflected his limitations, able to see Progressivism's demands but lacking the tool kit for leadership that would fulfill them.

Stepping back from the particulars of these three presidents, how do their experiences of leadership in the Progressive Era relate to the presidency's development in subsequent decades? It is tempting to conclude this investigation of the progressive presidents with the claim that this book illuminates the beginning of the modern presidency.[9] The claims to support that conclusion seem initially strong. Here are presidents of great influence on successors up to the present time. And here is a period of activism that asserts for the first time in American history what we can call a presidentialist politics, and these presidents govern at the outset of a new structure of power in American politics, an emerging pluralist system replacing the party period.[10]

However, for all its appealing simplicity in conceptualizing a twentieth-century presidency, the modernity hypothesis does not account for important aspects of our story. It overlooks the contingencies we have uncovered in the Progressive Era's presidency. It fails to recognize the counterfactual possibilities within the period. To directly link the progressive presidents and the modern presidency also misses the centrality of institutionalization within the latter development. Note also that the modernity hypothesis ignores the obvious problem that progressive presidential leadership was not in chronological sequence with the later, modern presidents. Rather it seems an interlude, with the presidency's role later demoted by the return of normalcy in 1920 and a resurgence of standpat Republicans and congressional government.[11] But it would also miss the most important implication of the progressive presidents to see them as a mere interlude of activism within the long period of Republican control, small presidents, and limited national government, from the end of the Civil War to 1933.

From Hyper-Contingency to Institutionalized Modernity

There is no neat punch line to conclude my examination of the Progressive Era presidents. This sequence of presidents began with the bang of Roosevelt's spectacle and ended, in the years beyond this book's domestic scope, with the whimper of Wilson's failure to win the treaty battle with the Senate after World War I. But while the Progressive Era's reform agenda and presidential leadership were trumped by the exigencies of war, the experiences of the progressive presidents marked a period of remarkable executive leadership and extraordinary contingency in the conduct of that leadership.

After 1900 the emergent structure of pluralist power shifted the balance among institutions, leaving the presidential role with fewer constraints and new possibilities. Thus great changes in presidential leadership after 1901 were contingent upon the way incumbents used opportunities and deployed leadership skills to secure political resources. Had Roosevelt not succeeded to the presidency in 1901, it is unlikely that we would be considering William McKinley's experiment in progressive leadership. Had Taft not seemed to fail at the challenge of progressive leadership, we would not have Wilson leading his Democratic majority to fulfill much of the progressives' legislative wish list. Also consider other counterfactuals presented by the period. What if Roosevelt had correctly predicted that his new party could be victorious in 1912? What if Wilson had been successful in forging a stable electoral bond between Democrats and Progressives? Either of those events would have dramatically changed electoral politics into the future and the presidency as well.

Additionally, we see nothing in the purposes and actions of these presidents to suggest they were thinking of a future presidency rather than calculating what means they had at hand to affect policies, move Congress, and influence the public. Roosevelt did not circumvent the navy's hierarchy to gain information for the purpose of institutionalizing presidential advising. He was, rather, improvising to gain resources necessary to achieve his own policy goals. Wilson did not address Congress on the tariff to initiate a new practice of presidential rhetoric. Rather, he sought a means to influence the Democratic majority and promote public support for the agenda to which the party and the president were committed.

After 1920 the presidency seemed more affected by immediate contingency and micro-level events than some larger developmental logic toward modernity. Warren G. Harding's "normalcy" returned presidents to subordination in the Republican Party and to Congress and put into office incumbents with no ambition for stretching the executive role. So potent was the return to normalcy that even Herbert Hoover, the least conventional of the 1920s presidents, could not muster his technocratic expertise to escape Republican orthodoxy in the face of economic collapse.[12]

Yet, during the 1920s the presidency's organizational setting was changing, cumulating new potential resources for incumbents. An expanded executive branch posed new complexities that could only be solved by administration from the top, and the 1921 budget act and the budget bureau presented new possibilities for presidents with sufficient ambition to use them.[13] Thus new possibilities for presidential leadership were emerging, but they were not yet pieces of a modernizing presidency. Rather, they were available and their utility was contingent upon how presidents would use them.

Franklin Roosevelt entered office amidst economic crisis and pushed the role beyond anything seen in the 1920s, not on a path forward as much as back to the freewheeling experimentation of the Republicans Roosevelt and Wilson.

The Democratic Roosevelt's performance into the late 1930s was more like the progressive presidents than it was akin to a highly organized modern presidency. Until 1937 he experimented to solve a gaping incongruence between his goals and the limited powers and resources of the office. The consequence was a brilliant improvisation of policy experimentation, public appeals, prime ministerial leadership, and bargaining. Roosevelt's "three ring circus" was an extension of progressive presidential leadership far more than it was "modern." It had little structure. Roosevelt built no large, stable staff within the presidency. Rather, his success was in his agile leadership style along with his talent for acquiring external resources to resolve incongruence.

This is where my story of the progressive presidents ends and the modern presidency begins. In 1936 Franklin Roosevelt created the President's Committee on Administrative Management to plan an organizational structure and resources on tap, so to speak, to support expanded presidential leadership. Its recommendations led to the institutional innovations that would end Roosevelt's organizational improvisations and institutionally expand the presidency.[14] At that point the progressive presidency's asymmetry between large responsibilities and few resources was ending and the modern presidency was beginning.

Notes

Chapter One. The Progressive Era and the Presidency

1. "The New Nationalism," a speech at Osawatomie, Kansas, August 31, 1910, at www .theodore-roosevelt.com/trnationalismspeech.

2. Quoted in John Morton Blum, *The Progressive Presidents* (New York: Norton, 1980), 16.

3. Blum, *The Progressive Presidents*, 17.

4. It is appropriate to use gender neutrality referring to presidents in the present and future. But the male gender will be used referring to past presidents.

5. Herbert Croly, *The Promise of American Life* (New York: Macmillan, 1909), 170.

6. Clifford Geertz, "Centers, Kings, and Charisma: Reflections on the Symbolics of Power," in Geertz (ed.), *Local Knowledge: Further Essays in Interpretive Anthropology* (New York: Basic Books, 1983), 120.

7. See Stephen Skowronek, *Building a New American State: The Expansion of National Administrative Capacities, 1877–1920* (New York: Cambridge University Press, 1982), esp. chaps. 6 and 8.

8. Michael McGerr, *The Decline of Popular Politics: The American North, 1865–1928* (New York: Oxford University Press, 1986).

9. See Morton Keller, *Affairs of State: Public Life in Late Nineteenth Century America* (Cambridge, Mass.: Harvard University Press, 1977); and Richard McCormick, *The Party Period and Public Policy: American Politics from the Age of Jackson to the Progressive Era* (New York: Oxford University Press, 1986).

10. On the relationship between selection mode and presidential leadership, see James Ceaser, *Presidential Selection: Theory and Development* (Princeton, N.J.: Princeton University Press, 1979).

11. Samuel Kernell, *Going Public: New Strategies of Presidential Leadership*, 3d ed. (Washington, D.C.: CQ Press, 1997), 21.

12. Melvin Laracey, *Presidents and the People: The Partisan Story of Going Public* (College Station: Texas A&M University Press, 2002).

13. For an analysis of this role played out by an exceptionally activist party period president, James K. Polk, see Stephen Skowronek, *The Politics Presidents Make: Leadership from John Adams to George Bush* (Cambridge, Mass.: Harvard University Press, 1997), 155–176. For a conceptualization of factionalism in American parties and its relationship to presidential selection, see Howard L. Reiter, "Factional Persistence within Parties in the United States," *Party Politics* 10, no. 3 (2004): 251–271.

14. In distributive policies government produces disaggregated benefits to discrete beneficiaries while entailing no clear costs to other individuals or interests. See Theodore J. Lowi, "American Business, Public Policy, Case-Studies, and Political Theory," *World Politics*

16, no. 2 (July 1964): 677–715; and Theodore J. Lowi, *The Personal President: Power Invested, Promise Unfulfilled* (Ithaca, N.Y.: Cornell University Press, 1985), 23–28.

15. Henry Jones Ford, *The Cleveland Era: A Chronicle of the New Order in Politics* (New Haven, Conn.: Yale University Press, 1919), 59–60.

16. Keller, *Affairs of State,* chap. 9.

17. For a contemporary account of the role of patronage in party organization and operation, see Moise Ostrogorski, *Democracy and the Organization of Political Parties,* vol. 2 (Garden City, N.Y.: Anchor Books, 1964 [1903]).

18. Because 1876 and 1888 saw the Electoral College victories lose the popular election, the mean average popular winning margin in these five presidential elections is −.53. Data drawn from Gary King and Lynn Ragsdale, *The Elusive Executive: Discovering Statistical Patterns in the Presidency* (Washington, D.C.: CQ Press, 1988), 436.

19. Data drawn from King and Ragsdale, *The Elusive Executive,* table 7.20. Republican control of the presidency and Senate was assured by the party's control of the state admission process in the period after the Civil War, before the Southern Democrats regained control of their state's congressional representation. Peter H. Argersinger, "The Transformation of American Politics, 1865–1910," in Byron E. Shafer and Anthony J. Badger (eds.), *Contesting Democracy: Substance and Structure in American Political History, 1775–2000* (Lawrence: University Press of Kansas, 2001), 124–126.

20. Lowi, *The Personal President,* 27.

21. Keller, *Affairs of State,* 311.

22. Rutherford B. Hayes, *The Diary of Rutherford B. Hayes,* ed. T. Harry Williams (New York: McKay, 1964), 137.

23. Michael Les Benedict, "A New Look at the Impeachment of Andrew Johnson," *Political Science Quarterly* 88, no. 3 (September 1973): 349–367. Herein is an illustration of a process that Orren and Skowronek suggest poses the challenge for explaining institutional change: "The institutions that constitute the polity . . . will abrade against each other and . . . drive further change"; Karen Orren and Stephen Skowronek, "Beyond the Iconography of Order: Notes for a 'New Institutionalism,'" in Lawrence C. Dodd and Calvin Jillson (eds.), *The Dynamics of American Politics* (Boulder, Col.: Westview, 1994), 321.

24. Sean Dennis Cashman, *America in the Gilded Age,* 2d rev. ed. (New York: New York University Press, 1988), 163.

25. For the argument of McKinley as a transitional figure to a modern presidency, see Louis L. Gould, *The Modern American Presidency* (Lawrence: University Press of Kansas, 2003), chap. 1.

26. Jeffrey Tulis, *The Rhetorical Presidency* (Princeton, N.J.: Princeton University Press, 1987); Laracey, *Presidents and the People,* 134–138.

27. Keller, *Affairs of State,* 580.

28. McKinley, "Inaugural Address," in James D. Richardson (ed.), *A Compilation of the Messages and Papers of the Presidents* (New York: Bureau of National Literature, 1917), 13:6240.

29. McKinley, "Inaugural Address," and 1888 Republican platform, in Kirk Porter and Donald Bruce Johnson, *National Party Platforms, 1840–1956* (Urbana: University of Illinois Press, 1956), 80.

30. Gould, *The Modern American Presidency*, 2.

31. Keller, *Affairs of State*, 297. For more detail, see Leonard White, *The Republican Era* (New York: Macmillan, 1958), chaps. 2 and 3.

32. Woodrow Wilson, *Congressional Government: A Study in American Politics* (Baltimore: Johns Hopkins University Press, 1885), 47–48.

33. Henry Jones Ford, *The Rise and Growth of American Politics* (New York: Macmillan, 1898), 334; Robert C. Lieberman, "Ideas, Institutions, and Political Order: Explaining Political Change," American Political Science Review, vol. 96, no. 4 (December 2002): 697–712.

34. Editorial, *Chicago Tribune*, March 10, 1893, 4.

35. "The President's Part," *New York Times*, August 4, 1893, 4.

36. Ford, *The Rise and Growth of American Politics*, 275.

37. Theodore Roosevelt, "Inaugural Address," March 4, 1905; http://www.presidency.ucsb.edu/inaugurals.php; accessed October 12, 2006.

38. Theodore Roosevelt, "Seventh Annual Message," December 3, 1907; http://www.presidency.ucsb.edu/sou.php; accessed October 12, 2006.

39. David Mayhew. "Presidential Elections and Policy Change: How Much Connection Is There?" in Harvey L. Schantz (ed.), *American Presidential Elections* (Albany: State University of New York Press, 1996), 158.

40. Woodrow Wilson, *Constitutional Government in the United States* (New York: Columbia University Press, 1908), 70.

41. Henry W. Bragdon, *Woodrow Wilson, The Academic Years* (Cambridge, Mass.: Harvard University Press, 1967), 132.

42. King and Ragsdale, *The Elusive Executive*, 88.

43. Daniel D. Stid, *The President as Statesman: Woodrow Wilson and the Constitution* (Lawrence: University Press of Kansas, 1998), 35–45.

44. "The Plain Way," *New York Times*, October 14, 1893, 4.

45. *New York Evening Post*, July 16, 1896; paraphrased in White, *The Republican Era*, 308.

46. Richard E. Welch Jr., *The Presidencies of Grover Cleveland* (Lawrence: University Press of Kansas, 1988), 48.

47. King and Ragsdale, *The Elusive Executive*, 88, 163–164. On the uses of executive orders, see Kenneth Mayer, *By the Stroke of a Pen: Executive Orders and Presidential Power* (Princeton, N.J.: Princeton University Press, 2001), chaps. 1–2.

48. Wilson, *Constitutional Government in the United States*, 65.

49. Gould, *The Modern American Presidency*, chap. 1.

50. Ideas of presidential modernization are also developed by Fred Greenstein (ed.), *Leadership in the Modern Presidency* (Cambridge, Mass.: Harvard University Press, 1988), see the first and last chapters.

51. James G. March and Johan P. Olsen, *Rediscovering Institutions: The Organizational Basis of Politics* (New York: Free Press, 1989), 8; also see Jon Elster, "Marxism, Functionalism and Game Theory: The Case for Methodological Individualism," *Theory and Society* 11, no. 4 (July 1982): 454.

52. C-Span's poll of viewers ranked Taft 24th. www.americanpresidents.org/survey/viewer/26.asp; accessed September 18, 2006.

53. Of course, in 1911 and 1912 Roosevelt worked feverishly to assure that Taft's reputation would be that of a do-nothing reactionary. See the discussion of their relationship in Gould, *The Modern Presidency*, chap. 2. Also, see Peri E. Arnold, "Roosevelt versus Taft: The Institutional Key to 'the Friendship That Split the Republican Party,'" *Miller Center Journal* 5 (spring 1998): 23–40.

54. Karen Orren and Stephen Skowronek, *The Search for American Political Development* (New York: Cambridge University Press, 2004), esp. chap. 3.

55. Stephen Skowronek, *Building a New American State: The Expansion of National Administrative Capacities, 1877–1920* (New York: Cambridge University Press, 1982), esp. 169–176. For relevant and related conceptualizations of institutional change, see Orren and Skowronek, "Beyond the Iconography of Order: Notes for a 'New Institutionalism.'" See also Kathleen Thelen, "Timing and Temporality in the Analysis of Institutional Evolution and Change," *Studies in American Political Development* 14 (spring 2000): 101–108.

56. See Morton Keller, *Regulating a New Economy: Public Policy and Economic Change in America, 1900–1933* (Cambridge, Mass.: Harvard University Press, 1990); Oliver Zunz, *Making America Corporate, 1870–1921* (Chicago: University of Chicago Press, 1990).

57. Keller, *Regulating a New Economy*, 24.

58. Alfred D. Chandler, *The Visible Hand: The Managerial Revolution in American Business* (Cambridge, Mass.: Harvard University Press, 1977); Martin J. Sklar, *The Corporate Reconstruction of American Capitalism, 1890–1916* (New York: Cambridge University Press, 1988).

59. For a powerful analysis of the implications of interest groups replacing party influence on policy formation, see Mancur Olson, *The Rise and Decline of Nations: Economic Growth, Stagflation, and Social Rigidities* (New Haven, Conn.: Yale University Press, 1982).

60. Samuel Hays, "Political Parties and the Community-Society Continuum," in William Nisbet Chambers and Walter Dean Burnham (eds.), *The American Party System: Stages of Political Development* (New York: Oxford University Press, 1975), 169.

61. Robert Wiebe, *The Search for Order* (New York: Hill and Wang, 1967), 129; Debby Applegate, "The Cultural Uses of the Spirit," in Burton J. Bledstein and Robert D. Johnston (eds.), *The Middling Sorts: The Explorations in the History of the American Middle Class* (New York: Routledge, 2001), 101–124.

62. Michael McGerr, *A Fierce Discontent: The Rise and Fall of the Progressive Movement in America* (New York: Oxford University Press, 2003), 73.

63. McGerr, *A Fierce Discontent*, 43; In the 1890 census, about a third of the population lived in communities with 8,000 or more population. John Garraty, *The New Commonwealth, 1877–1890* (New York: Harper & Row, 1968), 179.

64. Data from King and Ragsdale, *The Elusive Executive*, 430–435; and see Walter Dean Burnham, "The Changing Shape of the American Political Universe," *American Political Science Review* 59 (1965): 7–28.

65. Kernell, *Going Public*, 67.

66. Bureau of the Census, *Historical Statistics of the United States 1789–1945* (Washington, D.C.: U.S. Government Printing Office, 1961), 710; Skowronek, *Building a New American State*, chap. 3.

67. Daniel J. Tichenor, *Dividing Lines: The Politics of Immigration Control in America* (Princeton, N.J.: Princeton University Press, 2002), 116.

68. Grant McConnell, *The Decline of Agrarian Democracy* (Berkeley: University of California Press, 1953). For a more general treatment of the logic of interest group organization, see Grant McConnell, *Private Power and American Democracy* (New York: Knopf, 1966).

69. Elizabeth Sanders, *Roots of Reform* (Chicago: University of Chicago Press, 1999).

70. Robert Harrison, *Congress, Progressive Reform, and the New American State* (Cambridge, U.K.: Cambridge University Press, 2004).

71. Michael McGerr writes, "The middle class began to explore the implications of associational and social solidarity with others . . . it also looked to state power," *A Fierce Discontent*, 67.

72. Harrison, *Congress, Progressive Reform, and the New American State*, 274.

73. "The 'Administration Party' in Congress," *New York Times*, July 10, 1902, 8.

74. Gary J. Miller, "Abnormal Politics: Possibilities for Presidential Leadership," paper delivered at the Annual Meeting of the American Political Science Association, August 30– September 2, 1990, San Francisco, California.

75. John P. Burke and Fred I. Greenstein, with Larry Berman and Richard Immerman, *How Presidents Test Reality: Decision on Vietnam 1954 and 1965* (New York: Russell Sage Foundation, 1989), 9–10.

76. Harrison, *Congress, Progressive Reform, and the New American State*, 156.

77. Lewis L. Gould, *The Presidency of William McKinley* (Lawrence: University Press of Kansas, 1980), 241.

78. Ibid., 248–249.

79. Eric Rauchway, "William McKinley and US," *Journal of the Gilded Age and Progressive Era* 4, no. 3 (July 2005): 23.

80. March and Olsen, *Rediscovering Institutions*, 57.

81. Terry Moe, "The Politicized Presidency," in John Chubb and Paul Peterson (eds.), *The New Direction in American Politics* (Washington, D.C.: Brookings Institution, 1985), 237. For recent contributions to this research program, see William Howell, *Power without Persuasion* (Princeton, N.J.: Princeton University Press, 2003); and David Lewis, *Presidents and the Politics of Agency Design* (Stanford: Stanford University Press, 2003).

82. Moe, "The Politicized Presidency," 238.

83. Skowronek, *The Politics Presidents Make*, 229.

84. Ibid., 231.

85. Contrast that lack of resources to the modern presidency's organizational and staff resources. See Fred Greenstein, "Nine Presidents in Search of a Modern Presidency," in Greenstein, *Leadership in the Modern Presidency*, 296–354; and John P. Burke, *The Institutional Presidency* (Baltimore: Johns Hopkins University Press, 1992).

86. Charles Lindblom, "Still Muddling, Not Yet Through," *Public Administration Review* 39 (November/December 1979): 517–526.

87. K. J. Radford, *Strategic and Tactical Decisions,* 2d ed. (Toronto: University Press of Canada, 1988), 3.

88. Ceaser, *Presidential Selection*, chaps. 3 and 4.

89. See Alexander L. George and Juliette L. George, *Presidential Personality and Performance* (Boulder, Col.: Westview Press, 1998), esp. chap. 1; Fred Greenstein, *The Presidential Difference: Leadership Style from FDR to Clinton* (Princeton, N.J.: Princeton University Press, 2000).

90. My approach is influenced by Thomas Preston, *The President and His Inner Circle: Leadership Style and the Advisory Process in Foreign Affairs* (New York: Columbia University Press, 2001).

91. For reasons explained below, three issues are examined for Woodrow Wilson.

92. Skowronek, *The Politics Presidents Make*, 18.

93. Ibid., 24.

Chapter 2. The Political Education of Theodore Roosevelt: Partisan Loyalty, Reform, and the Politics of Self-Display

1. John Morton Blum, *The Republican Roosevelt* (Cambridge, Mass.: Harvard University Press, 1954), 4.

2. "More Troops for Montauk," *New York Times,* August 11, 1898, 2.

3. "The Rough Riders Land at Montauk," *New York Times,* August 16, 1898, 1.

4. "More Troops for Montauk," 2.

5. "The Rough Riders Land at Montauk," 1.

6. "The Cowboy Regiments," *New York Times,* April 28, 1898, 1.

7. Quoted in Leonard D. White, *The Republican Era: 1869–1901* (New York: Macmillan, 1958), 168.

8. H. W. Brands, *T.R.: The Last Romantic* (New York: Basic Books, 1997), 361–362.

9. Letter, Theodore Roosevelt to Henry Cabot Lodge, July 31, 1898, in Elting E. Morison (ed.), *The Letters of Theodore Roosevelt,* vol. 2 (Cambridge, Mass.: Harvard University Press, 1951), 863.

10. G. Wallace Chessman, *Governor Theodore Roosevelt, 1898–1900* (Cambridge, Mass.: Harvard University Press, 1965), 15–17.

11. "Roosevelt's Boom Grows," *New York Times,* August 20, 1898, 1.

12. John Milton Cooper, *The Warrior and the Priest* (Cambridge, Mass.: Harvard University Press, 1983), 70.

13. Sarah Watts, *Rough Rider in the White House* (Chicago: University of Chicago Press, 2003), 238–239.

14. "Roosevelt Home Jubilee," *New York Times,* September 22, 1898, 1.

15. Letter, Theodore Roosevelt to Francis E. Leupp, September 3, 1898, in Morison (ed.) *The Letters of Theodore Roosevelt,* 2:870–871.

16. "Teddy's Terrors," *Denver Republican,* reprinted in *New York Times,* August 28, 1898, 6.

17. Watts, *Rough Rider in the White House,* 191.

18. Michael McGerr, *A Fierce Discontent: The Rise and Fall of the Progressive Movement in America* (New York: Oxford University Press, 2003), xiv.

19. "Action of Independents," *New York Times,* September 10, 1898, 12.

20. Letter, Theodore Roosevelt to Henry Cabot Lodge, September 19, 1898, in Morison, *The Letters of Theodore Roosevelt*, 2:876–877; and Theodore Roosevelt to John Jay Chapman, September 22, 1898, ibid., 2:877.

21. "Roosevelt the Standard Bearer," *New York Times*, September 28, 1898, 1.

22. See Letters, Roosevelt to Lemuel Quigg, October 16 and October 21, 1898, in Morison, *The Letters of Theodore Roosevelt*, 2:884–887. On Roosevelt's balancing act between political orthodoxy and reform politics, see Blum, *The Republican Roosevelt*.

23. Theodore Roosevelt, *An Autobiography* (New York: Macmillan, 1913), 293–305.

24. These negative electoral consequences of Roosevelt's post-Montauk personal political performance foreshadows what Theodore Lowi argues is the highly fragile base of political support for the post–New Deal plebiscitary presidency. See Lowi, *The Personal President: Power Invested, Promise Unfulfilled* (Ithaca, N.Y.: Cornell University Press, 1985), chap. 5.

25. Roosevelt, *An Autobiography*, 298.

26. Letter, Roosevelt to James Rockwell Sheffield, January 29, 1900, in Morison, *The Letters of Theodore Roosevelt*, 2:1148–1149.

27. For example, see the letter to his sister, Roosevelt to Anna Roosevelt Cowles, April 30, 1900, ibid., 2:1276–1278.

28. Paul Grondahl, *I Rose Like a Rocket: The Political Education of Theodore Roosevelt* (New York: Free Press, 2004), 340–351.

29. Blum, *The Republican Roosevelt*, 22–23.

30. Ibid., 7.

31. See Stephen Skowronek, *Building a New American State: The Expansion of National Administrative Capacities, 1877–1920* (New York: Cambridge University Press, 1982); and Robert Wiebe, *The Search for Order, 1877–1920* (New York: Hill and Wang, 1967).

32. John Morton Blum, *The Progressive Presidents* (New York: Norton, 1980), 24.

33. Consider the civil service commission. Leonard White wrote that it was "chronically understaffed and not infrequently in danger of the total loss of its appropriation"; *The Republican Era* (New York: Macmillan, 1958), 313. Bartholomew Sparrow's "resource dependent perspective" in discussing the government's capacity building during World War II sheds light, as well, on the problems faced by administrative agencies in obtaining resources to sustain and strengthen their functions. See Sparrow, *From Outside In* (Princeton, N.J.: Princeton University Press, 1996), 17–22.

34. Examining agencies at the beginning of the administrative state, Daniel P. Carpenter shows the crucial role of bureaucratic leaders in building support for, and establishing the reputation of, their agencies. Carpenter, *The Forging of Bureaucratic Autonomy: Regulations, Networks, and Policy Innovation in Executive Agencies, 1862–1928* (Princeton, N.J.: Princeton University Press, 2001), chap. 1.

35. Max Weber, *The Theory of Social and Economic Organization* (New York: Free Press, 1964), 339.

36. See Patricia W. Ingraham, *The Foundation of Merit: Public Service in American Democracy* (Baltimore: Johns Hopkins University Press, 1995), chaps. 2 and 3. For an organization

theory perspective, see Ronald N. Johnson and Gary Libecap, *The Federal Civil Service System and the Problem of Bureaucracy* (Chicago: University of Chicago Press, 1994).

37. Roosevelt, *An Autobiography*, 144–145.

38. For a description of legislative efforts to undercut the commission, see Theodore Roosevelt, "Six Years of Civil Service Reform," in Roosevelt, *Administration—Civil Service* (New York: G. P. Putnam, 1902), 23–40. Also consult Ari Hoogenboom, *Outlawing the Spoils* (Urbana: University of Illinois Press, 1961).

39. See Roosevelt, *An Autobiography*, 151–154.

40. Letter, Roosevelt to Arthur Pue Gorman, March 1, 1891, in Morison, *The Letters of Theodore Roosevelt*, 1:239–240.

41. Richard D. White Jr., *Roosevelt the Reformer* (Tuscaloosa: University of Alabama Press, 2004), 26.

42. White, *The Republican Era*, 307.

43. Ibid., 306–307.

44. See letters, Roosevelt to Henry Cabot Lodge, July 11, 1889 and July 17, 1889, in Morison, *The Letters of Theodore Roosevelt*, 1:170–172 and 173–174.

45. Beginning with his state assembly service, Roosevelt had exhibited a moral style of political rhetoric. See Brands, *T.R.: The Last Romantic*, 133. However, what was, initially, just the preaching of "the dude," matured into a potent rhetorical appeal to Americans seeking reform leadership.

46. White, *The Republican Era*, 324.

47. "Of all the public departments . . . the most contaminated by the Machine is . . . the police, whose cooperation is particularly valuable to it." Moise Ostrogorski, *Democracy and the Organization of Political Parties*, vol. 2, *The United States*, edited and abridged by S. M. Lipset (Garden City, N.Y.: Anchor, 1964), 209.

48. It should be noted that the police commission also oversaw the city's health department.

49. Robert Gregg, "Uneasy Streets: Police Corruption and Anxiety in Bombay, London, and New York City," in Emmanuel Kreike and William C. Jordan (eds.), *Corrupt Histories* (Rochester, N.Y.: University of Rochester Press, 2004), 188.

50. Roosevelt, *An Autobiography*, 188.

51. New York's legislature was typically Republican and constrained the New York City mayor's power over the police because the city was usually dominated politically by the Democratic Tammany machine.

52. H. Paul Jeffers, *Commissioner Roosevelt: The Story of Theodore Roosevelt and the New York Police Commission, 1895–1897* (New York: John Wiley, 1995), 98–99.

53. "Roosevelt in Action," *New York Times*, July 12, 1895, 20.

54. Roosevelt, *An Autobiography*, 191.

55. Jacob Riis was a seasoned New York City reporter as well as the author of *How the Other Half Lives* (New York: Scribners, 1890), a sensational report on poverty in New York City.

56. "Police Caught Napping," *New York Times*, June 8, 1895, 16. See Eric Rauchway, *Murdering McKinley: The Making of Theodore Roosevelt's America* (New York: Hill and Wang, 2003), 138–150.

57. Roosevelt, *An Autobiography*, 185.

58. Ibid., 186.

59. See Jeffers, *Commissioner Roosevelt*, 125.

60. Watts, *Rough Rider in the White House*, 26.

61. Brands, *T.R.: The Last Romantic*, 280.

62. *Washington Post*, April 7, 1897, 1.

63. See Theodore Roosevelt to Henry White, March 8, 1897, in Morison, *The Letters of Theodore Roosevelt*, 1:583.

64. Thomas Platt, quoted in Brands, *T.R.: The Last Romantic*, 305.

65. Harold and Margaret Sprout, *The Rise of American Naval Power: 1776–1918* (Princeton, N.J.: Princeton University Press, 1944), 224–225.

66. Letter, Roosevelt to Long, August 13, 1897, in Morison, *The Letters of Theodore Roosevelt*, 1:649–650.

67. Speech quoted in "Naval War College Opened," *New York Times*, June 3, 1897, 2.

68. For one of the earliest letters he wrote Mahan after entering the navy department, see the document specified "personal and private," letter, Theodore Roosevelt to Alfred Thayer Mahan, May 3, 1897, in Morison, *The Letters of Theodore Roosevelt*, 1:607–608.

69. Roosevelt's communication with President McKinley about strategic issues can be inferred from his description to Henry Cabot Lodge of such a meeting with him on September 14, 1897. Letter, Theodore Roosevelt to Henry Cabot Lodge, September 15, 1897, in ibid., 1:676. For Roosevelt's influence on McKinley, and the president's use of Roosevelt, see Brands, *T.R.: The Last Romantic*, 312–329.

70. Roosevelt, *An Autobiography*, 230.

71. Ibid., 230–231.

72. Letter, Theodore Roosevelt to John Long, August 5, 1897, in Morison, *The Letters of Theodore Roosevelt*, 1:639–640.

73. Roosevelt was also immersed in a technical debate over military construction regarding the question of the mounts for the secondary batteries in the construction of the warships *Kentucky* and *Kearsage*. See Letters, Roosevelt to Richard Henry Dana, May 8 and May 21, 1897, in Morison, *The Letters of Theodore Roosevelt*, 1:609–610, 616–617.

74. "Navy Militia Report," *New York Times*, August 8, 1897, 10.

75. Report, Roosevelt to John Long, December 9, 1897, in Morison, *The Letters of Theodore Roosevelt*, 1:726–740.

76. "The Navy Reorganization Bill," *New York Times*, May 17, 1898, 6.

77. Harold and Margaret Sprout, *The Rise of American Naval Power*, 225.

78. Max Weber, "Politics as a Vocation," in David Hacket and Tracy Strong (eds.), *Weber, The Vocation Lectures* (Indianapolis: Hackett, 2004).

79. Here I define Roosevelt in terms drawn from Weber, "Politics as a Vocation."

80. Letter, Roosevelt to Bellamy Storer, April 21, 1899, in Morison, *The Letters of Theodore Roosevelt*, 2:992–993. Roosevelt's last successful election was in 1883, for his third one-year term in the New York State assembly.

81. Roosevelt, *An Autobiography*, 301.

82. Ostrogorski, *Democracy and the Organization of Political Parties*, 2:226.

83. Roosevelt, *An Autobiography*, 96; Lewis Gould, *The Grand Old Party: A History of the Republicans* (New York: Random House, 2003), 100–102.

84. Theodore Roosevelt, "Morality and Efficiency," in Roosevelt, *American Ideals* (New York: G. P. Putnam, 1904), 76–77.

85. Stephen Skowronek, *The Politics Presidents Make: Leadership from John Adams to Bill Clinton* (Cambridge, Mass.: Harvard University Press, 1997), 231.

86. Harold Gosnell wrote of Platt, when the governor "was concerned about the confirmation of a[n] . . . appointment . . . he . . . saw Platt." Gosnell, "Thomas C. Platt—Political Manager," *Political Science Quarterly* 38, no. 3 (September 1923): 444.

87. Ibid., 451.

88. "Payn, Roosevelt, and Root," *New York Times*, December 15, 1899, 6.

89. Chessman, *Governor Theodore Roosevelt*, 97.

90. "Payn in Line with Platt," *New York Times* (October 24, 1899), 1; and "Payne to Fight Governor," *New York Times*, December 14, 1899, 2.

91. Letter, Roosevelt to Henry Cabot Lodge, December 29, 1899, in Morison, *The Letters of Theodore Roosevelt*, 2:1121–1122.

92. Chessman, *Governor Theodore Roosevelt*, 99–108; Letter, Roosevelt to John Proctor Clarke, January 12, 1900, in Morison, *The Letters of Theodore Roosevelt*, 2:1131–1132.

93. Letter, Roosevelt to Florence Bayard Lockwood La Farge, January 22, 1900, in ibid., 2:1135–1136.

94. It is in the midst of Roosevelt's pressuring Platt over Payn that Senator Platt began to plot the means for ridding himself of Roosevelt by nominating the governor in 1900 for the vice presidency. Letter, Roosevelt to Henry Cabot Lodge, December 30, 1899, in ibid., 2:1123.

95. Letter, Roosevelt to James Rockwell Sheffield, January 29, 1900, in Morison, *The Letters of Theodore Roosevelt*, 2:1148–1149.

96. Chessman, *Governor Theodore Roosevelt*, 75.

97. Roosevelt, *An Autobiography*, 297–299.

98. Letter, Roosevelt to Benjamin Barker Odell, March 15, 1899, in Morison, *The Letters of Theodore Roosevelt*, 2:962.

99. For an excellent discussion of the progressive drive for controlling big business, see Michael McGerr, *A Fierce Discontent: The Rise and Fall of the Progressive Movement in America* (New York: Oxford University Press, 2003), chap. 5; and on regulating utilities and their franchises in that period, see Morton Keller, *Regulating a New Economy: Public Policy and Economic Change in America, 1900–1933* (Cambridge, Mass.: Harvard University Press, 1990), chap. 3.

100. "Governor Roosevelt Sends a Message to the Legislature," *New York Times*, March 28, 1899, 8.

101. For example, as Roosevelt was acting, an initiative for increased taxation of corporations also appeared in New Jersey. "Want to Tax Corporations," *Wall Street Journal*, January 23, 1899, 5.

102. Blum, *The Republican Roosevelt*, 17.

103. Roosevelt, *An Autobiography*, 325.

104. On March 28 Roosevelt called for a legislative committee to study the question of franchise taxation, and party leaders gave that as their reason for sidelining the Ford bill. "New York Legislature," *New York Times,* April 15, 1899, 10.

105. "Governor Roosevelt Reaches Chicago," *Chicago Tribune,* April 10, 1899, 1.

106. "Governor Roosevelt on Taxes," *New York Times,* April 17, 1899, 3.

107. Edwin R. A. Seligman, "The Franchise Tax Law in New York," *Quarterly Journal of Economics* 13, no. 4 (July 1899): 451.

108. "Franchises to be Taxed," *New York Times,* April 29, 1899, 1.

109. Letter, Platt to Roosevelt, May 6, 1899, quoted in Chessman, *Governor Theodore Roosevelt,* 149.

110. Letter, Roosevelt to Platt, May 8, 1899, in Morison, *The Letters of Theodore Roosevelt,* 2:1004–1009.

111. It is interesting that even years after the nomination, in his *Autobiography,* Roosevelt wrote without a hint of his own ambitions at the time about the push and pull of forces leading him to the nomination. In his narrative, his fate was like a cork on the water pushed one way and the other by the forces of Platt, Hanna, and the party's popular sentiment. For Roosevelt, the refusal to admit to personal motives was often a signal of strong personal motives. See *Autobiography,* 331–334.

112. The Rough Riders again served as Roosevelt's defining image in the 1900 election. As a former Rough Rider appealed to voters in a 1900 campaign speech: "Vote for my colonel. He will lead you, as he led us, like sheep to the slaughter!" Quoted in Watts, *Rough Rider in the White House,* 199.

Chapter 3. Constructing Leadership to Make History: Anti-Trust and the Navy

1. Theodore Roosevelt, *An Autobiography* (New York: Macmillan, 1913), 420–421.

2. Letter, Roosevelt to William Howard Taft, March 12, 1901, Papers of Theodore Roosevelt, series 2, vol. 28, reel 325, Microfilm Edition, Library of Congress.

3. "The New President," *Washington Post,* September 15, 1901, 1.

4. Even as vice president, Roosevelt sought to ease doubts about him among "the influential classes," as he explained to Elihu Root in a letter describing a dinner he gave for J. P. Morgan. "Hitherto, I have given dinners only to professional politicians or . . . wild-eyed reformers." Letter, Roosevelt to Elihu Root, December 5, 1900, Roosevelt Papers, series 2, vol. 26, reel 325, no. 380.

5. "President McKinley Death," *The Nation* 73, no. 1890 (September 19, 1901): 218.

6. "Roosevelt's Future," *Washington Post,* September 15, 1901, 3.

7. "President McKinley Death," 218.

8. Fred I. Greenstein, "Can Personality and Politics Be Studied Systematically," *Political Psychology* 13, no. 1 (1992): 123.

9. William Allen White, "Theodore Roosevelt," *McClure's Magazine* (November 1901): 42.

10. Mathew Crenson and Benjamin Ginsberg, *Presidential Power: Unchecked and Unbalanced* (New York: Norton, 2007), 117.

11. For examination of McKinley as a transitional figure, see Lewis L. Gould, *The Modern American Presidency* (Lawrence: University Press of Kansas, 2003), chap. 1; and Gould, *The Presidency of William McKinley* (Lawrence: University Press of Kansas, 1980).

12. Matthew Josephson, *The President Makers: The Culture of Politics and Leadership in an Age of Enlightenment, 1896–1919* (New York: Harcourt, Brace, 1940), 115. Wayne Morgan, "William McKinley as a Political Leader," *Review of Politics* 28, no. 4 (October 1966): 421.

13. Morton Keller, *Affairs of State* (Cambridge, Mass.: Harvard University Press, 1977), 297.

14. H. W. Brands, *T.R.: The Last Romantic* (New York: Basic Books, 1997), 543; and John Morton Blum observes that Roosevelt "was never more intent on achievement" than after his great victory in the 1904 election. John Morton Blum, *The Republican Roosevelt* (Cambridge, Mass.: Harvard University Press, 1954), 73.

15. "1900 Republican Platform," in Kirk H. Porter and Donald B. Johnson (eds.), *National Party Platforms, 1840–1956* (Urbana: University of Illinois Press, 1956), 122–123.

16. See Naomi Lamoreaux, *The Great Merger Movement in American Business, 1895–1904* (New York: Cambridge University Press, 1985).

17. "Roosevelt on the Trusts," *Washington Post*, October 27, 1900, 6.

18. "Teddy Making a Triumphal Tour," *Los Angeles Times*, September 8, 1900, 1.

19. Keller, *Affairs of State*, 434–435; see data presentation in Hans B. Thorelli, *The Federal Antitrust Policy: Origination of an American Tradition* (Baltimore: Johns Hopkins University Press, 1955), 275; more generally, see Sklar, *The Corporate Reconstruction of American Capitalism*, 1–33; and Lamoreaux, *The Great Merger Movement in American Business*.

20. John Milton Cooper Jr., *Pivotal Decades: The United States, 1900–1920* (New York: Norton, 1990), 11–12; and Thorelli, *The Federal Antitrust Policy*, chap. 6.

21. Thorelli, *The Federal Antitrust Policy*, 226; Sklar, *The Corporate Reconstruction of American Capitalism*, 105–117.

22. Thorelli, *The Federal Antitrust Policy*, 369–410. The most notorious of the labor cases was *In Re Debs* (1895), which sustained a federal injunction against striking railroad unions on the authority of the Sherman Act.

23. Charles McCurdy, "The *Knight* Decision of 1895 and the Modernization of American Corporation Law: 1869–1903," *Business History Review* 53 (1979): 304–342.

24. See Sklar, *The Corporate Reconstruction of American Capitalism*, 127–146; and Thorelli, *The Federal Antitrust Policy*, 445–448.

25. Sklar, *The Corporate Reconstruction of American Capitalism*, 117–133.

26. See ibid., 335–343.

27. Brands, *T.R.: The Last Romantic*, 427.

28. For example, Grover Cleveland introduced his 1893 annual message, "commending to the Congress a careful examination of the . . . reports of the heads of Departments who are chiefly charged with the executive work. . . . In an effort to abridge this communication . . . I shall supplement a brief reference to the contents of these departmental reports by the mention of such executive business and incidents as are not embraced therein and by such recommendations as appear to be at this . . . time appropriate." "First Annual Message," December 4, 1893, in James D. Richardson (ed.), *Messages and Papers of the Presidents, 1789–1897,*

vol. 9 (Washington, D.C.: U.S. Government Printing Office, 1898), 434. See Melvin Laracey, *Presidents and the People: The Partisan Story of Going Public* (College Station: Texas A&M University Press, 2002), 142–144.

29. Theodore Roosevelt, "First Annual Message," American Presidency Project at University of California, Santa Barbara, americanpresidency.org; accessed May 21, 2007.

30. Ibid.

31. Roosevelt, *An Autobiography,* 465–466.

32. John Patrick Diggins, *The Promise of Pragmatism: Modernism and the Crisis of Knowledge and Authority* (Chicago: University of Chicago Press, 1994), 34.

33. The essential core of pragmatism as the term is used here is well captured by James Livingston's characterization of Henry James's thought. Pragmatism is "this account of the truth as the profoundly contingent or functional relation between ideas and their impending objects." James Livingston, *Pragmatism and the Political Economy of Cultural Revolution, 1850–1940* (Chapel Hill: University of North Carolina Press, 1991), 200.

34. Entry for January 22, 1901, Diary, Papers of George C. Cortelyou, Library of Congress, Washington, D.C.

35. Letter, Theodore Roosevelt to Nicholas Murray Butler, October 1, 1901, series 2, vol. 31, reel 327, Roosevelt Papers, Microfilm Edition, Library of Congress.

36. Letter, Theodore Roosevelt to Brooks Adams, September 27, 1901, ibid.

37. Letters, Theodore Roosevelt to various recipients, September and October 1901, ibid.

38. Letter, Theodore Roosevelt to Senator Nelson Aldrich, September 30, 1901, ibid.

39. Letter, Theodore Roosevelt to George W. Ray, November 2, 1901, series 2, vol. 32, reel 327, Roosevelt Papers.

40. Letter, Theodore Roosevelt to Wayne MacVeagh, October 7, 1901, series 2, vol. 31, reel 327, Roosevelt Papers.

41. Letters, Theodore Roosevelt to various, series 2, vols. 30–32, reel 327, Roosevelt Papers.

42. Letter, Theodore Roosevelt to Senator Orville Platt, November 15, 1901, in Elting E. Morison (ed.), *The Letters of Theodore Roosevelt*, vol. 3 (Cambridge, Mass.: Harvard University Press, 1951), 198.

43. Letter, Theodore Roosevelt to Paul Dana, November 18, 1901, in ibid., 200.

44. Letter, Roosevelt to Douglas Robinson, October 17, 1901, in ibid., 167–177.

45. Letter, Roosevelt to Paul Dana, November 18, 1901, in ibid., 200.

46. Letter, William Taft to Charles Taft, December 3, 1905, series 1, reel 21, Papers of William Howard Taft, Microfilm Edition, Library of Congress.

47. Roosevelt, *An Autobiography,* 383.

48. "Opinions of Editors," *Chicago Tribune,* December 4, 1901, 12.

49. A legal history of the *Northern Securities* case can be found in Balthasar Meyer, "A History of the *Northern Securities* Case," *Bulletin of the University of Wisconsin: Economics and Political Science Series* 1, no. 3 (1906): 215–350. For a brief overview of the case, see R. W. Apple Jr., "The Case of the Monopolistic Railroadmen," in John A. Garraty (ed.), *Quarrels That Have Shaped the Constitution* (New York: Harper & Row, 1987), 175–192.

50. See Louis L. Gould, *The Presidency of Theodore Roosevelt* (Lawrence: University Press of Kansas, 1991), 213–218.

51. Sklar, *The Corporate Reconstruction of American Capitalism*, 342. For an informative discussion of the relationship between Roosevelt's *Northern Securities* suit and his effort for corporate regulatory legislation, see Arthur M. Johnson, "Antitrust Policy in Transition, 1908: Ideal and Reality," *Mississippi Valley Historical Review* 48, no. 3 (December 1961): 415–434.

52. "President's Action Startles Wall Street," *New York Times*, February 21, 1902, 1.

53. Ibid.

54. Philip C. Jessup, *Elihu Root*, vol. 1 (New York: Dodd, Mead, 1938), 414.

55. Richard Neustadt. *Presidential Power and the Modern Presidents* (New York: Free Press, 1990), 8–9.

56. G. Wallace Chessman, *Governor Theodore Roosevelt* (Cambridge, Mass.: Harvard University Press, 1965), 166.

57. Letter, Roosevelt to Herschel V. Jones, February 26, 1902, in Morison, *The Letters of Theodore Roosevelt*, 3:236.

58. The charge that Roosevelt acted with secrecy toward business, uncharacteristic of presidents, should be taken with a grain of salt, if only because the Interstate Commerce Commission in December 1901 had announced it would investigate Northern Securities' business model and its purposes. Gould, *The Presidency of Theodore Roosevelt*, 50.

59. Blum, *The Republican Roosevelt*, 119–122; William Henry Harbison, *Power and Responsibility: The Life and Times of Theodore Roosevelt* (New York: Farrar, Straus and Cudahy, 1961), 161; Gould, *The Presidency of Theodore Roosevelt*, 27.

60. Thorelli, *The Federal Antitrust Policy*, 421.

61. "Shall Blackmail Be Nationalized?" *New York Times*, May 3, 1901, 6.

62. "Oregon State Ticket and Platform," *Los Angeles Times*, April 3, 1902, 1.

63. "Peril to Capital," from the *Philadelphia Press*, reprinted in the *Washington Post*, April 18, 1902, 14.

64. G. Edward White, *Justice Oliver Wendell Holmes: The Law and the Inner Self* (New York: Oxford University Press, 1993), 299.

65. Letter, Roosevelt to Henry Cabot Lodge, July 10, 1902, in Morison, *The Letters of Theodore Roosevelt*, 3:288–290.

66. Quoted in Richard H. Wagner, "A Falling Out: The Relationship between Oliver Wendell Holmes and Theodore Roosevelt," *Journal of Supreme Court History* 27, no. 2 (2002): 120.

67. Letter, Theodore Roosevelt to Philander Knox, April 28, 1903, Papers of Philander Chase Knox, Library of Congress, Washington, D.C.

68. See the discussion of Supreme Court appointments in Henry J. Abraham, *Justices and Presidents: A Political History of Appointments to the Supreme Court*, 3d ed. (New York: Oxford University Press, 1992), chap. 7.

69. Meyer, "A History of the Northern Securities Case," 272–273.

70. *Northern Securities Co. v. U.S.*, 193 U.S. 197 (1904).

71. Dissenting opinion of Justice Holmes, *Northern Securities Co. vs. U.S.* What is curious about Holmes's dissent in *Northern Securities* is that it both belied his major theoretical premise as a jurist that the law is organic and contextual and is inconsistent with the pattern of his later and far more progressive tendencies. On the peculiarities of his dissent, see

R. Blake Brown and Bruce A. Kimball, "When Holmes Borrowed from Langdell: The 'Ultra Legal' Formalism and Public Policy of Northern Securities (1904)," *American Journal of Legal History* 45 (2001): 278–321.

72. Quoted in White, *Justice Oliver Wendell Holmes*, 307.

73. "War on Beef Trust," *Los Angeles Times,* April 9, 1902, 1.

74. "Beef and the Railroads," *Washington Post,* April 7, 1902, 6.

75. "The 'Beef Trust,'" *Washington Post,* April 4, 1902, 14.

76. "Mr. Roosevelt to the Rescue," *Washington Post,* April 26, 1902, 6.

77. Quoted from *The Commoner,* "W. J. Bryan's Open Letter," *New York Times,* June 6, 1902, 1.

78. Memorandum, Knox to Roosevelt, n.d. (103–104 in letter book), Papers of Philander Chase Knox, Library of Congress, Washington, D.C.; Letter, Roosevelt to Winthrop Murray Crane, October 22, 1902, in Morison, *The Letters of Theodore Roosevelt,* 3:359–366.

79. Letter, Roosevelt to Winthrop Murray Crane, October 22, 1902. Roosevelt's threat was never publicly announced but he had apparently identified a senior military officer to lead the operation, General John Schofield, and informed at least Secretary of War Root and Attorney General Knox of his plan. In turn, Root and Knox were negotiating with the owners and others, such as J. P. Morgan, and it is likely that Roosevelt's intention was communicated to them in some form because shortly afterward the owners came to the table to accept arbitration by a presidential commission. Gould, *The Presidency of Theodore Roosevelt,* 69–71.

80. William Henry Harbaugh, *Power and Responsibility: The Life and Times of Theodore Roosevelt* (New York: Farrar, Straus and Cudahy, 1961), chap. 10.

81. "The President's Great Work," *Washington Post,* October 17, 1902, 6.

82. Theodore Roosevelt, "Second Annual Message," December 2, 1902, at John Woolley and Gerhard Peters, *The American Presidency Project;* online at www.presidency.ucsb.edu; accessed June 6, 2007.

83. Sklar, *The Corporate Reconstruction of American Capitalism,* 346.

84. "Theodore Roosevelt, Second Annual Message," December 2, 1902 at American Presidency Project, online at www.presidency.ucsb.edu; accessed June 6, 2007.

85. For example, as court cases were pending and the administration was preparing legislation, Roosevelt arranged an interview for Knox with Henry Brown of the *New York Herald,* and a highly favorable story followed on February 2, 1903. Letter, George Cortelyou to Philander Knox, January 20, 1903, Papers of Philander Chase Knox, Library of Congress, Washington, D.C.

86. Letter, Joseph B. Bishop to William Taft, September 17, 1903, series 3, reel 40, Taft Papers.

87. Keller, *Affairs of State,* 437–438.

88. Quoted in White, *The Republican Era,* 159.

89. Harold and Margaret Sprout, *The Rise of American Naval Power, 1776–1918* (Princeton, N.J.: Princeton University Press, 1944), 191–201; and White, *The Republican Era,* chap. 8.

90. Theodore Roosevelt, *The Naval War of 1812* (New York: G. P. Putnam, 1882).

91. Harbaugh, *Power and Responsibility,* 98.

92. Speech quoted in "Naval War College Opened," *New York Times,* June 3, 1897, 2.

93. Gary Gerstle, "Theodore Roosevelt and the Divided Character of American Nationalism," *Journal of American History* 86, no. 3 (December 1999): 1281; Harbaugh, *Power and Responsibility*, 97–101; and Blum, *The Republican Roosevelt*, chap. 3.

94. Robert O'Connell, *Sacred Vessels* (Boulder, Col.: Westview, 1991); and Robert K. Massie, *Dreadnought: Britain, Germany, and the Coming of the Great War* (New York: Random House, 1991), 468–497.

95. Quoted in Harold and Margaret Sprout, *The Rise of American Naval Power*, 194.

96. Ibid., 234–235.

97. Ibid., 250.

98. Matthew M. Oyos, "Roosevelt and the Implements of War," *Journal of Military History* 60, no. 4 (October 1996): 633.

99. Donald W. Mitchell, *History of the Modern American Navy* (New York: Knopf, 1946), 133.

100. Ibid., 131–132.

101. Harold and Margaret Sprout, *The Rise of American Naval Power*, 249.

102. Letter, Roosevelt to William Eaton Chandler, November 1, 1901, in Morison, *The Letters of Theodore Roosevelt*, 3:186.

103. In this regard it is instructive to compare Roosevelt's first message to those of McKinley, Cleveland, and Harrison before him. McKinley's first message (December 6, 1897) made no mention at all of the navy, even though the message was concerned with maintaining neutrality regarding the Cuban insurrection against Spain. Cleveland's first message (second term, December 4, 1893), gave eight paragraphs to the navy, but wholly for the purpose of describing the navy secretary's report. And he closed with the caution that Congress should keep an eye on a depleted Treasury before authorizing any new ships. Harrison's first message (December 3, 1889) devoted two paragraphs to the navy. The first referred to the naval secretaries' report and recommendation for more ships, and the second expressed regret for a disaster suffered by a navy ship in the Pacific.

104. Theodore Roosevelt, "First Annual Message," December 2, 1901; John Woolley and Gerhard Peters, *The American Presidency Project,* online at www.presidency.ucsb.edu; accessed June 14, 2007.

105. Gould, *The Presidency of Theodore Roosevelt*, 123; for the list of secretaries and dates served, see Leonard W. Levy and Louis Fisher (eds.), *Encyclopedia of the American Presidency* (New York: Simon & Schuster, 1994), 4:1699.

106. Harold and Margaret Sprout, *The Rise of American Naval Power*, 259.

107. From the *Atlanta Journal*, printed as "Our Army and Navy," *Washington Post,* January 2, 1902, 6.

108. "The American Navy," *Los Angeles Times*, October 14, 1901, 6.

109. Alfred Thayer Mahan, *The Influence of Sea Power upon History: 1660–1789* (Boston: Little, Brown, 1890).

110. William E. Livezey, *Mahan on Sea Power* (Norman: University of Oklahoma Press, 1947), 77–92. Mahan's ideas were sufficiently esteemed that in 1902 he was elected president of the American Historical Association.

111. James R. Reckner, "TR and His Navy," *Naval History* 15, no. 1 (February 2001): 2.

112. Oyos, "Theodore Roosevelt and the Implements of War," 648.

113. John P. Burke, *The Institutional Presidency* (Baltimore: Johns Hopkins University Press, 1992), 12–23.

114. Mitchell, *History of the Modern American Navy*, 156. For the frustrations of William Sims, on whom Roosevelt heavily relied, see Elting E. Morison, *Admiral Sims and the Modern American Navy* (Boston: Houghton Mifflin, 1942).

115. Reckner, "TR and His Navy," 24.

116. Quoted in Reckner, "TR and His Navy," 28.

117. Letters, Key to Roosevelt, January 26 and April 13, 1906; and Memorandum, "Notes on Navy Personnel Legislation," October 31, 1907, series 1, reel 78, Roosevelt Papers, Library of Congress.

118. Quoted in Morison, *Admiral Sims*, 57.

119. Mitchell, *History of the Modern American Navy*, 146–147.

120. Morison, *Admiral Sims*, 57.

121. Letter, William Sims to Roosevelt, November 16, 1901, Special Correspondence: Theodore Roosevelt, 1901–1909, Papers of William Sims, Library of Congress, Washington, D.C.

122. Letter, Roosevelt to William Sheffield Cowles, December 12, 1901, in Morison, *The Letters of Theodore Roosevelt*, 3:206–207.

123. Roosevelt to William Snowden Sims, December 27, 1901, in ibid., 212.

124. Roosevelt, "First Annual Message."

125. Morison, *Admiral Sims*, 57.

126. Roosevelt, *An Autobiography*, 230.

127. Letter, Roosevelt to Henry Clay Taylor, December 27, 1901, in Morison, *The Letters of Theodore Roosevelt*, 3:212.

128. Roosevelt to St. Clair McKelway, January 16, 1902, in ibid., 217.

129. Roosevelt to Henry Clay Taylor, April 22, 1902, in ibid., 253–254.

130. Letter, Albert P. Niblack to William Sims, January 15, 1902, Box 76, Sims Papers.

131. Niblack's appointment was announced in the bureau of navigation's section (dated October 6, 1902) of *Annual Reports of the Navy Department for the Year 1902* (Washington, D.C.: U.S. Government Printing Office, 1902), 402.

132. Roosevelt, *An Autobiography*, 232.

133. Robert K. Massie, *Dreadnought: Britain, Germany, and the Coming of the Great War* (New York: Random House, 1991), 468. And generally, see O'Connell, *Holy Vessels*.

134. Kenneth J. Hagan, *This People's Navy: The Making of American Sea Power* (New York: Free Press, 1991), 193–197.

135. The American fleet's weakness in battleships is evident when these early examples are compared to British ships launched about the same time. The *H.M.S. Trafalgar* (1890) displaced 11,940 tons, the *H.M.S. Mars* (1896) displaced 14,900 tons, and the *H.M.S. Formidable* (1898) displaced 15,0000 tons. http://www.battleships-cruisers.co.uk/battleships.htm; accessed June 15, 2007.

136. Each of the postwar ships displaced 14,948 tons. Harold and Margaret Sprout, *The Rise of American Naval Power*, 218, 248–249.

137. Secretary of the Navy, *Annual Report, 1901* (Washington, D.C.: U.S. Government Printing Office, 1901), 14.

138. Secretary of the Navy, *Annual Report, 1901*, 6.

139. Mitchell, *History of the Modern American Navy*, 131 and 140.

140. Harold and Margaret Sprout, *The Rise of American Naval Power*, 265–270.

141. "President's Address to the Naval Cadets," *New York Times*, May 3, 1902, 3.

142. "President Supplements Monroe Doctrine Speech, *Washington Post*, September 2, 1902, 1.

143. "President Discusses the Monroe Doctrine," *New York Times*, April 3, 1903, 1.

144. Roosevelt, *An Autobiography*, 592.

145. Roosevelt, *An Autobiography*, 593–594.

146. Mitchell, *History of the Modern American Navy*, 132.

147. Ibid., 132.

148. See Morison, *Admiral Sims*, 158–161.

149. Letter, Roosevelt to Sims, October 5, 1904, series 2, reel 335, Roosevelt Papers, Library of Congress.

150. Letter, Sims to Sec. of Navy Truman Newbury, February 18, 1909, Sims Papers. This document constitutes a long memorandum that relates to the secretary the history of Sims's analyses of gunnery, naval organization, and naval architecture. It was prepared as part of a defense to respond to possible charges of insubordination lodged after Roosevelt left office.

151. Morison, *Admiral Sims*, 161.

152. Massie, *Dreadnought*, chap. 26.

153. Harold and Margaret Sprout, *The Rise of American Naval Power*, 262–263.

154. Secretary of the Navy, *Annual Report of the Navy Department* (Washington, D.C.: U.S. Government Printing Office, 1908), 568.

155. Mitchell, *History of the Modern American Navy*, 138.

156. "Building Bigger Warships," *Boston Globe*, April 4, 1907, 10.

157. Morison, *Admiral Sims*, 162–163.

158. Alfred Thayer Mahan, "Reflections, Historical and Other, Suggested by the Battle of the Sea of Japan," in U.S. Congress, Senate, *Size of Battleships*, 59th Cong., 2d Sess., 1907, Senate Doc. No. 213.

159. Letter, Sims to Roosevelt, September 17, 1906, series 1, Roosevelt Papers.

160. William S. Sims, "The Inherent Tactical Qualities of All-Big-Gun, One Caliber Battle Ships of High Speed, Large Displacement and Gun Power," in U.S. Congress, Senate, *Size of Battle Ships*.

161. "The 'All-Big-Gun' Battleship," *New York Times*, February 7, 1907, 8; "The Size of Battleships," *Washington Post*, January 17, 1907, 6.

162. Letter, Sims to Roosevelt, January 10, 1907, series 1, reel 71, Roosevelt Papers.

163. Letter, Roosevelt to Rep. George Foss, January 11, 1907, in Morison, *The Letters of Theodore Roosevelt*, 5:545.

164. Albert Key to Navy Department, Memo on Construction of *South Dakota*, June 9, 1908, Albert Key File, Sims Papers; Letter and Memo, Key to Roosevelt, June 9, 1908, series 1, reel 83, Roosevelt Papers; Letter, Sims to Roosevelt, June 25, 1908, ibid.

165. Interestingly, a year earlier Sims had urged that Roosevelt go public on a naval issue. He said: "It seems to me that the most effective way of influencing the persons . . . who do

not wish to be convinced would be to bring the pressure of public opinion upon them." Letter, Sims to Roosevelt, January 10, 1907, ibid.

166. Henry Reuterdahl, "The Needs of Our Navy," *McClure's Magazine* (January 1908): 251–263.

167. Morison, *Admiral Sims*, 183.

168. Letter, Sims to Roosevelt, July 10, 1908, Subject File: Relations with TR, 1908, Sims Papers.

169. Gould, *The Presidency of Theodore Roosevelt*, 264.

170. U.S. Committee on Administrative Management, *Report* (Washington, D.C.: U.S. Government Printing Office, 1937), 5.

171. Morison, *Admiral Sims*, 263.

172. Stephen Skowronek, *The Politics Presidents Make: Leadership from John Adams to Bill Clinton* (Cambridge, Mass.: Harvard University Press, 1997), 259.

173. "Overloading the President," *The Nation* 74, no. 1938 (June 12, 1902): 458.

Chapter 4. The Political Education of William Howard Taft: Toward a Brilliant Career

1. Quoted in Henry Pringle, *The Life and Times of William Howard Taft* (New York: Farrar & Rinehart, 1939), 57.

2. "The Next President," *Los Angeles Times*, June 19, 1908, II:4.

3. For example, see Michael Korzi,"Our Chief Magistrate and His Powers: A Reconsideration of William Howard Taft's 'Whig' Theory of Presidential Leadership," *Presidential Studies Quarterly* 33, no. 2 (June 2003): 305–320.

4. Quoted in Pringle, *The Life and Times of William Howard Taft*, 16.

5. Quoted in ibid., 22.

6. Quoted in ibid., 35.

7. Quoted in Ishbel Ross, *An American Family: The Tafts, 1678 to 1964* (Cleveland: World Publishing, 1964), 106.

8. Quoted in Pringle, *The Life and Times of William Howard Taft*, 19.

9. Ibid., 96.

10. Frederick N. Judson, "Taft as Judge and His Labor Decisions," *American Monthly Review of Reviews* (August 1907): 212–217.

11. Letter, William H. Taft to Alphonso Taft, July 29, 1889, reel 17, series 1, Papers of William Howard Taft, Library of Congress Microfilm. Unless otherwise noted, subsequent archival references are to Taft Papers, Library of Congress.

12. Letter, Horace Taft to William H. Taft, May 9, 1889, reel 17, series 1.

13. Letter, William H. Taft to Alphonso Taft, July 6, 1889, ibid.

14. Letter, William H. Taft to Alphonso Taft, September 14, 1889, ibid.

15. *Los Angeles Times*, April 29, 1889, 4.

16. Letter, William H. Taft to Alphonso Taft, August 10, 1889; and Letter, William H. Taft to Alphonso Taft, August 20, 1889, reel 17, series 1.

17. Joseph B. Foraker to William Henry Harrison, September 23, 1889, reel 30, series 3. ibid.

18. Letter, William H. Taft to Alphonso Taft, September 15, 1889, reel 17, series 1.

19. Letter, William H. Taft to Alphonso Taft, March 18, 1891, ibid.

20. Letters, Benjamin Butterworth to William H. Taft, January 24 and 26, 1890, reel 30, series 2.

21. "Work of Congress," *Washington Post,* January 31, 1900, 7.

22. Quoted in Carl Sferrazza Anthony, *Nellie Taft: The Unconventional First Lady of the Ragtime Era* (New York: William Morrow, 2005), 96

23. Letter, Alphonso Taft to William H. Taft, February 3, 1890, reel 17, series 1.

24. James Easby-Smith, *The Department of Justice: Its History and Functions* (Washington, D.C.: W. H. Lowdermilk, 1904), 19–20.

25. Letter, William H. Taft to Alphonso Taft, February 26, 1890, Taft Papers, reel 17, series 1.

26. Letter, William H. Taft to Alphonso Taft, February 14, 1891, reel 17, series 1.

27. Pringle, *The Life and Times of William Howard Taft,* 110.

28. Alpheus Thomas Mason, *William Howard Taft: Chief Justice* (New York: Simon and Schuster, 1964), 18.

29. The figure of eleven wins comes from a letter from William H. Taft to Alphonso Taft, January 28, 1891, Taft Papers, reel 17, series 1. The figure of eighteen cases and two losses comes from Pringle, *The Life and Times of William Howard Taft,* 119. There is some discrepancy between Pringle's figures and the Taft Papers.

30. Helen Taft, *Recollections of Full Years* (New York: Dodd, Mead, 1914), 28.

31. Letter, William H. Taft to Hiram Peck, December 14, 1890, reel 640, series 21, vol. 1.

32. Telegram, Hiram Peck and others to Benjamin Harrison, March 2, 1891, reel 30, series 3.

33. Letter, Charles Taft to William H. Taft, November 6, 1891, reel 17, series 1.

34. Letter, William H. Taft to Hiram Peck, October 12, 1891, reel 640, series 21, vol. 1.

35. Letter, William H. Taft to Paul Charlton, April 23, 1890, reel 1, series 17 .

36. Letter, William H. Taft to Alphonso Taft, March 18, 1891, reel 17, series 1.

37. Helen Taft, *Recollections of Full Years,* 30.

38. Judith Icke Anderson, *William Howard Taft: An Intimate History* (New York: Norton, 1981), 60.

39. "Seven New Judges," *Chicago Daily Tribune,* December 17, 1891, 1.

40. Quoted in Mason, *William Howard Taft: Chief Justice,* 18.

41. Theda Skocpol, *Protecting Soldiers and Mothers* (Cambridge, Mass.: Harvard University Press, 1992), 285–293.

42. Quoted in Pringle, *The Life and Times of William Howard Taft,* 141.

43. *United States v. E. C. Knight,* 156 1 15 S. Ct. 249 (1896).

44. Martin J. Sklar, *The Corporate Reconstruction of American Capitalism, 1890–1916* (Cambridge, U.K.: Cambridge University Press, 1988), 123–131.

45. "Iron Pipe Trust Illegal," *New York Times,* February 15, 1898, 1.

46. "Sustained the Commission," *Washington Post,* November 15, 1899, 2.

47. For example, Mason, *William Howard Taft,* 41–52.

48. Letter, John Harlan to William H. Taft, November 13, 1892, reel 30, series 3.

49. Quoted in Pringle, *The Life and Times of William Howard Taft,* 125,

50. Letter, Charles Taft to William H. Taft, January 6, 1896, reel 18, series 1.

51. Letter, Henry Taft to William H. Taft, January 14, 1899, ibid.

52. Letter, William H. Taft to Henry Taft, January 23, 1899, ibid.

53. Ralph Eldin Minger, *William Howard Taft and United States Foreign Policy: The Apprenticeship Years, 1900–1908* (Urbana: University of Illinois Press, 1975), 1.

54. Helen Taft, *Recollections of Full Years* (New York: Dodd, Mead, 1914), 32.

55. Philip C. Jessup, *Elihu Root* (New York: Dodd, Mead, 1938), 353.

56. Minger, *William Howard Taft and United States Foreign Policy*, 3–4.

57. Taft, *Recollections of Full Years*, 32–34.

58. Letter, Horace Taft to William H. Taft, January 31, 1900, reel 18, series 1

59. Letter, Henry Taft to William H. Taft, January 30, 1901, ibid.

60. Letter, Henry Taft to William H. Taft, January 30, 1901, ibid.

61. Taft, *Recollections of Full Years*, 35.

62. Minger, *William Howard Taft and United States Foreign Policy*, 22.

63. Pringle, *The Life and Times of William Howard Taft*, 161.

64. Letter, William H. Taft to Charles Taft, May 8, 1900, reel 18, series 1.

65. Minger, *William Howard Taft and United States Foreign Policy*, 50.

66. Rowland T. Berthoff, "Taft and MacArthur, 1900–1901: A Study in Civil-Military Relations," *World Politics* 5, no. 2 (January 1953): 196–213.

67. Taft gave a detailed description of MacArthur's views of his own expansive authority in Letter, William Taft to Elihu Root, March 17, 1901, reel 19, series 1.

68. Letter, William H. Taft to Charles Taft, November 15, 1900, ibid.; Taft, *Recollections of Full Years*, 110.

69. Letter, Elihu Root to William H. Taft, January 21, 1901, reel 19, series 1.

70. Quoted in Pringle, *The Life and Times of William Howard Taft*, 185–186.

71. Letter, William Taft to Elihu Root, March 17, 1901, reel 19, series 1.

72. Quoted in Pringle, *The Life and Times of William Howard Taft*, 194

73. Taft, *Recollections of Full Years*, 125.

74. Ibid., 125–126.

75. Letter, William H. Taft to Henry Taft, October 21, 1901, reel 19, series 1.

76. Letter, William Taft to Horace Taft, April 12, 1901, ibid.

77. Letter, William Taft to Charles Taft, January 29, 1901, ibid.

78. "Secretary Root's Report," *The Outlook* 69, no. 14 (December 7, 1901): 854.

79. Letter, William Taft to Elihu Root, February 8, 1901, reel 19, series 1.

80. On Taft's initiatives on colonial government, see Minger, *William Howard Taft and United States Foreign Policy*, 55–101.

81. Quoted in ibid., 85.

82. Pringle, *The Life and Times of William Howard Taft*, 223.

83. Letter, Archbishop P. L. Chapelle to William H. Taft, April 13, 1901, reel 19, series 1.

84. Letter, William H. Taft to Elihu Root, October 14, 1901, ibid.

85. Letter, William Taft to George N. Wolfe, March 27, 1903, reel 39, series 3.

86. Letter, William Taft to James F. Smith, March 26, 1903, reel 39, series 3.

87. Theodore Roosevelt, "Governor William H. Taft," *The Outlook* 69, no. 3 (September 21, 1901): 166–167.

88. The solicitor-general's office was high office in the sense that it was second in justice to the attorney general. However, its scope of activities was narrow. Its staff was tiny, and its public visibility low.

89. See Letter, William H. Taft to Charles Taft, November 6, 1900, reel 19, series 1.

90. Philip C. Jessup, *Elihu Root* (New York: Dodd, Mead, 1938), 354.

91. Quoted in ibid., 354.

92. Quoted from 1901 war department annual report, in Jessup, *Elihu Root,* 357.

93. Letter, Elihu Root to William H. Taft, January 21, 1901, reel 19, series 1.

94. Pringle, *The Life and Times of William Howard Taft,* 240.

95. Letter, William Taft to Charles Taft, November 11, 1902, reel 20, series 1.

96. Anthony, *Nellie Taft,* 158–160, 185–191.

97. "Taft May Succeed Shiras," *Washington Post,* December 10, 1902, 2.

98. "Taft Puts Duty above Ambition," *Chicago Tribune,* January 13, 1903, 3.

99. Letter, William Taft to Harry Taft, November 26, 1902, reel 20, series 1.

100. Letter, William Taft to Charles Taft, January 7, 1903, ibid.

101. Taft's wife saw in these appointment offers the possibility that Roosevelt hoped to eliminate Taft as a potential competitor for the 1904 presidential nomination. In turn, Taft made sure to signal to Secretary Root that he was absolutely uninterested in seeking the presidency. Donald Anderson, *William Howard Taft* (Ithaca, N.Y.: Cornell University Press, 1973), 9–10.

102. Letter, Henry Taft to William Taft, January 10. 1903, reel 20, series 1.

103. Letter, William Taft to Charles Taft, January 26, 1903, ibid.

104. Taft, *Recollections of Full Years,* 267–268.

105. Letters, Henry Taft to William Taft, January 22 and March 2, 1903, reel 20, series 1.

106. Letter, Charles Taft to William Taft, February 24, 1903, reel 20, series 1.

107. Letter, Horace Taft to William Taft, March 2, 1903, ibid. Besides being the family intellectual, Horace was also the family Mugwump, having voted for Cleveland. He was also a free trader and civil service reformer. "The Campaign of Intellect," *Washington Post,* December 30, 1888, 4.

108. Letter, Henry Taft to William Taft, March 2, 1903, reel 20, series 1.

109. For example, "Taft as Roosevelt's Running Mate," *Salt Lake Telegram,* July 20, 1903, in reel 40, series 3.

110. Jessup, *Elihu Root,* 411.

111. Pringle, *The Life and Times of William Howard Taft,* 252.

112. Letter, William Taft to Howard Hollister, September 21, 1903, reel 40, series 3.

113. Helen Taft, *Recollections of a Full Life,* 269.

114. The governor's compensation was equivalent $447,000 in 2006 dollars, and the secretary of war salary was equivalent to $180,000 in 2006 dollars. These conversions use the historical conversion formula at www.minneapolisfed.org/research/data/us/calc/hist1800.cfm; accessed November 12, 2007.

115. Roosevelt's advice to Taft is described in Letter, William Taft to Howard Hollister, September 21, 1903, reel 40, series 3.

116. Pringle, *The Life and Times of William Howard Taft,* 254.

117. See Jessup, *Elihu Root*, 215–407; and Philip L. Semsch, "Elihu Root and the General Staff," *Military Affair* 27, no. 1 (spring 1963): 16–27.

118. Letter, William Taft to Horace Taft, February 6, 1904, reel 21, series 1.

119. Minger, *William Howard Taft and United States Foreign Policy*, 110.

120. "Platt on the Issues," *Washington Post*, September 14, 1904, 1.

121. "Taft on the Philippines," *Washington Post*, October 2, 1904, 1.

122. Pringle, *The Life and Times of William Howard Taft*, 272–274.

123. See Minger, *William Howard Taft and United States Foreign Policy*, 139–148.

124. John Gilbert Reid, "Taft's Telegram to Root, July 29, 1905," *Pacific Historical Review* 9, no. 1 (March 1940): 69.

125. For a breezy account of the journey, see Ross, *An American Family*, chap. 14.

126. Letter, William Taft to Charles Taft, December 3, 1905, reel 21, series 1.

127. William Taft to Charles Taft, December 3, 1905, ibid.

128. Letter, William Taft to Horace Taft, January 29, 1906; and Horace Taft to William Taft, February 23, 1906, ibid.

129. "Taft Will Go On to Supreme Bench," *Washington Post*, March 10, 1906, 1.

130. Letter, Charles Taft to William Taft, March 10, 1906, reel 21, series 1.

131. Letter, Horace Taft to William Taft, March 13, 1906, ibid.

132. "Taft Family Council," *New York Times*, March 14, 1906, 1.

133. "Taft to Wait Awhile; May Be Chief Justice," *New York Times*, March 17, 1906, 7.

134. Letter, Theodore Roosevelt to William Taft, May 15, 1906, reel 21, series 1.

135. Taft wrote: "Never in any two weeks have I endured such a strain as that of the last two weeks in trying to settle this wretched Cuban business." Letter, William Taft to Charles Taft, October 4, 1906, ibid. On the Cuban negotiations generally, see Ralph Eldin Minger, "William H. Taft and the United States Intervention in Cuba in 1906," *Hispanic American Historical Review* 41, no. 1 (February 1961): 75–89.

136. Letter, William Taft to Helen Taft, September 22, 1906, reel 25, series 2.

137. Reprint, "Secretary of Peace," *Washington Post*, October 28, 1906, E4.

138. Letter, William Taft to Charles Taft, November 1, 1901, reel 21, series 1.

139. About the need for immediate organization of the campaign, William wrote to Charles, "I bow to your judgment, and am deeply grateful to you." Letter, William Taft to Charles Taft, March 21, 1907, ibid.; Pringle, *The Life and Times of William Howard Taft*, 318–323.

140. On the controversy among Republicans over the Brownsville case, see John D. Weaver, *The Senator and the Sharecropper's Son* (College Station: Texas A&M University Press, 1997).

141. Letter, William Taft to Charles Taft, January 1, 1907, reel 21, series 1.

142. Helen Taft, *Recollections of Full Years*, 308.

143. "Taft Will Speak Often," *Washington Post*, May 18, 1907, 4.

144. Letter, William Taft to Charles Taft, August 18, 1907, reel 21, series 1.

145. Taft, *Recollections of Full Years*, 311–312.

146. James Ceaser, *Presidential Selection* (Princeton, N.J.: Princeton University Press, 1979), 133.

147. Letter, Theodore Roosevelt to William Taft, September 12, 1907, reel 21, series 1.

148. "Presidential Booms," *Washington Post*, June 11, 1907, 6.

149. "Standpatters Attack Taft," *Washington Post,* May 13, 1907, 6; and "Stand Patters Fearful of Taft," *New York Times,* August 10, 1907, 4.

150. Letter, Theodore Roosevelt to William Taft, September 3, 1907, reel 21, series 1.

151. Psalm 58, *The Holy Bible* (King James).

152. Quoted in Pringle, *The Life and Times of William Howard Taft,* 57–58.

153. Moise Ostrogorski, *Democracy and the Organization of Political Parties,* vol. 2, *The United States,* edited by S. M. Lipset (New York: Doubleday Anchor, 1964), 188.

154. Pringle, *The Life and Times of William Howard Taft,* 261.

155. Ibid., 2:758.

156. Mason, *William Howard Taft: Chief Justice,* 16.

157. Donald F. Anderson, *William Howard Taft,* 296.

158. Ibid., 290–291.

159. Ibid., 292.

160. Roosevelt, *An Autobiography* (New York: Macmillan, 1913), 512.

161. Pringle, *The Life and Times of William Howard Taft,* 272; also see Anderson, *William Howard Taft,* 86.

162. For a good example, see Letter, William Taft to Charles Taft, December 3, 1905, reel 21, series 1.

163. Letter, Theodore Roosevelt to William Howard Taft, May 15, 1906, ibid.

164. William Howard Taft, "The Duties of Citizenship Viewed from the Standpoint of a Recent Graduate of a University," in David H. Burton (ed.), *The Collected Works of William Howard Taft,* vol. 1 (Athens: Ohio University Press, 2001), 13.

165. "Return of Taft," reprint, *Washington Post,* December 20, 1907, 6.

166. Richard Neustadt, *Presidential Power and the Modern Presidency* (New York: Free Press, 1990), 152.

167. Pringle, *The Life and Times of William Howard Taft,* 107.

Chapter 5. Improvising For Continuity: The Tariff and the Blow-Up at Interior

1. Letter, Theodore Roosevelt to Howard Hollister, April 11, 1910, Theodore Roosevelt and Henry Cabot Lodge, *Selections from the Correspondence of Theodore Roosevelt and Henry Cabot Lodge,* vol. 2 (New York: Charles Scribner's Sons, 1925), 367.

2. On the currency issue, see Gretchen Ritter, *Goldbugs and Greenbacks: The Antimonopoly Tradition and the Politics of Finance in America, 1865–1896* (New York: Cambridge University Press, 1997).

3. Quoted in Michael Kazin, *A Godly Hero* (New York: Knopf, 2006), 151.

4. "Campaign Lacks Dominant Issue," *Chicago Daily Tribune,* October 11, 1908, 1.

5. "Taft Pledges Square Deal," *Los Angeles Times,* November 6, 1908, 14.

6. "First Taft Speech in Ohio," *Chicago Daily Tribune,* September 7, 1908, 2; and Henry Pringle, *The Life and Times of William Howard Taft* (New York: Farrar & Rinehard, 1939), 366.

7. "Tariff Revision Taft's Keynote," *Chicago Daily Tribune,* September 30, 1908, 6.

8. "Through a Day's Work with Taft On His 'Special,'" *New York Times*, November 1, 1908, SM7.

9. However, Bryan drew many more contributors than Taft. Kazin, *A Godly Hero*, 156.

10. Letter, Theodore Roosevelt to Henry Cabot Lodge, October 21, 1908, in *Selections from the Correspondence of Theodore Roosevelt and Henry Cabot Lodge*, 2:323.

11. The year 1896 broke the pattern of close post–Civil War elections. Gary King and Lynn Ragsdale, *The Elusive Executive* (Washington, D.C.: CQ Press, 1988), 436.

12. "Taft Pledges Square Deal," *Los Angeles Times*, November 6, 1908, 14.

13. Pringle, *The Life and Times of William Howard Taft*, 378.

14. Quoted in Judith Ickes Anderson, *William Howard Taft: An Intimate Portrait* (New York: Norton, 1981), 26.

15. K. J. Radford, *Strategic and Tactical Decisions*, 2d ed. (Toronto: University Press of Canada, 1988), 3.

16. Michael E. McGerr, *The Decline of Popular Politics* (New York: Oxford University Press, 1986), 13.

17. William H. Taft, "The Duties of Citizenship Viewed from the Standpoint of a Recent Graduate of a University," in David Burton (ed.), *The Collected Works of William Howard Taft* (Athens: Ohio University, 2001), 19.

18. Ibid., 18.

19. William G. Shade and Ballard C. Campbell (eds.), *American Presidential Campaigns and Elections* (Armonk, N.Y.: Sharpe Reference, 2003), 2:610.

20. "Lincoln Like Roosevelt," *New York Times*, February 13, 1908, 5.

21. Letter, Theodore Roosevelt to Henry Cabot Lodge, April 11, 1910, *Selections from The Correspondence of Theodore Roosevelt and Henry Cabot Lodge*, 369.

22. Letter, Theodore Roosevelt to William H. Taft, November 29, 1908, reel 321, series 4A, Papers of William Howard Taft, Microfilm Edition, Library of Congress. Subsequent references to archive papers are to Taft Papers unless otherwise specified.

23. Eric F. Goldman, *Charles J. Bonaparte: Patrician Reformer* (Baltimore: Johns Hopkins University Press, Studies in Historical and Political Science, 1943), 93.

24. Donald F. Anderson, *William Howard Taft* (Ithaca, N.Y.: Cornell University Press, 1973), 96.

25. "Tafts in Virginia," *Washington Post*, November 7, 1908, 1.

26. "Taft's Winter Plans," *Washington Post*, November 10, 1908, 4.

27. *Los Angeles Times*, November 10, 1908, 14.

28. Letter, Horace Taft to William H. Taft, December 1, 1908, reel 22, series 1.

29. "The Men Who Will Probably Be in Mr. Taft's Cabinet,'" *New York Times*, February 10, 1909, SM1.

30. Pringle, *The Life and Times of William Howard Taft*, 383–384.

31. Letters, Theodore Roosevelt to William H. Taft, December 10, 1908; Theodore Roosevelt to William H. Taft, December 15, 1908, reel 321, and Letter, William H. Taft to Theodore Roosevelt, January 8, 1909, reel 322, series 4A.

32. For example, entries in the Diary of James R. Garfield, December 22 and 23, 1908, and January 4, 11, and 25, 1909, box 8, Papers of James R. Garfield, Library of Congress. The

entry of January 11: "Nothing from Taft. I am utterly at sea—if he wishes me to stay he should ask me soon. . . . All the cabinet members are being treated in the same way."

33. "The Taft Cabinet as Completed," *Chicago Tribune*, February 26, 1909, 3.

34. Anderson, *William Howard Taft*, 63.

35. Knox had been Roosevelt's attorney general in the *Northern Securities* suit. Wickersham was eager for vigorous enforcement of anti-trust and rate regulations. Pringle, *The Life and Times of William Howard Taft*, 2:604.

36. Letter, William H. Taft to Philander C. Knox, December 22, 1908, Letterbook no. 6, 868, Papers of Philander C. Knox, Library of Congress, Manuscript Division.

37. Taft's address was 5,433 words and Harrison's was 8,445. "Presidential Inaugural Addresses: Length and Date of Speech, at www.infoplease.com/ipa/A0878085.html; accessed September 17, 2007.

38. The novelty of Taft's speech is seen by comparison with Roosevelt's brief and unspecific 1904 address and McKinley's longer and vague first-term inaugural. All references to the inaugural address drawn from William H. Taft, "Inaugural Address," March 4, 1909, in Burton, *The Collected Works of William Howard Taft*, 3:44–55.

39. "Taft to Clinch Roosevelt's Policies," *New York Times*, September 9, 1908, 3.

40. See Robert F. Bruner and Sean D. Carr, *The Panic of 1907: Lessons Learned from the Market's Perfect Storm* (New York: John Wiley, 2007).

41. William H. Taft, "A Pledge of Tariff Reform," in Burton, *The Collected Works of William Howard Taft*, 2:101.

42. A treatment of change across time in inaugural addresses is Michael J. Korzi, *A Seat of Popular Leadership* (Amherst: University of Massachusetts Press, 2004), chap. 4.

43. Letter, William H. Taft to Theodore Roosevelt, May 26, 1910, reel 322, series 4A.

44. Helen Taft suffered a stroke with paralysis two months after the inauguration.

45. Paulo Coletta wobbles between seeing Taft as a conservative (108–109) and, more perceptively, seeing him caught among interests and factions (for example, 121–122). *The Presidency of William Howard Taft* (Lawrence: University Press of Kansas, 1973).

46. Ibid., 122.

47. Letter, Henry Cabot Lodge to Theodore Roosevelt, November 30, 1909, in *Selections from the Correspondence of Theodore Roosevelt and Henry Cabot Lodge*, 2:353–355.

48. Martin J. Sklar, *The Corporate Reconstruction of American Capitalism, 1890–1916* (New York: Cambridge University Press, 1988), 376.

49. See Pringle, *The Life and Times of William Howard Taft*, 2:32; Coletta, *The Presidency of William Howard Taft*, chap. 6; Sklar, *The Corporate Reconstruction of American Capitalism*, 333–334. On administrative reform see Peri E. Arnold, *Making the Managerial Presidency* (Lawrence: University Press of Kansas, 1998), chap. 2.

50. Bureau of the Census, *Historical Statistics of the United States* (Washington, D.C.: U.S. Government Printing Office, 1961), 712 and 720.

51. See Paul Wolman, *Most Favored Nation: The Republican Revisionists and U.S. Tariff Policy, 1897–1912* (Chapel Hill: University of North Carolina Press, 1992), chap. 1.

52. John Gerring, "Party Ideology in America: The National Republican Chapter, 1828–1924," *Studies in American Political Development* 11 (1997): 44–108; and Lewis L.

Gould, *The Grand Old Party: A History of the Republicans* (New York: Random House, 2003).

53. "Who Wants Tariff Revision," *New York Times*, February 3, 1908, 8.

54. Theodore Roosevelt to James Ford Rhodes, November 29, 1904, in Elting Morison (ed.), *The Letters of Theodore Roosevelt* (Cambridge, Mass.: Harvard University Press, 1952), 3:1049. Morison suggests that Roosevelt raised the tariff issue as a bargaining chip for his railroad legislation. See note, 1028.

55. Bureau of the Census, *Historical Statistics of the United States*, 126 and 127. Average earnings for all workers increased 35 percent during this period, *Historical Statistics*, 91.

56. Letter, Horace Taft to William H. Taft, December 1, 1908, reel 22, series 1.

57. "Men Who Map Out Issues for Taft," *New York Times*, June 14, 1908, 3.

58. "Interest Fixed on Platform," *Washington Post*, June 12, 1908, 1.

59. "Uncle Joe Brings His Ax," *Chicago Daily Tribune*, June 15, 1908, 2.

60. William H. Taft, "Inaugural Address," March 4, 1909, in Burton, *The Collected Works of William Howard Taft*, 3:45–46.

61. *Chicago Daily Tribune*, March 7, 1909, 1.

62. Quoted in Robert Harrison, *Congress, Progressive Reform, and the New American State* (Cambridge, U.K.: Cambridge University Press, 2004), 180.

63. Pringle, *The Life and Times of William Howard Taft*, 1:421.

64. Letter, Henry Cabot Lodge to Theodore Roosevelt, end of March 1909, in *Selections from the Correspondence of Theodore Roosevelt and Henry Cabot Lodge*, 2:331–332.

65. Pringle, *The Life and Times of William Howard Taft*, 1:429.

66. Quoted in Wolman, *Most Favored Nation*, 93.

67. Letter, Horace Taft to William H. Taft, December 1, 1908, reel 22, series 1.

68. "Peace with Cannon," *Washington Post*, December 2, 1908, 1.

69. Coletta, *The Presidency of William Howard Taft*, 61.

70. "Taft Is Neutral in Rules Fight," *Chicago Daily Tribune*, March 10, 1909, 1; see Anderson, *William Howard Taft*, 99–101.

71. Letter, Roosevelt to Taft, March 19, 1903, in Morison, *The Letters of Theodore Roosevelt*, 3:453.

72. Letter, Archibald Butt to his sister, Clara, March 10, 1909, in *Taft and Roosevelt: The Intimate Letters of Archie Butt*, vol. 1 (Garden City, N.Y.: Doubleday, Doran, 1930), 3. This was the same person who remarked on Taft's style as secretary of war: "He has a wonderfully well-trained mind and seems to have none of the trouble of so many . . . in deciding questions." Letter, Archibald Butt to his mother, June 30, 1908, in Lawrence F. Abbott (ed.), *The Letters of Archie Butt* (Garden City, N.Y.: Doubleday, Page, 1924), 52.

73. Letter, William H. Taft to Charles Taft, March 21, 1909, reel 124, series 3.

74. Quoted in Anderson, *William Howard Taft*, 179.

75. Coletta, *The Presidency of William Howard Taft*, 61.

76. Letter, William H. Taft to Horace Taft, June 27, 1909, reel 124, series 3.

77. Anderson, *William Howard Taft*, 105.

78. Letter, Archibald Butt to Theodore Roosevelt, August 17, 1909, in *Taft and Roosevelt*, 1:178.

79. Letter, William H. Taft to Helen Taft, July 16, 1909, reel 26, series 2.

80. Letter, William H. Taft to Helen Taft, July 9, 1909, ibid.

81. Letter, William H. Taft to Helen Taft, July 8, 1909, ibid.

82. Taft described these machinations to his brother in Letter, William H. Taft to Horace Taft, June 27, 1909, reel 124, series 3.

83. On the role of veto threats, see Charles M. Cameron, *Veto Bargaining: Presidents and the Politics of Negative Power* (New York: Cambridge University Press, 2000).

84. Butt, *Taft and Roosevelt: The Intimate Letters of Archie Butt,* 40.

85. Letter, J. D. Brannan to William H. Taft, June 29, 1909, reel 452, series 7.

86. Coletta, *The Presidency of William Howard Taft,* 62–63.

87. Memo, Assistant Secretary of the Treasury, n.d., reel 327, case 5, series 5.

88. Letters, William H. Taft to Helen Taft, July 22 and July 28, 1909, reel 26, series 2.

89. Letter, William H. Taft to Horace Taft, June 27, 1909, reel 124, series 3.

90. Letter, William H. Taft to William A. White, March 30, 1909, reel 124, series 3.

91. William H. Taft, "The Tariff," Winona, Minnesota, September 17, 1909, in Burton, *The Collected Works of William Howard Taft,* 3:179–180.

92. Ibid.

93. "Taft Reads Rebels Out," *Boston Globe,* September 18, 1909, 1.

94. "The Winona Tariff Speech," *Chicago Tribune,* September 19, 1909, B4.

95. Coletta, *The Presidency of William Howard Taft,* 75.

96. Eight months after Taft signed the Payne-Aldrich Act, Roosevelt wrote, "It is not possible . . . to expect the tariff to be well handled by representatives of localities." Letter, Roosevelt to Henry Cabot Lodge, April 6, 1910, in *Selections from the Correspondence of Theodore Roosevelt and Henry Cabot Lodge,* 366.

97. The best treatment of the case is James Penick Jr., *Progressive Politics and Conservation: The Ballinger-Pinchot Affair* (Chicago: University of Chicago Press, 1968).

98. Ironically, Garfield had proposed Ballinger to Roosevelt for the land office job. Entries of January 10 and 11, 1907, Diary of James Garfield, James R. Garfield Papers, Library of Congress, Manuscript Division.

99. Pinchot suggested to Roosevelt that "he put me in for six months to clear up" the land office. Entry for October 22, 1906, Diary of Gifford Pinchot, Microfilm, reel no. 2, Papers of Gifford Pinchot, Library of Congress, Manuscript Division.

100. Gifford Pinchot, *Breaking New Ground* (New York: Harcourt, Brace, 1947), 391.

101. M. Nelson McGeary, *Gifford Pinchot: Forester-Politician* (Princeton, N.J.: Princeton University Press, 1960), 88–89.

102. Penick, *Progressive Politics and Conservation,* chap. 2.

103. Pinchot, *Breaking New Ground,* 408.

104. See Pringle, *The Life and Times of William Howard Taft,* 1:26; and Coletta, *The Presidency of William Howard Taft,* chap. 4.

105. Alpheus Thomas Mason, *Bureaucracy Convicts Itself: The Ballinger-Pinchot Controversy of 1910* (New York: Viking Press, 1941), 74.

106. Robert M. LaFollette, *LaFollette's Autobiography* (Madison: University of Wisconsin Press, 1960), 195.

107. On Progressivism's diverse aims, see John D. Buenker, "The Progressive Era: A Search for a Synthesis," *Mid-America* 51 (1969): 175–193. On the centrality of conservation, see Michael McGerr, *A Fierce Discontent: The Rise and Fall of the Progressive Movement in America* (New York: Oxford University Press, 2003), 164–169.

108. See Samuel Hays, *Conservation and the Gospel of Efficiency* (Cambridge, Mass.: Harvard University Press, 1959).

109. Gifford Pinchot, *The Fight for Conservation* (Seattle: University of Washington Press, 1967 [1910]), 23.

110. McGeary, *Gifford Pinchot*, 19–69.

111. Ibid., 86. Also see Daniel P. Carpenter, *The Forging of Bureaucratic Autonomy Reputations, Networks and Policy Innovation in Executive Agencies, 1862–1928* (Princeton, N.J.: Princeton University Press, 2001), chap. 8.

112. "The Forest Reserves," *Los Angeles Times*, March 5, 1907, 1:14

113. Pinchot, *Breaking New Ground*, 358.

114. Letter, Archibald Butt to his mother, October 21, 1908, in Abbott, *The Letters of Archie Butt*, 147.

115. Letter, William H. Taft to Theodore Roosevelt, December 24, 1908, reel 321, series 4A.

116. "Ballinger Will Continue All Prosecutions Planned by Garfield," *Chicago Daily Tribune*, March 29, 1909, 3.

117. Pinchot, *Breaking New Ground*, 388–389.

118. See Taft's special message to Congress, "Conservation of National Resources," January 14, 1910, in Burton, *The Collected Works of William Howard Taft*, 3:426–434.

119. See Morton G. White, *Social Thought in America: The Revolt against Formalism* (New York: Viking Press, 1949).

120. Conflict over land withdrawals had become public during May 1909. Letter, W. H. Taft to Hulbert Taft, May 12, 1909; and "Tale of Two Cops," *Cincinnati Post*, May 6, 1909, reel 124, series 3.

121. Penick, *Progressive Politics and Conservation*, 113.

122. Ibid., 113.

123. Ibid., 116–117.

124. For example, "Taft Takes a Hand in Public Land Row," *New York Times*, August 26, 1909, 5.

125. Letter, William H. Taft to Horace Taft, September 11, 1909, reel 124, series 3.

126. "The Ballinger Letter," *Washington Post*, September 17, 1909, 6.

127. Letter, William H. Taft to Horace Taft, September 11, 1909, reel 124, series 3.

128. Letter, William H. Taft to Helen Taft, October 15, 1909, reel 26, series 2.

129. "Ballinger Wires Conge to Glavis," *Chicago Daily Tribune*, September 17, 1909, 5.

130. McGeary, *Gifford Pinchot*, 146.

131. Pinchot describes the meeting in *Breaking New Ground*, 432–439; Taft private thoughts, in Letter, William H. Taft to Helen Taft, October 1, 1909, reel 26, series 2.

132. See John Milton Cooper, *Pivotal Decades: The United States, 1900–1920* (New York: Norton, 1990), 80–89.

133. McGeary, *Gifford Pinchot*, 151.

134. *New York Times,* November 10, 1909, 1.

135. Letter, Archibald Butt to his sister Clara, March 22, 1909, in *Taft and Roosevelt*, 18.

136. Letter, William H. Taft to Helen Taft, July 14, 1909, reel 26, series 2.

137. "Ballinger or Pinchot's Job," *Chicago Daily Tribune,* November 12, 1909, 2; Penick, *Progressive Politics and Conservation*, 131.

138. "Ballinger or Pinchot's Job," *Chicago Daily Tribune,* November 12, 1909, 2.

139. Anderson, *William Howard Taft*, 75.

140. Letter, Archie Butt to his sister Clara, December 19, 1909, in *Taft and Roosevelt*, 235.

141. "Taft for Inquiry in Land Dispute," *Washington Post,* December 21, 1909, 1.

142. "Pinchot Defends Glavis against Taft," *New York Times,* January 7, 1910, 1.

143. Brandeis received $25,000 from *Collier's.* This is the equivalent of about $560,000 in 2009 dollars.

144. Letter, Louis D. Brandeis to Alfred Brandeis, February 28, 1910, in Melvin I. Urofsky (ed.), *The Letters of Louis D. Brandeis* (Albany: State University of New York Press, 1972), 2:324.

145. Letter, Louis D. Brandeis to Regina W. Goldmark, March 2, 1910, in ibid., 325.

146. "Mr. Ballinger's Defense," *New York Times,* May 1, 1910, 10.

147. See Letters, Louis D. Brandeis to Alfred Brandeis, April 18 and 24, 1910; Louis D. Brandeis to James R. Garfield, April 26, 1910; Louis D. Brandeis to Henry Watterson, May 25, 1910, in Urofsky, *The Letters of Louis D. Brandeis*, 2:330–338.

148. "Says President Did Not Write Glavis Letter," *Chicago Daily Tribune,* May 15, 1910, 1.

149. "Taft Told Lawler to Prepare Report," *New York Times,* November 16, 1910, 1.

150. Archibald Butt to his sister Clara, May 15, 1910, in *Taft and Roosevelt*, 349.

151. Letter, Theodore Roosevelt to Henry Cabot Lodge, May 5, 1910, in *Selections from the Correspondence of Theodore Roosevelt and Henry Cabot Lodge*, 379.

152. Quoted in McGeary, *Gifford Pinchot*, 183.

153. Henry Cabot Lodge to Theodore Roosevelt, April 29, 1909, in *Selections from the Correspondence of Theodore Roosevelt and Henry Cabot Lodge*, 2:334–335.

154. Letter, William H. Taft to Theodore Roosevelt, May 26, 1910, reel 322, series 4A.

155. Erwin Hargrove, *The President as Leader: Appealing to the Better Angels of Our Nature* (Lawrence: University Press of Kansas, 1998), vii.

156. Letter, Archibald Butt to his sister Clara, November 14, 1909, in *Taft and Roosevelt*, 202.

157. Harvey C. Mansfield Jr., *Taming the Prince* (New York: Free Press, 1989), 278.

158. Letter, Archibald Butt to his sister Clara, March 22, 1909, in *Taft and Roosevelt*, 27.

Chapter 6. The Political Education of Woodrow Wilson:
Interpretive Leadership and Expediency

1. "The Ministry and the Individual," address at McCormick Theological Seminary, November 2, 1909, in Arthur S. Link (ed.), *The Papers of Woodrow Wilson,* vol. 19 (Princeton: N.J.: Princeton University Press, 1975), 476.

2. Arthur S. Link, *Wilson: The Road to the White House* (Princeton, N.J.: Princeton University Press, 1947), 143.

3. January 5, 1911 address, quoted in ibid., 229

4. Wilson's idea of interpretive leadership is detailed in a paper he wrote in 1890, early in his teaching career at Princeton. "You Must Lead Your Own Generation, Not the Next," in E. David Cronon (ed.), *The Political Thought of Woodrow Wilson* (Indianapolis: Bobbs-Merrill, 1965), 20–27. Wilson's ideas about responsible leadership are found in his first published article, "Cabinet Government in the United States," *International Review* 7 (August 1879): 146–163.

5. Link, *Wilson: The Road to the White House*, 16–17.

6. Woodrow Wilson, *Congressional Government* (Boston: Houghton, Mifflin, 1885), 56.

7. Ibid., 106.

8. Ibid., and xi.

9. Wilson, "You Must Lead Your Own Generation, Not the Next," in Cronon, *The Political Thought of Woodrow Wilson*, 25.

10. Ibid., 43.

11. Ibid., xvi.

12. "Cabinet Government in the United States," in Cronon, *The Political Thought of Woodrow Wilson*, 29–53.

13. Ibid., 6.

14. Wilson to Ellen Axson, February 24, 1885, quoted in Link, *Wilson: The Road to the White House*, 19.

15. Wilson to Ellen Axson, October 30, 1883, in Cronon, *The Political Thought of Woodrow Wilson*, 6.

16. "From Wilson's Confidential Journal," October 20, 1887, in Link, *The Papers of Woodrow Wilson*, 5:619.

17. Grover Cleveland, "Third Annual Message," December 6, 1887, in James D. Richardson (ed.), *A Compilation of the Messages and Papers of the Presidents, 1789–1897*, vol. 8 (Washington, D.C.: U.S. Government Printing Office, 1898), 584, 590.

18. Woodrow Wilson, *A History of the American People*, vol. 5 (New York: Harpers, 1901), 191.

19. Ibid., 192.

20. Ibid., 232.

21. Daniel D. Stid, *The President as Statesman: Woodrow Wilson and the Constitution* (Lawrence: University Press of Kansas, 1998), 36–37.

22. Ibid., 41.

23. Terri Bimes and Stephen Skowronek, "Woodrow Wilson's Critique of Popular Leadership: Reassessing the Modern-Traditional Divide in Presidential History," *Polity* 29, no. 1 (fall 1996): 30–31.

24. Woodrow Wilson, *Constitutional Government in the United States* (New York: Columbia University Press, 1908), 54.

25. Ibid., 57.

26. Ibid., 58–59.

27. Ibid., 60.

28. Ibid., 68.

29. Ibid., 70.

30. Link, *Wilson: The Road to the White House*, 96.

31. Ibid., 107; see "From the Diary of William Starr Myers," May 8, 1908, in Link, *The Papers of Woodrow Wilson*, 18:293.

32. Woodrow Wilson, "An Address on Political Reform to the City Club of Philadelphia," November 18, 1909, in ibid., 19:518.

33. Jeffrey Tulis, *The Rhetorical Presidency* (Princeton, N.J.: Princeton University Press, 1987).

34. Cronon, *The Political Thought of Woodrow Wilson*, 25.

35. Ibid., 28.

36. Bimes and Skowronek, "Woodrow Wilson's Critique of Popular Leadership," 48.

37. Wilson, *Constitutional Government*, 66.

38. Cronon, *The Political Thought of Woodrow Wilson*, 28.

39. John Morton Blum, *Woodrow Wilson and the Politics of Morality* (Boston: Little, Brown, 1956), 23.

40. James Axtell, *The Making of Princeton University from Woodrow Wilson to the Present* (Princeton, N.J.: Princeton University Press, 2006), 35–48.

41. Letter, Woodrow Wilson to Thomas Raynesford Lounsbury, July 16, 1902, in Link, *The Papers of Woodrow Wilson*, 14:20.

42. Woodrow Wilson, "To the Board of Trustees of Princeton University," October 21, 1902, in ibid., 150–161. Wilson's goal was the equivalent of about $300 million in current dollars.

43. Link, *Wilson, The Road to the White House*, 90.

44. Ibid., 91.

45. Henry Bragdon, *Woodrow Wilson: The Academic Years* (Cambridge, Mass.: Harvard University Press, 1967), 337.

46. Woodrow Wilson, "Princeton in the Nation's Service," October 25, 1902, in Link, *The Papers of Woodrow Wilson*, 14:176. On Wilson as academic leader, see Laurence R. Veysey, "The Academic Mind of Woodrow Wilson," *Mississippi Valley Historical Review* 49, no. 4 (March 1963): 613–634.

47. Axtell, *The Making of Princeton University*, 48.

48. Bliss Perry, *Gladly We Teach* (Boston: Houghton Mifflin, 1935), 157–158.

49. Hardin Craig, *Woodrow Wilson at Princeton* (Norman: University of Oklahoma Press, 1960), 66–67.

50. Bragdon, *Woodrow Wilson*, 274–277.

51. Letter, Woodrow Wilson to Ellen Axson Wilson, April 21, 1904, in Link, *The Papers of Woodrow Wilson*, 15:263–265.

52. Bragdon, *Woodrow Wilson*, 293.

53. Ibid., 293.

54. Letter, Woodrow Wilson to Ellen Axson Wilson, April 26, 1904, in Link, *The Papers of Woodrow Wilson*, 15:295–297.

55. Perry, *And Gladly We Teach*, 153–159.

56. Axtell, *The Making of Princeton University*, 39.

57. Craig, *Woodrow Wilson at Princeton*, 90.

58. Bragdon, *Woodrow Wilson*, 304.

59. Axtell, *The Making of Princeton University*, 65.

60. Letter, Charles Williston McAlpin to Wilson, October 24, 1902, in Link, *The Papers of Woodrow Wilson*, 14:168.

61. Axtell, *The Making of Princeton University*, 50.

62. Ibid., 59.

63. "New Princeton," *Boston Daily Globe*, May 5, 1905, 3.

64. "A News Report of Two Speeches in Albany, New York," February 16, 1904; and "A News Report of an Address in Syracuse, New York," February 17, 1904, in Link, *Papers of Woodrow Wilson*, 15:168–173.

65. "Princeton's New Way," *New York Times*, July 5, 1905, 6.

66. Link, *The Road to the White House*, 44.

67. "His Man for President," *New York Times*, February 4, 1906, 4.

68. Kendrick A. Clements, *Woodrow Wilson: World Statesman* (Boston: Twayne Publishers, 1987), 52.

69. "Good for a Presidential Platform," *Wall Street Journal*, April 3, 1906, 1.

70. "News Report: From *New York Evening Post*," October 2, 1906, in Link, *The Papers of Woodrow Wilson*, 16:454–455.

71. Quoted in Bragdon, *Woodrow Wilson*, 320.

72. Ibid., 317.

73. "Wilson to Abolish Clubs at Princeton," *New York Times*, June 25, 1907, 16.

74. Perry, *Gladly We Teach*, 157–158.

75. "Princeton Rejects Quad," *New York Times*, October 18, 1907, 3.

76. Bragdon, *Woodrow Wilson*, 326.

77. Letter, Woodrow Wilson to John Van Antwerp MacMurray, March 9, 1908, in Link, *The Papers of Woodrow Wilson*, 18:12.

78. "An Address to the Princeton Club of Chicago," March 12, 1909, in ibid., 17–34.

79. Bragdon, *Woodrow Wilson*, 270, 314.

80. Perry, *And Gladly We Teach*, 158.

81. Bragdon, *Woodrow Wilson*, 354.

82. Woodrow Wilson to Moses Pyne, December 22, 1909, in Link, *The Papers of Woodrow Wilson*, 19:620.

83. Woodrow Wilson to Herbert Brougham, February 1, 1910, in ibid., 20:69–71.

84. Bragdon, *Woodrow Wilson*, 379.

85. James Kerney, *The Political Education of Woodrow Wilson* (New York: Century, 1928), 32–33.

86. John Gerring, *Party Ideologies in America, 1828–1996* (New York: Cambridge University Press, 1998), 226.

87. Bragdon, *Woodrow Wilson*, 349; see Link, *Wilson: The Road to the White House*, 83–91; and Blum, *Woodrow Wilson and the Politics of Morality*, 34.

88. "That State and the Citizen's Relation to It," December 28, 1909, an address, in Link, *The Papers of Woodrow Wilson*, 19:642.

89. Ibid., 643.

90. "An Address at the Inauguration of Henry Harbaugh Apple as President of Franklin and Marshall College," January 7, 1910, in Link, *The Papers of Woodrow Wilson*, 19:742–743.

91. For example, Harvard's president wrote that he learned that Wilson was approaching resignation. Abbott Lawrence Lowell to Woodrow Wilson, March 21, 1910, ibid., 20:276–277.

92. Link, *Wilson: The Road to the White House*, 140–142.

93. Ibid., 142; and note in Link, *The Papers of Woodrow Wilson*, 20:146–148; and also Kerney, *The Political Education of Woodrow Wilson*, 27–42.

94. John Maynard Harlan to Woodrow Wilson, June 11, 1910, in Link, *The Papers of Woodrow Wilson*, 20:519–520; and Wilson to Harlan, June 23, 1910, in ibid., 540–541.

95. Quoted in Link, *Wilson: The Road to the White House*, 159–160.

96. "A Speech Accepting the Democratic Gubernatorial Nomination," in Link, *The Papers of Woodrow Wilson*, 21:91–94.

97. Quoted in Kerney, *The Education of Woodrow Wilson*, 55.

98. Ibid.

99. "Wilson Calls for Control of Trusts," *New York Times,* October 1, 1910, 1.

100. "Lied About, Says Wilson," *New York Times,* October 6, 1910, 3.

101. "A News Report of Campaign Addresses in Camden," from the *Philadelphia Record,* October 25, 1910, in Link, *The Papers of Woodrow Wilson,* 22:415.

102. Kerney, *The Political Education of Woodrow Wilson*, 72.

103. Link, *Wilson: The Road to the White House*, 190.

104. Ransom E. Noble Jr., "George L. Record's Struggle for Economic Democracy," *American Journal of Economics and Sociology* 10, no. 1 (October 1950): 76–77.

105. Kerney, *The Political Education of Woodrow Wilson*, 70–71.

106. Wilson to George Record, October 11, 1910, in Link, *The Papers of Woodrow Wilson*, 21:296.

107. George Record to Wilson, October 17, 1910, in ibid., 338–347.

108. Wilson to George Record, October 24, 1910, in ibid., 406–411.

109. Link, *Wilson: The Road to the White House*, 195.

110. Kerney, *The Political Education of Woodrow Wilson*, 76.

111. Joseph Howell to Wilson, October 26, 1910, in Link, *The Papers of Woodrow Wilson,* 21:443–444.

112. George Harvey to Wilson, October 25, 1910, in ibid., 433.

113. John Morton Blum, *Joe Tumulty and the Wilson Era* (Boston: Harper, 1951), 34.

114. "Smith in the Lead for Jersey Senator," *New York Times,* November 11, 1910, 3.

115. "Plenty of Time, Says Ex-Senator Smith," *New York Times,* November 21, 1910, 18.

116. Link, *Wilson: The Road to the White House*, 208.

117. Blum, *Joe Tumulty and the Wilson Era*, 24–25.

118. Kearney, *The Political Education of Woodrow Wilson*, 81.

119. Blum, *Joe Tumulty and the Wilson Era*, 26; Kearney, *The Political Education of Woodrow Wilson*, 93.

120. "Statement on the Senatorship," December 8, 1910, in Link, *The Papers of Woodrow Wilson*, 22:153–154.

121. Joseph Tumulty to Wilson, December 15, 1910, in ibid., 200.

122. Wilson to Mary Ellen Peck, December 17, 1910, in ibid., 210.

123. Blum, *Joe Tumulty and the Wilson Era*, 26.

124. "Woodrow Wilson's Victory," *New York Times,* January 26, 1911, 10.

125. Kerney, *The Political Education of Woodrow Wilson*, 95.

126. Saladin M. Ambar, "An 'Unconstitutional Governor': Woodrow Wilson and the People's Executive, 1885–1913," paper presented at the Miller Center Fellowship Spring Conference, University of Virginia, Charlottesville, Virginia, May 2008.

127. "A Campaign Speech in Woodbury, New Jersey," October 5, 1910, in Link, *The Papers of Woodrow Wilson*, 21:247.

128. Ibid., 250.

129. "An Inaugural Address," January 17, 1911, in ibid., 22:345–354.

130. Link, *Wilson: The Road to the White House*, 248–253.

131. "News Report of a Conference with the Democratic Assemblymen of New Jersey," *Trenton Evening Times*, March 7, 1911, in Link, *The Papers of Woodrow Wilson*, 22:481–482.

132. Blum, *Joe Tumulty and the Wilson Era*, 27–29.

133. Link, *Wilson: The Road to the White House*, 267.

134. Quoted in "Study of Gov. Wilson," *Washington Post,* April 27, 1911, 4.

135. "Two Governors with One Bee," *Los Angeles Times,* May 19, 1991, 15.

136. "Gov Wilson's Trip," *Boston Daily Globe,* April 27, 1911, 12.

137. Kerney, *The Political Education of Woodrow Wilson*, 146–147.

138. "Woodrow Wilson," *Outlook* 98, no. 6 (June 10, 1911): 273.

139. "Wilson Tells Why Progressive Policies Will Redeem Government for People," Norfolk, Virginia *Landmark* (April 30, 1911), in Link, *The Papers of Woodrow Wilson*, 22:594.

140. Quoted in Link, *Wilson: The Road to the White House*, 278.

141. Link, *The Papers of Woodrow Wilson*, 23:170.

142. Ibid.

143. Ibid., 177.

144. Blum, *Joe Tumulty and the Wilson Era*, 36–37.

145. For example, "Victory for Wilson on Election Law," *New York Times,* April 14, 1911, 2.

146. "An Annual Message to the Legislature of New Jersey," January 9, 1912, in Link, *The Papers of Woodrow Wilson*, 24:18–25.

147. "A Campaign Speech in Woodbury, New Jersey," October 5, 1910, in Link, *The Papers of Woodrow Wilson*, 22:250.

148. Blum, *Woodrow Wilson and the Politics of Morality*, 46.

Chapter 7. A Parliamentary Presidency: The Tariff, Bank Reform, and Anti-Trust

1. "Inaugural Address," March 4, 1913, in Arthur Link (ed.), *The Papers of Woodrow Wilson* (Princeton, N.J.: Princeton University Press, 1978), 27:151.

2. Eric Goldman, *Rendezvous with Destiny* (New York: Knopf, 1952), 213.

3. Wilson to Mary Ellen Hulbert Peck, December 10, 1911, in Link, *Papers of Woodrow Wilson,* 23:590.

4. A concise narrative of the 1912 election can be found in James Chace, *1912: Wilson, Roosevelt, Taft and Debs—The Election That Changed the Country* (New York: Simon and Schuster, 2004).

5. The Roosevelt-Taft break leading to the party split had no single cause. However, the steel anti-trust case was important because in 1907 Roosevelt had assured the firm's backers that the government would not act against its acquisition of Tennessee Coal and Iron, a move that was part of the emergency measures by J. P. Morgan's combine to quell the panic of 1907. On the Roosevelt-Taft break generally see Lewis L. Gould, *Grand Old Party: A History of the Republicans* (New York: Random House, 2003), chap. 5.

6. Arthur Link, *Wilson: The Road to the White House* (Princeton, N.J.: Princeton University Press, 1947), 415.

7. Ibid., 402.

8. Debs was the Socialist Party's 1908 nominee.

9. Wilson to Edward M. House, March 15, 1912, in Link, *The Papers of Woodrow Wilson*, 24:248. The end of George Harvey's "love affair" with Wilson and the subsequent opposition from leading Bourbon Democrats gave Wilson's suspicion some credence.

10. In particular see Alexander George and Juliette George, *Woodrow Wilson and Colonel House: A Personality Study* (New York: Dover, 1964); and Alexander George and Juliette George, *Presidential Personality and Performance* (Boulder, Col.: Westview Press, 1998).

11. Michael E. McGerr, *The Decline of Popular Politics: The American North, 1865–1928* (New York: Oxford University Press, 1986), chap. 2; and Joel H. Silbey, *The American Political Nation, 1838–1893* (Stanford: Stanford University Press, 1991).

12. See Lewis Gould, *Four Hats in the Ring: The 1912 Election and the Birth of Modern American Politics* (Lawrence: University Press of Kansas, 2008). Also for close examination of the intellectual positions of the candidates and parties in 1912, see Sidney M. Milkis, *Theodore Roosevelt, the Progressive Party, and the Transformation of American Democracy* (Lawrence: University Press of Kansas, 2009).

13. Patricia Sykes, "Party Constraints on Leaders in Pursuit of Change," *Studies in American Political Development 7*, no. 1 (1973): 151–176; Milkis, *Theodore Roosevelt*, chap. 5.

14. Wilson to Richard Heath Dabney, November 16, 1911, in Link, *The Papers of Woodrow Wilson*, 23:550–552; Kerney, *The Political Education of Woodrow Wilson* (New York: Century, 1926), 207–211.

15. Link, *Wilson: The Road to the White House*, 345.

16. See Michael Kazin, *A Godly Hero* (New York: Knopf, 2006), chap. 8.

17. Charles Wayland Bryan to Wilson, July 29, 1911, in Link, *The Papers of Woodrow Wilson*, 23:237–239.

18. Link, *Wilson: The Road to the White House*, 313–314; Kerney, *The Political Education of Woodrow Wilson*, 133.

19. See Godfrey Hodgson, *Woodrow Wilson's Right Hand: The Life of Colonel Edward M. House* (New Haven, Conn.: Yale University Press, 2006).

20. Edward M. House to Wilson, October 16, 1911, in Link, *The Papers of Woodrow Wilson*, 23:458.

21. Edward M. House to Wilson, November 18, 1911, in ibid., 552.

22. Hodgson, *Woodrow Wilson's Right Hand,* 66–68.

23. Link, *Wilson: The Road to the White House,* 488.

24. Goldman, *Rendezvous with Destiny,* 138.

25. Josephus Daniels, *The Wilson Era: Years of Peace, 1910–1917* (Chapel Hill: University of North Carolina Press, 1944), 542–543.

26. For example, see Brandeis to Theodore Roosevelt, April 13, 1908, Melvin Urofsky and David W. Levy (eds.), *The Letters of Louis D. Brandeis* (Albany: State University Press of New York, 1972), 2:124; and David P. Thelen, *Robert M. La Follette and the Insurgent Spirit* (Madison: University of Wisconsin Press, 1985), 109–110.

27. Louis Brandeis to Norman Hapgood, July 3, 1912, in Urofsky and Levy, *The Letters of Louis Brandeis,* 2:633.

28. Louis Brandeis to Robert La Follette, July 3, 1912, in ibid., 638.

29. "Two News Reports: Gov. Wilson Agrees with Mr. Brandeis," August 28, 1912, from *New York Times,* August 29, 1912, in Link, *The Papers of Woodrow Wilson,* 25:57.

30. Hodgson, *Woodrow Wilson's Right Hand,* 59

31. Louis Brandeis to Alfred Brandeis, August 29, 1912, in Urofsky and Levy, *The Letters of Louis Brandeis,* 2:660–661.

32. On this difference between Wilson and Brandeis, see John Milton Cooper, *The Warrior and the Priest: Woodrow Wilson and Theodore Roosevelt* (Cambridge, Mass.: Harvard University Press, 1983), 193–195.

33. John Gerring, *Party Ideologies in America, 1828–1996* (New York: Cambridge University Press, 1998), 67–68, 199, 217.

34. See Theodore Roosevelt, "The New Nationalism," a speech at Osawatomie, Kansas, August 31, 1910 at www.theodore-roosevelt.com/trnationalismspeech; accessed August 4, 2008.

35. "A Confession of Faith," August 6, 1912, at http://www.theodore-roosevelt.com/trarmageddon.html; accessed August 4, 2008.

36. "Democratic Platform of 1912," in Kirk H. Porter and Donald B. Johnson (eds.), *National Party Platforms, 1840–1956* (Urbana: University of Illinois Press, 1956), 169.

37. "A Speech Accepting the Democratic Nomination," August 7, 1912, in Link, *The Papers of Woodrow Wilson,* 25:11. See Kendrick A. Clements, *Woodrow Wilson: World Statesman* (Boston: Twayne, 1987), 80–82.

38. "A Labor Day Address in Buffalo," September 2, 1912, in Link, *The Papers of Woodrow Wilson,* 25:73–75.

39. Letter, Louis Brandeis to Woodrow Wilson (and enclosure), September 30, 1912, in ibid., 287–304.

40. See Robert F. Bruner and Sean D. Carr, *The Panic of 1907: Lessons Learned from the Market's Perfect Storm* (Hoboken, N.J.: John Wiley, 2007).

41. Clements, *Woodrow Wilson World Statesman,* 52–53.

42. "Democratic Platform of 1912," in Porter and Johnson, *National Party Platforms, 1840–1956,* 171.

43. "Speech Accepting the Democratic Nomination," in Link, *The Papers of Woodrow Wilson,* 25:14.

44. "A Labor Day Address," September 2, 1912, in ibid., 78.

45. "A Speech to Businessmen in Columbus, Ohio," September 20, 1912, in ibid., 202–203. On Wilson's view that there is a moral basis to business and banking reform, see Blum, *Woodrow Wilson and the Politics of Morality*, 39–40.

46. Letter, Samuel Untermyer to Wilson, July 31, 1912, and Charles S. Hamlin to Wilson, August 1, 1912, in Link, *The Papers of Woodrow Wilson*, 24:577 and 581.

47. Sidney Milkis and Daniel J. Tichenor, "Direct Democracy and Social Justice, the Progressive Party Campaign of 1912," *Studies in American Political Development* 8 (fall 1994): 282–340.

48. Cooper, *The Warrior and the Priest*, 160.

49. "Inaugural Address," March 4, 1913, in Link, *The Papers of Woodrow Wilson*, 27:148–152.

50. Stephen Skowronek, *The Politics Presidents Make* (Cambridge, Mass.: Harvard University Press, 1997), 45.

51. Dwight Eisenhower represents the best example of such adaptation by a preemptive president to dominant party policy commitments. See Skowronek, *The Politics Presidents Make*, chap. 3; and Fred I. Greenstein, *The Hidden Hand Presidency* (Baltimore: Johns Hopkins University Press, 1994).

52. "Wilson Considering Mooser for Cabinet," *New York Times*, January 10, 1913, 6.

53. "More Cabinet Suggestions," *Boston Daily Globe*, January 23, 1913, 4.

54. Link, *Wilson: The New Freedom*, 11–14; "Getting Busy with the Cabinet," *Los Angeles Times*, November 6, 1912, 15; and, for example, "Massachusetts Hears about Brandeis for the Cabinet," *Wall Street Journal*, February 11, 1913, 6.

55. Arthur Link, *Wilson: The New Freedom* (Princeton, N.J.: Princeton University Press, 1956), 1–20.

56. Josephus Daniels, *The Wilson Era: Years of Peace—1919–1917* (Chapel Hill: University of North Carolina Press, 1944), 151.

57. Kendrick A. Clements, *The Presidency of Woodrow Wilson* (Lawrence: University Press of Kansas, 1992), 53.

58. Blum, *Woodrow Wilson: The Politics of Morality*, 68.

59. "From the Diary of Colonel House," January 8, 1913, in Link, *The Papers of Woodrow Wilson*, 27:20–24.

60. "Oscar Underwood to Wilson," January 13, 1913, ibid., 44–45.

61. "From the Diary of Colonel House," January 17, 1913, in ibid., 26:61–64.

62. "Would Wilson be Welcome?" *Boston Daily Globe*, February 27, 1913, 2.

63. Arthur Link, *Woodrow Wilson and the Progressive Era, 1910–1917* (New York: Harper & Brothers, 1954), 35; Lewis L. Gould, *The Modern American Presidency* (Lawrence: University Press of Kansas, 2003), 47; David Sarasohn, *The Party of Reform: Democrats in the Progressive Era* (Jackson: University of Mississippi Press, 1989), 167–168.

64. "Wilson at Capitol Again," *New York Times*, May 8, 1913, 8.

65. Link, *Wilson: The New Freedom*, 20–21.

66. Cooper, *The Warrior and the Priest*, 229–232; and Morton Keller, *America's Three Regimes* (New York: Oxford University Press, 2007), 183.

67. Elizabeth Sanders, *Roots of Reform* (Chicago: University of Chicago Press, 1999), 225–226; Link, *Wilson: The New Freedom*, 178.

68. Sanders, *Roots of Reform*, chap. 2.

69. Oscar Underwood to Wilson, February 20, 1913, in Link, *The Papers of Woodrow Wilson*, 27:123; "Democratic Split on Tariff Reported," *New York Times*, February 20, 1913, 1.

70. Wilson to Oscar Underwood, March 14, 1913, and Underwood to Wilson, March 17, in Link, *The Papers of Woodrow Wilson*, 27:177, 192.

71. Sara Fisher Ellison and Wallace P. Mullin, "Economics and Politics: The Case of Sugar Tariff Reform," *Journal of Law and Economics* 38, no. 2 (October 1995): 335–366.

72. "From the Diary of Colonel House," April 1, 1913, in Link, *The Papers of Woodrow Wilson*, 27:250–251.

73. Diary entry for April 4, 1913, *The Cabinet Diaries of Josephus Daniels 1913–1921*, ed. E. David Cronon (Lincoln: University of Nebraska Press, 1963), 21–22.

74. Ibid., 15–17, 21–22, 25–26.

75. An Address on Tariff Reform to a Joint Session of Congress," in Link, *The Papers of Woodrow Wilson*, 27:269–272.

76. Scott James, *Presidents, Parties and the State* (New York: Cambridge University Press, 2006), 141–143.

77. For an example of Wilson's negotiations with Underwood on rates for specific goods, see Oscar Underwood to Wilson, April 22, 1913, in Link, *The Papers of Woodrow Wilson*, 27:347.

78. Sanders, *The Roots of Reform*, 226–228.

79. "Senate Stands with President," *Boston Daily Globe*, May 19, 1913, 18.

80. Cronon, *Diary of Josephus Daniels*, 224.

81. "Hearkens to Lobby," *Los Angeles Times*, May 7, 1913, 11; "Democrats Desperate," *Los Angeles Times*, May 13, 1913, 11.

82. See George Juergens, *News from the White House: The Presidential-Press Relationship in the Progressive Era* (Chicago: University of Chicago Press, 1981), 151–153.

83. "Remarks at a Press Conference," May 26, 1913, in Link, *The Papers of Woodrow Wilson*, 27:471–473.

84. "A Statement on Tariff Lobbyists," May 26, 1913, in ibid., 473.

85. Cummins Asks Lobby Inquiry," *Boston Daily Globe*, May 28, 1913, 20.

86. "Democrats Agree to Lobby Inquiry," *New York Times*, May 29, 1913, 1.

87. "Lobby on Tariff Faces Exposure: Inquiry Ordered," *Chicago Tribune*, May 30, 1913, 1.

88. "Wilson Blames Revision's Foes," *Chicago Daily Tribune*, June 5, 1913, 7; "Hold Lobby Exists but of a New Kind," *New York Times*, June 5, 1913, 2.

89. Karen E. Schnietz, "The 1916 Tariff Commission: Democrats Use of Expert Information to Constrain Republican Tariff Protection," *Business and Economic History* 23, no. 1 (fall 1994): 176–189.

90. Quoted in Link, *Wilson: The New Freedom*, 194.

91. Sarasohn, *The Party of Reform*, 167; Sanders, *The Roots of Reform*, 227.

92. On this point, see Robert Harrison, *Congress, Progressive Reform, and the New American State* (Cambridge, U.K.: Cambridge University Press, 2004), 274.

93. Charles Forcey, *The Crossroads of Liberalism: Croly, Weyl, Lippman, and the Progressive Era* (New York: Oxford University Press, 1961), 195.

94. "An Address on Tariff Reform to a Joint Session of Congress," in Link, *The Papers of Woodrow Wilson*, 27:272. Despite Wilson's expectations, and for reasons unrelated to the tariff law, the economy sank into recession during his first two years in the White House. Unemployment measured 5.2 percent in 1912 and rose to 8 percent in 1914. Bureau of the Census, *Historical Statistics of the United States* (Washington, D.C.: U.S. Government Printing Office, 1963), 73.

95. "Currency Bill up to Public," *Boston Daily Globe*, June 17, 1913, 10.

96. David F. Houston, *My Years with Wilson's Cabinet* (Garden City, N.Y.: Doubleday, Page, 1926), 1:18–20.

97. "Democratic Platform of 1912," in Porter and Johnson, *National Party Platforms: 1840–1956*, 171.

98. See H.R. Rep. No. 1593, 62d Cong., 3d Sess., 39 (1913); Louis Galambos and Joseph Pratt, *The Rise of The Corporate Commonwealth: United States Business and Public Policy in the 20th Century* (New York: Basic Books, 1988), 66–67.

99. For a detailed description of the plan, see Paul Warburg, *The Federal Reserve System: Its Origin and Growth* (New York: Macmillan, 1930), 1:56–80.

100. Sanders, *The Roots of Reform*, 258.

101. There is long-standing debate among historians interpreting the forces and motives underlying the Federal Reserve's creation. But our focus here is on the information and purposes immediately accessible to Wilson, his advisers, and the Democratic legislators. For all of them the immediate issues of private/public control and degrees of centralization/decentralization comprised the matrix within which the policy debate unfolded. Regarding the historical interpretive debates, from one perspective the reform was the result of money-centered bankers seeking to limit access to the banking industry. See Gabriel Kolko, *The Triumph of Conservatism* (New York: Free Press, 1963). Contrariwise, James Livingston argues that the reform was a product of financial capitalism's structural development and requirement for expanded, orderly banking mechanisms. See Livingston, *Origins of the Federal Reserve System* (Ithaca, N.Y.: Cornell University Press, 1986). More recently, the political scientist J. Lawrence Broz argues that the political coalition that made the bank reform possible was formed of those businessmen needing the U.S. currency system to acquire the characteristics necessary for international exchange. See Broz, *The International Origins of the Federal Reserve System* (Ithaca, N.Y.: Cornell University Press, 1997).

102. See Henry Parker Willis, *The Federal Reserve* (Garden City, N.Y.: Doubleday, Page, 1915), 43–48.

103. J. Laurence Laughlin, *The Federal Reserve Act: Its Origins and Problems* (New York: Macmillan, 1933), 127–128; and Warburg, *The Federal Reserve System*, 81–104.

104. Public control raised bankers' and conservatives' justifiable fears it would subject credit and currency policies to the immediate interests of whatever political party was in control of government. Livingston, *Origins of the Federal Reserve System*, 219–223. For a contemporary progressive view reflecting fears about party control, see J. Allen Smith, *The Spirit of American Government* (New York: Macmillan, 1907), 211.

105. "From the Diary of Colonel House," January 8, 1913, in Link, *Papers of Woodrow Wilson*, 27:21; Link, *Wilson: The New Freedom*, 204–205.

106. Kazin, *A Godly Hero*, 225–226.

107. "Remarks at a Press Conference," May 29, 1913, in Link, *The Papers of Woodrow Wilson*, 27:483–487.

108. "Henry Warns of Wall Street," *Boston Daily Globe*, June 14, 1913, 8.

109. "Oppose Reopening of Money Inquiry," *New York Times*, May 31, 1913, 13; Kazin, *A Godly Hero*, 226.

110. "Currency Bill to Public," *Boston Daily Globe*, June 17, 1913, 10.

111. "Presidency Cites Currency Need," *Chicago Daily Tribune*, June 24, 1913, 4.

112. "Wilson Poses as Mediator,"*Los Angeles Times*, July 23, 1913, 14.

113. For example, Tumulty to Wilson, July 14, 1913, in Link, *The Papers of Woodrow Wilson*, 90.

114. Livingston, *Origins of the Federal Reserve System*, 223; Stid, *The President as Statesman*, 109.

115. Wilson to John Sharp Williams, October 11, 1913, in Link, *The Papers of Woodrow Wilson*, 28:389.

116. Bryan to Wilson, October 7, 1913, in ibid., 367–370.

117. Link, *Wilson: The New Freedom*, 227–238; and Thelen, *Robert M. LaFollette*, 102–104.

118. "A Tremendous Power," reprinted in *Washington Post*, June 22, 1913, ES4.

119. "Remarks upon Signing the Federal Reserve Bill," in Link, *The Papers of Woodrow Wilson*, 28:64.

120. Porter and Johnson, *National Party Platforms: 1840–1956*, 169.

121. Sarasohn, *The Party of Reform*, 142.

122. Martin J. Sklar, *The Corporate Reconstruction of American Capitalism* (New York: Cambridge University Press, 1988), 117–154.

123. Thomas K. McCraw, *Prophets of Regulation: Charles Francis Adams, Louis D. Brandeis, James M. Landis, Alfred Kahn* (Cambridge, Mass.: Harvard University Press, 1984), 102–109.

124. Herbert Croly, *The Promise of American Life* (New Brunswick, N.J.: Transaction Publishers, 1993 [1909]), 358–359.

125. Sanders, *Roots of Reform*, 277–282.

126. "A Campaign Address in Sioux City, Iowa," September 17, 1912, in Link, *The Papers of Woodrow Wilson*, 25:154.

127. "A Campaign Address in Burlington, New Jersey," October 31, 1912, in ibid., 25:496.

128. "Remarks at a Press Conference," November 3, 1913, in ibid., 28:487.

129. Peter S. Grosscup, "Can Republicans and Progressives Unite?" *North American Review* (March 1914): 353.

130. "Trust Task First," *Washington Post*, January 13, 1914, 1.

131. "Leaders Accept Wilson Trust Plan," *New York Times*, January 15, 1914, 1.

132. "President Asks Rigid Trust Curb," *Chicago Daily Tribune*, January 15, 1914, 1.

133. "An Address on Antitrust Legislation to a Joint Session of Congress," January 20, 1914, in Link, *The Papers of Woodrow Wilson*, 29:153–158; Wilson reiterated this description of his commission proposal in "Remarks at a Press Conference," January 26, 1914, in ibid., 29:175.

134. Davies to Wilson, with Enclosure, December 27, 1913, in ibid., 29:83–84.

135. Samuel J. Graham to Wilson, with Enclosure, January 6, 1913, in ibid., 27:107.

136. William Redfield to Wilson, December 18, 1914, and David Benton Jones to Wilson, December 23, 1914, in ibid., 27:31, 40–44, and 67–69.

137. James, *Presidents, Parties, and the State*, chap. 3.

138. "From the Diary of Colonel House," January 16, 1914, in Link, *The Papers of Woodrow Wilson*, 29:135.

139. "President Wilson and the Trade Commission," *Outlook*, January 31, 1914, 233.

140. Sanders, *Roots of Reform*, 278–279.

141. McCraw, *Prophets of Regulation*, 102–105.

142. "Four of Wilson's Trust Bills Out," *New York Times*, January 23, 1914, 1.

143. For a very thoughtful critique that synthesizes the Republican and Progressive perspectives, see Grosscup, "Can Republicans and Progressives Unite?" 353.

144. "Wilson Welcomes Aid on Trust Bills," *New York Times*, February 13, 1914, 2.

145. "Wilson to Rush Trust Measures," *New York Times*, January 31, 1914, 7; "Wilson Ignores Underwood: Anti-Trust Bills Must Pass," *Chicago Daily Tribune*, June 20, 1914, 1.

146. Wilson to William Redfield, April 21, 1914, in Link, *The Papers of Woodrow Wilson*, 29:478.

147. Wilson to Franklin P. Glass, May 13, 1914, in ibid., 30:28.

148. For an example of Wilson's inclusion in the process of shaping the bills, see Francis G. Newlands to Wilson, April 29, 1914, in ibid., 29:535.

149. William C. Adamson to Wilson, April 23, 1914, in ibid., 29:496–497.

150. "Assail Trust Bills," *Washington Post*, June 4, 1914, 1; "Price Regulation Danger of Bills before Congress," *Chicago Daily Tribune*, June 10, 1914, 17.

151. Arthur Link, *Wilson: The New Freedom*, 427–433; "A News Report: Threaten Wilson unless He Agrees to Exempt Labor," April 30, 1914 (from New York *World*), in Link, *The Papers of Woodrow Wilson*, 29:537–538.

152. Henry Hollis to Wilson, May 29, 1914, in ibid., 30:110.

153. See Eric McClure, *Earnest Endeavors: The Life and Public Work of George Rublee* (Westport, Conn.: Greenwood Press, 2003).

154. See memo summarizing call from Brandeis to Wilson, later on the day of June 10. "From the White House Staff," June 10, 1914, in Link, *The Papers of Woodrow Wilson*, 30:166.

155. Link, *Woodrow Wilson: The New Freedom*, 438–439.

156. Ibid.

157. *Chicago Daily Tribune*, June 11, 1914, 18; *Wall Street Journal*, June 11, 1914, 2.

158. "Democrats Firm for Trust Bills," *Chicago Daily Tribune*, July 1, 1914, 4.

159. "First to Pass Senate," *Washington Post*, August 6, 1914, 10.

160. "Senate Passes Clayton Bill," *Chicago Daily Tribune*, September 3, 1914, 5.

161. "Reed Attacks Clayton Bill," *Boston Daily Globe*, September 29, 1914, 2.

162. Link, *Wilson: The New Freedom*, 444.

163. See Kolko, *The Triumph of Conservatism*, chap. 10; and Sklar, *The Corporate Reconstruction of American Capitalism*, 309–333.

164. James, *Presidents, Parties, and the State*, chap. 3.

165. For his thoughts on this point, see the letter he wrote at the close of the session that was used as a campaign document. Wilson to Oscar Underwood, October 17, 1914, in Link, *The Papers of Woodrow Wilson*, 31:168–174.

166. For the same observation from quite different perspectives, see Link, *Wilson: The Path to the White House;* and Alexander George and Juliette George, *Wilson and House.*

167. Albert B. Cummins, "The President's Influence a Menace," *The Independent* 78, no. 3417 (June 1, 1914): 350.

168. Cooper, *The Warrior and the Priest*, 229.

Chapter 8. The Progressive Presidents and the Modern Presidency

1. "What Is Included in the Making of a National Budget," paper delivered at the annual meeting of the Efficiency Society, New York City, January 28, 1913. In the files of the President's Commission on Economy and Efficiency, 030.2, RG 51, National Archives.

2. For the leading book dealing with more than one of the progressive presidents, see the comparative study on Roosevelt and Wilson by John Milton Cooper, *The Warrior and the Priest* (Cambridge, Mass.: Harvard University Press, 1983).

3. "The New Nationalism," a speech at Osawatomie, Kansas, August 31, 1910; www .theodore-roosevelt.com/trnationalismspeech; accessed September 21, 2008.

4. Clifford Geertz, "Centers, Kings, and Charisma: Symbolics of Power," in Geertz (ed.), *Local Knowledge: Further Essays in Interpretive Anthropology* (New York: Basic Books, 1983), 122.

5. Michael Beschloss, "Imperial Presidency," *Newsweek,* January 9, 1995, 45.

6. Joel H. Silbey, *The American Political Nation, 1838–1893* (Stanford: Stanford University Press, 1991), 236.

7. Theodore J. Lowi, *The Personal President: Power Invested, Promise Unfulfilled* (Ithaca, N.Y.: Cornell University Press, 1985), chap. 5.

8. Steven J. Diner, *A Very Different Age* (New York: Hill & Wang, 1998), 217.

9. For this conception of a linear development of the twentieth-century presidency, see Lewis L. Gould, *The Modern American Presidency* (Lawrence: University Press of Kansas, 2003); and Fred I. Greenstein, "Nine Presidents in Search of a Modern Presidency," in Greenstein (ed.), *Leadership in the Modern Presidency* (Cambridge, Mass.: Harvard University Press, 1988), 296–354.

10. Stephen Skowronek, *The Politics Presidents Make: Leadership from John Adams to George Bush* (Cambridge, Mass.: Harvard University Press, 1997), 52–58.

11. See Morton Keller, *America's Three Regimes* (New York: Oxford University Press, 2007), chap. 9.

12. Skowronek, *The Politics Presidents Make,* 260–286.

13. Peri E. Arnold, *Making the Managerial Presidency: Comprehensive Reorganization, 1905–1996,* 2d rev. ed. (Lawrence: University Press of Kansas, 1998), chap. 3; and Sidney M. Milkis, *The President and the Parties: The Transformation of the American Party System since the New Deal* (New York: Oxford University Press, 1993).

14. See Matthew Dickinson, *Bitter Harvest: FDR, Presidential Power, and the Growth of the Presidential Branch* (New York: Cambridge University Press, 1997); Arnold, *Making the Managerial Presidency,* chap. 4.

Bibliography

Primary Sources

Abbot, Lawrence F., ed. 1924. *The Letters of Archie Butt.* Garden City, N.Y.: Doubleday.
Boston Daily Globe
Bureau of the Census. 1961. *Historical Statistics of the United States.* Washington, D.C.: U.S. Government Printing Office.
Burton, David, ed. 2001. *The Collected Works of William Howard Taft.* 6 vols. Athens: Ohio University Press.
Butt, Archie. 1930. *Taft and Roosevelt: The Intimate Letters of Archie Butt.* 2 vols. Garden City, N.Y.: Doubleday, Doran.
Chicago Daily Tribune
Cortelyou, George. Papers, Library of Congress, Manuscript Division.
Cronon, David E., ed. 1963. *The Cabinet Diaries of Josephus Daniels, 1913-1921.* Lincoln: University of Nebraska Press.
———. 1965. *The Political Thought of Woodrow Wilson.* Indianapolis: Bobbs-Merrill.
Garfield, James R. Papers, Library of Congress, Manuscript Division.
Hayes, Rutherford B. 1964. *The Diary of Rutherford B. Hayes,* ed. T. Harry Williams. New York: McKay.
Houston, David F. 1924. *My Years with Wilson's Cabinet.* 2 vols. Garden City, N.Y.: Doubleday.
The Independent of Kansas City, Missouri
Knox, Philander Chase. Papers, Library of Congress, Manuscript Division.
LaFollette, Robert M. 1960. *LaFollette's Autobiography.* Madison: University of Wisconsin Press.
Link, Arthur, ed. 1966-1994. *The Papers of Woodrow Wilson.* 69 vols. Princeton, N.J.: Princeton University Press.
Los Angeles Times
Morison, Elting E., ed. 1951. *The Letters of Theodore Roosevelt.* Cambridge, Mass.: Harvard University Press.
The Nation
New York Times
North American Review
The Outlook
Pinchot, Gifford. Papers, Library of Congress, Manuscript Division.
———. 1947. *Breaking New Ground.* New York: Harcourt, Brace.
———. 1967 [1910]. *The Fight for Conservation.* Seattle: University of Washington Press.
Porter, Kirk, and Donald Bruce Johnson, eds. 1956. *National Party Platforms, 1840-1956.* Urbana: University of Illinois Press.

Bibliography

Reuterdahl, Henry. 1908. "The Needs of Our Navy." *McClure's Magazine,* 251–263.

Richardson, James D., ed. 1897. *A Compilation of the Messages and Papers of the Presidents, 1789–1897.* Washington, D.C.: U.S. Government Printing Office.

Roosevelt, Theodore. Papers, Library of Congress (Microfilm).

———. 1882. *The Naval War of 1812.* New York: G. P. Putnam.

———. 1902. *Administration—Civil Service.* New York: G. P. Putnam.

———. 1904. *American Ideals.* New York: G. P. Putnam.

———. 1913. *An Autobiography.* New York: Macmillan.

———. 1925. *Selections from the Correspondence of Theodore Roosevelt and Henry Cabot Lodge.* 2 vols. New York: Charles Scribner's Sons.

Ross, Ishbel. 1964. *An American Family: The Tafts, 1678 to 1964.* Cleveland: World Publishing.

Secretary of the Navy. 1901. *Annual Report.* Washington, D.C.: U.S. Government Printing Office.

———. 1902. *Annual Report.* Washington, D.C.: U.S. Government Printing Office.

———. 1908. *Annual Report.* Washington, D.C.: U.S. Government Printing Office.

Shade, William G., and Ballard Campbell, eds. 2003. *American Presidential Campaigns and Elections.* 3 vols. Armonk, N.Y.: Sharpe Reference.

Sims, William. Papers, Library of Congress, Manuscript Division.

Taft, Helen. 1914. *Recollections of Full Years.* New York: Dodd & Mead.

Taft, William Howard. Papers, Library of Congress (Microfilm).

Urofsky, Melvin I., and David M. Levy, eds. 1971–1978. *The Letters of Louis D. Brandeis.* 5 vols. Madison: University of Wisconsin Press.

U.S. Committee on Administrative Management. 1937. *Report.* Washington, D.C.: U.S. Government Printing Office.

U.S. Congress. Senate. 1907. *Size of Battleships.* 59th Cong. 2d. Sess. Washington, D.C.: U.S. Government Printing Office.

Wall Street Journal

Washington Post

White, William Allen. 1901. "Theodore Roosevelt." *McClure's Magazine,* November.

Wilson, Woodrow. 1879. "Cabinet Government in the United States." *International Review* 7: 146–163.

———. 1885 [1981]. *Congressional Government: A Study in American Politics.* Baltimore: Johns Hopkins University Press.

———. 1908. *Constitutional Government in the United States.* New York: Columbia University Press.

Books and Articles

Abraham, Henry J. 1992. *Justices and Presidents: A Political History of Appointments to the Supreme Court.* 3d ed. New York: Oxford University Press.

Ambar, Saladin M. 2008. "An 'Unconstitutional Governor': Woodrow Wilson and the People's Executive, 1885–1913." Paper presented at the Miller Center Fellowship Conference. University of Virginia, Charlottesville.

Anderson, Donald F. 1973. *William Howard Taft.* Ithaca, N.Y.: Cornell University Press.

Anderson, Judith Icke. 1981. *William Howard Taft: An Intimate History.* New York: Norton.

Anthony, Carl Sferrazza. 2005. *Nellie Taft: The Unconventional First Lady of the Ragtime Era.* New York: William Morrow.

Apple, R. W. 1987. "The Case of the Monopolistic Railroadmen." In *Quarrels That Have Shaped the Constitution,* ed. John A. Garraty. New York: Harper & Row.

Applegate, Debby. 2001. "The Cultural Uses of the Spirit." In *The Middling Sorts: The Explorations in the History of the American Middle Class,* ed. Burton J. Bledstein and Robert D. Johnston. New York: Routledge.

Argersinger, Peter H. 2001. "The Transformation of American Politics, 1865–1910." In *Contesting Democracy: Substance and Structure in American Political History,* ed. Byron E. Shafer and Anthony J. Badger. Lawrence: University Press of Kansas.

Arnold, Peri. 1998. *Making the Managerial Presidency: Comprehensive Reorganization, 1905–1996.* 2d rev. ed. Lawrence: University Press of Kansas.

———. 1998. "Roosevelt versus Taft: The Institutional Key to 'the Friendship That Split the Republican Party." *Miller Center Journal* 5, no. 1: 23–40.

Axtell, James. 2006. *The Making of Princeton University from Woodrow Wilson to the President.* Princeton, N.J.: Princeton University Press.

Benedict, Michael Les. 1973. "A New Look at the Impeachment of Andrew Johnson." *Political Science Quarterly* 88, no. 3.

Berthoff, Rowland T. 1953. "Taft and MacArthur, 1900–1901: A Study in Civil-Military Relations." *World Politics* 5, no. 2: 196–213.

Beunker, John D. 1969. "The Progressive Era: A Search for a Synthesis." *Mid-America* 51: 175–193.

Bimes, Terry, and Stephen Skowronek. 1996. "Woodrow Wilson's Critique of Popular Leadership: Reassessing the Modern-Traditional Divide in Presidential History." *Polity* 29, no. 1: 27–63.

Blum, John Morton. 1951. *Joe Tumulty and the Wilson Era.* Boston: Harper.

———. 1954. *The Republican Roosevelt.* Cambridge, Mass.: Harvard University Press.

———. 1956. *Woodrow Wilson and the Politics of Morality.* Boston: Little, Brown.

———. 1980. *The Progressive Presidents.* New York: Norton.

Bragdon, Henry W. 1967. *Woodrow Wilson: The Academic Years.* Cambridge, Mass.: Harvard University Press.

Brands, H. W. 1997. *T.R.: The Last Romantic.* New York: Basic Books.

Brown, R. Blake, and Bruce A. Kimball. 2001. "When Holmes Borrowed from Langdell: The 'Ultra Legal' Formalism and Public Policy of Northern Securities." *American Journal of Legal History* 45: 278–321.

Broz, J. Lawrence. 1997. *The International Origins of the Federal Reserve System.* Ithaca, N.Y.: Cornell University Press.

Bruner, Robert F., and Sean D. Carr. 2007. *The Panic of 1907: Lessons Learned from the Market's Perfect Storm.* New York: John Wiley and Sons.

Burke, John P. 1992. *The Institutional Presidency.* Baltimore: Johns Hopkins University Press.

Bibliography

Burke, John P., and Fred I. Greenstein, with Larry Berman and Richard Immerman. 1989. *How Presidents Test Reality: Decisions on Vietnam 1954 and 1965*. New York: Russell Sage Foundation.

Burnham, Walter Dean. 1965. "The Changing Shape of the American Political Universe." *American Political Science Review* 59: 7–28.

Cameron, Charles. 2000. *Veto Bargaining: Presidents and the Politics of Negative Power*. New York: Cambridge University Press.

Carpenter, Daniel P. 2001. *The Forging of Bureaucratic Autonomy: Regulations, Networks, and Policy Innovation in Executive Agencies, 1862–1928*. Princeton, N.J.: Princeton University Press.

Cashman, Sean Dennis. 1988. *America in the Gilded Age*. 2d rev. ed. New York: New York University Press.

Ceaser, James. 1979. *Presidential Selection: Theory and Development*. Princeton, N.J.: Princeton University Press.

Chace, James. 2004. *1912: Wilson, Roosevelt, Taft and Debs—The Election That Changed the Country*. New York: Simon and Schuster.

Chandler, Alfred D. 1977. *The Visible Hand: The Managerial Revolution in American Capitalism, 1890–1916*. Cambridge, Mass.: Harvard University Press.

Chessman, G. Wallace. 1965. *Governor Theodore Roosevelt, 1898–1900*. Cambridge, Mass.: Harvard University Press.

Clements, Kendrick A. 1987. *Woodrow Wilson: World Statesman*. Boston: Twayne Publishers.

———. 1992. *The Presidency of Woodrow Wilson*. Lawrence: University Press of Kansas.

Coletta, Paulo. 1973. *The Presidency of William Howard Taft*. Lawrence: University Press of Kansas.

Cooper, John Milton. 1983. *The Warrior and the Priest*. Cambridge, Mass.: Harvard University Press.

———. 1990. *The Pivotal Decades: The United States, 1900–1920*. New York: Norton.

Crenson, Mathew, and Benjamin Ginsberg. 2007. *Presidential Power: Unchecked and Unbalanced*. New York: Norton.

Croly, Herbert. 1909. *The Promise of American Life*. New York: Macmillan.

Daniels, Josephus. 1944. *The Wilson Years: Years of Peace, 1910–1917*. Chapel Hill: University of North Carolina Press.

Dickinson, Matthew. 1997. *Bitter Harvest: FDR, Presidential Power, and the Growth of the Presidential Branch*. New York: Cambridge University Press.

Diggins, John Patrick. 1994. *The Promise of Pragmatism: Modernism and the Crisis of Knowledge and Authority*. Chicago: University of Chicago Press.

Diner, Steven J. 1998. *A Very Different Age*. New York: Hill & Wang.

Easby-Smith, James. 1904. *The Department of Justice: Its History and Functions*. Washington, D.C.: W. H. Lowdermilk.

Ellison, Sara Fisher, and Wallace P. Mullin. 1995. "Economics and Politics: The Case of Sugar Tariff Reform." *Journal of Law and Economics* 38: 335–366.

Elster, Jon. 1982. "Marxism, Functionalism and Game Theory: The Case for Methodological Individualism." *Theory and Society* 11, no. 4: 453–482.

Forcey, Charles. 1961. *The Crossroads of Liberalism: Croly, Weyl, Lippman, and the Progressive Era.* New York: Oxford University Press.

Ford, Henry Jones. 1898. *The Rise and Growth of American Politics.* New York: Macmillan.

———. 1919. *The Cleveland Era: A Chronicle of the New Order in Politics.* New Haven, Conn.: Yale University Press.

Galambos, Louis, and Joseph Pratt. 1988. *The Rise of the Corporate Commonwealth: United States Business and Public Policy in the 20th Century.* New York: Basic Books.

Garraty, John. 1968. *The New Commonwealth, 1977–1890.* New York: Harper & Row.

Geertz, Clifford. 1983. "Centers, Kings, and Charisma: Reflections on the Symbolics of Power." In *Local Knowledge: Further Essays in Interpretive Anthropology,* ed. Clifford Geertz. New York: Basic Books.

George, Alexander L., and Juliette George. 1964. *Woodrow Wilson and Colonel House: A Personality Study.* New York: Dover.

———. 1998. *Presidential Personality and Performance.* Boulder, Col.: Westview Press.

Gerring, John. 1997. "Party Ideology in America: The National Republican Chapter, 1828–1924." *Studies in American Political Development* 11: 44–108.

———. 1998. *Party Ideologies in America, 1828–1996.* New York: Cambridge University Press.

Gerstle, Gary. 1999. "Theodore Roosevelt and the Divided Character of American Nationalism." *Journal of American History* 86, no. 3: 1280–1307.

Goldman, Eric. 1952. *Rendezvous with Destiny.* New York: Knopf.

Gosnell, Harold. 1923. "Thomas C. Platt—Political Manager." *Political Science Quarterly* 38, no. 3: 443–469.

Gould, Lewis L. 1980. *The Presidency of William McKinley.* Lawrence: University Press of Kansas.

———. 1991. *The Presidency of Theodore Roosevelt.* Lawrence: University Press of Kansas.

———. 2003. *The Grand Old Party: A History of the Republicans.* New York: Random House.

———. 2003. *The Modern American Presidency.* Lawrence: University Press of Kansas.

———. 2008. *Four Hats in the Ring: The 1912 Election and the Birth of Modern American Politics.* Lawrence: University Press of Kansas.

Greenstein, Fred I., ed. 1988. *Leadership in the Modern Presidency.* Cambridge, Mass.: Harvard University Press.

———. 1992. "Can Personality and Politics Be Studied Systematically." *Political Psychology* 13, no. 1: 105–128.

———. 1994. *The Hidden Hand Presidency.* Baltimore: Johns Hopkins University Press.

———. 2000. *The Presidential Difference: Leadership Style from FDR to Clinton.* Princeton, N.J.: Princeton University Press.

Gregg, Robert. 2004. "Uneasy Streets: Police Corruption and Anxiety in Bombay, London, and New York City." In *Corrupt Histories,* ed. Emmanuel Kreike and William C. Jordan. Rochester, N.Y.: University of Rochester Press.

Grondahl, Paul. 2004. *I Rose Like a Rocket: The Political Education of Theodore Roosevelt.* New York: Free Press.

Harbison, William Henry. 1961. *Power and Responsibility: The Life and Times of Theodore Roosevelt.* New York: Farrar, Straus and Cudahy.

Bibliography

Hargrove, Erwin. 1998. *The President as Leader: Appealing to the Better Angels of Our Nature.* Lawrence: University Press of Kansas.

Hagan, Kenneth J. 1991. *This People's Navy: The Making of American Sea Power.* New York: Free Press.

Harrison, Robert. 2004. *Congress, Progressive Reform, and the New American State.* Cambridge, U.K.: Cambridge University Press.

Hays, Samuel. 1959. *Conservation and the Gospel of Efficiency.* Cambridge, Mass.: Harvard University Press.

———. 1975. "Political Parties and the Community-Society Continuum." In *The American Party System: Stages of Political Development,* ed. William Nisbet Chambers and Walter Dean Burnham. New York: Oxford University Press.

Hodgson, Godfrey. 2006. *Woodrow Wilson's Right Hand: The Life of Colonel Edward M. House.* New Haven, Conn.: Yale University Press.

Hofstadter, Richard. 1955. *The Age of Reform: From Bryan to F.D.R.* New York: Knopf.

Hoogenboom, Ari. 1961. *Outlawing the Spoils.* Urbana: University of Illinois Press.

Howell, William. 2003. *Power without Persuasion.* Princeton, N.J.: Princeton University Press.

Ingraham, Patricia W. 1995. *The Foundation of Merit: Public Service in American Democracy.* Baltimore: Johns Hopkins University Press.

James, Scott. 2006. *Presidents, Parties and the State.* New York: Cambridge University Press.

Jeffers, H. Paul. 1995. *Commissioner Roosevelt: The Story of Theodore Roosevelt and the New York Police Commission, 1895–1897.* New York: John Wiley.

Jessup, Philip C. 1938. *Elihu Root.* Vol. 1. New York: Dodd, Mead.

Johnson, Arthur. 1961. "Antitrust Policy in Transition, 1908: Ideal and Reality." *Mississippi Valley Historical Review* 48, no. 3: 415–434.

Johnson, Ronald N., and Gary Libecap. 1994. *The Federal Civil Service System and the Problem of Bureaucracy.* Chicago: University of Chicago Press.

Josephson, Matthew. 1940. *The President Makers: The Culture of Politics and Leadership in an Age of Enlightenment, 1896–1919.* New York: Harcourt, Brace.

Judson, Frederick N. 1907. "Taft as Judge and His Labor Decisions." *American Monthly Review of Reviews* (August): 212–217.

Juergens, George. 1981. *News from the White House: The Presidential-Press Relationship in the Progressive Era.* Chicago: University of Chicago Press.

Kazin, Michael. 2006. *A Godly Hero: The Life of William Jennings Bryan.* New York: Knopf.

Keller, Morton. 1977. *Affairs of State: Public Life in Late Nineteenth Century America.* Cambridge, Mass.: Harvard University Press.

———. 1990. *Regulating a New Economy: Public Policy and Economic Change in America, 1900–1933.* Cambridge, Mass.: Harvard University Press.

———. 2007. *America's Three Regimes.* New York: Oxford University Press.

Kernell, Samuel. 1997. *Going Public: New Strategies of Presidential Leadership.* 3d. ed. Washington, D.C.: CQ Press.

Kerney, James. 1928. *The Political Education of Woodrow Wilson.* New York: Century.

King, Gary, and Lynn Ragsdale. 1988. *The Elusive Executive: Discovering Statistical Patterns in the Presidency.* Washington, D.C.: CQ Press.

Kolko, Gabriel. 1963. *The Triumph of Conservatism.* New York: Free Press.

Korzi, Michael. 2003. "Our Chief Magistrate and His Powers: A Reconsideration of William Howard Taft's 'Whig' Theory of Presidential Leadership." *Presidential Studies Quarterly* 33, no. 2: 305–320.

———. 2004. *A Seat of Popular Leadership.* Amherst: University of Massachusetts Press.

Lamoreaux, Naomi. 1985. *The Great Merger Movement in American Business, 1895–1904.* New York: Cambridge University Press.

Laracey, Melvin. 2002. *Presidents and the People: The Partisan Story of Going Public.* College Station: Texas A&M University Press.

Laughlin, J. Laurence. 1933. *The Federal Reserve Act: Its Origins and Problems.* New York: Macmillan.

Lewis, David. 2003. *Presidents and the Politics of Agency Design.* Stanford: Stanford University Press.

Lieberman, Robert C. 2002. "Ideas, Institutions, and Political Order: Explaining Political Change." *American Political Science Review* 96, no. 4: 697–712.

Lindblom, Charles. 1979. "Still Muddling, Not Yet Through." *Public Administration Review* 39, no. 5: 517–526.

Link, Arthur S. 1947. *Wilson: The Road to the White House.* Princeton, N.J.: Princeton University Press.

———. 1954. *Woodrow Wilson and the Progressive Era, 1910–1917.* New York: Harper & Brothers.

———. 1956. *Wilson: The New Freedom.* Princeton, N.J.: Princeton University Press.

Livezey, William E. 1947. *Mahan on Sea Power.* Norman: University of Oklahoma Press.

Livingston, James. 1986. *Origins of the Federal Reserve System.* Ithaca, N.Y.: Cornell University Press.

———. 1991. *Pragmatism and the Political Economy of Cultural Revolution, 1850–1940.* Chapel Hill: University of North Carolina Press.

Lowi, Theodore J. 1964. "American Business, Public Policy, Case Studies, and Political Theory." *World Politics* 16, no. 2: 677–715.

———. 1985. *The Personal President: Power Invested, Promise Unfulfilled.* Ithaca, N.Y.: Cornell University Press.

Mahan, Alfred Thayer. 1890. *The Influence of Sea Power upon History: 1660–1789.* Boston: Little, Brown.

Mansfield, Harvey C., Jr. 1989. *Taming the Prince.* New York: Free Press.

March, James G., and Johan P. Olsen. 1989. *Rediscovering Institutions: The Organizational Basis of Politics.* New York: Free Press.

Mason, Alpheus. 1941. *Bureaucracy Convicts Itself: The Ballinger-Pinchot Controversy of 1910.* New York: Viking Press.

———. 1964. *William Howard Taft: Chief Justice.* New York: Simon and Schuster.

Massie, Robert K. 1991. *Dreadnought: Britain, Germany, and the Coming of the Great War.* New York: Random House.

Bibliography

Mayer, Kenneth. 2001. *By the Stroke of a Pen: Executive Orders and Presidential Power.* Princeton, N.J.: Princeton University Press.

Mayhew, David. 1996. "Presidential Elections and Policy Change: How Much Connection Is There?" In *American Presidential Elections,* ed. Harvey L. Schantz. Albany: State University of New York Press.

McClure, Eric. 2003. *Earnest Endeavors: The Life and Public Work of George Rublee.* Westport, Conn.: Greenwood Press.

McConnell, Grant. 1953. *The Decline of Agrarian Democracy.* Berkeley: University of California Press.

———. 1966. *Private Power and American Democracy.* New York: Knopf.

McCormick, Richard. 1986. *The Party Period and Public Policy: American Politics from the Age of Jackson to the Progressive Era.* New York: Oxford University Press.

McCraw, Thomas K. 1984. *Prophets of Regulation: Charles Francis Adams, Louis D. Brandeis, James M. Landis, Alfred Kahn.* Cambridge, Mass.: Harvard University Press.

McCurdy, Charles. 1979. "The *Knight* Decision of 1895 and the Modernization of American Corporation Law: 1869–1903." *Business History Review* 53: 304–342.

McGeary, M. Nelson. 1960. *Gifford Pinchot: Forester-Politician.* Princeton, N.J.: Princeton University Press.

McGerr, Michael. 1986. *The Decline of Popular Politics: The American North, 1865–1928.* New York: Oxford University Press.

———. 2003. *A Fierce Discontent: The Rise and Fall of the Progressive Movement in America.* New York: Oxford University Press.

Meyer, Balthasar. 1906. "A History of the Northern Securities Case." *Bulletin of the University of Wisconsin: Economics and Political Science Series* 1, no. 3: 215–350.

Milkis, Sidney M. 1993. *The President and the Parties: The Transformation of the American Party System since the New Deal.* New York: Oxford University Press.

———. 2009. *Theodore Roosevelt, the Progressive Party, and the Transformation of the American Democracy.* Lawrence: University Press of Kansas.

Milkis, Sidney M., and Daniel J. Tichenor. 1994. "Direct Democracy and Social Justice, The Progressive Party Campaign of 1912." *Studies in American Political Development* 8: 282–340.

Miller, Gary J. 1990. "Abnormal Politics: The Possibilities for Presidential Leadership." Paper presented at the Annual Meeting of the American Political Science Association. San Francisco, California.

Minger, Ralph Eldin. 1961. "William H. Taft and the United States Intervention in Cuba in 1906." *Hispanic American Historical Review* 41, no. 1: 75–89.

———. 1975. *William Howard Taft and United States Foreign Policy: The Apprenticeship Years, 1900–1908.* Urbana: University of Illinois Press.

Moe, Terry. 1985. "The Politicized Presidency." In *The New Direction in American Politics,* ed. John Chubb and Paul Peterson. Washington, D.C.: Brookings Institution.

Morgan, Wayne. 1966. "William McKinley as a Political Leader." *Review of Politics* 28, no. 4: 417–432.

Morison, Elting E. 1942. *Admiral Sims and the Modern American Navy.* Boston: Houghton Mifflin.

Neustadt, Richard. 1990. *Presidential Power and the Modern Presidents.* New York: Free Press.

O'Connell, Robert. 1991. *Sacred Vessels.* Boulder, Col.: Westview.

Olsen, Mancur. 1982. *The Rise and Decline of Nations: Economic Growth, Stagflation, and Social Rigidities.* New Haven, Conn.: Yale University Press.

Orren, Karen, and Stephen Skowronek. 1994. "Beyond the Iconography of Order: Notes for a 'New Institutionalism.'" In *The Dynamics of American Politics,* ed. Lawrence C. Dodd and Calvin Jillson. Boulder, Col.: Westview Press.

———. 2004. *The Search for American Political Development.* New York: Cambridge University Press.

Ostrogorski, Moise. 1964 [1903]. *Democracy and the Organization of Political Parties.* Vol. 2, *The United States.* Edited and abridged by S. M. Lipset. Garden City, N.Y.: Anchor Books.

Oyos, Matthew M. 1996. "Roosevelt and the Implements of War." *Journal of Military History* 60, no. 4: 631–655.

Penick, James, Jr. 1968. *Progressive Politics and Conservation: The Ballinger-Pinchot Affair.* Chicago: University of Chicago Press.

Perry, Bliss. 1935. *And Gladly We Teach.* Boston: Houghton Mifflin.

Preston, Thomas. 2001. *The President and His Inner Circle: Leadership Style and the Advisory Process in Foreign Affairs.* New York: Columbia University Press.

Pringle, Henry. 1939. *The Life and Times of William Howard Taft.* 2 vols. New York: Farrar & Rinehard.

Radford, K. J. 1988. *Strategic and Tactical Decisions.* 2d ed. Toronto: University Press of Canada.

Ransom, Noble E., Jr. 1950. "George L. Record's Struggle for Economic Democracy." *American Journal of Economics and Sociology* 10, no. 1: 71–83.

Rauchway, Eric. 2003. *Murdering McKinley: The Making of Theodore Roosevelt's America.* New York: Hill and Wang.

———. 2005. "William McKinley and US." *Journal of the Gilded Age and Progressive Era* 4, no. 3: 234–253.

Reid, John Gilbert. 1940. "Taft's Telegram to Root, July 29, 1905." *Pacific Historical Review* 9, no. 1: 66–70.

Reiter, Howard L. 2004. "Factional Persistence within Parties in the United States." *Party Politics* 10, no. 3: 251–271.

Reckner, James R. "TR and His Navy." *Naval History* 15, no. 1: 41–45.

Riis, Jacob. 1890. *How the Other Half Lives.* New York: Scribners.

Ritter, Gretchen. 1997. *Goldbugs and Greenbacks: The Antimonopoly Tradition and the Politics of Finance in America, 1865–1896.* New York: Cambridge University Press.

Sanders, Elizabeth. 1999. *The Roots of Reform: Farmers, Workers, and the American State, 1877–1917.* Chicago: University of Chicago Press.

Bibliography

Sarasohn, David. 1989. *The Party of Reform: Democrats in the Progressive Era.* Jackson: University of Mississippi Press.

Schnietz, Karen E. 1994. "The 1916 Tariff Commission: Democrats Use of Expert Information to Constrain Republican Tariff Protection." *Business and Economic History* 23, no. 1: 176–189.

Seligman, Edwin R. A. 1899. "The Franchise Tax Law in New York." *Quarterly Journal of Economics* 13, no. 4: 445–452.

Semsch, Philip L. 1963. "Elihu Root and the General Staff." *Military Affair* 27, no. 1: 16–27.

Silbey, Joel. H. 1991. *The American Political Nation, 1838–1893.* Stanford: Stanford University Press.

Sklar, Martin J. 1988. *The Corporate Reconstruction of American Capitalism, 1890–1916.* New York: Cambridge University Press.

Skocpol, Theda. 1992. *Protecting Women and Soldiers.* Cambridge, Mass.: Harvard University Press.

Skowronek, Stephen. 1982. *Building a New American State: The Expansion of National Administrative Capacities, 1877–1920.* New York. Cambridge University Press.

———. 1997. *The Politics Presidents Make: Leadership from John Adams to George Bush.* Cambridge, Mass.: Harvard University Press.

Smith, J. Allen. 1907. *The Spirit of American Government.* New York: Macmillan.

Sparrow, Bartholomew. 1996. *From the Outside In.* Princeton, N.J.: Princeton University Press.

Sprout, Harold, and Margaret Sprout. 1944. *The Rise of American Naval Power: 1776–1918.* Princeton, N.J.: Princeton University Press.

Stid, Daniel D. 1998. *The President as Statesman: Woodrow Wilson and the Constitution.* Lawrence: University Press of Kansas.

Thelen, David. 1985. *Robert M. La Follette and the Insurgent Spirit.* Madison: University of Wisconsin Press.

Thelen, Kathleen. 2000. "Timing and Temporality in the Analysis of Institutional Evolution and Change." *Studies in American Political Development* 14, no. 1: 101–108.

Thorelli, Hans B. 1955. *The Federal Antitrust Policy: Origination of an American Tradition.* Baltimore: Johns Hopkins University Press.

Tichenor, Daniel J. 2002. *Dividing Lines: The Politics of Immigration Control in America.* Princeton, N.J.: Princeton University Press.

Tulis, Jeffrey. 1987. *The Rhetorical Presidency.* Princeton, N.J.: Princeton University Press.

U.S. Bureau of the Census. 1961. *Historical Statistics of the United States, 1789–1945.* Washington, D.C.: U.S. Government Printing Office.

Veysey, Laurence R. 1963. "The Academic Mind of Woodrow Wilson." *Mississippi Valley Historical Review* 49, no. 3: 613–634.

Wagner, Richard H. 2002. "A Falling Out: The Relationship between Oliver Wendell Holmes and Theodore Roosevelt." *Journal of Supreme Court History* 27, no. 2: 114–137.

Warburg, Paul. 1930. *The Federal Reserve System: Its Origin and Growth.* 2 vols. New York: Macmillan.

Watts, Sarah. 2003. *Rough Rider in the White House.* Chicago: University of Chicago Press.

Weaver, John D. 1997. *The Senator and the Sharecropper's Son.* College Station: Texas A&M University Press.

Weber, Max. 1964. *The Theory of Social and Economic Organization.* New York. Free Press.

———. 2004. "Politics as a Vocation." In *Weber, The Vocation Lectures,* ed. David Hacket and Tracy Strong. Indianapolis: Hackett.

Welch, Richard E., Jr. 1988. *The Presidencies of Grover Cleveland.* Lawrence: University Press of Kansas.

White, G. Edward. 1993. *Justice Oliver Wendell Holmes: The Law and the Inner Self.* New York: Oxford University Press.

White, Leonard D. 1958. *The Republican Era: 1869–1901.* New York. Macmillan.

White, Morton G. 1949. *Social Thought in America: The Revolt against Formalism.* New York: Viking Press.

White, Richard D., Jr. 2004. *Roosevelt the Reformer.* Tuscaloosa: University of Alabama Press.

Wiebe, Robert. 1967. *The Search for Order, 1877–1920.* New York: Hill and Wang.

Willis, Henry Parker. 1915. *The Federal Reserve.* Garden City, N.Y.: Doubleday, Page.

Wolman, Paul. 1992. *Most Favored Nation: The Republican Revisionists and U.S. Tariff Policy, 1897–1912.* Chapel Hill: University of North Carolina Press.

Zunz, Oliver. 1990. *Making America Corporate, 1870–1921.* Chicago: University of Chicago Press.

Index

Index

Index

Index

Index